Shout Out

Out

Women of color respond to violence

edited by María Ochoa and Barbara K. Ige

SEAL PRESS

Shout Out
Women of Color Respond to Violence

Copyright © 2007 Edited by María Ochoa and Barbara K. Ige

Published by Seal Press
A Member of the Perseus Books Group
1400 65th Street, Suite 250
Emeryville, CA 94608

Library of Congress Cataloging-in-Publication Data

p. cm.
Includes bibliographical references.
ISBN-13: 978-1-58005-229-0
ISBN-10: 1-58005-229-0
1. Minority women--Violence against. 2. Minority women--Crimes against. 3. Family violence. 4. Rape. 5. Violent crimes. I. Ochoa, Maria. II. Ige, Barbara K.

HV6250.4.W65S534 2008
362.82'920820973--dc22
2007032582

Cover design by Susan Koski Zucker
Interior design by Tabitha Lahr
Printed in the U.S.A.

For my *prima* Virginia Hernández (1947 – 1980), a bright star.

—— **M.O.**

As my first teachers, mentors, role models, and

inspiration for all that is strong and good in the world,

I dedicate this work to my mother, Sue Hatsuko Ige,

and in memory of my father, Takemori Ige.

—— **B.K.I.**

Contents

Chapter I.
Strength in the Service of Vision

Chapter 2.
Articulating a Global Ethic

Chapter 3.
Speaking Truth to Power

Chapter 4.
Messages of Pain

Chapter 5.
Defining a Principled Peace

Foreword

Chitra Lekha Divakaruni

I am honored to be writing a foreword for this important and timely anthology, which examines with stark honesty and deep compassion many aspects of violence against women. I am particularly impressed by the diversity and originality presented here.

The editors of *Shout Out* are to be commended for searching out so many never-before-published works that span a number of genres—from poetry and performance pieces to critical essays—and touch upon numerous aspects of this violence. They have made it a point to choose writers that come from different communities and countries, different races and generations, different political and economic backgrounds, and play different roles in the violent acts they describe. (Not all are the usual victims or witnesses, which I found to be an unexpected and refreshing element.) But, in all cases, their voices are powerful and persuasive as they draw our attention (often in very unusual ways) to crimes against women—which, as the editors rightly point out, are crimes against all of humanity.

Most importantly, the book does not stop with underscoring the problems. While acknowledging how complex and deeply rooted the causes of these violent crimes are, it suggests solutions that are at once practical, empowering, and healing, and thus leave us with a sense of hope and a desire to do what we can to improve the situation for women, both in our communities and halfway across the globe.

Reading the collection, I was moved to tears a number of times. In spite of my years of working with violence against women and writing about it, I learned many new things here, things that I hadn't considered before in quite this way.

Reader, this is my recommendation: Open your heart to this book; it has the potential to change how you look at life—and how you live it.

—Chitra Lekha Divakaruni

Count Down

Adrianne Shown Deveney

Introduction

Hopeful Insistence,
Informed Resistance

hout Out: Women of Color Respond to Violence is a collection that draws from the well of hope. These pages contain critical examinations, creative nonfiction, poetry, spoken word expression, and visual art that explore a range of responses to the injustices that women of color sustain in the conduct of their daily lives. More than fifty women and girls contributed to this anthology and give voice to the precarious conditions faced by women and girls around the world. The writing and visual representations serve as witness to some of the remarkable and inspiring individuals and organizations working to end war, rape, murder, slavery, the sex trade, domestic violence, poverty, and other forms of oppression.

Contributors chose to share their struggle, pain, and knowledge in order to educate and to eradicate the maltreatment of women. Each piece of writing and each work of art is unique to the vision of the author or artist. When read together, these expressions point to the complex relationship born of cultural work, social agency, and collective identity. What these works share in common is the demonstration of how collective agency is a powerful force that refutes and resists the violence perpetrated by individuals and institutions. Each piece reveals how the relationship of gender to culture affects the different forms of resistance that are created by women of color.

As editors, we received hundreds of responses to our call for submissions. As we pored over achingly stark expressions that told of countless forms of violence and oppression, we continually pondered, "How is it that so many women and girls are murdered daily around the world, and yet there is no public outcry great enough to halt the femicide? How do so many women survive the violence of their daily lives? Where do women find the wellspring of hope in the reality of such unrelenting generational conditions of economic poverty, physical and emotional enslavement, cultural obliteration, social injustice, and bodily danger? How might we ('we' meaning a collective self that comes from a caring and a desire for action that extends beyond the personal) change these conditions?"

There is no singular response, reaction, remediation, or recourse. However, in the aggregation of such stories—personal and collective, critical and creative—the ability to turn away, to deny that such mayhem takes place is made more difficult. The assemblage of material such as that found in this book permits readers the opportunity to learn, in part, about the severity of conditions faced by women of color around the world.

We acknowledge that this book reflects but a portion of the oppression and violence that women of color endure. We know that there is more to be said, examined, understood, and acted upon than is possible to be contained within these pages. There is more to be done to halt the escalating violence against women and girls, especially those whose ethnicity, cultural traditions, social status, religion, or sexual orientation make them targets of heinous acts. It is our hope that this collection will occasion the blossoming of other expressions that illustrate the courage of those who struggle daily to bring compassionate justice to their families and their communities.

Contributors to *Shout Out* are women and girls committed to illustrating the challenges and successes they encounter as they work to create a more peaceful world for all people. This book contains material about Latin American, Eastern European, Pacific Islander, Middle Eastern, and Southeast Asian women, as well as African American, Asian American, Indo-American, Chicana, and American Indian women. The anthology interlaces the voices of young women still in high school with women of Generations X and Y, baby boomers, and women in their senior years.

There are five chapters in this book, each addressing a set of questions or themes related to violence against women and girls of color. There is a work of visual art that opens each chapter and provides a moment of reflection. The first chapter contains writing that increases our understanding of contemporary issues regarding domestic violence in the United States. The second chapter presents a range of international perspectives about the sexual trafficking of women and girls, suicide, and the distortion of issues that mainstream media promulgates regarding women of color. The third chapter reflects on how war and other military actions contribute to institutionalized rape, murder, and the oppression of women. Literary expressions as forms of liberation and healing are closely examined in the fourth chapter. The book concludes in the fifth chapter with a series of works that call for a more peaceful world for women of color, and for all who dwell on the earth.

Our inspiration to organize this book around the critical and creative representations of women of color came from the writer, scholar, and activist Gloria Anzaldúa, who rests now with the ancestors but whose influence is still present. Gloria's precedent-setting books bridged multiple forms of expression and indelibly altered the ways in which feminists of color would come to frame the realities of their lives. The content and format of *Shout Out* grew from our conscious effort to create historical, literary, and activist links to her work by placing creative nonfiction, poetry, visual art, and critical analyses in an integrated arrangement. This book is an *ofrenda* to Gloria and serves as our honoring of her work and legacy.

Thank you, Gloria, for pointing the way to new creative and intellectual endeavors. Thank you for creating a vision that permits us to work, imagine, create, and argue in the space and embrace of solidarity. Thank you for teaching us the everlasting importance of hopeful insistence and informed resistance.

María Ochoa   Barbara K. Ige

Chapter I.

Strength in the Service of Vision

Sarah's Family

Keina Davis-Elswick

Introduction

*When I care to be powerful—to use my strength in the service of my vision—
then it becomes less and less important whether I am afraid.*

—Audre Lorde

Stepping forward to identify, articulate, and carry out strategies for crafting a comprehensive response to domestic violence requires a special vision. Domestic violence is a form of harm that frequently takes place without public comment, because it occurs within the boundaries of an intimate relationship, behind closed doors. The situation for women of color who find themselves in abusive relationships is compounded by cultural and religious traditions, immigration status, economic conditions, language barriers, and social isolation.

In this chapter, contributors speak about abuse and activism from a variety of experiences. We hear from African American women who, in a groundbreaking study, identified the cultural, social, and economic support necessary for the rebuilding of their lives as survivors. A Chicana traces, in essay form, her journey from an abusive marriage to her completion of her undergraduate studies and to her work as a campus coproducer of Eve Ensler's *Vagina Monologues*. An African American spoken word artist crafts a poignant poem that conveys the regrets of an overworked, slightly impatient hotline worker. A historical outline of the centuries-long violence against American Indian women helps us to contextualize and to develop relevant contemporary interventions. A one-of-a-kind collection of interviews with activists that created culturally sensitive services for South Asian women in the United States during the '80s and '90s brings to light important details about the history of the movement against domestic violence. And the chapter concludes with the findings from a first-of-its-kind study that documents domestic violence among Afghan immigrant women and that discusses the issues of living in hostile domestic and public worlds.

Peace begins within each individual, and the stories in this chapter teach us how to move from the personal to collective agency in the effort to end systemic violence.

"What Is It about the Walls?"

A Summary Report of African American Women's Experiences of Domestic Violence in Lincoln, Nebraska

Venita Kelley, Principal Investigator

Abstract

This essay reflects perspectives gained from focus group and personal interviews with African American women living in the area of Lincoln, Nebraska, who experienced domestic violence. Women ages thirteen to fifty-four, representing socioeconomic statuses from the "prison to the PhD" (as one participant termed it) took part. During the study, the authors of this piece became aware that a theme of "fighting with" their abusers emerged among participants. A sense of intrigue about what that phrase implied about African American women's lives prompted this exploration.

Report Summary

In 2003 the authors of this essay conducted a study about the domestic violence that African American women experienced in the Lincoln, Nebraska, area. The title of the study, "'What Is It about the Walls?' A Report on the Domestic Violence Services African American Women Receive in the Lincoln, Nebraska, Area," arose from the mouths of the women in a focus group in the study. The question both described and encapsulated a reoccurring theme in the stories of the women who participated in it.

The study reveals that abusers have a keen sense of the dramatic. In the experiences of some participants, walls were literally used as stages to reinforce the terror and

4

domination abusers would inflict: The walls were a "set" to throw a woman against, punch holes around her head, press on her body and smash as she was held against it, holler for her to stay up against, or ensure that she was physically trapped. The walls became a crucial character necessary to the scenario of the assault that the abuser constructed. Some found that there were invisible walls within shelters for accessing transitional assistance, although they sometimes witnessed European American women residents pass through them with less resistance. Walls also were found in the Black churches and in mosques. Many women indicated that their pastor or imam had counseled them to remain with their abuser, and most Lincoln ministers were unresponsive to Kelley, who coordinated the project, when she attempted to conduct a focus group about the ways these spiritual leaders helped the women in their congregations (a common occurrence by the church in all communities). Walls were also in evidence with law enforcement, as attitudes and nonverbal "assessments" conveyed to participants that they were being faulted for the assaults they suffered.

The study also revealed a wall of silence about domestic violence in the African American community in general, and specifically in the women's families. In fact, many of the women said that it took them some time to even find the words to describe what was happening in their homes because they found no meaningful vocabulary in the African American community with which to describe their experience of violence. Finally, women talked about the walls of isolation from friends, from other women, and the shame related to domestic violence.

Still, the study's participants often sought assistance from domestic violence service providers, law enforcement, the legal system, correctional facility programs, faith-based organizations in the African American community, and other institutions designed for assistance. The study's participants found their efforts for assistance complicated both by images of themselves within the microculture of African American society, and by mediated images of them in the larger society. The results of such images (and African American women are not the major innovators of these images) are matrices of domination, power, and control that African American women must negotiate for their daily survival and sense of self. Thus we found that there is additional danger and trauma that domestic violence imposes upon the already vulnerably positioned African American female. The report stemming from the focus groups tried to represent the women's experiences and concerns, and to clarify aspects of the danger matrices that frame African American women's lives. Certainly those matrices affect the options and the means of solutions that African American women might use to address domestic violence in their lives.

This essay is a summary of that larger report and tries to privilege the voices and experiences of the women. It organizes the participants' oral and written responses to focus group, personal interview, and survey questions about the domestic violence they had experienced, witnessed, or been engaged in as a part of an abused woman's support system. The study has made clear that there must be a continual refinement in understanding and eliminating domestic violence, its issues, and its related traumatic contexts. There can be no absolutes in terms of perceptions of domestic violence and whom it affects, or in terms of the efficacy of solutions to eliminate it.

The phenomena associated with domestic violence are constantly reshaped as society shifts; thus, reflective thinking, reevaluation, and readjusting procedures and responses must become normative procedure. Eliminating domestic violence must be thought of as an evolving process, where once-useful solutions are understood to no longer be so; or where structures set in place to establish order are recognized as contributing to disorder; or where mechanisms of empowerment are recognized as having been subverted to the point that they operate to disempower and disenfranchise those who were meant to be helped.

Key Findings

The experience of domestic violence (as defined by participants) encompasses sexual, physical, verbal, mental, and spiritual assault that, by the earliest report, began at age thirteen and still affected participants aged fifty-four in the present day. In general, the study of the domestic violence services that African American women receive in the Lincoln area revealed a need for greater awareness of how domestic violence itself affects and is perceived by African Americans.

It also revealed the need for awareness and support of African American women experiencing domestic violence in six primary institutions in the Lincoln area. The women themselves identified the six institutions: domestic violence service providers, correctional facilities, city and governmental agencies, law enforcement, faith-based organizations, the media, and, to a lesser extent, medical institutions.

Narrative of Findings Related to
Domestic Violence Service Providers

Outreach to African American women could be increased. Written material about shelters is not currently being placed in areas that African American women frequent, such as grocery stores, African American–owned beauty salons, and church vestries. Furthermore, women who had previously been in shelter said that thirty days was not enough for African American women "living in a racist society" to find a job, become economically independent, and establish a secure family environment for their children. Women said they needed more time in shelter, better access to transitional housing, job-location assistance, family counseling, and family assistance when transitioning out of correctional facilities. Women also acknowledged that they felt that some of the European American staff in shelters saw African American women's problems as their own fault and stereotyped them to be drug abusers or women who did not want to work. The women said that they were more quickly written up in shelter than were European American women, and that they were less likely to be told about available resources, or provided with guidance about practical survival matters, such as signing up for family aid and navigating new neighborhoods.

African American women who were on staff at shelters stated that they were misunderstood, viewed as intimidating, resented in the context of their work. Some had interactions involving overt censure and suspicion, experienced passive-aggressive undermining of their efforts, and were subtly ridiculed among their colleagues—especially when their methods, while succeeding with the women they worked with, did not meet the established structure of the shelter or provider context. Participants stated that the power and control cycle is in strong evidence in the shelter environment, both with African American women as staff colleagues and in what participants view as the inflexible structures of the shelters themselves.

Participants found also that shelter staff's willingness to listen and share personal experiences or knowledge with them helped them feel less isolated. One participant was grateful for the shelter's cosigning for a phone for her. The classes and educational materials were useful for women—either by giving them a perspective about what they were experiencing, or as tools for planning their exit from the abusive situation and for evaluating the emotional states of an abuser.

Narrative of Findings Related to Correctional Facilities

Participants in correctional services said that their imprisonment was a part of the domestic violence cycle; "they are all related: domestic violence, alcohol, drugs, prison," said one participant at the Nebraska Correctional Center for Women (NCCW). Several of the women were in prison for defending themselves from further domestic assault, resulting in the abuser's death. Other women said they felt that previous domestic violence counseling had been a "setup." When they exit the prison, one woman said, they are given their children and still don't have a job. When they turn to a man for support, he is often from a former relationship, and the cycle begins again. "We need ninety days, during which time we are in contact with our kids but not totally responsible for them," one woman said.

The women noted that programs for support related to domestic violence have not been in place for at least two years at NCCW, and do not exist at Lincoln Correctional Center (LCC). The NCCW program became de facto defunct when the person who staffed the program left the NCCW context.

There are no counseling (or staff) personnel of African American or other woman of color descent in place at the correctional facilities. The sentiment that European American personnel were not interested and were not able to relate to the issues and perspectives of African American women was also expressed by correctional facility residents. Racism, "overpolicing," and distrust of potential service providers (due to self-reported past experiences of betrayal) were also cited by the women as challenges within their environment.

A number of participants voiced the belief that Nebraska has no self-defense law; therefore, responses to abuse that directly contributed to their incarceration were not considered in their convictions. Despite personal research and inquiries, Kelley was unable to confirm whether any self-defense law was indeed lacking. If it is fact that there is no self-defense law, our concern is that the judicial system is de facto supporting domestic violence through inadequate understanding of the dimensions of the problem.

Perhaps not surprisingly, power and control dynamics are in evidence for women in correctional facilities. Participants stated that guards have been known to say, "I need a crackhead to empty the trash," to solicit women for work detail. Comments and approaches like these were reported to be a part of daily interaction between the women and correctional facility staff. Abusive contexts such as these would then increase incarcerated African American women's distrust and disdain for staff and programs in the facilities, were they in place.

We were not able to return to NCCW to interview other potential participants interested in being in the study. Participants stated that other NCCW women from the Lincoln area were also interested in being interviewed but had not been identified to the researchers by NCCW staff because they were not favored. Staff at NCCW were felt to have had some say in which imprisoned women would be allowed to participate in the study.

Narrative of Findings Related to City and Governmental Agencies

These findings are related to policy-creating entities such as educational institutions, police departments, and state institutions such as departments of social services and state legislatures. Participants stated that, at present, educational institutions such as public schools do nothing to warn girls about the dangers of domestic violence or about the "red flags" that can be spotted early on in a relationship. In addition, participants stated that when school officials interact with children who enter schools near the shelter environment, they ask the students about circumstances unrelated to their education or personal safety ("Why did your mom have to move so suddenly?" and "None of your family has any clothes anymore?" and "Do you all use food stamps?" and "Do you ever take a bath?"), thus contributing to an environment of shame and humiliation for the children.

African American women are more likely to have to rely on local police in a domestic violence crisis, because they are statistically less likely to be financially able to remove themselves from the abuser's locale. But most participants who had experienced domestic violence found officers to be of little help, either in referring them to shelters or in stopping the abuse for more than a few minutes. In some cases, the police added to women's fearfulness, as they threatened to arrest both her and the abuser. In a few cases, an officer tried to make sexual or romantic overtures to the women in crisis.

However, a set of officers—an African American male and a European American female—offered great emotional support to one woman who was plotting her way out of her domestic violence situation. The team was always the one to respond to calls to her home. They did not offer her any information about shelters, however. "He was my strength," the woman said of the African American officer who, while interviewing her away from the abuser, quietly gave encouragement and perspective to her about how she could change her situation. After their first call to her home, they began to refer to her by her name, and she never sensed they were judging her. Another woman stated that an African American male officer listened to her patiently and offered encouragement and a view about how she should be treated.

In general, participants in this study experienced a high level of distrust with social and human services workers. At times, participants stated that when they did approach the workers about domestic violence assistance, the workers seemed more interested in reporting that a man had spent the night in the home (and potentially causing a web of economic problems in the form of cuts in aid) than in helping the women and their children. Furthermore, a recent Nebraska law allows the state to place children who have witnessed domestic violence into foster care. Therefore, in reporting the domestic violence, African American women risk losing custody of their children. One participant said, "Once your children are gone into that system, it's like hell to get them back. They look at *you* as the unstable one, even though you were not the perpetrator. Meanwhile, he's walking around free and easy, with no worries about a child on his mind."

This Nebraska law, then, is a major hindrance to reporting domestic violence in the African American community and may serve to further empower abusers. A few participants stated that ineffective experiences with social and human services as children or youths contributed to their reluctance or refusal to seek services as adults.

Narrative of Findings Related to Faith-based Organizations

The faith-based response for African American women mirrors the general faith-based response to domestic violence in the larger society. Most participants expressed ambivalence and outright discouragement about the Black church's and Muslim mosque's responses to their situations of domestic violence. Participants stated they were often counseled to stay with their abusers and were targeted as creating the problem in their situations, particularly if they sought divorce. A few participants had direct ties to leaders in the churches and mosques, and found that they themselves were again focused upon as the problem, or that the religious leaders used their organizational positions to breach the women's confidentiality and whereabouts.

One participant—who had gone to a Christian minister and to a Muslim imam several times—said, "I cannot justly capture what I am trying to say in words, but it seemed as if ministers have an attitude that implies that God has personally told them how to address the issue of domestic violence. Moreover, it is up to the member to humbly seek this revelation [from the minister]."

Several participants stated that they began to seek answers for their situation through their own reading of the Bible or Koran. They stated that there is an incomplete application of scripture to their situations: Women are encouraged to submit to the male leadership in the house; whereas in the Bible, husbands are told to "love their wives like Jesus loved the church" and, in the Koran, that Allah instructs that a woman should be cherished and not struck. Thus, the women's own reports attest that their personal understanding of scripture and doctrine evolve at odds with instruction from leaders in the faith-based community. Although their own understanding is at odds with that of their leaders, women survivors of domestic abuse opt to believe the words of the texts they investigate rather than words they may receive from a faith community leader, thus often become distanced from the institutional structures of churches and mosques.

Yet participants do find aid in the faith community. One participant engaged in marital counseling with her husband and their pastor. A year after her husband cursed the pastor out and left a counseling session, the minister aided her with funding for a divorce. It should be noted that in that year she was still subjected to physical and emotional abuse. In a focus group specifically for religious leaders, the one participant who came, a minister, covered a number of issues and concerns among the pastoral community: Ministers are in denial about the seriousness of domestic violence; ministerial duties influence them to counsel toward keeping families together; ministerial training mirrors societal gender biases; ministers are actively involved in issues related to domestic violence but operate in isolation; ministers are reluctant to place themselves in the middle of family circumstances; there is no ministerial training related to a therapeutic way to address domestic violence.

Narrative of Findings Related to African American Women Who Have Not Sought Services

Some participants who said that they have not previously sought services or that they did not call the police said that they fear "getting him into trouble" or contributing to the abuser's death at the hands of overzealous officers. This finding indicates that African American women are constantly negotiating multiple and conflicting levels of societal realities, which then result in their experiencing paradoxes that either "paralyze" their options or further entrap them in the domestic violence circumstances.

Participants frequently cited financial dependence (either on the part of the abuser or the participant) as the reason behind their fear of his being incarcerated. Some of the women said that they did not want to "turn against him to the white man." After some discussion, participants explained that they see the historical oppression of African American people as ongoing and do not want to become a part of that societal system of degradation. The primary reason for their hesitancy was their distrust of the legal system, of law enforcement, and of social and human services systems as advocates for African American people in general and African American families in particular.

One facilitator described African American women in domestic violence situations as being so busy "managing the perception of African American people in the eyes of white people" that they do not know how to solicit and accept assistance from those same persons. Kelley talked about a need to "unpack the dual consciousness" in order to help African American women neutralize their self-negation under false notions of being "true to the race."

Narrative of Findings Related to the Media

Participants stated that until the wife of O. J. Simpson was slain and her experiences with domestic violence publicized, the media had largely ignored this social problem. Further, the persons identified as victims were then "only white." We determined that long-standing media portrayals of African American women—as strong, unfeminine, ugly, not worthy of respect, loud, masculine; as domestics and as literal and emotional servants to others—have affected African American women's self-image and have shaped ideas about African American women in the larger society. Those ideas both strengthen and weaken African American women's ability to respond to issues and crises such as domestic violence.

Participant Recommendations

The most important policy recommendation stems from the participants' identification of the primary reason that they remain in domestic violence situations: economic need. Indeed, Maslow's theory of the hierarchy of human needs states that physiological needs (food, shelter, etc.) are first. Safety needs (security, protection from physical and emotional harm) are second, and social needs (affection, belonging, acceptance, friendship) are third.

African American women's societal positioning largely confers the idea that physiological and safety needs are all that they deserve and should desire—and those only minimally. As a result, African American women may be more likely to endure short-term or cyclic periods of violence in their homes, because, in their view, at least they have an actual space to live in terms of providing for themselves and their children. Ironically, within their bounded, socially contextualized situation in the larger society, they understand institutional structures and their own necessities, but may often feel forced to forgo those personal needs in order to serve the needs of the African American microsociety, which has its own safety needs and which also insulates the women themselves in multiple ways. The recommendations that follow stem from participants' awareness of their positioning, and their perspectives in light of that awareness.

Domestic Violence Service Providers

The women overwhelmingly stated that a shelter run by women of color, or with women of color "involved at every level of decision-making" would enhance domestic violence services for them. Their perceptions indicated that European American women staff sometimes acted as if they had a "missionary complex" and were superior to the women seeking assistance.

Miscellaneous Practical Suggestions

- Provide bus passes to women in shelters so they can maintain jobs and family duties (such as taking children to school), or develop shuttle services.
- Install motion detectors around all vulnerable areas of shelters [where an abuser might hide or lie in wait for a woman's arrival].
- Keep a supply of new underwear that women can be given upon arrival at the shelter.
- Make sure shelter walls have pictures and art that reflect African American women, including cultural art.
- Make sure that African American magazines such as *Essence* and *Jet* are available for women to read in a shelter environment.
- Make certain the shelter's resource library has books and materials specifically addressing African American women (Iyanla Vanzant's series of books, Hopson and Hopson's *Friends, Lovers, and Soulmates,* etc.). Materials like these would be of use in helping women redefine relationship and self-care expectations.
- Create a written resource packet related to rental procedures and setting up utilities, and that includes names and contact information for area African American counselors and psychologists, etc.; present this to women upon their arrival to provider services and to women who will be residing in shelters.

Shelter Practices

- Establish a shelter run by and for women of color.
- Assist European American providers in recognizing their societal conditioning as being "superior," which becomes a filter that operates in their provider and collegial work with African American women. European American providers should actively seek training, counseling, and education or engage in an in-depth reading program that would familiarize them with African American culture and perspectives.
- Report organizational breaches of confidentiality (such as from church leadership) to judges and law enforcement.
- When a woman calls in crisis, share the shelter's criteria for assessing her situation for (immediate) emergency entry earlier on in the crisis call.
- Establish support groups for children residing in shelters.

- Encourage and help women in shelters to become lay or paracounselors for one another.
- Establish tutors and paraeducators in the shelters so that children will not be humiliated in new-school situations and to lessen the chance of children's exposure to the abuser, who may visit the school.
- Establish an on-site health facility for vision and dental checks, vitamins, etc.
- Never conduct an intake interview in front of a woman's children.
- Establish a process where women are allowed to go through, or are taken through, a "detox" time (unrelated to substance abuse)—"something like a twelve-step program" when entering a shelter or other programs. Compare the shock and trauma treatment that emergency patients receive in hospitals, but create a human services equivalent to it. This "detox" process should likely be created with the help of domestic violence survivors, so that they are able to inform and shape it for effectiveness.

Cultural Outreach

- Establish or support culture-specific support groups for African American women experiencing domestic violence.
- Develop culturally appropriate shelter intake questions.
- Give training in African American rapport-building, in interpersonal contexts, to shelter personnel and professionals.

Public Outreach

- Establish a media campaign that specifically focuses upon African American women, using culturally appropriate language and images. The campaign should include statistics ("Once it starts, it rarely stops") and escape route outlines.
- Establish and maintain a public campaign for hotel soaps, shower caps, and shampoos that then are offered to women in crisis upon arrival at shelter.

In-Community Environments

- At the checkout stands of grocery and women's clothing stores, post business-size cards (easily palmed) that identify shelter numbers, define domestic violence, and provide an outline for escape plans.
- Post information and business-size cards in hair salons frequented by African American women.
- Make greater efforts to involve the African American religious communities in the elimination of domestic violence.
- Identify and "recruit to the cause" community ministers and imams as allies and liaisons.
- Establish links with community centers, which then would provide information about domestic violence providers and services, resource packets, and a community-based locale for domestic violence trainings and programs.

"Providers as Colleagues"

- Facilitate professional networking with other African American and women of color providers.
- Avoid making African American colleagues the "exotic other."
- Invite and incorporate suggestions and practices that differ from established shelter structures, particularly when methods are useful to women.
- Train and educate providers about female-to-female competitive strategies, including power and control dynamics across race and culture lines.

Correctional Facilities

- Open more women-only halfway houses for domestic violence survivors transitioning out of prison.
- Establish a halfway house staffed by women of color to assist transition back into public society.
- Establish and maintain grief, family, and domestic violence support groups.

- Establish a domestic violence advisory board, which may include former correctional residents and which will work closely with correctional facilities to design and steer appropriate projects.

City and Governmental Agencies

LAW ENFORCEMENT

- As often as possible, the same investigation team should respond to domestic violence calls within a given family or living situation: Such familiarity can strengthen court testimony.
- Establish a public information policy whereby officers responding to calls hand a business-size card with shelter information and a general definition of domestic violence to women. Codes for the types of assault should also be on the card.
- Establish a public information standard script whereby officers responding to calls inform women about medical care, provider services, and support groups.
- Establish a policy of dismissal for officers who are found to use their law enforcement positions to aid abusers or harass victims.
- Refine policies of dual arrest in domestic violence situations.
- Raise the number of times that law enforcement will attempt to serve an abuser. Currently they cease trying to serve after two attempts. Another alternative would be to create warrants and restraining orders that are logged into the system "in perpetuity" so that they are always active and can be invoked against an abuser whenever he is found or comes out of hiding from the police.
- Inform officers of related statistics, such as the fact that African American women leave an abusive situation an average of ten times before they can manage to stay away.
- Offer monetary rewards for information on abusers who are on the run from arrest.
- Establish a link with the phone company whereby a woman can call and document that she is experiencing abuse. For instance, she might be in the abusive situation, but can call "# 2" to alert correctional officers to a domestic violence need-for-assistance call.

EDUCATION

- Establish a policy that school officials respect children's rights to privacy.
- Establish a progressive education curriculum about domestic violence, which would start firstly alongside sexual education in the fourth grade, then as part of health classes in middle and high schools.

MEDICAL

One of the oldest study participants, a woman who had suffered domestic violence repeatedly in the 1970s, and who subsequently became dependent on the medicine (valium, etc.) prescribed to calm her nerves, critiqued the medical field's response to her crises by saying that the medical response "shouldn't just be 'Do [you] need stitches?' but 'Do [you] need counseling?'" She linked the 1970s medical response of giving valium and other depressants to women as the starting point of her drug habit: "Come to think of it, I *did* begin abusing prescription medicine first. . . . [They] gave me] what I describe as "'the black people's domestic violence counseling.'" This participant eventually wound up in prison for actions related to supporting her drug habit.

LEGAL SYSTEM

- Establish a self-defense law for victims of domestic abuse.
- Repeal or revise laws and policies that place children in foster care as a result of situations of domestic abuse.
- Refine laws related to dual arrest.
- Establish criteria to assess when a woman should not be legally responsible for the bills of her abuser.
- Establish practices that make the abuser accountable for abuse: jailed if child support orders are ignored; paychecks garnished to pay child support; child support payments made to social services network (and then distributed to the woman) when the woman needs her location to be secret for safety reasons; mandatory attendance at battering men's groups (with driver's license points, community service, or jail time if there is noncompliance).

Faith-based Organizations

- Engage faith leaders in training and education related to domestic violence.
- Use sermons to address domestic violence as a sin against "God's sacred vessel."
- Incorporate domestic violence as a concern in interfaith organizational contexts.
- Take action to close the gulf between congregational sufferers of domestic violence and counseling and other services.
- Eliminate the assumption that the feminist movement is responsible for African American women's protest against and seeking relief from domestic violence within churches and mosques. (As in "African American women who don't want to suffer abuse, and who speak out, are brainwashed and being mouthpieces for European American women who participate in domination scenarios all African Americans suffer from [but particularly African American men], thus African American women who 'complain' are operating as agents for domination by European American society.")
- Establish the churches and mosques as safe places for women to seek or be connected to services.

Media

African American women seeking redress from domestic violence need to be included in mainstream social images of domestic violence. A concerted effort to eliminate stereotypical images of African American women is needed.

Culturally Significant Differences in Terms of African American Women's Experience of Domestic Violence

These ideas emerge as possible differences in how African American women evaluate and respond to domestic violence in culturally relevant contexts. Identifying these areas may be useful in developing culturally appropriate services, campaigns, and educational infrastructures.

- Women's use of the term "fighting" indicates a different positioning regarding how they see themselves as women—not passively accepting victimization, but willing (or expected) to engage in hand-to-hand combat between equals, for instance (though the women are routinely brutalized). Or there is verbal engagement at the level of resistance talk: "We was fighting." This woman does not say "He was yelling at me" and acquiesce to being dominated; she reveals a sense of personal agency ("we" rhetorically indicates she sees herself as just as viable as her abuser) as she relates that she and her abuser were arguing, prior to his "kicking my butt."

- An emotional/psychological dichotomy often exists in the mind of the woman, where the abuser is both good and evil, but where the good is enough to redeem his abusive behavior, even after exiting the relationship: "I know all in all he's a good guy, but he'll never change." (This finding would be related to sexist and racist conditioning for African American women in the United States, where African American women have had to settle for "a little bit of good" because the "bad" is so often a part of their societal positioning. Being involved with a man, then, who is able to exhibit good or endearing traits alongside or out of context of the abuse he delivers would be a noteworthy part of an African American woman's daily reality. Again, the historical context for this kind of "splitting" of consciousness can be well inferred. In addition, the African-based cultural philosophy of "nothing in itself is bad; it's what's done with a 'thing' that makes it or the doer bad" can be seen at work/odds with the woman's experience of abuse.)

- The abuser is often chronically unemployed and forces, castigates, or manipulates the woman into taking care of him.

- The woman is often culturally positioned as the protector of the abuser: "I lied a lot . . . told police he was gone . . . [would] bond [my] husband out . . . say he was 'gone in love. . . .'"

- African American women are often positioned—both culturally (they are "invisibilized" but held accountable for the culture's survival and viability) and by their abuser—as the (sole) economic provider.

- Some women paradoxically support or try to establish their self-esteem, and assert or discover their worth, through physically engaging the abuser: "I got off on self-defense [physically fighting back with the abuser]."

- African American women suffer from or are afraid of accusations of being traitors to the race, to religious communities and faiths, and to African American men when seeking redress from domestic violence.

- Young (college) African American women place men in the "king" role as an outcome of their incomplete learning about African-centered thought.
- Young (college) African American women view African American women who are abused as "weak" and "at fault" for the abuse they suffer, commenting that the legitimacy of an abused woman's womanhood is at stake. (This would constitute psychological and emotional subversion of empowerment structures for women.)
- African American women are overburdened in terms of the roles they are expected to accept or that are "left to them," within both the microsociety and the larger society.

African American Women's Personal Concerns upon Leaving the Abusive Situation

- Had no phone
- Was assigned delinquent bills because of legal obligations due to marriage to abuser (which means being able to establish a life independent of abuse also means a ruined credit rating)
- Lack of education
- Lack of programs to transform underground economy skills into mainstream economy assets/skills
- Lack of adequate substance-abuse counseling
- Lack of information that would help them to understand what domestic violence is and provide language to define the experience
- Overload of paperwork and information in paper form when seeking domestic violence assistance from providers and correctional officers
- Lack of knowledge on how to establish utilities
- Not enough time nor an adequate support system to transition from abusive situation or incarceration
- No clothes or personal care items: "I had no brush, no hair grease, no comb, no sanitary products . . . just me and my two babies, on the bus."
- No money to exit the abusive situation, due to the abuser's control of the economic situation: "I didn't even have a dollar for the bus."

Conclusion

While domestic violence crosses all communities and does not discriminate according to race, class, region, or other differences, it is clear there are differences in the women's experiences of violence. What it means to be a woman has additional sets of circumstances and realities for different cultures and classes of women. These realities attest to the fact that a one-size-fits-all approach to addressing domestic violence is not useful for servicing diverse groups of women. African American women's experiences with domestic violence cannot be taken out of the context of the African American experience, including modern-day and historical relationships with institutions.

African American women hold a strong distrust and fear of many of the institutions that are integral to the delivery of domestic violence services. Their distrust and fears are grounded in the contemporary and historical realities of the relationships between those institutions and the African American community. In terms of law enforcement, an African American woman's trusting officers to "do the right thing" is often a choice made at the point of desperation rather than according to belief that the institution itself will offer real solutions. With the criminal justice and legal systems, African American women still find laws, policies, and practices that protect the perpetrators and make them and their children vulnerable to misaligned and systemically inadequate forms of regulation. The medical community's efforts often sabotage their efforts for solutions beyond physical relief. Notably, African American women may associate domestic violence services with general social services, wherein their assessments of these services are informed by previous distrust issues with societal institutions.

As for the faith institutions, nearly every one of the women expressed a belief, faith, and practice in a "higher being." Unanimously, their faith and practice evolved beyond, and existed in alienation from, faith-based organizations. According to the study's participants, African American women consistently find that religious institutions and communities operate under the beliefs that the Bible and Koran sanction violence. When they discover, often on their own, that in fact there is no religious doctrine to support the abuse they suffer, they are often further isolated from the faith community and the potential solutions it may offer to their dilemmas. The Black church and other religious organizations are philosophically and factually the major institutions in the African American community. Institutions are the primary means by which a society establishes and maintains its existence. By their lack of adequate response and consideration of domestic violence realities, the core institutions an African American woman relies upon for evidence and practice of her connection to her culture, faith, and community serve to undermine her feelings of belonging, visibility, and viable humanity.

In addition, cultural representations of African American women impact and prevent them from seeking domestic violence services. While African American women are often viewed intraculturally and portrayed in media as strong and resilient, this imposed conditioning to "be resilient" may prompt them to resist seeking outside services and to deal with domestic violence problems on their own. This response can have both positive and negative outcomes for women. Positively, she may discover depths of resourcefulness that help her to live a fuller life of her own design. Negatively, she may find herself, her family, and her culture at the mercy of penal and human services systems that react to and interact with her as though she is responsible for the conditions of the abuse. The burden of the interwoven blaming and the practice of diminishing her sense of her self and her (culturally contextualized) womanhood keep her isolated, vulnerable, and keenly aware of her unprotected status in the larger society. The larger society's views have had an impact, and her viability and agency are also under attack at increasing levels in African American microsociety. Besides the dire survival circumstances created for African American women in general, we have found that this social positioning makes a direct contribution to African American women's incarceration.

On the other hand, the valor of African American women is an enormous asset, and their resoluteness can have a positive impact on their escape from the violence. We found women who carefully plotted their escape and were successful, without jail or prison time being a part of their experience. It should be kept in mind that these women made their escape in isolation from any services or institutional means of assistance. Yet the resulting positive self-concept and assurance about their ability to design their own life and negotiate challenges cemented their conviction to speak out, establish healthy relationships, provide healthy roles and instruction to their children, and claim their own forms of womanhood. Clearly, one challenge for those concerned with how domestic violence affects African American women becomes providing women with the tools, information, and supportive means to replicate this outcome and to help women best use their resilient spirits to combat the multiple power and control dynamics they face in life.

For reasons related to the above ideas, we feels it is time to acknowledge that there is a tenet of assumption that "the feminist movement" is responsible for African American women's protest against sexism and other forms of female subjugation in the African American microsociety. Besides horribly distorting the impact that African American women (such as Paula Giddings, Alice Walker, Anita Hill, and Patricia Hill Collins) have had on equality, equity, and ideas and practices of egalitarianism in the United States, the idea as related to domestic violence is that an African American woman who seeks relief from domestic violence—who speaks out about it and what she suffers—is deemed "brainwashed" and is accused of being a mouthpiece for a European American agenda of domination and oppression of all African Americans (but particularly affecting African American men).

Therefore, as a mechanism of controlling their words and actions in the microsociety, African American women who complain about their microsociety's oppressed state are castigated for operating as agents of the entrenchment of the domination and destruction of African American people by European American society. This has tragic results, as it affects African American women's efforts for redress in their communities: There is no separation of the historical, political, and sociological evidence of that mainstream domination agenda with the domination of the female agenda that now exists within African American communities. We feel that the need to extricate this idea from African American women's struggle for a safe, healthy, and thriving humanity is intimately tied into the harmonious existence of African American society in the United States.

To finalize, African American women find themselves at the crossroads of being the coprotectors and cosustainers of their culture without the safeguards to ensure that they have the best chance to build a whole personhood that would allow them to fulfill these roles. African American women are needed to preserve all that is magnificent about the culture. However, the culture no longer evenly enacts its own philosophical notion that their life is one that "no man should rend asunder."

African American women, then, often become the scapegoats for the cultural and societal stressors that affect African Americans as a whole, and they often suffer the physical, emotional, spiritual, and economic outcomes related to that social positioning. The African American woman endures and endeavors constantly against both subtle and overt power and control dynamics in the larger societal culture and within her own microculture. Rather than dismissing these interlocking areas of existence, solutions should begin by placing African American women at the center of solution practices and considerations, including the development and/or alteration of current programs and policies created to address their particular circumstances. To ignore these intersections and to employ a one-size-fits-all mentality is to directly contribute to the violence that African American women face. Courageous holistic considerations and solutions related to domestic violence against African American women must be painstakingly considered nonnegotiable and attainable.

Sixteen

Aya de Leon

I am waiting for a phone call. A young woman's phone call.
Maybe a million guys would like this young woman to call them
dozens have asked her for her phone number
maybe even hundreds

She is a doe-eyed sixteen with a pepsodent
smile, a set of boom! pow! curves to fill out
her tight coolgirl clothes and a chronic case of
aggressive makeup and thoroughly systematized
hair.

She is the girl the guys wanna get with
and the other girls wanna be.

But I am the one waiting for her phone call.
Not a lover or a would be suitor.
Not a pretty girl who likes to be seen
with other pretty girls at the mall
But me, a stressed out youth counselor
on my day off.

Her voice was soft, but she didn't whisper
I think they said I need an adult
to pick me up afterwards, she said.
I asked what day the procedure would be
Saturday.

We were in the hallway at the high school between classes.
Students rushed past in a blur of fashion.
I was running late
had too many things in my hands
was trying to damage control on a mistake the school had made.

There was chaos all around us
we were both in a rush but now
I am worried.
I told her to call me.
Didn't I say I thought I could pick her up?
Is she not calling because she has another ride?
Because she decided she wants to be a teen mom?

Or could it be because I was not clear enough?
Could she tell I was stressed out
had a hard week
and didn't want to give her my Saturday?

Why didn't I say
Yes, I will help you
I will be there
I will pray with you
I will drive you home
I will give you a charm to ease the grief
you won't even acknowledge
I will reassure you if you are afraid
I will tell you from my heart
I do not believe God will be mad at you
I will not condescend/disapprove/patronize/lecture

But I didn't say that.
Instead I
gave her my card
in a rush
told her to call.
Give me the number.
I need the details.
What time Saturday?
Let me know when you'll be done.

I am waiting for a phone call.
Her message on the voice mail will tell me
You did it right
I trust you
You were clear enough
available enough
welcoming enough.

I am waiting for a phone call.
I am afraid this young woman will be bleeding
for three hours on two buses
maybe with a girlfriend chatting about shoes and hair and nails
to fill the space
maybe with a sullen boyfriend looking away
or maybe all alone.

I am waiting for a phone call.
I am really waiting for God to call up and say
Don't worry, I've taken care of everything
It's okay, you can relax now
I've set it up so young women can be safe
won't be preyed upon, exploited, shattered

It's all right.

You can stop being so vigilant every fucking minute.

Yes God it's you I need to speak to
I don't understand this
Why does it have to be so hard for young women? For all women?
It just doesn't seem right.
And yet I trust you because
I have no other choice.
It's all in your hands anyway so
please watch over this young woman, and all young women.
Please bless them and keep them because
I am not equal to the task
and my phone is not ringing. . . .

After *Violation* in a Most Vicious Way

Teresa Pedrizco Romero

This year I'm celebrating the seventh anniversary of my "liberty." More importantly, I am celebrating my new life with a determination for something better for myself and other women. My determination and energy took me to the Women's Resource Center at San José State University. Recently I took a leave from my work to spend time as the producer of *The Vagina Monologues* on V-Day, a global movement to increase awareness and raise money for anti-violence organizations. As an ardent feminist advocate, I work on a daily basis for women's rights. Yet this wasn't always the case. I wasn't always the outspoken activist that I am today.

My ex-husband (X) and I met at work. I guess after working together for a long time, we started to like each other. We started dating, even though his family, especially his father, did not want him to date someone like me—whatever that entailed. We dated for three and a half years. At the beginning, he was not violent however, this gradually changed. It started with his jealousy—he asked me not to talk to male friends. It escalated when he began pushing and shoving me, and then pulling my hair. After getting married, all of that behavior continued. The abuse escalated to the point where I was in complete isolation; eventually it was followed by spousal rape.

X "guided the boat," and I had to do as told. I was not allowed to talk to friends and could only see my family on timed and supervised (by him) visits. He accused me of having an affair with my manager, and he asked me to stop working. He wanted me to be at home at all times so I "would not have any temptations." He wanted me to spend more time with him; he wanted me to be a full-time housewife. He wanted me to devote myself to wife-chores and school. I eventually stopped working full-time and started working only on weekends.

Despite what I went through with X, I still had hope that he would change. However, all hope vanished when his obsessive jealousy arose again, and he beat me so severely that the physical scars lasted for almost three months. I felt a desperate need to talk to someone. I knew that if he found out that I was telling someone about our "personal problems," it automatically meant I was going to get beaten again. I was not only terrified that he would find out if I *did* talk about what was going on, but I was also embarrassed to talk about it. I knew I wasn't going to be believed, because people always told me, "Oh, X is so nice. He is a very nice person. You are so lucky to have him as your husband."

Despite the shame, I had to let it out. It was a heavy load to carry all by myself. The desperation that I felt took me to Gaby, a friend of mine who I had been prohibited to talk to for a couple of years. X absolutely prohibited that I visit or talk to Gaby because he assumed she had been unfaithful to her husband and that she would be a "bad influence" for me.

Since I was working only on the weekends and her house was on my way home, I thought X would not notice the mileage difference—as he constantly monitored the miles I drove—and I stopped at Gaby's house. Well, I was definitely wrong. After I vented with Gaby for a few minutes, I got on the road and headed home. Once I got in the car, I noticed that X had called me on the cell phone multiple times. I thought he was going to be furious, so I drove home without returning his call. I thought of just dealing with it when I got home.

When I got home, X was not there; he had gone out looking for me. Minutes after I got home, the phone rang. It was X. When I answered, he did not hesitate to tell me, "If you don't get out of the house, I'm going to kick your ass." Wishfully, I told myself, *He won't do it. He promised already not to do it again,* and I proceeded to change my working clothes for more-comfortable sweats. Even though I was in complete denial about his violent behavior, I hid the gun he had—just as precaution. The gun was always in its casing, hanging on the pole of the floor lamp, next to our bed. It was a constant reminder for me to "behave." That night I listened to my instincts and put the gun under the carpet in a different room of the house.

As soon as I heard X parking his car in the garage, I went to the living room to wait for him—that way he would not notice right away that the gun was not in its place. As soon as he got into the house, he started yelling and screaming, demanding to know "where in the hell" I had been. I felt worthless. I felt guilty for causing his temper. I was speechless. I just sat on the couch, looking down. However, X took this as an offense. He thought I was ignoring him. With one hand, he grabbed me by the hair and with the other hand, he held my face up so I would be looking at him in the eye. He continued pulling my hair, slapping me, and punching me. I did not know what would be worse, to tell him that I was with someone he had forbidden me to talk to, or to remain silent.

Silence wasn't helping, so I opted to make up a story to account for the time and the extra miles. I told X, "I gave a ride to a girl from work, and after that, I headed myself to Santa Cruz—for a walk on the beach and to clear my mind from all the problems we were having—and when I noticed it was getting late, I decided to drive back home." When I said that, he demanded to know why I had "disobeyed." He demanded to know the name and address of my coworker so he could verify my story. I just gave him the name of one of my coworkers. However, the violence did not stop there. He continued asking me if I had been in bed with someone as he beat me. I just covered my face with my hands and arms to avoid being hit in the face. In that moment I was thinking about the shame it would bring if people saw the marks on my face.

X was absolutely sure I had been with another person and kept punching me, shoving me against the walls and around the living room. Next, X removed his belt from his waistband and proceeded to whip me with it. X continued interrogating me about being unfaithful. Then, without warning, he pulled off my sweatpants and panties. He penetrated my vagina with his fingers to get evidence that I had been with someone. When he pulled his fingers out of my vagina, he put his hand a couple of inches away from my face and, rubbing his fingers together, he said, "See, you are wet, you must have been with somebody." Now I think, *How ignorant and paranoid he was.* After he inserted his fingers in my vagina, I felt horrible. I felt worthless. I felt trashed. I felt dishonored. I felt humiliated. I felt that my inner me had been violated. As X attempted to do it again, and even though I was unable to do much, I tightly closed my legs to keep him from inserting his fingers again. Crying, I begged him to leave me alone. However, he did not listen to my pleas. I could not escape from his whipping. I attempted to use a blanket that was on the couch to shield myself, but X would move it aside and continue his assault on me. He struck me on my back, abdomen, legs, and arms, which resulted in welts and bruises. He said that I "earned the punishment for being unfaithful."

When X hit my knee with the buckle, I crunched together and continued to beg him to stop hitting me. Instead of stopping, X pushed me through the hallway toward our bedroom. He insisted that since any man could have sex with me, he had "the right to do it too, because he was my husband." I was afraid that he would do it as he had done many times in the past. At that time, I did not know that was spousal rape.

As he shoved me through the hallway, I tried to grab onto what I could so he wouldn't get me to the room. I scratched the wall; I screamed; I begged. Finally, I was able to hold on to the laundry room doorknobs and sat on the floor so X would not take me to the room. I knew that if he took me to the room, he would "do it." That he would *rape* me—*rape* me as he did many times. I was not only terrified that he would rape me, but that he would notice that the automatic pistol was not there. I was successful in avoiding being dragged into the room. However, he walked to the room and saw that the gun was not there. He started kicking me as I was on the floor holding on to the doorknob, demanding to know where the gun was.

I don't remember for how long the "punishment" went on, but I remember that X calmed down and offered to take me to Santa Cruz for a walk on the beach. Obviously, I rejected the invitation because of the nightmare I had just gone through. When I heard him asking me, I thought I was going to faint. I could not believe what I was hearing. I was going nuts. I couldn't believe that he violated my person in a way I never thought possible and was now asking me to go for a "romantic walk" at the beach. The psychological trauma was so intense, I thought I was going to go crazy. After I refused to go, he said, "See, who can understand you? First, you wanted to go." After hearing him, I realized that if I did not go with him, I was going to be listening to that all night long, so I just went along.

Once in Santa Cruz, and while we were walking on the beach, he asked me to look up to the "romantic moon." My bloody knee hurt and made it hard to walk. And when X put his arm around my shoulder as we walked on the beach, it felt as if my back were going to shatter into pieces. The pain he caused by putting his arm over the welts was intolerable, yet I could not express it. I could not stand the pain. I could not stand the psychological torture. There was a point when I thought of just walking into the water to drown. I really wanted to put an end to this internal agony, and that was the only way I could.

After the walk on the beach, X drove home, and once we were in our bed, he whispered in my ear, "You know, I don't like it. But you make me do things I don't like to do." The next day, he wanted to find out where the pistol was. At first, I refused to tell him, but after he told me that it was going to be worse if he found it on his own, I opted to give it to him.

In the time following that cruel and inhumane beating, I had no desire to have sex, yet X wondered why I was "so cold." He interpreted my "coldness" as I was having someone else to "please" me. Every time he took my clothes off, so HE could have sex, it brought all the terrible memories from that night. Even though it was terrible, I tried to put it behind me, just as I did many instances before. However, I couldn't. The cut on my knee and the bruises and welts on my arms, legs, and abdomen made it very difficult to forget. Even though I was in denial, I could not avoid seeing and feeling the marks on my body when I showered—the wounds hurt as the water fell on my body.

The emotional distress that those purple and bloody lines all over by body caused eventually pushed me to finally seek help. The wounds were not only physical, but also emotional and psychological. I would jump off the chair if the phone rang. I would get scared and cry when the dog barked. In addition, it affected my academic potential. It was very hard to concentrate on the school material. I was afraid that X would show up at school and that everything could happen all over again. It became extremely difficult to live with the marital problems and still try to concentrate in class. Out of desperation, I ended up letting one of my professors know what I was going through. He suggested I talk to a campus counselor.

After I saw the counselor, I found out about Support Network for Battered Women, in Mountain View, where I managed to go without X finding out. After I reached out for help, I learned that the relationship I was trying to hold on to—and which I was in for too many years, and which I thought was "normal"—was unhealthy. I made the decision to separate from X. One evening, I told X I was leaving. As one might have expected, he automatically blamed me and said, "Is it for another man? That is why you never wanted to give me a baby." His nonsense conclusion did not intimidate me any longer, and I stood up to my difficult decision.

When X realized how firm I was on our separation, he told me that he was NOT going to move out of the house, because it was "his own," and that if I wanted my "liberty," I was the one who had to move out. The decision was already made, and there was no going back. I wasn't willing to play his game anymore. I did not want to go back to my mother's house—because I did not want her to say "I told you so." She didn't know about the abuse, but she had never liked. Thanks to the goddesses, my mother let me move in with her.

X made my life miserable until the very last day we were under the same roof. That night, X insisted that I should be "romantic for the last time." Of course I refused. However, he kept placing his hands on me. Like so many times before, what I wanted did not matter, and he proceeded to undress me, forced my legs open, and got on top. When he was on top of me, I felt used and hopeless. I just lay there as tears came down my face; I did not want to get hurt even more. I did not want to do anything that would make him even more violent. I knew the light at the end of the tunnel was a few hours away. I told myself, *Tomorrow. Tomorrow I'm gone.* After he ejaculated on my stomach, he just lay back on the bed as if nothing had happened.

After I told a coworker of the incident, she suggested that I report the rape. Despite my fear, I went to the police station and reported what happened. I felt that the male police officers were not taking me seriously and instead were judging me. I felt they were questioning the truthfulness of my version. While I was there, giving my testimonial, I told myself, *This is why I never called the police.* The police officer asked me if X forced me to have sex, and then he asked me to describe it. I told him that X had asked me to be "romantic for the last time" and that after I refused he just got on top of me and penetrated me. Then the officer said, "So he had sex by himself." That is when I felt that my situation was not taken seriously, that there was no sense of urgency. The officer asked me if X had ejaculated, and I said "Yes." Then he asked, "Inside?" I said "No, outside. On my stomach." He kept on taking notes, but never asked to take a DNA sample, or some evidence along those lines. It was about a year later that I found out that a DNA sample could have been taken, even though I reported the incident about eighteen hours after it happened.

At that point, I still did not know about "spousal rape." I just wanted to report the incident so that there would be some kind of record in case X came back to hurt me or even kill me. The questioning continued, and the officer asked me if I wanted X to be arrested. Before I could answer, many questions flashed through my mind, questions such as, *If he gets arrested, who is going to make the car and mortgage payments?* I was completely dependent on him. So I responded, "No." At that time, I definitely felt guilty for talking about our "personal problems" and for the potential harm that I was going to cause X.

↯

When I got out from that relationship, I dedicated myself to healing my physical and psychological wounds. I learned about domestic violence (DV), the power and control dynamics. The more that I learned about DV, the more I was intrigued and wanted to learn even more. I found out that the abuse of women was not found just within marriages but emerged from social circumstances. I came to the conclusion that the way society treats women is reflected in the home. After educating myself, I realized that violence against women, or any other disadvantaged group, was not something new; that there is a history of abuse in the world. For instance, I relate my domestic violence experiences with slavery, especially with those slaves who were whipped by their masters. X did not want me to talk to anyone, because he knew that as soon as I educated myself, I would run as fast and as far away from him as I could. By keeping me ignorant, he kept control over me.

Now, as a conscious survivor, I do what I can to make a difference not only in my life, but also in the lives of others. My experience with domestic violence has been completely transformed into activism. I believe that only those of us who have experienced certain trauma can understand and sympathize with those who are currently going through something similar. We who are survivors have to demand change. However, in these demands, we have to find a connection with other oppressed groups.

Now that I'm trying to fight the constant political, social, and cultural violence against women, I consider myself extremely lucky, because I got out of it alive. I broke the cycle, and I am doing all that is in my power to break the cycle for other individuals. I paid a way-too-high price to learn what I know now. I regret that no one in my family or high school ever spoke about violence against women. I am sorry that there was no open dialogue about domestic violence and the choices we women have. Social expectations were that I marry, and I did. Social expectations were that I have someone to "protect" me, and that the person be a male. I expected to be protected in my marriage, but I wasn't. I now know that I have choices: I can remarry, stay happily single forever, have biological children, or adopt if I so please. Now I have the power to question societal norms and to decide to follow that body of knowledge, or form new ones. I acknowledge the advantages that I have as a heterosexual. I have no idea what would have happened if I were a lesbian and had to deal with the social and family pressure of staying in a marriage. I paid an extremely high price to learn what I know now. However, it doesn't have to be the same for others.

The Evolution of Domestic Violence and Reform Efforts Across Indian Country

Victoria Lucia Ybanez

Introduction

In order to end domestic violence in all its forms, we must understand why it exists in Indian Country today and assess our current challenges in addressing the issue. When we examine the reasons behind the presence of domestic violence in Native communities, we must first consider its historical origins.

Domestic violence in Native society came about over the course of centuries of change. Examining the history of oppression that laid the groundwork for the rise of violence against Native women shows us that efforts to end the domestic violence faced by women across Indian Country today are still in their infancy.

You must be able to see where you have been before you can possibly know where you want to go.

—Muscogee Creek saying

Precontact Societies

1. Native people occupying the land now known as the United States had complex societal structures that shaped the way they lived their lives. Some researchers estimate indigenous precontact populations at more than forty-five million, while

others approximate twenty million. The United States government estimates it at around half a million.[1]

2. In spite of the disagreement regarding the numbers, one fact remains commonly understood: Native people held women as sacred. In many societies, women were universally honored and respected for their life-giving powers.[2] Their ability to create life likened them to Mother Earth. Their communities respected and honored them. Acts of violence such as rape were uncommon, and when they did occur, they evoked fear and horror, because Native respect for women arose from the belief that women had power over life and death.[3] By many accounts, domestic violence was rare in indigenous societies prior to European contact and only became common after the onset of colonization.

Colonization and the Early Erosion of Tribal Societies

European contact began in large part in 1492 and led to a historic and tragic change in the lives of indigenous people: the beginning of the loss of culture and the change in the status of Native women.

1. During the 17th century, tales of the New World spread through Europe, and explorers arrived and lay claim to territories and riches for their homelands abroad. These colonizers held the common view that it was not only their divine right, but also their responsibility to take and use the land and its resources without regard for the rights of the indigenous people living there at the time.[4] This threatened Native values and imposed the notion of ownership (a concept foreign to Native ways of life), which brought the ideas of men's entitlement and of women as property.

2. Prior to 1684, tribes were viewed as independent nations by foreign entities with the exception of Spain. Spain viewed the Native occupants as citizens and therefore as subject to Spanish rule. This was the onset of the erosion of tribal sovereignty and the eventual loss of Native women's sovereignty.

3. By the 18th century, European exploration of the New World had spread across the eastern and western seaboards and as far north as Alaska, creating far-reaching avenues that had an impact on the values and roles of Native women and men.

Confrontation of Tribal Ways of Living

The traditional Cheyenne saying "A people is not defeated until the hearts of its women are on the ground" reflects the destructive practices of the colonizers.

1. The 18th and 19th centuries were times of significant suffering for indigenous people. The values of traditional Native society were being undermined by practices aimed at gaining control of the land and resources, exposing and imposing a values system that was foreign to Native societies and that relegated women to the position of substandard citizens.

2. Native people were viewed as "barbarian," "savage," and "not human"; the Native way of life was being destroyed. This labeling was a tool used to enable the widespread destruction of Native people and is commonly used today as a tactic by batterers to control and dehumanize women. There are tales of small pox-infected blankets, strychnine-infected biscuits, slaughters of herds of bison, massacres of hunting parties, and slaughters of Native women and children.

3. In 1800, the buffalo population was estimated to be at about forty million; less than a century later, in 1895, it was at one thousand.[5] The slaughter of buffalo, a tactic used to starve Native people into extinction or submission, defiled Native societies with values that permitted waste and caused detachment from their relationship with animals—concepts that were previously virtually unknown.

4. The systematic destruction of Native cultures included a particular degradation of Native women. In many ways, the conquest of Native nations by Anglo-Europeans was accomplished by making war on Indian women.[6] Native women were raped, abused, and killed in order to seize land and force the assimilation of Native people.

5. By the mid-19th century, U.S. policy makers and military commanders were stating—openly, frequently, and in plain English—that their objective was no less than the "complete extermination" of any Native people who resisted being dispossessed of their lands, subordinated to federal authority, and assimilated into the colonizing culture.[7] As Native societies were repeatedly exposed to the values of the colonizers, Native men and women were being changed. The process of internalizing those values was under way. It led to the eventual belief that men have a right to certain entitlements in their relationships with women and a right to enforce or control a woman's behavior.

6. The 1883 Supreme Court decision in *Ex Parte Crow Dog* allowed the United States to interfere with the structure of tribal courts and the process by which tribes develop their own laws.[8] The Major Crimes Act led the way for complicating the jurisdictional issues still found today in Indian Country:

> *On the Sioux Reservation in Dakota Territory, Crow Dog shot to death Spotted Tail. The tribal system restored harmony to the two families; however, the United States criminal justice system did not honor the tribal system's decision. The case went all the way to the Supreme Court, where tribal sovereignty was upheld, and it was affirmed that the U.S. courts lacked criminal jurisdiction over crimes committed between Native people in Indian Country. As a result, the United States Congress passed the Major Crimes Act, extending federal jurisdiction over certain crimes committed in Indian Country.[9]*

The Era of Termination and Assimilation: 1870 to 1958

1. Forced relocation led to the decimation of thousands of Native people as they were rounded up and force-marched across the country in the early 19th century in order to open up tribal lands in the southeastern United States to white settlement and slavery. The most well-known of these instances is the relocation of seventeen thousand Cherokees, who were compelled to walk the Trail of Tears. More than 25 percent died of malnutrition, disease, and exposure along the way.[10] By 1837, most members of the five southeastern nations (Cherokee, Creek, Choctaw, Chickasaw, and Seminole) had been relocated west from their land, which was east of the Mississippi, opening up twenty-five million acres. This began a process of relocation and removal that took place across the country, forcing Native people to leave their homelands either through coercion or through the results of wars: Manifest Destiny.

2. The United States government also attempted to assimilate indigenous people into the mainstream of American life by changing customs, dress, occupations, language, religion, and philosophy. Boarding schools were a federally sanctioned practice that transpired over the course of a hundred years. In 1928, the Merriam Report to

Congress outlined the harsh treatment of Native children in boarding schools and the outrageous behavior of school authorities toward Indian children.[11] Native people have been raised by institutions (the boarding schools) and subjected to inhumane treatment for multiple generations. This has led to the loss of traditional cultural values, Native identity, and the internalization of oppression.

3. Iroquois women influenced the early suffragette movement by providing a model of women who lived liberated lives with rights, freedoms, and a voice in government.[12]

> *Surely these white women living under conditions of virtual slavery did not get their vision in a vacuum. Somehow they were able to see from point A where they stood corseted, ornamental, legally nonpersons, to point C, the regenerated world gauge predicted in which all repressive institutions would be destroyed. They caught a glimpse of the possibility of freedom because they knew women who lived liberated lives, women who had always possessed rights beyond their wildest imaginations, Iroquois women.[13]*

4. The year 1924 saw the mandatory citizenship of Native people.

5. In 1934, the Indian Reorganization Act allowed tribes to develop tribal justice codes and operate court systems enforcing tribal laws thusly enacted.[14] Because the laws and regulations of the tribal courts had to be approved by the Bureau of Indian Affairs, the tribes were under great pressure to incorporate Western types of judicial procedure into their own judicial systems.[15]

6. The 1950s saw the Bureau of Indian Affairs identify more than a hundred tribes to be singled out for "termination" under the federal government's policy to end its relationship of trust with tribes,[16] relinquishing itself of its treaty obligations of responsibility.

7. A major step toward termination was the enactment of Public Law 280, in 1953. It transferred federal criminal jurisdiction in Indian Country to certain states. Initially placed on six states, PL 280 allowed other states an opportunity to apply for jurisdiction over tribes, without the consent of the tribal governments. Ten states were granted optional jurisdiction. It was amended in 1968, partly to prohibit this situation from occurring without tribal consent; there has been almost no expansion of PL 280,[17]

and three states have retroceded jurisdiction or returned jurisdiction to the federal government. PL 280 further complicates jurisdiction and enforcement issues across Indian Country.

The 1970s

1. Early organizing around violence against women in the mainstream society followed on the heels of women's participation in the civil rights and antiwar movements. The antirape movement was one of the earliest components of the movement to address violence against women.[18]

2. In 1978, the Indian Child Welfare Act (ICWA) was adopted by Congress in order to preserve the integrity of Indian tribes and ensure their future. Before 1978, as many as 25 to 35 percent of the Indian children in certain states were removed from their homes and placed in non-Indian homes by state courts, welfare agencies, and private adoption agencies. By enacting ICWA—which requires that Indian children, once removed, be placed in homes that reflect their unique traditional values—Congress was acknowledging that no nation or culture can flourish if its youngest members are removed.[19]

3. No one knows for sure today how many Native women were sterilized during the 1970s. Eugenics, which literally means "well born," is a movement that promoted the elimination of so-called inferior people from spreading their inferiority upon the stock of the nation.[20] Sterilization reached its popularity in Indian Health Services during the 1970s and was the last official eugenic effort. Native women of childbearing age numbered around a hundred thousand, and as of 1982, it was estimated that 42 percent of Native American women were sterilized, having a significant impact on Native nations' ability to reproduce its small population.[21] While efforts to end violence against women were growing, state-sanctioned violence such as this continued to be practiced.

4. The White Buffalo Calf Women's Society (WBCWS), the first shelter created to serve battered Native women living in the country, opened in 1977 on the Rosebud Sioux Reservation in South Dakota. A group of Native women came together to develop the shelter. The purpose of WBCWS was to create a safe place for women that honored them in their own culture, their inherent right as women to be respected and to be held

as sacred. It continues to work to reduce domestic violence by providing services and a safe environment to enable domestic violence victims to leave their abusers.

5. Contrary to the common perception that the United States is a country founded on religious freedom, it was not until 1978 that the Indian Religion Freedom Act was passed by Congress. Central in tribal societies, many ceremonies and spiritual practices were lost as a result of government laws against certain Native spiritual practices. Many ceremonies and spiritual practices were outlawed until twenty-five years ago. Native communities are working to reclaim and protect those spiritual practices that do remain.

6. Early organizing saw Native leadership working to bring the voices of Native women to the domestic violence movement. Tillie Blackbear, a grandmother in the movement, was one of the founding mothers of the National Coalition Against Domestic Violence (NCADV) and the South Dakota Coalition Against Domestic Violence and Sexual Assault (SDCADVSA). In 1978, the NCADV formed when battered women's advocates from all parts of the nation attended the U.S. Commission on Civil Rights hearing on battered women in Washington, D.C., hoping to address common problems.[22] The SDCADVSA formed in 1978 as a result of organizing efforts, assisted by the South Dakota Commission on the Status of Women, bringing together more than seventy-five women at the first meeting, which was held on the Rose Bud Reservation.[23]

The 1980s

Early work in Indian Country was slow to start, compared to the mainstream movement to end violence against women. However, as Native leadership in the movement expanded, significant efforts were being developed to create Native-specific responses that went beyond replicating mainstream programming.

1. The American Indian Women's Circle against Abuse (AIWCA) was formed in 1982 as the first Native coalition, with representation from ten of the eleven tribes in Minnesota and all the Native advocates working in battered women's programs. The AIWCA provided a range of training to Native communities and battered women's programs. However, the coalition was defunded in 1993 and eventually dissolved.

2. Women of Nations (WON) in Minneapolis, Minnesota, formed in May 1982 as a volunteer community advocacy program, originally supported by member contributions from their own pockets. In 1989, it became the first urban Indian shelter for battered women in the United States. Organizing members secured the shelter's existence by obtaining a legislative appropriation of more than $100,000 to open its shelter doors.

3. The pro-arrest code (now known as the mandatory arrest code) was passed in 1989 on the Pine Ridge Reservation, making it the first reservation to adopt a mandatory arrest policy. The code made it against the law to assault or abuse an intimate partner and included further protections such as mandatory arrest, no bond until arraignment, and mandatory sentencing.[24]

The 1990s

1. In 1990, a group of Indian advocates and community members from the Fond Du Lac Reservation, concerned about the level of violence against Indian women, formed to begin a dialogue on domestic violence. As a result, Mending the Sacred Hoop was created. The organization's goals were to 1) develop an intervention model that would coordinate reservation and nonreservation agencies to work collectively on policy and procedure changes, 2) to educate off-reservation court systems and law enforcement agencies about the myths and beliefs related to Indian people and domestic violence, 3) to coordinate a Council on Nonviolence, which would consist of judges, prosecutors, probation officers, law enforcement, public defenders, advocates, counselors, reservation service providers, and representatives of the business committee, and 4) to provide training to reservations on developing an intervention project.

2. In 1994, the Violence Against Women Act (VAWA)—a part of the Federal Crime Control Bill—gave federal support to develop and strengthen law enforcement and prosecution strategies to combat violence against Indian women and children and to develop and strengthen victim services, particularly those related to violent crimes against women.[25]

3. In 1995, the VAWA created the Violence Against Women Office (VAWO)—now known as the Office of Violence Against Women—within the Office of Justice Programs

(OJP) of the Department of Justice. It was a historic acknowledgement by the federal government that the occurrence of violent crime targeted women.

4. The Office of Victims of Crimes (OVC) provided resources for domestic violence victims prior to the creation of the VAWO. The OVC delivered its federal funds by way of a state pass-through. Because of tribal sovereignty, many tribes were unwilling to seek funding from the states. In 1998, the OVC eliminated its state pass-through of federal funds to the tribes, which had proven to be less than ideal.[26]

5. Funding was slow to reach Indian Country. Advocating for change, a vocal group of Native women campaigned for set-aside VAWA funds to be designated for tribes as to ensure that resources reached them. As a result, the STOP Violence against Indian Women Grant Program was created. This program encouraged tribal governments to develop and strengthen the tribal justice system's response (including law enforcement, prosecution, victim services, and courts) to violence against Indian women and to improve services to victims of domestic violence, sexual assault, and stalking. In reaffirming the United States' unique relationship with Native American tribal governments, Executive and Justice Department policy requires OJP to work on a government-to-government basis with Indian tribes.[27]

6. As resources to stop violence grew across Indian Country, domestic violence responses expanded. The mid- to late 1990s saw a growth in domestic violence programs, coordinated community responses, and changing tribal codes. Some tribal communities engaged in working to reclaim traditional values in their efforts to end violence against Indian women.

7. Two significant resources were created for work in Indian Country. Mending the Sacred Hoop's STOP Violence against Indian Women Technical Assistance Project provides technical assistance to recipients of the STOP Violence against Indian Women Discretionary Grants with a purpose of working to ensure the safety of victims and their families and to create accountability within the systems. Grantees are provided training and consultation. The Sacred Circle National Resource Center is one of six national resource centers in the United States addressing domestic violence, and it provides support primarily to 562 federally recognized American Indian/Alaskan Native tribes across the United States.

8. According to "American Indians and Crime," a study by the Department of Justice released in 1999, Native Americans are far more likely to be victims of violent crimes than members of any other racial group. The rate of violent crime experienced by Native women is nearly 50 percent higher than that experienced by black males. The Alaska Native Women Sexual Assault Committee was formed in January 1999 after the Federal Bureau of Investigation ranked Alaska number one in incidents of rape. Alaska had been at the top of that crime category for about two-thirds of the previous two decades.[28]

9. The year 1999 saw the onset of new advances with Native coalitions. The Oklahoma Native American Coalition was formed; it brings together twelve tribes to stop domestic violence and sexual assault against Native American women and children.

Current Issues

Ahead of us is an overriding challenge to undo a history that supports rape and violence against Native women, and to create one that strives toward both the physical and cultural survival of Native people.

Navajo poet Luci Tapahonso read the following during the 1991 Modern Language Association's annual convention:

> *I am, I am*
> *In wisdom I walk*
> *In beauty may I walk . . .*
> *In beauty it is restored.*
> *The light, the dawn.*
> *It is morning.*

As she read, my heart was lifted in recognition of our power, our magnificent life.

> *I am Laguna, woman of the lake, daughter of the dawn, sunrise, kurena. I can see the light making the world anew. It is the nature of my blood and heritage to do this. There is surely cause to weep, to grieve; but greater than ugliness, the endurance*

of tribal beauty is our reason to sing, to greet the coming day and the restored life and hope it brings.[29]

Developing relevant responses that work toward reclaiming precontact values that restore harmony and balance to Native communities, which have been shaken by a history of oppression, is on the forefront for progressing the work to end violence against Indian women.

1. Developing Native-specific programs that intervene in men's use of violence must adapt an educational approach that centers around the belief that violence is a learned behavior, evolving from a history of oppression, and that it can be unlearned. Much of the work in men's groups that work with Native men needs to emphasize the relationships within family and community by incorporating teachings of respect, by acknowledging and honoring the roles of men and women, and by restoring natural ways of living.[30]

2. Sexual assault in Indian communities is an issue that is barely addressed, while Native women report that it is rampant in their communities. Work in this area has been slow, but Native women are beginning to organize. Sexual Assault Programs and Sexual Assault Tribal Coalitions are becoming resources for training and support for many advocates and victims.[31]

3. Good work is being done to address stalking in Indian Country, but there is still much left to do.[32] As 17 percent of Native American and Alaskan Native women have been stalked (compared with 8.1 percent of women in the general population, and 2 percent of men), it is of the utmost importance that we keep the issue in the front of our minds. Developing and implementing tribal antistalking codes is barely in its infancy and must continue and should infuse sovereignty and tribal values.[33]

4. With well over five hundred federally recognized tribes, there are barely twenty-six Native-specific shelters in existence today, with only a few more in development. Efforts must support the development and ongoing operation of shelters across Indian Country.

5. In the work to end violence against Indian women, many Native nations are finding that shelter options alone do not provide the time or the stability women need to create a solid base for change in their lives. Longer-term housing and affordable permanent

housing that goes "beyond the physical structure" need to create opportunities for battered women leaving abusive relationships to live in a community that extends safety, support, and a place to work toward reclaiming their connections with themselves and each other.

6. There are many jurisdictional complexities and limitations in Indian Country. The confusing division of authority among tribal, federal, and state governments—which results in a jurisdictional maze—is complicated by the lack of tribal courts' criminal jurisdiction over non-Indians, which is the practical impact of PL 280 and other limitations on tribal criminal jurisdiction. The difficulty of determining jurisdiction, and provisions for the concurrent jurisdiction of certain cases, can cause conflict and confusion for law enforcement, prosecution, courts, service providers, and crime victims in Indian Country.[34]

7. State coalitions have not been effective in bringing voice to Native issues. As a result, Native coalitions are being developed across Indian Country. Efforts to continue forming and expanding the reaches of Native coalitions across the country will support the efforts to strengthen domestic violence responses, training, and leadership.

8. Struggles around the effectiveness of criminal justice responses (its historical legacy, which has a disproportionate number of Native Americans incarcerated in the United States), as well as a search for alternative justice solutions, poses significant challenges for future work. A restorative justice movement is growing in both mainstream and indigenous communities, and it brings significant concerns that must be weighed heavily in deciding if and how this work ties to domestic violence efforts. There are concerns about how restorative justice or community justice efforts place greater power with the community. A culturally appropriate justice system cannot simply be achieved by ensuring that more community members are involved.[35] While restoring community responsibility affirms traditional Native values, many communities lack the social structure to support shifts of power into the hands of their community. In addition, the power imbalance in relationships where domestic violence is taking place precludes an ability to involve victims of domestic violence in processes where they have equal footing with their abuser. There are a significant number of issues to be examined; exploring restorative justice alternatives must consider these issues heavily before deciding if it is an appropriate alternative.

Maybelline War Paint

Deidra Suwanee Dees

Oppression
> you make my
> mouth
> bleed

reclusive
> staying indoors on
> the rez when the
> wounds are really big

facades
> hiding
> behind my wardrobe
> of Indian faces

pretense
> Maybelline war paint
> covers
> battered traces

frightened
> hoping they won't
> see the scars of
> my shame

waiting
> for you to leave me
> so I can die in the
> middle of my pain

Voices of the Pioneers: The Origin of the South Asian Domestic Violence Movement in the United States

Lakshmy Parameswaran

In loving memory of Jothi (Jo) Viswanathan

Introduction

A cross the United States, there are more than twenty major South Asian organizations working to end personal and societal violence against women. I am a founder of one of them: Daya, which is located in Houston. The majority of the founders of these organizations are like me, women who migrated to America in their youth and came of age on Western soil. Pursuing many roles—professionals, activists, and homemakers— these women quietly shoulder their commitment to end violence.

In the last twelve years of my association with the leaders of these organizations, I have discovered that their experiences represent the collective growth and development of South Asian women in America—and more specifically, the evolution of the South Asian domestic violence movement in this country. I believe it is important to record their experiences, for they provide a backdrop to this growing movement of twenty-five years and testify to the strength of South Asian women as a group. Using the voices of four pioneers of the movement, I narrate the history of the South Asian antiviolence movement.

A Glance at the Early Days

A newly arrived and upwardly mobile migrant group in America, South Asians began organizing in the early 1970s[1] by establishing associations based on their religious and regional similarities. "Indian identity; American commitment," stated the 1971 slogan of the New York–based Association of Indians in America.[2] The role of women in these organizations, which were mostly spearheaded by men, was limited to duties such as arranging potluck dinners and children's programs. Issues of South Asian women's rights remained unaddressed, even at a time when the feminist movement was rising in America. Feeling marginalized by the mainstream women's movement, South Asian women drew inspiration from the third world feminist groups, which exposed the problems of dowry deaths and female feticide and questioned the gender-based norms in the institutions of marriage and family.[3] By the early 1980s, many South Asian women had begun to voice their observations and experiences of personal and structural oppression as immigrants from South Asia.

In the spring of 1982, Jo Viswanathan, a social worker in Houston, organized a meeting to voice her concerns that depression, isolation, and relational conflicts—problems hidden behind the wrinkle-free image of South Asians—had begun to surface and threaten their well-being as they settled on American soil. I was among a handful of Indian women who were present, in the back room of that library, to listen to Jo and ponder her idea of forming a support network for us.

Only years later would I recognize the significance of this meeting as a turning point in our lives. I did not know then that migration to America had altered our identities and environment, and that there were women like Jo in other cities, women who were concerned about the same problems in their communities and entertaining the same solutions. It had not occurred to me that their collective vision would birth a nationwide South Asian movement against domestic violence, significant enough to be noted in the history of immigration to America.

Despite Jo's efforts in 1982, it took an unfathomable domestic violence tragedy to startle Houston into joining the movement that was spreading across America. On March 22, 1996, twenty-eight-year-old Nirmala Katta shot and killed her violent husband of eight years and her three young children, and then set her suburban house on fire before shooting and killing herself. The *Houston Chronicle* ran a Sunday front-page exposé on this tragedy, entitled "When Hope Dies."[4] Nirmala, although educated and employed, had not sought serious help from anyone for her terrible ordeal, perhaps because she felt there was no one she could turn to. Had Jo's vision of a support system for South Asian women materialized, Nirmala's tragedy might have been avoided.

Realizing this, seven Indian American women, including myself, founded Daya (which means "compassion"), and it began operating in July 1996. Through counseling, advocacy, and community education, Daya empowers Houston's South Asian victims of family violence. Jo died of cancer in 2002, but her handprint remains on the organization.

Covering the Basics

The basis of this article is formed by in-depth telephone interviews with four founders: Prem Sharma, of Apna Ghar, in Chicago; Shamita Das Dasgupta, of Manavi, in New Jersey; Kalpana Sutaria, of Saheli, in Austin; and Srilakshmi (Sri) Renganathan, of South Asian Women's Empowerment and Resource Alliance (SAWERA), in Portland, Oregon. In addition, the basis of this article is formed by the responses I received from a few other advocates, who completed a questionnaire.

I selected these four women based on their willingness to share information and to be quoted publicly. However, I have chosen not to identify the individuals by name when I actually quote them. I want each woman to speak without her identity shadowing her narration, so readers can "hear" her true voice. I have selected the quotes from our conversations and organized them into four major categories: Marriage and Migration, Double Isolation of Immigrants, Advocacy in a South Asian Context, and Challenges. Utilizing the founders' own narratives, the categories project a sort of "slide show" that depicts the lives of women in India, their passage as immigrants to America, and their subsequent efforts to safeguard their rights and live in an atmosphere of nonviolence in the new society.

Additionally, I have inserted excerpts from the *Houston Chronicle* article "When Hope Dies," in which Mike Tolson, through extensive interviews with people in India and Houston, explored the multidimensional causes of Nirmala Katta's victimization. Rereading the report after ten years, I was struck by the passages that reiterate the burden of the hyphenated South Asian–American identity. Nirmala's tragedy signifies the reasons for the origin of Daya, and for that of the South Asian domestic violence movement in general.

Founders: A Sample

Prem, Shamita, Kalpana, and Sri represent a diversity of experiences as founders of South Asian antiviolence groups. Like Jo and me, Prem and Shamita are part of the first wave of immigrants from South Asia that arrived on American shores subsequent to the passing of the Immigration and Nationality Act of 1965, which provided economic opportunities for Asian professionals. As early settlers, Prem and Shamita had to begin their advocacy from the ground up. Thanks largely to their initiative, Kalpana and Sri, who migrated a decade or two later, had a base from which to launch their work.

A self-described professional volunteer, Prem Sharma of Chicago was instrumental in establishing a helpline in 1983 that took calls from Indians in distress. Realizing how domestic violence dominated the spectrum of issues they dealt with, the helpline led to the opening of Apna Ghar (Our Home) in 1989.

Shaped by the women's movement of the 1970s, community worker Shamita Das Dasgupta opened the doors of her New Jersey home in 1985 to establish Manavi (Primal Woman). Since then, Shamita's home telephone doubled as Manavi's hotline number for many years. Of all the problems (immigration status, discrimination, and violence) for which the callers sought help, domestic violence matters predominated.

Architect and activist Kalpana Sutaria was among the core group of about eight women who conceived the idea of a helpline for Austin South Asians. Each of those eight women knew someone who was struggling with domestic violence. Deriving encouragement from groups like Manavi, Kalpana acted on her conviction and established Saheli (Women Friends) in 1992.

Even before the creation of SAWERA, South Asian women were sharing their tales of abuse with Sri Renganathan and seven other cofounders of the Portland organization. A software engineer, Sri saw the surge in the South Asian population in the high-tech Pacific Northwest, and she knew there had to be more such tales. The time for SAWERA had arrived. Founded in May 1997, SAWERA received its first call in June.

Today, Apna Ghar has joined the ranks of mainstream organizations, with a shelter for battered women and a child-visitation center; Manavi maintains its leadership role with innovative strides toward advocacy and awareness; SAWERA, within its short life span, has become a vital force in the greater Portland community; and Saheli has earned respect for its activism to create social change.

Diversity in Unity

Prem, Shamita, Kalpana, and Sri—four women as varied as the dialects of India—are united by one common goal: to serve and strengthen South Asian women in America. Similarly, their organizations—Apna Ghar, Manavi, Saheli, and SAWERA—have remained distinct while sharing a mainstream mission to end violence against women. Reflective of this diversity in unity, the founders unanimously expressed how "different" they felt while growing up in India.

> *I was the different one in my family. My siblings don't do [this work]. [For me], it has been a continuous process from second grade. I have never taken a back seat. I [always] take a stand. [Even] in my school, I'd have a* bhel-puri *stall to make money for some cause or other. It is a frame of mind, I think. You see the world differently.*

> *I felt different right from age eight. I was one sister among three brothers. I could play cricket with boys; I had a bike just like my brothers. I remember clearly, I was thirteen or fourteen, some girl made a comment that I was like a boy [because] I was only interested in studies. Still, I [knew] I was in an environment that [had] double standards. I'd do housework, while my brothers were not required to.*

The following experiences show that, at times, their feelings of being different might be linked to extenuating circumstances, which can bring an awareness to one's uniqueness.

> *The last child is the smartest one, my mother used to say; they take all the knowledge from the womb. I was the youngest; I had seven siblings. My youngest brother was eight years older than me. I was already way behind [my siblings]. [Besides], my mother was superstitious. I was born in November—very cold in Simla. My mother blamed me for my father's asthma, because it happened right after I was born. It was difficult, but you find your way in a large family. I became mature before I grew up, under the shade of a large tree, not a little plant.*

My father was in a transferable service, so my family moved [around].
[Therefore], I didn't go to a formal school until I was ten; I didn't have the
opportunity to make friends. I was a loner. My early education was through reading,
observing nature. I was left to myself; my parents didn't show any compunction over
my socialization or education.

Ultimately, their feelings of being different—more so than the circumstances that
made them feel different—seem to have guided the founders toward their chosen path.

The Influences

FROM THE *HOUSTON CHRONICLE* ARTICLE:

[An Indian] woman's identity comes first from her father and later from her
husband, to whose family she now belongs. As a dependent and subordinate partner,
she can exert little control over her destiny.[5]

The range of power a woman can wield within this secondary status depends
on her own resourcefulness. The founders exemplified this truth when they spoke of
their mothers, who, even while disempowered, were able to influence their daughters
strongly.

My father called me his "fourth son" and gave me [equal] freedom. But my
mother could never speak up. [Yet] she taught me to speak up [and] was glad that
I'd speak up. She'd talk about how she wanted to be a doctor. She cherished the fact
that she had ambitions and was proud of it.

My mother was a victim of her own beliefs, [but] she was a very dynamic
woman. She was a reformer. She got rid of the veils we [women] had to wear in
my community. She got rid of the joint family [we were living in]. She asked her
sons and daughters-in-law to [move] separately. I adopted her ways [except for her
superstitious beliefs]. She became my mentor.

The founders felt that such influences, although significant, were not enough to prepare them for adulthood, especially as immigrants to America.

Women need time and resources to develop skills and independence so they can get out of a bad situation quickly. I didn't have them, and I was unaware of the importance [of having them]. As a result, I did struggle when I came to this country [as a young wife] in 1968.

I understood the thinking that [makes] our clients take [the] abuse and [not] do anything about it. I had a hunch about it from the way I was raised as a daughter, even though my father would call me his "fourth son." If the atmosphere [in India] were conducive to raising sons and daughters equally without putting daughters down, I might have become different.

The founders' words also revealed how the double standards of their upbringing were wedged in their thoughts, regardless of their accomplishments.

I chose a career [usually] pursued by males, and my parents supported me. Even in America, parents don't encourage girls [toward] "male" professions. Still, my awareness about women comes from [seeing others] treat women as emotional [beings]. They say in my language that women's brains are at their ankles.

Marriage and Migration
FROM THE *HOUSTON CHRONICLE* ARTICLE:

Nirmala's parents considered [Ashok, Nirmala's husband] a good catch. Indian men living in the West, with its greater earning potential, usually are. The couple married in February 1988 . . . Nirmala's disillusionment began almost the moment she arrived in Houston [in April 1990, after she obtained her visa] . . . her loving husband of memory seemed cold to her, almost hostile.[6]

The founders' stories of migration to America were reflective of the times they came of age in India (the '60s, '70s, and '80s) and of the erosion of a long-cherished tradition—the tradition of the family's input and involvement in every aspect of a girl's marriage.

> *I came to this country in 1968, when I was nineteen, and I was already married for three years. It was an arranged marriage; happened quickly after I finished school. I did fight against it, [although] it was a futile fight. My husband came as a student, and I followed him. I felt lonely here; no money for me to go to college. It was difficult, but being young has its advantages. I started [college] in 1973, [after] I had had my daughter.*

By the mid-1970s, however, the allure of migration to America began to outshine the desire of parents (in educated, middle-class homes) to see their daughters married traditionally, and at an "appropriate age."

> *My mother didn't want me to go to America [for higher studies] without getting married. My family was looking for a professional match from the same caste. I said no; I had decided that I would marry not because I was [twenty something], but when I find someone who will treat me with respect. I met my husband here. He was my professor. But in the late '70s, when I told them I wanted to marry a divorced man with two kids, my family was very upset.*

> *I came in 1988 to study in the East Coast. That was where I met my husband; never finished the PhD I was supposed to . . . [laughs]. Prior to my [leaving], my father had put my horoscope in a "horoscope drum" [from which you pick potential matches]; not even one [profile] came out filling my requirements for an ideal husband. So my father permitted me to go abroad and study [since my time to marry hadn't come]. My sister married someone who was in the U.S., but my parents in India arranged their meeting. [Unlike] our clients, [my sister] lucked out [because her husband is not abusive].*

Nirmala, who experienced rejection from the moment she landed in Houston, certainly would have been one such client for whom the promise of migration to America turned out to be a series of nightmares.

Family Structure and Abuse Dynamics
FROM THE *HOUSTON CHRONICLE* ARTICLE:

> *In letters to her parents, [Nirmala] complained of being left in the apartment for long stretches. Ashok worked days and nights and would not tell her where he was. She had no car and no friends. . . . "Daddy I don't know what to do," Nirmala wrote. "I am alone here" . . . "I beg you Daddy. Help me, help me, help me."*[7]

The members of an Indian nuclear family, small or large, identify themselves with a much larger extended family network.[8] Thus, even for a newly married South Asian woman, there is usually a group made up of kin compensating for any lack of affection on the part of her spouse. The same network of people also acts as a mechanism of social control in case the husband turns out to be violent.[9] This may be a reason why all four founders reported not having witnessed ongoing or severe physical abuse in India.

While the inclusive and, at times, intrusive Indian family structure might help in containing the most brutal forms of family violence, it does not stop all forms of abuse. Indian families, like families in other cultures, contribute to and endure various forms of abuse. Our founders' families were not exempt from such abuse nor the denial that often accompanies it.

> *My father had anger problems that sometimes turned into emotional abuse. But I could talk to him, and he listened when he was calm. Eventually he reduced [his temper], because his kids were growing up. I had an access to him that my mother and brothers didn't have, which helped.*

> *Oppression of women was all around me. I have been noticing it since I was little. I knew my mom and aunts were tremendously oppressed [by their*

families and communities]. But they couldn't get out. They didn't have the means and the opportunity. It was not just individual oppression; I could [also] see structural oppression.

My mom's sister was an abused wife. Still [the family] put up with my uncle, didn't do anything about it. My uncle is dead now. In spite of what he did, his daughter—my cousin—wanted to name her new house after him. My aunt couldn't bear it. She said no; his treatment of her [had] affected her deeply.

Double Isolation of Immigrants

FROM THE *HOUSTON CHRONICLE* ARTICLE:

Though no note of explanation was left [by Nirmala], the scraps that remained beneath the charred veneer of her life tell an inexorably tragic tale—one of cruelty and betrayal, of isolation and the inescapable tug of old India.[10]

Isolation is a key characteristic of an abusive relationship, and it aptly describes the plight of new immigrants. While South Asians formed associations based on religion and language to mitigate their cultural isolation, these groups were ignorant of the pain of personal isolation caused by spousal abuse. The leaders of these cultural groups operated on the premise that migration to an egalitarian Western society, in and of itself, has elevated the status of South Asian women, equalizing, more or less, the gender disparities of South Asian culture.[11] The first step for the founders was to question the validity of this assumption.

In 1978, I started a social club so we could form friendships, not because [I thought] we had issues. The Indian community was looking good then. We even collected dues. [Then] I heard a friend was going through divorce. It was shocking news then; "divorce" was a word unfamiliar to Indians. I am sure there was abuse. That's when I realized our community needs some real help. So from social club, we went to social service. When we thought of the crisis line, I was still not sure.

As the process of assimilation unfolded, the distinct nature of the two forms of isolation—isolation from one's culture and from one's marriage, a double isolation—experienced by South Asian victims of abuse began to emerge more clearly, as did the limitations of mainstream and ethnic organizations in addressing this multi-layered alienation.

> *I spoke with people from other organizations, like Sakhi, in New York. They told me they were getting calls from [my hometown]. Women were calling [New York] to talk to a South Asian advocate instead of calling local agencies or their own cultural groups. So I knew something was needed [in my hometown]. We [the founders] thought we should begin by doing a survey, but everyone in the room already knew someone who [was] being abused. So, we [thought], we will start [the organization], and the women will come, and they did. It was the best thing we did for our community.*

Advocacy in a South Asian Context
FROM THE *HOUSTON CHRONICLE* ARTICLE:

> *[I]t would have been out of character for Nirmala to seek assistance. An Asian woman, private by nature, doesn't often turn to strangers, especially if she thinks they might suggest divorce.*[12]

Advocating for South Asian battered women is a complex task. Trained in the West, the founders see the merits in empowering clients discreetly, by inducing them to change their own atmosphere. As Indian women, however, they are aware of the possible ineffectiveness of this hands-off approach with their clients. This is because South Asian women are traditionally accustomed to the involvement of the extended family in resolving serious personal problems.

Psychologist Jyotsna Vaid points out that the philosophy of South Asian organizations draws on the model of an Indian extended family: a *ma-behen* (kinship) approach that rejects the provider-client premise of the West.[13] In essence, this approach encourages an advocate to shed the formalities of a "professional" and approach the client as an aunt or sister in order to establish trust and intervene effectively. The founders understand this cultural premise.

> I [have] always opened my house for the [organization]. The client confidentiality does not apply to my immediate family. I have brought clients to my house; police have come to my house. My mom goes to clients' homes with food; my husband comes to all our [organization's] events.

> There was no help for South Asian women in the early days. Some of us started our organizations at home, using our home phone numbers. We made it up as we went along, how to help. My organization is well established now. I have cut down my involvement with it. Women [clients] still call me at home. We cannot uniformly apply Western rules on boundaries and distancing with our women. They need some leeway.

Challenges

Professor Margaret Abraham notes the gradual change in attitude among South Asians toward accepting the mission of the women's organizations and lending them moral and financial support.[14] The shift that Abraham describes resonates with one of the founders.

> We [the founders] are not a group of women working alone; there are men who are involved. [We have] a male member who is always present in court whenever there is a case involving one of our clients. There are some who help with grant writing. We feel our community is behind us.

Despite this encouraging trend, the founders felt that such shows of community support were infrequent and inadequate. Early on, they had to face a reluctant community that rose to deny the reality of domestic violence. A founder of New York–based Sakhi had observed responses ranging from wide-eyed surprise to vehement denial in the form of hate mail.

As one advocate of California-based Narika noted, some people saw the founders as "home breakers" putting ideas into women's heads, thus causing breakup of families. Even after two decades of dedicated service, the founders perceived opposition from their own communities as an ongoing issue.

> It is a love-hate relationship we have with [our] community. We've been kicked out of conferences and meetings. They see our services as baseless, controversial. It was very hostile till the mid-'90s. Even now, there is only grudging acceptance, even though they know we are here to stay.

> I see total denial from the community. [Once], an Indian merchant started calling us names [because] we [were exploring claims] from Indian beauticians that they see affluent Indian women with bruises on their bodies. We are the butt of jokes in social gatherings. Even clients' families have ridiculed us, using four-letter words.

> The message that it is okay to leave an unsafe marriage should be a coordinated message; it should come from parents and the community. As it is, our community intimidates [and] isolates parents who tell their daughters not to put up with abusive husbands.

Since victims often assume responsibility for the abuse and fear societal ostracism, the impact of an appropriate community response cannot be overemphasized. It is a crucial element in breaking through the denial that keeps the cycle of violence spinning.

FROM THE *HOUSTON CHRONICLE* ARTICLE:

> [Indian] women don't even want rumors of a troubled marriage to leak out, so corrosive are they to reputation. In letter after letter, Nirmala implored her father not to tell anyone of her woes—"Everyone will insult me."[15]

It is to bring attention to such fears that the advocates continue to distribute leaflets, hold talks, produce plays, and screen movies about the reality of domestic violence. Still, the following remark (as noted by Vaid in 1989), by the New York–based Association of Asian Indian Women in America, about the tepid community response seems to hold true today: "Community awareness is 60 percent; community participation is 10 percent."[16]

Fitting It All In

"Lack of support from [members'] spouses" was cited as the reason for the internal controversies of the Los Angeles–based Asian Indian Women's Network.[17] The founders acknowledged the inevitable role their husbands play in their commitment to fight male-dominated abuse.

> *Among the core group of women who founded this organization, those who didn't have 100 percent support of their husbands left. They couldn't continue, because the level of commitment [needed] was beyond the comfort zone of their partners. Whenever I get discouraged and talk of quitting, my husband reminds me of my strengths.*

> *I was quite clear and open about my feminism from early on. I don't think I gave my husband a choice. So my husband had to accept it, and he eventually did. Over the years, he has become involved in my work, but in his own way.*

The chosen mission of Prem, Shamita, Kalpana, and Sri might have been tough, but it was interesting to see how their mission had given them a unique view on family bonding.

> *It might be too late if you wait for your children to grow [up] before embarking on such important work. Whenever I have a [organization-related] meeting, I make sure my daughter has some activity to go to. It is enriching when we share our [different] experiences. My time away [for this work] also allows my daughter to be [with] her dad. He is a very good influence on her. I don't believe in this [idea of] "quality time" [laughs]. We don't need to sit around the dining table to know each other.*

I never excluded my daughter from my activities; I have taken her around since she was a baby. I didn't have to teach her about empowerment; for her it was a no-brainer. She is a very politically involved professional now; she had her skills in place before she got married and had a family.

The Mission Continues

Apna Ghar, Manavi, Saheli, and SAWERA will always remain a force in the lives of Prem, Shamita, Kalpana, and Sri, respectively. Their commitment to their organizations is strong, and equally strong is the love they feel for the women who rely on them. After a quarter century of struggle, Prem confirmed this with the following reminiscence, tinged with remorse:

It was 1984. I remember clearly. The call came at four in the morning from a local donut shop. She said she was Indian; eighteen, abused and pregnant, and running away from home. I told her to stay put; I'd call back in a few minutes with shelter information. And I did. But she was not there. I remember wishing we had a shelter of our own. The idea for Apna Ghar came because of this girl, although I couldn't help her.

And Sri reiterated:

I cry a lot. The client sitting in front of me is the reality created by oppression. She cries; I cry with her. I tell her I'm glad we are in this together. Strength comes because we are involved; we are figuring a way out, she and I. We are not crying helplessly; ours is not a cry in failure.

Conclusion: Voices of the Pioneers

In my conversations with Prem, Shamita, Kalpana, and Sri, I did not hear any wrenching confessions of abuse that motivated these women to commit to ending the violent treatment of women. Rather, it was the experience of belonging to an oppressive society—and of migration to a seemingly liberated one—that poised women like Prem and Shamita to search for a new South Asian female identity with due rights at a time when women all over the world were questioning their place in society.

In analyzing the founders' narratives in the context of their pasts and presents—as Indians and Indian-Americans, respectively—I see that, like Jo, they felt a sense of urgency, perhaps induced by the awareness that as new immigrants, they were at an unfamiliar intersection in an alien society. This intersection, as for all women, cut on the lines of gender and class; for South Asian immigrants, however, it also cut on the lines of ethnic and cultural differences from the mainstream. In this richest and most advanced country of immigrants, the founders realized, freedom and respect were not a given for any woman.

Recognizing the mirage of equality and liberation, the founders became painfully aware of the void in their lives created by the process of immigration. They felt the absence of a viable identity and a place in society—even a subordinate one—that their predecessors would have passed on to them had they remained in India. With the crucial link to their past missing, they began their own quest for a rightful place, as products of two distinctly different cultures.

The quest challenged them to face tough issues of gender inequality and cultural stereotypes. In a woman like Nirmala, the founders could have sensed the double jeopardy: the trap of an abusive marriage and the trap set by two patriarchal yet opposing societies—West and East, modern and traditional. The resulting cultural schizophrenia can very well lead to catastrophes like Nirmala's. Without question, South Asian women needed a niche of their own on this new soil, a niche where they could reconcile such conflicting cultural expectations and feel safe, sane, respected, and accepted. With over twenty organizations across the country presently working to realize this need, no one will doubt the vision of these and other pioneering women. They are responsible for this movement, which has been gaining momentum since the 1980s, incorporating more and more South Asian women from the early as well as later generations.

Although this article does not address the involvement of young South Asian women—including the second-generation daughters—in organizations like Saheli and Daya, it is important to note their rising participation. The Junior Board of Apna Ghar is but one example of the youth involvement in the South Asian domestic violence movement. A number of the board, staff, and volunteer positions in a majority of these organizations are held today by women of the second generation.

Through the voices of Prem, Shamita, Kalpana, and Sri, I have attempted a collective flashback into the lives and times of a special group of women who envisioned an equal and violence-free South Asian society in America. The movement they began may only be a short chapter in the migration history of South Asians to America but, undoubtedly, it is an important one. I hope this brief account will act as a bookmark for upcoming generations to identify the turning point and perhaps to continue to trace the rest of the path. I hope this bookmark will also be a fitting tribute to Jo.

The Prevalence of Domestic Violence in Afghan Households

Hosai Ehsan

Domestic violence is a major predicament in Afghan households today. It is an issue that has a long history, sees no barriers, and impinges on Afghan women's well being in Afghanistan as much as on Afghan-American women in the United States. Although the United States has a large number of domestic violence cases of various magnitudes recorded annually, it is not known how many of them have occurred in Afghan households. Similarly, the issue has not been investigated in Afghanistan, thus making the frequency a large mystery.

Although in the United States "race is a standard factor examined in national surveys on [domestic] violence, most of the minority research is on black or Latino populations," leaving much to be wondered about other ethnicities.[1]

Violence in women's lives is typically conceptualized as a series of abusive, horrible, or tragic events; and domestic violence is explained as a cycle of violence.[2] The cycles, however, occur at different stages of the women's lives, and moreover, all women do not experience domestic violence equally or in the same ways.[3] Violence against women has many interconnected sources, ranging from male dominance, traditionally inherited gender biases, economic dependency, and strict anti-divorce cultural guidelines. Exposure to domestic violence imperils the development of children as well, as they attempt to form their own intimate relationships throughout life.[4]

Looking at households of Middle Eastern and South Asian descent, we find that males are (and have been) the primary breadwinners and decision makers of the family. Similar to historic western culture, women and children are considered the chattel or the property of men.[5] Dasgupta argues that many white Americans presume that "other" cultures, especially minority ones, are far more accepting of domestic violence than the U.S. culture.[6] American mainstream society still likes to believe that the abuse is limited to minority ethnic communities, lower socio-economic strata, and individuals with dark skin colors. It is important to comprehend that, more importantly, gender roles and male patriarchy influence women's understanding and tolerance of domestic violence.[7] Although patriarchy is found across all cultures, immigrant women are more likely to become vulnerable to experiencing detrimental expressions of patriarchy.[8]

Misinterpreted and contradictory (in meaning) Quranic text, classism, racism, and sexism, shape male perceptions of dominance and patriarchy. The Koran and Hadith emphasize equality between men and women as individuals and as worshipers. Furthermore, the writings also advocate women being able to conduct business or attain an education without consent from their husbands. But they also allow for male polygamy-thus giving women lower inheritance shares-and valuing women's testimony in court only half as much as males.[9] True, most Afghans are Muslims, but Islam alone is only one of the factors influencing Afghan women's intimate partner relationships. Afghan traditional values, history, socioeconomic status, male hierarchy, and cultural stereotypes need also be considered, when attempting to investigate domestic violence and the reasons for its acceptance.

In countries like Morocco, Pakistan, Iran, Saudi Arabia, northern India, Bangladesh, and Afghanistan, males remain the primary financial contributors of the household, and their social standing highly depends on keeping their women secluded from the public view. Politicians use this seclusion of women as a way to express political agendas related to the preservation of cultural identity and traditions.[10] Looking at Afghanistan under the ruling of the various political regimes, control over women's movement and autonomy is a way to express and impose political agendas and power.[11] Although this study is specific to Afghan-American families who physically no longer live in Afghanistan, their ideology continues to be that of male dominancy and female subordination. Factors of national political instability, immigration, loss of family-based support system, inaccessibility to education, failing to gain cultural capitol as well as financial dependence influences the gender based dominant and subordinate position and becomes a catalyst to domestic violence.

For centuries, Afghan women have been victims of war, socioeconomic struggles, lack of education, and most other resources. The past thirty years of Afghanistan's political upheavals have magnified these struggles, placing Afghan women at socially, politically, economically, and even physically disadvantaged positions. According to the *CIA World Fact Book*, only 7.4 percent of women in Afghanistan are literate, marriages are most often arranged (not to be confused with forced) and generally take place in the early teen years. Access to health care and other resources is often controlled by the male household leaders (husband, father, brother-in-law), which places women's social and psychological well being in great jeopardy. Although Afghan women who have been raised in California tend to have more education, have some say about their marriages and can access resources more freely, domestic violence continues to occur in their lives.

Most often it is believed that migration to the United States automatically improves women's status and safety; this is not actually true.[12] In her work "Women's Realities: Defining Violence against Women by Immigration, Race and Class," Dasgupta refers to the South Asian community and raises a question of why a community, which can be oppressive at times, is so important to immigrant women.[13] A suitable answer inscribed well within her work illustrates that escaping from the community can deprive them from the support that community offers. Such support could include but is not limited to, translation services, link to social and economic resources, family or friends' interference, and even providing temporary shelter and escape in the case of violence.[14]

Another issue that exacerbates the problem is that the Afghan communities in California have no women's shelters, hotlines, or any other resources of similar sort for battered women. Often Afghan women are faced with having to weigh the cost versus the benefits of staying with abusive partners. The highest cost of physical and emotional distress abused Afghan women face cannot defeat the benefits of avoiding cultural burdens of shame and dishonor synonymous with divorce.

Methods

Data for this research paper was collected through availability data sampling, snowball sampling, key informant interviews, and a mix of other methods in order to increase the validity of the findings. Since there are not specific places where Afghans work or live in dense populations, it was not viable to use a random sampling method. I asked two community organizations, whom I knew had a large Afghan membership, to provide me with membership lists that I could use to conduct the survey at random. Due to the sensitivity of the issues addressed in the questionnaire, both organizations apologetically denied my request. For the aforementioned reasons of topic sensitivity, possible mass-retaliation from the public and thus in turn concern for my own safety caused me to refrain from conducting the survey in mosques, and several other large-scale community events that took place over the summer.

As a viable option, I used availability sampling-where I approached Afghans at various smaller-scale community gatherings, shops, and parks to conduct surveys. Further, I used snowball sampling where I asked each respondent if they knew of people who might be willing to take the survey. A total of 140 surveys, in equal proportions, were distributed among female and male Afghans, age 18 years and older. Respondents reported residing in counties as far north as Humboldt, as far east as Sacramento down to San Diego, California. The survey included 28 closed-ended questions. Item 29 on the survey was left open for additional comments. The survey addressed questions related to demographics, couple relationships, marriage, and domestic violence among Afghans in the United States.

In order to preserve confidentiality, the survey respondents were reassured that there were no identifying marks on the surveys. They were further instructed to place the completed survey in an attached blank envelope, and return it to me personally or mail it to the address indicated on the survey. Each participant was fully informed about the nature of the research, what is required, as well as any possible stresses and benefits. They were also given the option to withdraw at any time.

Domestic violence was defined as intentionally attempting to physically abuse (slap, kick, punch, push, grab) and/or injure a female spouse/partner. The survey had a surprising return rate of 58% for females and 45% for males. The data collected from the surveys were analyzed using line graphs, pie charts, and tables.

In addition, I conducted eleven key informant interviews with six female and five male adult Afghans. I conducted the interviews in English, Pashto, and Farsi, depending on the preferred language of the subjects. Key informants tend to be the type of people that the community has trust in and looks up to for a variety of reasons. They are also the ones families (especially women) tend to approach in the event they decide to seek help concerning violence within their households. The research did not require key informants to share personal experiences of family violence, but rather give information about the community-tell stories they might have heard, talk about cases they might have observed and give any information they might know regarding domestic violence among Afghans.

The key informant respondents I interviewed had a minimum of five to a maximum of twenty years of experience serving the Afghan community in various professional and personal levels in California. They ranged from people with no education, to those who had attained postgraduate degrees in medicine, agriculture, social sciences, and education. Their ages ranged from twenty-six years to sixty-seven years. One female key informant interviewee was single due to divorce, while others were married, or remarried to Afghans.

A series of eleven open-ended questions were asked during the key informant interviews. Their responses were transcribed. Despite its elevated prevalence, discourses surrounding domestic violence are kept hidden in the Afghan culture, and therefore all respondents were prudent about not revealing their identities. All but one male and one female respondent asked to be interviewed anonymously. The data collected from the key informant interviews were analyzed using coding schemes that classified responses to categories that related to a single variable. For example, punching, kicking, pushing, pulling, and slapping were all related to the variable of hitting in the coding scheme.

Results

PREVALENCE/ACCEPTANCE

The total sample size of 72 respondents is considered as the results are analyzed. Let it be understood that numbers appearing in parenthesis next to various factors are based on the 72 (out of 140) survey responses received. It refers to the total number of respondents agreeing on a variable. For example, a majority of females (34) feel that violence should be reported to the police: means that 34 females agreed that violence against women should be reported to the police. Responses from the key informant interviews are used to enhance and support the research design. In order to preserve the confidentiality of the people whose stories have been told in the interviews minor details that do not affect survey outcome have been altered.

The rates of prevalence versus acceptance of domestic violence in Afghan households are described. A majority of respondents believe that domestic violence against women occurs in most households (31) or in some households (30), and that it is culturally accepted in most homes. It was also found that Afghan women often (35) do not report violence against them to the law enforcement. However, a greater majority of females (34) as opposed to a minority of the males (8) feel that it should always be reported. Nine key informants stated that U.S. law and prevention programs are not culturally sensitive and, therefore, are not a viable option for intervention in Afghan household matters.

Female and male attitudes towards family violence are further described. It is made evident that a larger number of respondents (48) consider males to be responsible for violence in Afghan households; and a surprisingly moderate number of respondents (43) considered females to be at least somewhat responsible for the violence. Overall, males are thought to be mainly the perpetrators and, therefore, more accountable for aggression against their female partners.

It is indicated that a slight majority of respondents (37) agreed that Afghan women in the United States are not less likely to fall victim to domestic violence, yet 50 respondents stated that it has not ever and does not occur in their own households. Three key informants did, however, report having been victimized by male partners.

"How about I tell you my own story," a female key informant began nervously. She continued,

> My husband and I argued over various issues. When he got upset he would slap me, pull my hair, kick and punch me and curse me out. He would also disrespect my family. My children would cry and beg for us to stop fighting. One of my children recently told me that he attempted to commit suicide at one point because he could no longer bear to see the fighting and arguing. My children eventually grew up, and stood up for me. My husband is still mean, but after 23 yeas the physical abuse has

stopped. I'm glad, because divorce was never an option for us as it brings shame on the family.

Key informants dissect the issue of family violence in Afghan households in the United States. They report having heard of or seen numerous cases of mild to severe physical female partner abuse, involving pushing, pulling, slapping, kicking, punching, breaking bones, causing miscarriages, black eyes, killing and using weapons such as guns and knives. Frequent psychological abuse including minimizing, cursing, disrespecting, controlling, and stalking were reported as well. The key informants retold many case-stories. They all mimicked each other, summing up an overall rigid picture of Afghan-American intimate partner relationships.

The story here realistically exemplifies the prevalence and acceptance of family violence in Afghan households: An Afghan couple had two children and the third was on the way. The family was received welfare. The mother-in-law who lived with the couple caused many problems. She and her son wanted to save as much money as possible in order to send it back home. Every time the wife made an issue out of this her husband beat her. Once the beating was so severe that she went into shock and ended up having a miscarriage. The neighbor and I called the ambulance, despite the husband's persistence in convincing us not to. He argued that going into shock was normal for his wife during pregnancy. When the wife recovered, she denied the abuse to the law enforcement and continues to be married to the same man today.

Effects on Children

Survey respondents agree 100 per cent that domestic violence negatively affects Afghan children. Key informant interviews indicated that Afghan children most often witness domestic violence, as it occurs in their households. They further explain that such experiences cause children to have low self-esteem, lower academic achievement, and slower performance in daily tasks, alienation, deviance, as well as depression. One respondent even reported her child attempting suicide as an escape from his abusive household. Several key informants agree that family violence is a learned trait. They believe that Afghan boys who are raised in abusive households mimic the father and become abusive later in life, while Afghan girls who are raised in abusive households learn to tolerate abuse from their future partners-much like their mothers did. Key informants further report that most cases of family violence involve children getting physically and psychologically harmed or kidnapped by either one or both parents.

A Key informant remembers a case from years ago:

> *A woman arranged her daughter's marriage with her nephew from back home. He came to California and the couple began having major problems. He was very closed-minded and she was raised here so she was Americanized. During one fight the couple pulled their baby from each other and broke nine of his bones. The emergency room doctors called the police and the couple went to jail.*

Causes

The rates of various socioeconomic, cultural, religious, and male partner dependencies on domestic violence is described. It is evident that patriarchy (52), followed by female lack of education (35), female financial dependency (28), and lack of resources (22) are the major factors influencing prevalence of family violence in Afghan households. Culture (14), religion (5), and female immigration status (4) were considered least influential causes of violence against women. A majority of respondents reported that arranged marriages were somewhat (53) common, and somewhat (53) responsible for domestic violence amongst Afghan couples in the United States.

Key informants emphasize that factors of patriarchy, male favoritism, victim-blaming, low self-esteem, lack of trust, education/awareness, communication, prevention/intervention resources, and stressors (where the male is under socioeconomic stress) are tightly coiled within the cycle of violence. The case described here is a direct example of the use and misuse of Afghan male privileges-rewarded by misinterpreted cultural and religious ideology:

A couple had several children, some of whom were disabled. When an argument between the spouses arose, the husband beat the wife. The wife depended fully on her husband because all her family was in Afghanistan, she was illiterate, didn't speak English, and couldn't drive. The man eventually married a second woman. Despite all of the abuse and polygamy the first wife never called the police on him nor did she ask for a divorce.

He divided his time between the two wives as convenient for him. He ended up having two children with the second wife who he had also physically abusing since the beginning of their marriage. Eventually, she second wife called the police on him and ended up divorcing him. He now lives with the first wife-fulltime.

Prevention/Intervention/Resources

Various intervention and prevention techniques and programs that are assumed to be successful are stated by respondents. Let it be known that a great majority of respondents (53) state that there are no resources within the Afghan community for women facing family violence. Most respondents believe that seeking help via counseling (60), extended family (41), shelters (40), friends (38), and community organizations geared towards helping Afghan women (35) would be helpful entities in the fight against domestic violence. Religious groups (20) are rarely considered helpful in prevention of domestic violence.

Key informant interviews clarify that Afghans are enigmatic about their intimate partner relationships. The preliminary element of uncovering the issue places the researchers and the respondents in great danger. Such was the case with a community member who attempted to raise awareness of the issue of intimate partner abuse in order to form a support group. Public retaliation and physical attacks caused him to refrain from proceeding, as told by a key informant. The people in the community feel that raising awareness will help women recognize the problem and, therefore, increase the divorce rate. "Divorce of course will break homes and bring a bad name upon the family," comments a key informant.

Preservation of self and family reputation and Afghan traditional values are key factors preventing Afghan women from seeking help. Women who do seek help are stigmatized and lose respect within the community. Divorced women are considered a burden on the family for financial and social reasons, and have a much lower chance of remarrying. Key informants stress the fact that awareness, education and readily available resources are critical in preventing domestic violence against women. Prevention and intervention methods need be strategically in place in order to begin uncovering this vital issue.

Conclusion

In this study, patriarchy was found to be a direct cause of domestic violence against women in Afghan households in California. Other factors contributing to the prevalence of violence were Afghan traditional values, educational level, socioeconomic status, financial dependency, loss of community based support, and lack of available prevention programs. Based on data collected from surveys and key informant interviews forty to fifty percent of households were believed to be facing domestic violence and a majority of these cases are not reported to law enforcement. Burdens of cultural shame and honor are dominant reasons keeping women and children from speaking out and seeking help.

Causes of domestic violence in Afghan households in California run the gamut of traditional values, socioeconomic statuses, male hierarchy, immigration, loss of family/community based support, inaccessibility to education, failure to gain cultural capitol, and financial dependence. When women's positions are pessimistically shadowed, they become more vulnerable to violence. They cannot separate from the abusive partner because that will bring shame on the family. Furthermore, most of them do not have the financial independence or cultural capitol to survive on their own, thus being obligated to remain with their abusive partners.

Children who are exposed to domestic violence face emotional disorders such as depression, low self-esteem, lower academic success rates, and are likely to mimic or be subject to learned violent traits in their own relationships. These children are found to be aggressive, depressed, have low self-esteem, perform poorly in academics, have poor problem solving skills, and may suffer from posttraumatic stress disorder.[15] When mothers are victims of violence, they are less likely to be emotionally available and responsive to their children's needs. The lack of such basic trust and security, which is the foundation of a healthy development, causes youth to substitute family peer groups such as gangs, where learned violence is repeated in dealing with disputes and frustration.[16]

The lack of available resources remains a leading threat to the unveiling and combating of the issue of domestic violence in Afghan communities throughout California. Shelter programs specific to minority communities are either nil (as is the case for the Afghan community) or grassroots efforts.[17] Furthermore, cultural insensitivity and language barriers prevent Afghan women from reaching intervention programs in California. Implementation of programs focusing on teaching cultural competency of mainstream sources and creating community-based sources are essential to the Afghan-American communities.[18] Afghan women must first be able to take advantage of "exosystem intervention programs" where they learn how to escape from further violence.[19] A more advanced and later step would be to combat the causes of spousal abuse in an effort to enable women to gain full control over their bodies and acquire the power to be free beings. It is absolutely crucial to begin advocacy campaigns that unveil the reticent issue of violence against women in the Afghan communities throughout California. Furthermore, it must be reiterated that the issue of domestic violence is not specific to only Afghan households, but holds true to all cultures across the globe. Great care must be taken when drawing conclusions about Afghan women, men, and their intimate relationships. In addition, it should be understood that this study was based on a small sample size, and that results may vary if the sample size is increased.

Chapter 2.

Articulating a Global Ethic

Pushing the Borders

Anida Yoeu Ali

Introduction

The world needs a global ethic with values which give meaning to life experiences and, more than religious institutions and dogmas, sustain the nonmaterial dimension of humanity.

—Wangari Maathai

In order to create a global ethic, we must first identify and address those issues that perpetuate the subordination and exploitation of women and girls of color. This chapter addresses some of these complex issues by recognizing how all nations in the world and, by extension, all people in the world have a responsibility in understanding how their behavior might cause or perpetuate the enslavement of women and girls of color.

In this chapter, a spoken word performance created by a Filipina Muslim woman powerfully illustrates the first step necessary to agency: self-identification. In another piece, a critique of trafficking describes the various forms of struggle applied by Thai women and girls in their refusal to accept their enslavement as sex workers. An essay draws connections between the desire for cheap labor in the United States and the sale of girls by focusing on a case study of the powerful forces that conspired to halt a group of Southeast Asian women seeking to bring an end to this type of exploitation. Another compelling work discusses how the mainstream media in the United States perpetuates a dangerous stereotyping of East Indian women in the context of domestic violence, which contributes to the ongoing debasement and socially sanctioned stereotyping. A poem evokes an indigenous Philippine musical form whose melodious language brings succor to the painful litany of stories found in this chapter. A paper poses the startling, yet compelling, argument that Sri Lankan women's resort to suicide may be read as an act of resistance against practices of social control. A final piece addresses how more than five hundred Mexican women and girls have been murdered en route between home and job in the Mexican city of Juárez—and how not a single case has been solved.

Globalization seeks to increase markets and capital in an ever-widening circle of distribution and consumption. We must seriously question and resolve to end the oppression of women and girls in this cycle of exchange.

What's in a Name?

Anida Yoeu Ali

My name is

2,000 years of history present in 1 body

     3 decades of civil unrest awake in 3 syllables

          5 letters dense of "Birth" "Blood" "Islam" "Peace" "Khmer" "Story"

    2 letters away from "Refugee"

1 letter short of "Home"

My name knows my mother labored

     screaming for hours

          only to mourn a year later

as she buried her sorrow.

A baby boy

     empty of breast milk

     born into famine instead of family.

          (2 letters and war separate the difference)

My mother buried the pains from her first labor

     along with her grief,   knowing

          her son had learned the word for hunger

               before he was able to call her "mother" or speak her name.

     She labored a second time, and my name was born.

My name unexpectedly inherited first-child honors.

My name echoes the same shahadah* whispered to early newborns

     carves legacy into intricate ancient mountains

thrives as a rice field of shallow graves
        escaped from a land kissed by American bombs.

When you say my name
      it is a prayer   a mantra   a call

when you say my name
      when you whisper it
            when you cry it
                  when you desire it

I respond.

Before countries bounded themselves into borders
      before cities became governments
           even before the nations of hip hop
it is the original call and response that all people claim.

So, I take issue with *your* inarticulate mangling of my name
      she refuses to disintegrate
            into a colonized tongue.

In America, she's just another foreign name.
My name survived racism before she knew what it was called.
Picture this:
A small child sinks deeper into her seat
      into her shame
          into her difference
             into *their* laughter
         into *their* stares
     into *their* sneers
into a classroom of white kids

with white teachers

with white tongues

with perfectly pronounceable white American names

like Katy, Courtney, Jennifer,

Michael, Bobby, Doug,

Mrs. Smith, Mrs. Nelson

Mr. How-do-you-say-your-weird-name-again?

Miss I'm-sorry-I-just-can't-seem-to-say-it-right!

Every mispronunciation is like a mouth shooting bullets

the spit of syllables building from a gullet turn barrel

triggering *precise* memories attached to *precise* feelings

like shame inflected in my parents' broken English

the guilt of witnessing daily sacrifices by my mother and father

their dreams and youth slaughtered for money, food, *my* perfect English.

Every misplaced tongue targets *my* foreignness, *my* unbelonging, *my* vulnerabilities.

So when I get angry or curse you for your mispronunciation

Please don't tell me I can't do that

Don't tell me to take it easy

Don't scold me afterwards for making a point of it in public

Don't shrink me down any further

Please just listen.

Allow me to own this one thing:

The rights to my name.

to say her correctly

to have her said correctly

to come when she calls me

to come to her defense

to honor her legacy.

She is my only refuge when I am stripped naked.

She is my bloodline to mothers who have labored before me.

She is My Name. The echo of Home I long to remember.

My name is Anida

daughter of Souraya

who is the daughter of Abidah

who is the daughter of Fatimah

who is the daughter of a woman whose name I do not know

who are all daughters of Hawwa

daughters of life

sisters of survival

women of resistance

daughters of the earth

water

breath

fire

dreams.

shahadah — a Muslim's declaration of faith

Spirits in Traffic:
Transient Community
Formation in Opposition
to Forced Victimization

Elena Shih

I n order to move beyond the simplistic portrayals of victimhood that are presented through U.S. antitrafficking discourse, it is important to place trafficking within the context of globalization, where multiple factors influence intersecting historical, economic, social, and political levels. Contextualizing human trafficking within the globalization paradigm lends itself to a more comprehensive engagement with trafficked women, which recognizes the diverse forms of agency and resistance that are crucial for individual women's survival.

Kevin Bales's text *New Slavery* describes how contemporary slavery—slavery of the past fifty years—differs from previous forms of slavery.[1] Bales notes that in countries that are currently trying to rebuild during their respective postcolonial eras, colonial legacies have fostered lasting economic disparities. These disparities have resulted in the distribution of immense wealth to the country's elite by contributing to the increased poverty of the poor. In the new form of slavery, poverty is the underlying driving force, and "behind every assertion of ethnic difference is the reality of economic disparity." Bales's assertion holds true for the vast majority of trafficking cases, and I plan to address these economic factors within this chapter.

Neferti Tadiar's work *Fantasy Production: Sexual Economies and Other Philippine Consequences for the New World Order* also defines trafficking within the context of globalization. She calls for a move toward the term "new-industrial slavery," which refers to the way human trafficking is directly related to transnational flows within newly industrializing economies.[2]

In this chapter, I reference Thailand as a relevant case study, because it represents a primary origin, transit, and destination country of human trafficking. I recognize certain elements of Thailand's relation to the globalized economy as a means of moving toward a more nuanced understanding of a trafficked woman's subjectivity in relation to legacies of colonialism and imperialism. Thus this chapter does not aim to provide an overview of trafficking in women from Thailand, but rather highlights the ways in which trafficking in the Thai context must be framed within a politics of globalization.

The Globalized Sex Sector

A study conducted in 2000 by the Coalition to Abolish Slavery and Trafficking estimated that human trafficking is a $9-billion-a-year industry; a more recent analysis, conducted by the federal government, claims that in the past three years, trafficking has grown to a $13-billion-a-year industry. One author writes:

> *The traffic in women starkly illuminates the nature of global market economy; its very illegality casts an oblique light on the mechanisms, which are now the object of universal acceptance—the sanctification of the market as the supreme means of answering human need. . . . In many ways, women are the perfect commodity.[3]*

Globalization increases the fluidity of transactions across borders, and the proliferation of new goods and services is not limited to the technology or apparel industries. Rather, we see evidence of what Lim Leam Lin has termed "the sex sector,"[4] a global economy that commodifies women. The growing accessibility of sex as a global commodity—facilitated through the Internet, global sex tours, and porous borders—has allowed the sex sector to become what economist Edward Herman describes as "one of the booming markets in the New World Order—a multibillion dollar industry with finders, brokers, syndicate operations, and pimp 'managers' at the scene of action."[5]

Third world women become subject to the trends of capitalist development because they are, to use Kevin Bales's term, the most "disposable" members of the global community. The trade of women is an ideal economic undertaking, for there is very low investment, very low chance of being caught and prosecuted, and a very high return. Bales notes that "unlike drugs, where the product can be sold only once, when you commodify a human being, she can be sold over and over again." Once a woman is deemed unusable—either because of sexually transmitted diseases, old age, or pregnancy—younger recruits can easily replace her. In order to meet the demands of the growing globalized market, third world women supply the labor force in service occupations such as domestic work, sweatshops labor, and prostitution. This has very little to do with their inherent abilities as third world women or any kind of inherent moral flaws; rather, it is directly linked to the capitalist-driven globalization that seeks profit at any expense to others.[6]

Trafficking History

The history of trafficking women in Thailand traces back to the 19th century, when a free trade agreement between Thailand and the United Kingdom encouraged the importation of foreign labor. A large flow of overseas Chinese and Thai migrant workers responded to the demand for labor, and women who migrated for the purpose of marriage and prostitution often accompanied these laborers. Sex trafficking and labor migrations have remained closely connected phenomena to this day.[7]

Thailand currently is recognized as one of the primary hubs of trafficking in the world as a destination, origin, and transit country of trafficked populations. Thus, trafficking within the Thai context occupies a host of complexities: It is an origin country to trafficking cases in the United States and Japan; a transit country for Chinese women trafficked to the United States; and a destination country for Myanmar, Laotian, and Cambodian women; also, it reports large incidences of domestic (rural to urban) trafficking cases. Because I am focusing primarily on trafficking discourse and policy with relation to the United States/First World, I reference case studies that deal with instances where Thailand is an origin country of trafficked women.[8]

The U.S. State Department's annual Trafficking in Persons (TIP) report has consistently ranked Thailand a Tier 2 nation, out of a three-tiered ranking system that assesses antitrafficking work based on prevention, protection, and prosecution efforts. The 2006 report criticizes the Thai government for being complicit in sex trafficking through the governmental support of the sex tourism industry. While prostitution is officially illegal in Thailand, the sale of sexual services is readily available because these laws are rarely enforced. As a result, sex tourism is Thailand's most widely developed tourist platform and generator of GDP. In large-scale economies where tourism, in particular sex tourism, plays such a large role in nations' wealth, trafficking can be easily underreported or overlooked. Governments are thus less likely to be held accountable for trafficking that falls under the radar of broader economic development platforms.[9]

The TIP report's ranking and critique of Thai governmental complicity is not unfounded; however, it ignores the United States' historical role in developing Thailand's flourishing sex sector, which must be addressed in order to pose fair judgment and responsibility for the present-day situations that enable trafficking to occur.[10]

Sex Tourism

Since the 1960s, Thai development policies have been closely linked to international economic policies. These international economic policies are modeled around the objectives of the United States—a nation that historically employs the assistance of global policing agents like the International Monetary Fund (IMF) and World Bank.[11]

The promotion of the sex tourism industry traces back to the Indochina War, during which Secretary of Defense Robert McNamara encouraged the Thai government to support "Rest and Recreation" facilities for foreign military servicemen stationed in Indochina. These "Rest and Recreation" campaigns normalized the identity of an Asian woman as a sexual commodity.[12]

In 1975, based on the recommendations of the IMF and World Bank, Thailand instituted a National Plan of Tourist Development that implemented a shift from agriculture-based development to tourism. Thailand was encouraged to pursue an export-led strategy to promote growth, which was based around sex tourism as the primary engine of growth.

While tourism-based development has alleviated Thailand's international debt, it has fundamentally altered the Thai labor market, with serious gendered implications. By 1986, more than 70 percent of the five million tourists who went to Thailand were single men, and this gendered model of tourist development continues to this day.

Currently, there exists an extensive body of literature that supports the sex tourism industry; authors publish extensive manuals about sex tourism within Thailand, referencing notorious sex districts in Bangkok and Phuket.

This historical legacy has normalized a fetishized sexual relationship between the white male and Asian female. Bishop and Robinson note that the sex tourism industry promotes a commodification of Thai culture in which "the rhetoric of tourism leads to the belief that the natives don't have a 'real' culture." Glamorous lights, tourist attractions, and sensationalized sex tourist areas "confirm the first world view that the whole city is an erotic theme park."[13]

Bishop and Robinson's critique of Thailand's hypersensationalized sex industry illustrate Trinh Minh T. Ha's discussion of fabricated authenticity, which argues that the perpetuation of mythologies that Thai women are inherently sexualized, beautiful, and exotic feeds into a form of "planned authenticity" that meets first world demands. Authenticity, in the context of sex tourism, "turns out to be a product that one can buy, arrange to one's liking, and/or preserve."[14]

Thus while Thailand was never physically occupied as a colony, we can see the lasting effects of a history of U.S. imperialism in Southeast Asia. This legacy has affected all aspects of Thai society, and in particular, the unequal distribution of wealth has had direct influences on global sex trafficking. The history of U.S. involvement in Southeast Asia reflects the devastating effects of postcolonial legacies. The U.S. legacy as an imperialist regime is still felt in Southeast Asia and remains one of the primary reasons why criticism in the TIP report is incomplete. For while the report recognizes that sex tourism provides one of the fundamental backbones for sex trafficking, it does not acknowledge the United States' own role in the industry and thus does not acknowledge the United States' responsibility to eradicate it.

International Matchmaking Organizations

The history and present-day sex tourist economy is one of the primary facilitators of Thailand's trafficking industry. Bales notes that "migration for employment and also the export of female labor as important sources of foreign exchange earnings may have indirectly encouraged the growth of prostitution, and perhaps even trafficking in women."[15] While the sex tourist industry functions as an inadvertent supporter of trafficking, the same case can also be made for other "peripheral" industries that support the commodification of women as sexual objects. The recent growth in popularity of International Matchmaking Organizations (IMOs), commonly referred to as the "mail order bride" industry, also reveals the influence of contemporary globalizing forces on trafficking.

In a 1998 Report to Congress, International Matchmaking Organizations were defined as "a corporation, partnership, or other legal entity, whether or not organized under the laws of the United States or any state, that does business in the United States and for profit offers to residents of this state dating, matrimonial, or social referral services involving citizens of a foreign country or countries who are not residing in the United States." These organizations are primarily based on the Internet and facilitate intercontinental marriages by offering a selection of photographs and descriptions of women, and by selling the contact information for these women. These organizations often charge a monthly or yearly access fee with unlimited access to photos, descriptions, addresses, and phone numbers; others sell contact information at the cost of $2 to $5 per address.[16]

IMOs are not currently regulated by law and are only accountable for violations under federal criminal statutes if they participate in marriage fraud, trafficking in women, involuntary servitude, or prostitution. Oftentimes the syndicates that control the IMO's operation are so far removed from these prosecutable offenses that they are not held accountable for instances in which a relationship that originated from the IMO website results in a criminal situation.[17]

The growing popularity of the Internet reveals the potential for the changing state of trafficking to adapt to contemporary means of global commodification and transaction. IMOs, while often not perceived to be primary functionaries of trafficking, help place trafficking within a transnational globalization paradigm. The facility with which consumers can access prospective brides, maids, domestic workers, or sex slaves assists in the widespread commodification of women.

The popularity of the sex tourism and mail order bride industries has significantly altered the Thai economy. The labor market has shifted so that the majority of available jobs are within the sex sector. Rural women with low skills turn to prostitution, given the high demand for Thai prostitutes. Penn and Nardos tie the notion of economic inequality with the term "structural violence," insisting that existing gender biases—which establish unequal workloads, wage gaps, and access to labor—provide the backbone for forms of female subordination.[18]

This structural inequality has a great impact on the economic burdens of third world women, especially on the lives of those who are trafficked. Cases of Thai trafficking reveal that victims represent a diverse range of backgrounds, nations, genders, ages, and classes. Thai women come both from poor rural areas and large cities. They are drawn to prostitution and sex work for a variety of reasons, including poverty, the glamorization of the work in the Western entertainment industry, and potential escape from domestic violence and other abusive situations. However, the majority of Thai women are trafficked for motivations related to economic necessity.[19]

Trafficking Functionaries as Transnational Corporations

The aforementioned cases of U.S. involvement represent only one instance in which a transnational economic network supports the existence of trafficking. Examining the complex network of traffickers within a global context is interesting, because it enables one to draw numerous parallels between transnational corporations and trafficking functionaries. Just as women are transnational commodities, their movement throughout the transnational marketplace is facilitated by a multifaceted group of trafficking functionaries. The focus on industrializing the Thai sex services industry has resulted in the growth of intricate transnational networks of trafficking, which have varying degrees of support from the Thai government and other high-level officials.

Arrangers/Investors

At the very primary stages of trafficking lies an actor or group of actors who have very limited interaction with victims of trafficking. Arrangers/investors provide the capital that is necessary to transport human beings—financing anything from actual transportation costs to bribes—and oversee the entire trafficking process. Most often, their level of involvement is so limited that traffickers often do not know who these arrangers/investors are; one author notes, "an organizational pyramid structure insulates the arrangers, who stand back and are not easily connected with the commission of specific criminal offenses." The people who fill this role provide the backbone for the sustainability of trafficking. It is problematic to internationally prosecute their role, because their anonymity throughout the process, despite their integral role as financers, provides a convenient shield. As the overseers of entire trafficking operations, they can quickly and easily recoordinate new trafficking schemes after one has been discovered and tried.[20]

Currently, Asian crime syndicates operate such intricate webs of connections with trafficking rings that their participation makes the law enforcement of trafficking very difficult. These international crime rings participate in all aspects of trafficking, including recruitment, transportation, and management once in the United States. In California, over 80 percent of Asian brothels are controlled by Asian street gang syndicates, including Black Dragons, Orange Boys, Kool Boyz, Wah Ching, Red Door, United Bamboo, Mongolian Boy Society, and V Boyz.[21]

Recruiters

While arrangers/investors are the actors who make up the top of a pyramid, recruiters are recognized as the actors who compose the next level down. Recruiters serve as liaisons between the arranger and the customers of the criminal enterprise. Oftentimes the recruiter is an individual who has close connections with the local community from which the trafficked women are drawn. Their close relationship with the community gives their recruitment a certain level of legitimacy. A study completed by Human Rights Watch suggests that most women are initially approached by a "relative, neighbor, or other acquaintance." This personal relationship makes the women more inclined to trust the promises of the recruiter.[22]

One victim of trafficking remembers how a recruiter functioned as a member of her community:

> *The neighbors were talking about jobs in the United States. . . . I was getting more desperate trying to earn enough money. I asked them, "Who is that person who arranges jobs in the United States?" I had to pay a man 5,000 baht for introducing me to the woman who was looking for workers. When I went to see*

the recruiter, she told me that I was qualified, because I had been working, sewing in a factory in Bangkok, and because I was young and healthy.[23]

Because recruiters live with the populations that they hope to recruit, they are often aware of, and therefore have the advantage to play upon, recruits' personal weaknesses. Most often, recruiters are aware of which community members are experiencing the greatest financial difficulty, and they strategically target this population. Recruits are often promised large sums of money:

They promised to pay about $1,000 or $1,200 a month. That was a good amount. Transferred to Thai currency, it is about 30,000 baht a month. In Thailand, I could only earn about 7,000 baht. Of course, they did not pay you more than $10 to $20 a day, and we worked eighteen hours a day, every day of the month.[24]

The wealth and income disparities between the first and third worlds create a pull for women to seek migration to other countries. Many trafficked women send home remittances to help pay for children's education, healthcare, or housing. Remittances have become an integral aspect of the Thai economy because they aid not only the growth of individuals and families, but also larger economic institutions that enable the international transfer of funds. The growing link between overseas remittances and the development of national economies and local banking systems leads economists to claim that the remittances from migrant workers aid in structural economic development, which decreases a government's interest in supporting safe migratory practices.[25]

Debt Collectors and Transporters

The final two functionaries, debt collectors and transporters, form the base of the hierarchical pyramid because of their limited interaction with the overall structure and planning of the entire transaction. Because their involvement with trafficking is highly specialized and limited, they remain separated from individuals at the top of the pyramid, such as arrangers/investors. This complicates the process of prosecution, for most individuals involved in all levels of the hierarchical pyramid have little sense of either the nature or extent of the total trafficking process in which they are involved. Given this fragmented participation, it is difficult to target and prosecute more than one link in the vast transnational network.[26]

Transporters are persons who work in the country of origin to help migrants move within and exit the country of origin. In cases of trafficking where migrants are selected from rural areas, transporters may move them to larger, often capital, cities, where they will either work for a brief period of time or find transportation out of the country. Transporters fulfill an extremely specific role and as a result do not receive information about the larger criminal structures of organizations that employ them.

Transporters are responsible for finding effective ways of crossing borders. Using forged documents is one of the most common methods. Forged U.S. visas and passports are sold for anywhere between $5,000 and $10,000 in Asian countries. The most common cities of entry via air travel are New York, Los Angeles, San Francisco, Seattle, Las Vegas, Boston, and Honolulu. These cities are popular because they have multiple flights from Asia and are destinations for significant numbers of Asian populations. Traffickers attempt to arrange flights for particularly busy air travel days, with the hope that immigration officials will be less attentive to false documents.[27]

Debt collectors are crucial actors, because they enforce the element of coercion by asserting a sense of debt bondage. Women who agree to follow their recruiters are often told that they must "work off" or "earn" the expenses that were incurred to traffic them to their destination. Penn and Nardos note that the debt "typically includes the expenses incurred for her housing and food, her purchase price, the money required for her 'transportation' from her home to the brothel, the cost of travel papers and passports, medical care, clothing, and protection money paid to the police."[28] Women are paid a small sum for the services they provide, but it is nearly impossible for them to ever earn back the money that they owe to traffickers; one *mamasan* (female brothel owner) admitted, "the captors have no intention of setting the women free until they are no longer useable."[29]

Because the process of trafficking involves so many different actors, it is difficult to hold functionaries responsible for the trafficking of individuals when their involvement may be relegated to a very limited task. Kempadoo sums up the vast interconnected network that supports international sex trafficking:

> The "success" of the sex industry is based on a "special relation" of shared interests amongst a complex network of military leaders, police officials, business tourist promoters, godfathers, and pimps. At the international level, airline and hotel chains have worked closely with the local business military elite to promote the sex tourist industry. The World Bank's support of an open economy and export-oriented development strategies translate to an institutionally supported sex tourist industry in the Thai case.[30]

Trafficking in women is supported by an extensive network of globalized actors who contribute to the forced and unforced trafficking of women. Yet beyond these extensive globalized networks and these deeply entrenched systems of traffickers, there is the story of the key elements of trafficked women's survival. Ong argues that the sex worker's occupation must be seen as a fluid and responsive occupational choice that is responding to a globalized economy. She notes that, within this context, "'flexible citizenship' refers to the cultural logics of capitalist accumulation, travel, and displacement that induce the subject to respond fluidly and opportunistically to political economic conditions."[31] The decisions made by women who are subject to the aforementioned inequalities are thus survival strategies, not real choices. Recognizing the complexities of the globalized economy—and how this structural inequality creates an unequal distribution of wealth and power—reveals how the Western notion of "choice" is not relevant to the lives of trafficked women. Despite this, it is crucial to examine the powerful strategies that Thai sex workers employ as a means of survival.

Reconceptualizing "Agency"

As examined earlier in this paper, U.S. antitrafficking discourse and policy construct third world women as natural victims and without agency. Ong's work on Malaysian factory workers and Tadiars's work on Filipina domestic helpers challenge the narrow recognition of agency in mainstream discourse. They reject the authenticating tropes that restrict expressions of agency to Western notions of resistance. Their respective arguments can also be applied to the case of trafficking, where the "authentic" manner in which trafficked women are supposed to represent their victim status does not give recognition to the other ways in which they achieve agency.

Through referencing certain trafficking case studies, I move away from the romanticized idea of the authentic native, who is allowed to speak insofar as the first world mandates that speech. These authenticating stereotypes herald third world voices only within a context of victimization, and thus do not engage the other ways in which these women speak out. This practice of authenticity functions within domains of feminism that Trinh outlines, thus relegating third world women's voices to the margins, and only privileging them to the extent that they support first world privilege and power.

Westwood and Phizacklea's *Transnationalism and the Politics of Belonging* focuses on giving voice and agency to these experiences by refusing to categorize all of the cases of trafficking as forced or duped trafficking. They refer to an interesting research study that interviewed seventy women who had recently migrated from Southeast Asia to the United States; their results show that these women's reasons for migration were remarkably diverse. Westwood and Phizacklea reference this case study to show that "despite the harrowing conditions experienced by many women in the sex and maids industries worldwide, their migration represents an attempt to bring a better life to themselves and their families in the face of prodigious external constraint." Thus, despite the fact that women are faced with daunting conditions within migration, they still are able to derive a form of agency from their choice or lack of choices.[32]

Satoko Watenabe's case study on migrant sex workers establishes Thai women as autonomous subjects who find economic independence through seeking out opportunities for global sex work. Watenabe conducted interviews with five Thai migrant sex workers who were trafficked to Japan between 1995 and 1996. They did not view themselves as sex slaves or victims, but rather saw liberation in economic autonomy. These sex workers differentiated between the sex as an occupation and sex for personal satisfaction, and saw the ability to do so as a fundamental tool in rebelling against male power and social control.[33]

The five subjects' economic autonomy was the result of being able to make more money working in Japan than in Thailand. All of these women sent remittances to their families in Thailand but were also able to save some of the money to purchase nice things for themselves. Through their earned wages, they were able to help their families purchase

Western-style houses and other goods. This reflects a direct response to the forces of globalization; by migrating for higher wages, these women refuse to be victims of an international wage hierarchy. Instead, they assert their economic autonomy and agency through seeking alternate methods of employment.[34]

Watenabe notes that one of the ways in which these trafficked women were able to establish agency is by creating networks of support with other Thai women in foreign lands. One of Watenabe's subjects, a woman named Sai, prided herself in her role as mentor to new or recently trafficked women. As one of the older women, she took care of younger workers by helping them gain access to housing and medical attention. Watenabe's study deconstructs the notion of the Thai woman as one without agency; Watenabe notes, "unlike the general view that Thai women are the most vulnerable group among migrant workers . . . these women have a network of friends."[35]

Pasuk Phongpaichit's overview of "Trafficking in People in Thailand" references a 1994 case of trafficking of Thai women to New York City. The trafficked women in this case were forced to work under the confinement of ruthless conditions. They worked from 11:00 AM to 4:00 AM, averaging two clients a day at $130 a client. However, as is often the case, their wages were given directly to the *mamasan,* in the name of paying off debt. The women were not permitted to leave the premises and were frequently beaten and assaulted. One woman's way of resisting this situation was to jump from this second-story brothel. Her suicide drew attention to the brothel and caused it to later be shut down. In this case, one could certainly make the case that this woman made a conscious choice, within a certain set of constraints, to resist the injustice she was experiencing.[36]

McMahon's case studies include a narrative by Khai, who describes her personal agency. Khai was trafficked to the United States to work in slavelike conditions as a domestic servant for many years. In Khai's case, she was able to assert her personal agency through speaking out against her trafficker, leading to the effective prosecution and eventual punishment of the perpetrator.

Undeniably, Khai's experience speaks to the importance of the T-visa provision that allows trafficked women to remain in this country if they agree to participate in the prosecution of their traffickers. However, U.S. policy often privileges speaking out over silence, as indicated through laws that are fundamentally based upon the availability of first hand testimonials. Currently, there are few provisions that give options to individuals who refuse to speak out either in fear of danger of retribution or because of personal and cultural aversion to disclosing personal trauma. Many women choose not to speak out because they fear retaliation by the extensive networks of people in their homeland. They have been coaxed against speaking out during their whole term of servitude, and this makes it difficult for them to trust law enforcement officials. Thus, the T-visa is ineffective for those who choose to claim agency through silence.[37]

Outside of the Thai-specific context, there are many grassroots-level activist projects that aim to provide Asian trafficked women with the means for self-sustainability. The Masala Project is a grassroots initiative that helps survivors of trafficking achieve economic self-sustainability through long-term employment. Through charitable donations, two survivors of trafficking worked with local Bombay NGOs to establish a spice factory, which is currently run and staffed by other survivors of trafficking. This is one example of a local initiative that negotiates spaces for female and individual agency through economic sustainability. The women who work in the spice factory support themselves and in turn serve as allies, mentors, and support systems for other survivors of trafficking.[38]

Another participatory-based empowerment project is the Sonagachi Project, located in Kolcata, and organized by the Durbar Mahila Samanwaya Committee, a committee of former or current sex workers. This effort focuses on HIV/AIDS education through a network of peer support, in which the majority of activists and educators are current or former sex workers. This survivor-centered project focuses on a "three Rs" approach that acknowledges respect, reliance, and recognition, as opposed to the U.S. State Department's government-centered "three Ps" approach, based on prevention, protection, and prosecution. The Sonagachi Project succeeds in deconstructing the prevalent trope of victimization found in reductive policies like the U.S. State Department's TIP report by restoring individual agency in global sex work. The project aims to respect women who are engaged in sex work by providing peer counseling from other sex workers or survivors of trafficking, thus recognizing not only the elements of choice and nonchoice in third world women's lives, but also how, in cases when the element of choice may not be available, agency can be achieved nonetheless.[39]

In Thailand, a global restructuring of capitalist production and investment—the roots of which are traceable to the 1970s—has had gendered implications on third world women's access to the global market. As corporate strategies to increase profit have become more centered around the movement of capital from industrial centers to countries with cheap labor, unemployment and wages in the third world are gravely affected—and these inequities disproportionately affect members of the third world. The corporate drive to increase production, consumption, and profit has led to a steady increase in the desires of the global market, and the legacies of sex tourism and Asian sexual commodification make Third World women bear the burden of this inequity.

Yet despite the imperialist history that has left the Thai economy reliant on both tourism (sex tourism in particular) and the intricate networks of transnational trafficking functionaries, Thai women carve spaces of agency that have meaningful implications in their daily acts of survival and within larger contexts of political resistance. The range and complexity of these forms of resistance and expressions of agency speak to a space for self-sustainability that can be achieved independent of first world heroism.

Culture and Truth: Learning from a Transatlantic Trafficking Case

Nalini Shekar and Mukta Sharangpani

Silicon Valley, the high-tech capital of the world, is home to an ever-increasing number of South Asians. While many of them are affluent engineers, doctors, and lawyers, a significantly large number work in manufacturing and low-tech jobs, as taxi drivers, and in the hospitality industry as waiters, cleaners, and kitchen staff. Contrary to the popular belief that regards the South Asian community as a model minority, this group is vulnerable to the same social dysfunctions as the rest of the country, even though the ways that these are experienced are very different.

Maitri, an agency based in the South Bay (San Francisco Bay Area), helps South Asian women and children in situations of domestic violence, cultural displacement, and unresolved family conflict. A group of women who understood the cultural needs and uniqueness of South Asian women in abusive relationships founded Maitri in 1991. Determined not to duplicate existing services and to assist clients in assimilating and integrating into the mainstream as smoothly as possible, the founders of Maitri designed the program to be a liaison between South Asian survivors and mainstream resources. Today, Maitri receives more than two thousand calls a year, operates a transitional home and a helpline, and boasts of a volunteer base that speaks more than fourteen South Asian languages, including Urdu, Hindi, Bengali, Singhalese, and South Indian languages such as Tamil, Kannada, and Telugu.

On Monday, January 10, 2004, a volunteer at Maitri responded to an email stating that the Berkeley police needed a Telugu translator for a homicide case. Little did we know

101

that our reply would open the floodgates to our increased involvement in a landmark trafficking case that involved many young women and minors, who were exploited for cheap labor and/or sex.[1] It is a case that exceeded, by far, all the financial, temporal, and human resource requirements of any of our previous cases. Today, nearly five years later, we are still struggling with the fallout of this case.

A Berkeley landlord, Lakireddy Bali Reddy, age sixty-two, was sentenced on June 20, 2001, for ninety-seven months in federal prison and was required to pay a $2 million restitution fee. The sentence was handed down by Judge Saundra Brown Armstrong following a guilty plea to one count of conspiring to commit immigration fraud, in violation of Title 18 U.S.C.§§ 371; two counts of transportation of minors for illegal sexual activity, in violation of Title 18 U.S.C.§§ 2423(a); and one count of a false tax return, in violation of Title 26, U.S.C.§§ 7206(1). In his plea agreement, the defendant admitted that between 1986 and January 2000, he arranged to bring Indian nationals into the United States using fraudulent visas.

In particular, Mr. Reddy admitted that he made arrangements to have Venkateswara Vemireddy enter the United States on a fraudulent visa, to bring Vemireddy's sister into the United States posing as his wife, and to bring two minor girls into the United States as their daughters. He admitted that he intended to have sexual intercourse with both girls, who were younger than sixteen years old. Another girl victim was reported to be thirteen years of age in 1991, when Mr. Reddy brought her into the United States with false documents; it was further believed that he intended to have sexual intercourse with her.

Mr. Reddy admitted that he and other defendants arranged for the entry into the United States of between twenty-five and ninety-nine Indian nationals based on fraudulent visas. At least some of these aliens were vulnerable victims, because they were young women and girls who came from poor families in India and who were dependent upon the defendant for employment, housing, sustenance, and income, both in India and in the United States.[2]

In India he was and is a powerful man. He is known to have converted his hometown village Velavadum[3], which was named "Little India" by then Andhra Pradesh Chief Minister Chandra Babu Naidu. He was the richest property owner in Berkeley, with one thousand flats and apartments. Moreover, he owned restaurants, as well as a construction company—all together valued at $60 million or more. His two sons, his brother, and his wife also received sentences for conspiracy and related charges. One family and a few individual survivors pursued a civil case for damages, and one family that lost their daughter, and one survivor, received $8.9 million in a settlement after four and a half years of struggle. The survivors that Maitri supported included five young women and one girl who were sexually abused and exploited. These young women are from his village. Most of them came from economically poor, socially disadvantaged groups, although one woman belonged to the same caste as Reddy. We also supported a woman and a man, who were qualified as computer engineers and who were exploited for their labor by Reddy.

From the beginning, the severity and urgency of the case was evident. The death of a young girl, Shanti, drew the attention of police, attorneys, officers of the Immigration and Naturalization Services (INS, now Immigration and Customs Enforcement, or ICE), activist agencies, and the public. What began as a five-hour-long translation service for two young women and a middle-aged couple from a small village in South India soon sprang out of control as the facts of the Reddy racket began to be unveiled. Four days after receiving a call at our office, Reddy was arrested on charges of sexual trafficking and immigration fraud.

Reddy's arrest left the South Asian community stunned. For the South Asian community—a group that was often perceived as "a model minority"; a group that has significantly contributed to the booming U.S. economy, used very few state resources, and seen very little criminal activity—the Reddy story was a fairytale gone sour. Many were outraged when stories of his activities became public. His sexual perversions left many stunned and shamed.

Yet an equally large percentage of the community preferred to remain silent. Reddy was a respected and wealthy member and leader of the community. He embodied the immigrant dream. Many modeled themselves after him and sought his blessings and support in their own business ventures. Because of his incredible wealth, Reddy had contacts in high places, both within the United States as well as in his home country. His arrest made headline news in Andhra Pradesh and Velvadum. His townsmen in India were shocked and angry at the news, for Reddy had achieved the status of an icon through his significant contributions to charitable institutions, hospitals, schools, and colleges. The week Reddy was arrested, a statue in his honor was scheduled to be erected in the town square.

Pointing fingers at Reddy meant pointing fingers at the entire South Asian immigrant community. The Reddy debate raged on, in print media, at dinner table conversations, and at companies. The president of the Indo American Chamber of Commerce of Northern California said she had known Reddy for twenty-five years and suggested that if Reddy had sex with any girls, it would have been consensual. "He's a bachelor," she said. "If they want to have fun, and he wants to have fun, no one in the world can stop that." Another executive was quoted as saying, "He's very decent and very well-known. He did help a lot of people. He's not a bum off the streets." Some of the human rights groups mentioned that they had heard complaints for more than a year about Reddy's treatment of new immigrants, including a number of young women who worked in his restaurant and at his rental properties.[4]

There were furious email exchanges on many Indian listservs at various high-tech companies, intense arguments against publicly condemning Reddy. Many emails said "he is not guilty until proven." The mixed response from the community was evident when Maitri and other activist agencies organized demonstrations outside Reddy's premiere business, the Santa Clara–based restaurant Pasand. The demonstration was a success. More than a hundred people showed up outside what might have been their own favorite family eating place to condemn the actions of Reddy through slogans, speeches, and songs. This showed the courage of a community that was, by condemning its own, reaching out toward a vision of true justice and humanity.

At Maitri, our anxieties about this case were increasing by the day. In addition to pressure from the community to remain silent and watch from the sidelines, we were grappling with providing technical resources for the case, as well as generating a consensus on how much and how far we would allow ourselves to get involved. The Reddy case threatened to swallow the agency whole, and one of our biggest challenges was to provide the necessary assistance for the case without shortchanging or compromising any of our other clients. As a small agency with limited financial and volunteer resources, we found ourselves doing work beyond the scope of our previous charter and agenda. We learned on the fly, burned the midnight oil, ploughed through mountains of bureaucratic paperwork, and pushed the limits of our endurance and energy.

We provided culturally sensitive consultation to the Berkeley police. We wrote and rewrote press releases. We spent hours each day providing interpretation and translation services. In spite of thousands of Telegu-speaking professionals living and working in the area, we had almost no interpreters other than our own volunteers. Most people were nervous about working against Reddy. News of the extent of his reach had filtered into the community. With no criteria in place for selecting volunteers, we struggled to find additional interpreters who were not linked in any way to the large Reddy-kinship network.

As the case progressed and public interest in the case dwindled, it was left to a handful of us to stretch to our maximum and aid not just the survivors, but also their families, the attorneys, and the government. As we had always worked with the government on our own terms and without accepting "strings attached" federal funds, this was our first experience working in partnership with the government. We learned firsthand the challenges of collaborative efforts, the difficulties posed by confidentiality issues that legal representations required, and the urgencies that necessitated decisions to be made in minutes. We also learned how multitasking—playing the roles of victim advocate; translator; and cultural adviser to the government, survivor's attorneys, and the collaborative—put us in awkward and trying situations.

Very few of us had training in sexual assault and child prostitution. Almost none of us had worked with survivors of sexual trafficking before. In addition, the survivors were young girls, barely out of their teenage years, and few of us had worked with that age group before. Working on this case meant having an almost nonexistent personal life, getting by on just a few hours of sleep, long journeys to various destinations, and considerable financial expense. One volunteer had to quit her job in order to be accessible for this case. Yet our services continued to be rendered pro bono in order for us to maintain equality and not get coopted by any group. The fact that the trafficker was powerful and well connected made any involvement with this case potentially dangerous. Our volunteers were stalked, threatened, and given implicit warnings to back off.

Within the agency, questions about ethics, charters and agendas, and the politics of definitions began to erupt. Who qualified as "victim"? Who deserved to benefit from our resources? How could we gather funds to aid these survivors without taking away opportunities for our regular clients? Did sexual trafficking qualify as domestic violence? Was that part of our charter? Yes, we would rise to the occasion this time, but would we take on a similar case in the future? Such queries abounded, and our meetings were fraught with debates and introspection.

The Reddy case blurred lines between those who were victimized and those who aided the perpetrator. A case in point was the (now imprisoned) woman who had posed as the mother of the two girls, helping Reddy to bring them to the United States. She was also in jail, and the government had not posed any charges on her. In confidence, she shared with us the manner in which she was exploited by her own brother, who assured her that what she was doing was completely aboveboard, that she was simply helping someone migrate to the United States, and that in the process, she could earn enough so that she herself could support her poor family in India. It is a common cultural practice to sign any document a male relative asks a woman to; in traditional homes, men are allowed to make decisions regarding many aspects of a woman's life. It took a great deal of effort on the part of Maitri to make sure that she was not charged with any crime. Yet there was divided opinion on this within the agency. Some insisted that she was aware that she was falsifying documents that stated that she was the mother of the two young women accompanying her.

This case taught us a lot—not only about how to help survivors of trafficking, but also about how to mobilize as an immigrant community in an atmosphere of anti-immigrant sentiment and alien laws and systems. We learned that to address cases such as this, one must look at the systemic inequalities that make such situations possible, that give rise to a desperation in which parents are forced to give up their children for a pittance, and that cause young girls to look upon their abusers as their protectors. It taught us to take the time to understand the ideology, philosophy, and interests of each collaborative partner, no matter how high profile the case. It has taught us the importance of carefully selecting interpreters and translators, screening their political ideology and understanding their sensibilities and emotional connections to the trafficker's community.

This case has reminded us of the opportunities as well as the limitations of the media to educate both the mainstream and the ethnic community. To cite an example, in early January 2000, a member of one of the agencies that was supporting Maitri by providing emergency services to the victims appeared on television with her face blurred so that she would not be recognized in the community. This put many of us in an ethical quandary. Here we were, asking victims to be unafraid and come forth with their stories. Yet we were hiding behind blurs ourselves. Victims needed to see people who looked like them and talked like them. Covering the face of a spokesperson and then asking others to come forward was unacceptable. We learned this lesson, and we never made the mistake again.

One of the greatest outcomes of the Reddy case was the birth of ASATA (Alliance of South Asians Taking Action). A highly impassioned and committed group of young (mostly second and third generation) South Asians galvanized into action, forming a platform that was able to make political statements and organize the community when needed. This case was the first time that the lines between first- and second-generation South Asians began to appear. Interestingly, support for organizations such as Maitri and condemnation for Reddy's activities was forthcoming primarily from this younger group of people. The first generation remained ambiguous, sat on the fence, and shrugged away any responsibility. Perhaps it was because the first generation continues to struggle with assimilating into the mainstream, while the younger and new first generations have been more assertive in demonstrating their roots and their cultural diversity.

What was interesting too was the fury that emerged among all South Asians when the defense lawyers used a cultural defense to condone Reddy's actions, implying that it was culturally acceptable in India for men to have sex with young girls. This caused the South Asian community to mobilize and, facilitated by ASATA, they began a series of letter-writing campaigns that reached the judge on the bench. The judge mentioned that she received close to five hundred letters from the community. The people who had been silent and indifferent to the plight of the young survivors were quick to protect the image of their home culture in their host country.

On June 20, 2001, Reddy was sentenced. It was on this day that the politics of color revealed itself to us. Not in court, but outside it. As we stood outside, giving the press our statement and our reactions to the sentence, we noticed a group of white women screaming anti-Reddy slogans. Repeatedly, they screamed, "Send him back home!" To these women, who called themselves feminists, deportation was the answer to this problem. But Reddy was a citizen of the United States; this country had benefited from him as much as he had benefited from being here. He had paid taxes, and he had contributed to the local positions, and this was his home. Yet he was being asked to leave, because he had another home, another place he could call home. To these slogan-screaming women, the entire argument was reduced to this one fact. They did not care what the survivors got as part of the plea bargain. They had no interest in seeing whether justice had been done for the victims. They only cared that Reddy be deported. It was confusing to see white feminists unable to go beyond the color of one's skin and work toward a larger principle of justice and equality for all, regardless of race.

The plea bargain did not satisfy any of us. We were certain that no amount of money would bring back to these women the priceless moments of innocence and childhood that were lost forever. Furthermore, we were nervous about how the legal system would continue to cause them pain. In this foreign land with a complicated legal system that is culturally far removed from everything they had ever seen or heard, could they stand up to the defense attorneys, who would tear their personal lives into pieces and strip their most private and intimate encounters in order to disprove their stories? We believed that it was in the best interest of the survivors to get them out of the legal system as soon as possible and provide them with an environment that would allow them to begin living their lives again.

While Reddy and his family had exploited many young women, both for their labor and for sexual purposes, the men they had trafficked for labor were now well settled in the United States and able to help their families back home. As a result, they were reluctant and unwilling to testify against Reddy. Many intermediaries had benefited from Reddy's criminal activities and were furious at his arrest. These intermediaries began to create an antisurvivor sentiment in their hometowns in India. They demonstrated their support to Reddy and mobilized village opinion against the survivors for disclosing their experiences to their authorities. The survivors and their families were targeted, ostracized, and socially boycotted. Stories of vandalism, threats, and acts of violence were communicated to us through women's rights agencies based in the region. Members of one such agency, Asmita, worked endlessly, often putting their own safety on the line, to gather facts about Reddy's property and connections that would assist the survivors' attorneys. It was an overwhelming task to get this information, as support for Reddy was overwhelmingly high in India, and political parties who had benefited from Reddy's money refused to assist in the project.

The hardest part of our work was the complex ambiguity demonstrated by the survivors themselves. Reddy had assumed gigantic proportions in their young minds. He was their protector; he was the man they had to please sexually and otherwise, and he was the person for whose favor they constantly competed. This led to feelings of intense jealousy and insecurity among the young women—so much so that in seeking Reddy's approval and affection, sisters and friends began to see each other as rivals. Even when freed from the trafficker, these emotions remained.

As service providers, we found ourselves falling into the "rescue" trap, as we tended to expect them to express the feeling of freedom and feel a sense of solidarity with others who shared their experience. Nevertheless, the reality was that they needed time and technical guidance in order to process their experience, rationalize their behavior, and create new friendships. This is always a major challenge when women are freed from a trafficker all at once. Reddy was so powerful in their hometown that it was perceived to be a privilege to be close to him. As traffickers do, Reddy conditioned them into loyalty and obligation by comparing the lives they led in the United States to the lives of poverty and deprivation they had led in their hometowns. Working through the young women's anxiety and confusion—which often manifests as anger, arrogance, resistance, or rebuffs—continues to be the hardest part of our work. Even today, while we strive toward assimilating and empowering them, we continue to struggle with questions of trust, betrayal, and anger. In a land where their own compatriot violated and exploited them, our attempt is to help them learn to trust, to share, and to care again.

Selective Storytelling: A Critique of U.S. Media Coverage Regarding Violence Against Indian Women

Sharmila Lodhia

In July 2003, Guljit Sandhu was shot and killed by her husband, Inderpreet Sandhu, in Milpitas, California. He killed himself minutes later. After the crime was committed, a family member was quoted as saying that Inderpreet had no choice but to kill his wife, who was attempting to leave him, because his "culture didn't allow divorce."[1] The local media latched onto this statement, and its coverage of the crime focused overwhelmingly on this unchecked assertion about a "cultural" prohibition on divorce as a justification for this violence.[2] News accounts presented the crime as a foreseeable outcome in a community where "marriages are arranged" and women are "second-class citizens."

In October 2003, Nisha Sharma, a woman from India, made international headlines when she had her would-be husband arrested for demanding $25,000 dollars as a dowry payment from her family shortly before their wedding was to take place. While her act was brave and has inspired other young women to challenge dowry demands, news coverage of the event was similarly riddled with generalizations about the so-called "status of women in India" and the motivations for the violence committed against them. In particular, a *60 Minutes* story by CBS correspondent Christiane Amanpour was filled with magnified accounts of the links between marriage, dowry harassment, and a form of domestic violence commonly referred to in India as "bride burning."[3]

In January 2004, Oprah Winfrey began her show with the following statement: "I always say that if you are a woman born in the United States, you are one of the luckiest

110

women in the world. Did you know that? Well, if you didn't know that, you're really going to believe me after this show. . . . Today I wanted to take you to the other side of the globe, so all of you soccer moms out there, here's a chance to go places you'd never normally see and have an opportunity to meet women you'd never meet."[4] What followed was a montage of images of violence inflicted upon women in the Global South that included, not surprisingly, a highly disturbing journey into the "horror of bride burning in India" that Winfrey warned her audience was "right out of the Dark Ages."[5] The show not only relied on oversimplifications that distorted many aspects of these forms of violence, but also noticeably ignored the very tangible similarities between these crimes and parallel crimes of domestic-violence-related homicide in the United States—similarities that might have raised doubts about how "lucky" American women really are.

Having watched these stories unfold over the past several years, I find myself once again feeling frustrated at the media's recurring, albeit short-lived, interest in the "status of Indian women." I am not the first South Asian woman to express frustration with the coverage of these issues, and, given the frequency of these episodic ventures to the East, I most certainly will not be the last.[6] These previously cited examples are indicative of the limited ways in which ideas about foreign violence against women get imported into the dominant Western imagination. In these storylines, "culture" is presented as monolithic, and religious diversity is disregarded in favor of distorted versions of what gendered violence signifies within the Indian community.[7] Several scholars and activists have explored the critical gaps in this reporting with respect to issues such as the history and significance of dowry in India; the supposed links between religion, culture, and violence in this context; and the ways in which Indian law effectively reinforces the idea that a failure to meet dowry demands is the single motivating factor behind these crimes.[8]

Despite this rich and multifaceted work, the previously cited examples are a telling reminder that scholarly critiques of "third world women" as perpetual victims of barbaric and backward cultures have yet to enter mainstream discourses on violence against women.[9] It is much easier for reporters to make claims that leave concepts like culture and race unproblematized and to focus instead on the heightened drama of "the burning bride."[10] While many communities attribute violence against women to cultures of patriarchy and sexism, I believe that these are far too narrow explanations, especially when what comes to represent "Indian culture" in these cases has been so uncritically embraced. What I find especially discouraging is the fact that, in these reports, the Indian community is faulted not only for its particular brand of domestic violence, but also for things like arranged marriages, lavish weddings, and rising consumerism—as if these phenomena have no parallels in the West. I suppose that those who come from the land of speed dating, bridezillas, and millionaire-seeking bachelorettes are insulated from allegations of this kind of "cultural" deviance.[11]

Scholarly discourses on violence against women have been vastly expanded within the past several years, and important critiques have emerged with respect to the way in which violence against certain groups of women—particularly those identified as "third world"—is characterized by the West.[12] Despite this evolution, media reports continue to pathologize Indian culture, thereby preventing a meaningful analysis of this violence in a way that either seeks to understand its complexities or speaks to the critical work being done by activists to address it. Instead, these reports reinforce the belief that Indian women are at risk of a unique incarnation of patriarchal violence that Uma Narayan describes as "death by culture."[13] Crimes such as "dowry deaths" and "bride burnings" can thus continue to be distinguished from other forms of domestic violence.

It is not difficult to understand why sensationalized discussions of violence within the Indian community have remained a staple subject for talk shows and news programs. Western audiences seem to derive a kind of voyeuristic pleasure in imagining the spectacle of "burning brides" and hearing lurid tales of deadly mothers-in-law, both of which are perceived as far more intriguing than acts of domestic violence that occur locally. In fact, if these reporters were to look more critically at the issues involved in these cases, they would not only gain a far more complete picture of why these kinds of crimes occur, but they would be forced to notice the striking similarities between these acts and those committed against women in the United States.[14] The weapons may differ, but the fact remains that women in many parts of the world are more likely to die at the hands of a boyfriend or husband than of a stranger. To single out the particular embodiment of lethal violence that one finds in the Indian context is to willfully blind oneself to this tragic reality.

Choosing to invoke ideas about culture exclusively within the context of violence against non-Western women performs several critical functions. One key historical function in the case of India was the desire to advance the goals and objectives of the British Empire. Not unlike what occurred during early European settlement in the United States, the idea of the "civilizing" mission of colonialism was used by the British Empire to justify imperial expansion into already inhabited lands. "In their rhetoric, the 'superiority of Western civilization' functioned as a rationale and justification for the colonial project, casting colonialism as, in part, an attempt to bestow the benefits of 'Western civilization' on colonized peoples."[15] By focusing overwhelmingly on issues such as female infanticide, *sati,* and dowry deaths, the British could present the diverse Indian subcontinent as so steeped in backwardness as to require salvation.[16] This enabled the British to take control of local economies and to masculinize property rights in a way that historian Veena Oldenberg has argued did far more to damage the social position of Indian women than the supposed "traditions" on which these societal ills were blamed.[17]

Elevating the role of "culture" in these cases also allows for important distinctions to be made between violence against "third world women" and violence against women from Western communities. "Women in the third world are portrayed as victims of their culture, which reinforces stereotyped and racist representations of that culture and privileges the culture of the West."[18] It is precisely because violence against Indian women is characterized as distinct from "domestic" forms of violence against women by the media that Oprah Winfrey can brazenly claim that Americans place greater value on women's lives.

Uma Narayan's critical analysis of what happens when violence travels across borders and becomes decontextualized should inform our thinking about comparisons between the United States and India.[19] In her work she examines how the national contexts of India and the United States differently shaped these violence discourses. In addition to pointing out the difficulty of comparing statistics when definitions of domestic violence are so varied, she also notes that while "there is a *visible category* of 'dowry-murder' that picks out a lethal form of domestic violence in the Indian context, there is no similar, readily available category that specifically picks out *lethal instances* of domestic violence in the United States."[20] In critiquing the popular construction of these crimes, she notes that "Indian women's murder-by-fire seems mysterious, possibly ritualistic, and one of those factors that is assumed to have something to do with 'Indian culture.'"[21] What scholars like Narayan and Oldenberg have pointed out, however, is that fire is simply more accessible in Indian households than other weapons, and that the use of fire to kill is "forensically expedient," because all evidence is destroyed.[22] Interestingly this exoticized violence seems to garner far more interest and support from feminists who are eager to "expose" the dismal conditions of women internationally, yet who are conspicuously absent in the activism being engaged in by women of color who experience violence within their own countries.

In reality many women in the United States are victims of domestic violence. In 2000, intimate-partner homicides accounted for 33.5 percent of the murders of women, as compared to less than 4 percent of the murders of men.[23] In 2004, 1,159 women were killed by their partners.[24] Additionally, the U.S. Department of Justice has found that women recently divorced or who have left battering relationships are at greater risk of fatal violence.[25] Pregnant women and women who have been pregnant recently are also more likely to be victims of homicide than to die by other causes, and evidence suggests that a large number of these women are killed by their intimate partners.[26] Women are also far more likely than men to be victims of rape, attempted rape, and stalking in their lifetimes.[27] According to findings of a National Violence against Women survey, approximately 1.5 million women are raped and/or physically assaulted by an intimate partner yearly in the United States.[28]

These figures indicate a serious problem of violence in the United States, and the fact that there is an increased likelihood of violence when a woman tries to leave a relationship or gets pregnant suggests that similar issues of pride, honor, patriarchy, and—dare I say it even—"culture" may be operating in these cases. We never use such language to describe these crimes, however, and instead these cases are viewed as anomalous breakdowns within a family. Law professor Leti Volpp has noted that while the culture of the "Other" is always described in very limited and ahistorical ways, Western culture is never singled out in the same manner. She argues that because "we tend to perceive white Americans as 'people without culture,' when white people engage in certain practices, we do not associate their behavior with a racialized conception of culture, but rather construct other, noncultural explanations."[29] These problematic *"bad behaviors"* are thus only inscribed on "the bodies of racialized immigrant subjects."[30]

Scholars and activists have pointed out that the way dowry violence has been singled out within Indian law has perpetuated the idea that all intimate-partner homicides in India are dowry-related killings.[31] The early women's movement in India focused significantly on the most extreme forms of violence against women and dowry-related harassment, and lawmakers effectively codified this link. Indian criminal law contains a refutable presumption that if a woman dies within seven years of her marriage, and if she was harassed for dowry by her husband or his relatives, that the death was caused by them.[32] There is also a provision against "cruelty" within the law, which can include but does not require an allegation of a dowry demand. Because dowry-related violence is singled out in this way, many have argued that the police, courts, and society view other types of violence as less serious or objectionable, and women are less likely to pursue action in such cases.[33] "By focusing attention so strongly on dowry violence, the criminalization strategy may unwittingly have reinforced the tendency of the courts, the police, society in general, and women themselves to view non-dowry-related spousal violence as less significant, or even as acceptable."[34] Because other types of violence are viewed as less serious or less objectionable, women are reluctant to pursue legal action in such cases.[35] Even where issues of dowry are not present in a complaint, advocates have indicated that women are advised to add allegations of dowry harassment to strengthen their claims.[36] In this manner, what Oldenburg has described as the "unidimensional" focus on dowry-related deaths is created and sustained by Indian law.[37]

Comprehensive statistics on the problem of domestic violence in India are very limited. Some of this is attributable to the different ways in which domestic violence has been defined by various governmental and nongovernmental organizations; it is also attributed to the simple fact that interpersonal violence often goes unreported. The few studies that have been conducted "suggest that physical abuse of Indian women is quite high, ranging from 22 percent to 60 percent of women surveyed."[38] Violence impacts women from all backgrounds and communities in India, and this research also suggests that demands for dowry are not the only causes of this violence. "While international attention has been focused on dowry deaths, perhaps the most dramatic manifestation of violence against women, it is only one part of the problem. Not all violence within the household can be reduced to dowry demand; domestic violence or wife battering is far more systematic and pervasive than previously acknowledged."[39] One multisite study found that "dowry harassment was a factor in 12 percent of those women surveyed."[40] Another study on violence in rural Gujarat found that inadequate dowry was a cause for abuse in only 1 percent of the cases, while more often, women reported issues such as "mistakes in running the household, complaints about meal preparation, not caring for children properly, and economic stress" as the triggering factors in abuse.[41] Other studies have identified causes for domestic violence that include spousal disparity in educational attainment level or marital age, lack of autonomy within the home, dowry pressure, childhood abuse, unemployment, alcoholism, allegations of infidelity, and issues of sexual control and sexuality.[42]

One of the major critiques of antiviolence laws in India has been the overwhelming failure of criminal law approaches with these crimes. Existing legal formulations of violence within the family are limited to criminal prohibitions against "cruelty" or a category of homicides that the law refers to as "dowry deaths." These formulations of intimate violence can only be invoked by a married woman, and in the rare cases where a conviction is secured, available remedies are extremely limited. In addition, these laws have been critiqued for focusing too narrowly on the dowry-related aspects of intimate violence. Inadequate law enforcement and judicial responses to violence against women serve to magnify the shortcomings of existing laws. Police and judges are notoriously unwilling to intervene in cases involving violence within a marital relationship, except in cases involving extreme brutality or death. When they do choose to intervene, their responses often involve urging women to reconcile with their husbands in order to "save" their marriages. These barriers highlight the risk of relying too heavily on the criminal justice system to address violence and have a direct bearing on the Indian feminist movement to secure a civil law on domestic violence.

In September 2005, after years of dedicated advocacy by women's groups, the Indian government passed the Protection for Women from Domestic Violence Act of 2005, and it went into effect in October 2006. This pioneering law covers not only wives but *any* woman residing in a shared household. This includes not only women in live-in relationships, but also sisters, mothers, daughters, widows, divorced women, and women in marriages that the law views as invalid.[43] One of the other striking features of the recently enacted civil law is its broad conceptualization of "domestic violence," which includes physical, sexual, verbal, emotional, and economic abuse. In addition, the law establishes a unique remedial framework for safeguarding the rights of women who are victims of violence, including a unique "right of residency" provision that allows a woman to remain within the family home, regardless of whether she has a legal claim or share in the property. The enactment of this law was a significant milestone in antiviolence activism for women in India, though critical questions remain about how well it will be implemented.

Beyond efforts toward legal reform, advocates in India have worked to develop a range of innovative nonlegal responses to violence against women in both urban and rural parts of India. In some areas, All-Women Police Stations have been established in an effort to make the police more accessible to women and in the hope of creating greater sensitivity around gender-based crimes.[44] Another distinct response to violence is the Self-Help Collectives" or "Village Sanghas." These small and self-governed women's groups focus their efforts on improving women's opportunities to gain economic and political power. "The hope . . . is that if women are given increased educational, economic, and political status through these village collectives, or *sanghas,* they will be in a better position to take a stand against domestic violence."[45]

These alternative methods are interesting, because they seek to create an integrated and multilayered approach to the problem of violence within the family. They offer hope for advocacy that extends beyond the boundaries of the criminal justice system and that seeks to address the critical social and economic dimensions of these crimes. The insights about Indian activism, obtained through regional research in India, are extremely valuable and might well inform U.S.-based responses to violence against women, particularly efforts aimed at women whose experiences of violence are magnified by factors such as race, class, or immigrant status. Examinations of violence that occurs outside the United States should not be undertaken in order to convince ourselves that we are more "safe" than other women, but rather in an effort to understand the complex reasons why violence against women persists globally, despite myriad efforts to address it. I would argue that only when we redirect our attention away from culture and focus instead on how violence against women is linked to issues such as globalization, reassertions of state power, shifting racializations, religious fundamentalisms, and increased militarism worldwide can we really begin to understand the true magnitude of this multifaceted problem.

Salidummay

Lisa Valencia-Svensson

Yet there is still so much pain to express
salidummay . . .

To express from the flesh what is old
To ex-press from the folds
To press into tangible form and meaning
ay ay salidummay . . .

So many tales yet to tell
Narrating away the thorns of agony
Hidden still among the petals of your eyes
ay ay salidummay . . .

How to sing the suffering into a
Cadence that will at once
Enrage the senses
Spark the kindling of our souls
ay ay salidummay . . .

I pull the banners of courage
From the inner refuge of your eyes
Spinning a protest that wraps us
In resolve
Shooting us straight to the moon
ay ay salidummay salidummay diway

April 10, 1994

This poem is dedicated to the strength of Asian indigenous women.

This poem was inspired by three things: my reading of the January–March 1993 issue of *Change* (published by the Cordillera Women's Education and Resource Center), which focused on the experiences of rape and sexual assault of indigenous women in the Philippines; the music of Grace Nono, a Filipina singer based in the Philippines; and the frequent use, by someone close to my heart, of the phrase *"suntok sa buwan."*

Salidummay: a traditional music form in the Cordillera region of the Philippines; a melodic tune or chant that conveys an idea or tells a story; it is often women who sing it and make improvisations depending on the occasion or circumstance; it has evolved into a contemporary protest and revolutionary musical form.

Suntok sa buwan: "Trying to hit the moon," a phrase referring to that which is impossible to accomplish.

Hidden Transcripts: Women's Suicide as Resistance in Sri Lanka

Nandini Gunewardena

Introduction

The spectacle of suicide that has drawn global attention to Sri Lanka over the past decade is due to the stream of suicide bombings carried out by the separatist group, the Liberation Tamil Tigers of Elam (LTTE), which is fighting for a Tamil homeland in the northeastern part of the island. On the transnational stage, the equation of suicide in Sri Lanka primarily with suicide terror is exemplified by the fact that an Internet search yields literally hundreds of sites with information on suicide terrorism in Sri Lanka, as compared to a mere handful of sites on the more pervasive problem of suicide as a form of deliberate self-harm.[1]

According to one estimate, women have carried out about one-third of the LTTE's suicide attacks,[2] with the most notable incident being the killing of former Indian President Rajiv Gandhi by an LTTE woman fighter known only as Dhanu, and popularized in the film *The Terrorist*. The gendered implications of this film's romanticized rendition of the impetus for suicide merits separate discussion, not only because of its lack of engagement with the paradox of agency and choice on the part of women cadres who have carried out these gruesome acts of terror, but also because it glosses over their positionality and social location, thereby obliterating their personal histories.[3]

An analysis of the impact of terror and women's instrumentality in liberation struggles is beyond the scope of this paper. Most relevant to this research is that this specter of violence has occupied center stage, captivating the attention of local and global audiences—including the Sri Lankan diaspora over the past two decades—while the very terms of daily existence in Sri Lanka have come to be defined by the context of terror. Public and scholarly discourse have also been preoccupied with interpreting the meanings of political violence for the projects of identity, nationalism, and representation. As a result, much of the recent feminist scholarship emerging from Sri Lanka has also focused overwhelmingly on the embodiment of political violence in terms of the nation's central, and hence hegemonic, locations (positionalities of power), including the gendered impact of militarism.

Beyond the pale of the public gaze, however, and at the physical, social, economic and symbolic margins of the society, scarcely noticed by the hegemonic centers of power and perhaps not entirely unrelated to the panorama of political violence, a parallel phenomenon of death and destruction has been unfolding—the alarming incidence of uncelebrated suicides taking place on a daily basis in many impoverished regions of the country. In 1996, Sri Lanka had one of the world's highest suicide rates, at 55.46 per 100,000 population.[4] It outranked Finland, the country with the third-highest suicide rate in the world, by showing double the Finnish suicide rate. Twenty-three persons commit suicide daily in Sri Lanka, and ten times that number attempt it. Suicide is the commonest cause of death in Sri Lanka in the age group of fifteen to twenty-five; three times more women than men attempt suicide, while twice more men than women succeed in completing a suicide.[5]

Available data[6] on the history of suicide in Sri Lanka reveals that it peaked in the 1980s in the north central province, among farming communities. These data show a steady rise in the incidence of suicide since then, tapering off somewhat since 1995. Due to the tendency to underreport suicides,[7] and misclassification[8] the currently available data are wholly inadequate to provide a full picture of the current suicide rates. Studies since the mid-1990s[9] reveal that suicides are concentrated in rural areas of the country, particularly among Dry Zone resettled populations, as well as in Jaffna and Kurunegala districts. Apart from the phenomenon of fatal suicides, there is the rising incidence of attempted suicide, which is estimated to be triple the number of suicide mortality. Pesticide poisoning is the commonest method of suicide in Sri Lanka. In agricultural districts, pesticide poisoning is a leading cause of death in hospitals. Considering that approximately 75 percent of Sri Lanka is rural and populated by farming communities, this figure is indeed cause for grave concern.

Although Sri Lanka shows some of the highest gender indicators in the South Asia region (e.g., the highest life expectancy rates, highest literacy and economic activity rates, and the lowest maternal mortality rates), sadly, they register the highest suicide rates for women in the region. For a country where the discourse of *sati* has no sway, and where dowry-related suicides are virtually nonexistent despite its proximity to India, the high suicide rates among Sri Lankan women represents a confounding dilemma. In the four decades between 1950 and 1990, female suicide (fatality) in Sri Lanka has risen from a rate of 4.4 to 28 per 100,000 population. While the rate of completed suicide by women lags behind that for men, the difference between the two is lower than in many other countries,[10] and has been narrowing since the 1970s.[11] Other trends of concern are that female suicide in Sri Lanka is concentrated primarily in the age range of fifteen to thirty-five,[12] mostly among married women with relatively lower literacy and educational attainment levels than the national average.

Located as it is in a symbolic and physical terrain of marginality, suicide in Sri Lanka has not been considered a topic worthy of consideration by the public or the scholarly community. Let me begin by outlining the framing issues. Outside the issue of organic illnesses implicated as a trigger for suicide, the foremost question of course is the perennial existential question of motivation: What prompts an individual to take his or her own life? But as Rajeswari Sunder Rajan remarks on the production of knowledge about *sati,* the phenomenon of quasi-suicide in India, the need to know what really happened is frustrated by the impossibility of knowing, for "when the individual woman's subjectivity is read in terms of intention, intentionality can only be a matter of conjecture and, finally, ideological conviction."[13] In probing the issues of intention, I have been concerned with exploring how women's suicide in Sri Lanka might inform us of the processes of domination and subordination operating at the periphery, the construction of woman as the penultimate subaltern, if you will, determined not only by patriarchal ideologies of gender, but also by class hierarchies that inflect a specificity to the localized experiences of power and its expression via the violence experienced by rural women living in poverty.

This paper aims to embark on a reading of the representation and construction of women's suicide in Sri Lanka within cultural idioms of femininity, and to trace how discourses about women's suicide inform us of ideologies and practices that impose a pervasive surveillance and containment of women's lives. I will discuss how women's resort to suicide may be read as a form of resistance against gendered norms and practices of social control. In many social contexts, we know that gender hierarchies are maintained and reinforced via practices of gender violence, including physical, psychological, and verbal abuse. Simultaneously, the imposition of gender norms that encode practices of sexual surveillance, disciplining, and control over every aspect of a woman's life culminate in the particular contours of oppression in such hierarchical gender systems. Inevitably, women's attempts to assert their social agency have been met with severe suppression in many societal contexts. My concern is to explore whether under conditions of poverty—where low-income women have fewer opportunities to "overcome" the gender subordination that women with more means may be able to maneuver—suicide becomes perceived as an escape valve by rural women who see no exit from the grinding poverty, physical abuse, and oppression in their lives, as a means of registering protest over the containment of their lives, or as a way of expressing their opposition to oppressive proscriptions that culminate at the nexus of class and gender.

One of the main questions I address is whether the resort to suicide is a reflection of a vehement protest against patriarchal oppression or an attempt by a woman to register agency in crafting an autonomous subject position. As such, my attempt is to depersonalize the expressions of suicide as individual acts and explore their implications for the collective subjectivities of impoverished women in Sri Lanka. Given the risk of physical annihilation implicit in a suicide attempt, how could suicide be construed as representative of action aimed at self-determination? My concern is to explore the extent to which the resort to suicide is not simply the expression of a death wish by women, but rather an attempt to reconfigure the repressive contours of their lives by flagging attention to the unbearable aspects of patriarchal domination at the intersection of socioeconomic inequities. Inherent to this analysis is my attempt to complicate the subjective experiences of Sri Lankan women by de-essentializing their locations at the intersection of class, power, and gender hierarchies. The intersection of gender with sociocultural marginality, political oppression, and family conflict confers a particular kind of situatedness of low-income women in the suicide equation. Drawing upon the growing body of postcolonial and transnational feminist scholarship, my attempt is to interrogate the embodiment of class-based gender difference in hierarchically placed geographical locations in Sri Lanka (the urban as the center, and the rural as the margin), and to unravel how class inequities are inherently woven into the fabric of gender difference.

I have been interested in unraveling the relationship between physical location and social location as it constitutes the marginal positionality assigned to rural populations, both in terms of their spatial placement as well as in terms of their place in the neocolonial power hierarchies of Sri Lankan society. The metaphor of marginality, I argue, is resonated in the geographical, social, and cultural marginality of rural populations, as well as in the expressions of suicide. After Foucault and Lefebvre, my concern is to trace the exercise of power and social domination inherent in the marginality of the rural. As cultural-geography theorists have recently argued, far from constituting a neutral domain of social interrelationships, social space *is* the embodiment of practices and relations of power. My interest therefore is to reveal how the urban and rural are not merely disparate geographical units, but rather reflect markers of difference and domination.[14] An exploration of how the challenges from the margins that disrupt the cultural, social, and economic domination imposed by the center is at the core of my research. The way in which the margins become sites for the contestation of power through subversive acts that undermine the established social order and the imposition of social hierarchies is a related issue.[15] An equally pressing concern in my research has been to explore how the reach of patriarchal power is experienced and negotiated by rural women in Sri Lanka as they navigate their double marginality of geography and gender. The resort to suicide, I suggest, exemplifies the larger struggle over domination and subordination that is encountered by Sri Lankan women in general.

Contextualizing Suicide: Gender, Location, and the Construction of Marginality

As mentioned above, the incidence of suicide is highest in the Dry Zone regions of Sri Lanka, primarily among resettled populations.[16] Vast and desolate, much of the Dry Zone is frontier land, bordering thick jungle and at the seams of contested territory. The harsh physical environment in the Dry Zone, its vulnerability to drought and wildlife encroachment, imposes severe economic hardship on settler populations. Crop damage by elephants and other wildlife is a constant threat for farming communities in these marginal settings. Outside the massive irrigated areas of the Mahaweli River project, there is no assurance of water on the kind of regular schedule required for rice cultivation. Unexpected drought can destroy the entire rice crop, leaving a family with no way of recovering their investment in the crop, nor with the means to feed themselves for the rest of the season. Even within the Mahaweli, water equity is not always guaranteed, as we know from the spate of literature on top-ender, tail-ender disputes. A consistent characterization of the Dry Zone that I have encountered and experienced myself is the sense of desolation that haunts the spaced reclaimed from thick jungle. Locals use the Sinhala word *hudakalawa* to describe this sense of isolation. Dry Zone "settlements" are just that—sites where people have set up houses but not homes, places where a clustering of dwellings exist but not a community—at least not in the sense of a civic locus that permits a sense of belonging and integration. Individual vulnerability in resettled locations is conflated by the isolation of the nuclear family, brought on by the distancing from extended kin in home villages who might have otherwise functioned as a protective resource, both in terms of financial and social support. This social isolation is compounded by the economic and social stressors that resettled populations experience, further aggravating the fissures and strains within and between households.

Whether the choice was theirs or otherwise, those who occupied settlement schemes were individuals with little or no land in their home villages. Yet the promise of prosperity offered in the shift to a new location can become increasingly elusive, as the challenges of adjustment to the new setting is complicated by financial burdens that are not offset by social support. In effect, although their departure from their villages of origin was due to landlessness, they are no better off in the new setting, where their marginality is replicated. This factor alone places the average settler in a marginal location vis-à-vis district and state officialdom. They have little bargaining power or political clout with which to negotiate services or resources. Their marginality along vertical social axes is duplicated by the marginality along horizontal axes, namely from connections to kin networks of support. The lack of immediate access to kin networks (as in kin-based villages), an essential ingredient for fostering a Durkheimian sense of social integration, I argue, is a contributory factor in escalating interpersonal tensions and in aggravating the fissures and strains among resettled populations.

Resettled groups experience economic vulnerability due to a shift in livelihood patterns, limited income, and the fragility of the local as well as national economy.[17] Indebtedness and poverty are endemic to resettled populations—partly because of their unsuccessful adaptation to the vagaries of the ecological conditions of the Dry Zone. There is also the issue of an inadequate or debilitated physical infrastructure, which delimits a well-functioning service infrastructure, so that health and education facilities in these settlement areas of the Dry Zone are meager. Often due to the nonexistence of paved and navigable roads and reliable transportation, a distance of five kilometers can take an hour in traveling time. Imagine the difficulty of quickly conveying a person who has ingested a pesticide to the nearest rural hospital under these circumstances.

Dry Zone villages are typically underserved with regard to every kind of health service, let alone mental health services. Even upon arrival at a rural health outpost, there is no guarantee that the facilities and equipment required to treat a case of poisoning is readily available. Worse still, the stigma attached to suicide, even in health settings, means that a suicider is rendered to a pariah status, so that care for them is not prioritized. Eddleston, Sheriff, and Hawton report that in Anuradhapura district in the north-central area of the Dry Zone, 2,559 adults (age range twelve to seventy-three years; 1,443 men and 1,116 women) were admitted to the hospital with acute poisoning, almost all as a result of deliberate self-harm, during 1995 and 1996.[18] Altogether 325 (12.7 percent) died in the hospital (246 men and 79 women; 17 and 7.1 percent of admissions, respectively). The poisons used were pesticides, yellow oleander *(Thevetia peruviana)* seeds, and medicinal or domestic agents. Organophosphate and carbamate pesticides caused 914 admissions to hospitals and 199 (21.8 percent) deaths, and oleander poisoning accounted for 798 admissions to hospital and 33 (4.1 percent) deaths over a twenty-one-month period. According to this report, over 40 percent of the hospital's intensive-care beds were occupied by patients with organophosphate poisoning in 1996. The fatality rate for those who have ingested such poisons is high in Sri Lanka as compared to more developed countries. For example, nearly 13 percent of patients admitted to Anuradhapura Hospital for self-poisoning died, compared to one to two percent in the United Kingdom. The fatality rate for men who have ingested organophosphate poisons reaches 60 percent during some months. The probable reasons for the high mortality is cited as "the toxic nature of the substances involved, the lack of antidotes, the long distances between hospitals, and overstretched medical staff."

This paper draws upon fieldwork I conducted in December 1999 and June through August 2000 in three Dry Zone villages, Kurunegala, Thanamalvila and Embilipitiya. The latter two sites are located at the furthest (deepest) ends of Ratnapura and Moneragala district in the southeastern region of the country, in an area considered no-man's land due to its harsh terrain and lack of water resources. This location, at the heart of the country, signifies more the distance to conveniences and services than a notion of security. The former site is similarly situated, in Kurunegala district in the northwestern part of the country. Elephant encroachment is a constant threat that communities in all three villages contend with year-round. Much of the population have settled in both areas without proper authorization and are thus classified "encroachers" *(anavasara)*. Given that livelihood security is deeply rooted in the notion of landownership, their lack of access to proper land titles is itself a source of worry and confusion to this population. The possibility of being ousted hangs ever so threateningly over them, while the challenge of eking out a living in the inhospitable terrain looms as an ever-present concern.

The Gendered Discourses on Suicide in Sri Lanka

Public understandings of suicide in Sri Lanka—fed and shaped by popular magazines, newspaper accounts, and other media reports—typically associate women's suicides with the break-up of a love affair, while men's suicides are attributed to matters related to finances, livelihood, and work or the lack thereof. As such, public discourse on suicide consists of narratives that construct female suiciders as gullible, naive, irrational, and overly invested in romantic attachments. Interviews I conducted with family members of individuals who have attempted or completed suicide, casual commentaries by members of the public at large, and media reportage all revealed the tendency to depict women's suicide as lying within the "emotive" sphere, while suicide by men is portrayed as a phenomenon of the "rational" realm. Sensationalized media accounts portray the female victim as a love-struck young woman who took her life after a love relationship was severed, either because of abandonment or parental coercion to end it. The typical script is one that heralds male agency—a young woman abandoned by a young man, who has been cajoled by his parents to end a relationship because she has been classified as "unsuitable" in terms of caste or class—both of which are vehicles for social mobility and are instrumental in marriage transactions, which are designed to advance family status. The narrative of coercion—more applicable to female suiciders—signifies the imposition of generational authority particularly on women, as exemplified in the typical case of a young woman whose parents have pressured her into ending her relationship with an "unsuitable" partner (with the unsuitability being determined along the same parameters).

A 1996 study by Marecek revealed a similar gendered discourse on suicide causality, characterizing women as "delicate, weak, or emotionally vulnerable." Marecek notes that "in accounting for women's risk of suicide, respondents invoked internal, enduring character traits, that is, female nature." In accounting for men's risk of suicide, most interviewees invoked the social context, specifically, the pressures and constraints in the external environment."[19] These representations correspond to the binary classifications attributed to male and female "nature" among middle-class Sri Lankans, classifications that cast aspersions about the unbridled "emotional" nature of women who are in general unable to control their emotions. They also inform us about the gendered construction of realms of work and authority, with the relegation of women to the domestic sphere and the assumption that the strains associated with livelihood concerns are less pertinent to them. Despite, and perhaps because of, the inconsistency of these discourses with the reality of evolving gender roles, such characterizations provide us clues to the tenacity of gender constructs, as they perpetuate idealized gender codes that have far outlived the emerging realities.

The attribution of causality for female suicides to love-related distress glosses over women's inner conflicts in assuming the culturally sanctioned roles of dutiful, self-sacrificing wives and daughters, as well as their resistance to the accompanying repertoire of self-negation that is implicit in the scripted norms of these gender roles. Beyond the appearance of romantic crises lies a vast field of issues related to personal autonomy, agency, resistance, and in many instances, protest over personal histories scattered with incidents of chronic gender violence. Beneath the surface of the reported causality of an overly emotional young woman taking her life because she simply could not live without her choice of life partner, for example, is an expression of protest about the imposition of parental choice over one's life decisions.

As such, the depiction of women's suicide as a response to thwarted love is complicit in relegating women's suicide to the personal domain. It permits the dismissal of the tensions and conflicts surrounding the transformation of gender constructs in Sri Lankan society, as well as the dismissal of women's attempts to expand the confines of traditional gender roles. Painting women's suicide with the brush of thwarted romantic attachment allows for its construction as a private dilemma of overly emotional young women, and hence its relegation to a social issue of nonconsequence. This tendency is also the equivalent of equating women with "natural" desire and emotion, as compared to the "rational" bearers of culture that men are deemed to be. These patterns are consistent with the portrayal of women in public culture as flighty creatures with unbridled emotions. Common sayings, such as "a woman's mind goes no further than the handle of a spoon," capture the characterization of women's purportedly limited capacity for rational thinking. Other folk sayings allude to women's "quarrelsome" nature by the verdict "two women can't cook on the same hearth," thereby attributing irrationality and preoccupied self-interest to female conduct. They imply that women's "nature" is subject to the narrow confines of her emotions, where she is unable to think rationally in terms of the common good and accommodate the interests of others—a notion entirely contravened by the reality.

Although there is a rural–urban divide in such gendered depictions—to the extent that they are primarily the purview of middle-class, urbanized populations—variations of such themes prevail in rural contexts too, despite the latter's more equitable construction of gender. The subtext of such characterizations is that while such discourse is framed in the idiom of "romantic" attachment, they are in reality referring to women's sexuality. In effect, commentary about women's emotions running away with them is a signifier invoking cultural gender ideals that emphasize female restraint and chastity, part of the Protestant Buddhist ethos that Obeyesekere (1997) has written extensively about. Reasons cited as the trigger for suicide among my study sample, however, tells another story. These data reveal that marital and family conflicts serve as the leading factor associated[20] with suicide among women (in 62 percent of the cases). Physical violence is implicated in nearly one-fourth (23 percent) of the female suicides; in most of those suicides, alcohol use or abuse by the husband or male kin is another associated factor. In total, half of the suicides in this sample are associated with alcohol abuse and the ensuing conflict between the spouses and/or extended family. Eight of the women's suicides I classify as "marital conflict" involve the use and/or abuse of alcohol by a woman's husband, which formed the background for a range of ensuing conflicts (a typical pattern being that an inebriated husband would return home to engage in verbal assaults directed at a woman and/or to abuse her physically too). Indebtedness and financial problems have been reported in association with a relatively small number of cases (11 percent of the female suicides, and 19 percent of the male suicides). I suspect this reflects more a problem with interviewees' inability to attribute financial problems as a trigger for suicides. In reality, financial strain is the backdrop for all suicides, as evidenced in the income data I obtained.

Surprisingly, only 11 of the 69 suicides by women in my sample showed any association with a love-related matter, and the circumstances surrounding these suicides suggest that, rather than women's overemotionality, it is the overregulation of their sexuality and their life choices, often via violent means, that worked as the breaking point. Contrary to the charge of women's overemotionality, however, I suggest that a range of underlying issues—including those related to family conflict over choice of marriage partner, the imposition of parental decisions over such choice (often via physical force), the threat of being ostracized from family and kin circles, and conflicted emotions over the pressures to comply to gender norms and acquiesce to parental wishes—are implicated in suicide among young unmarried women. As such, I argue that the imminent threat of violence as a means of imposing control over "disobedient" daughters and "wayward" wives serves as the backdrop for women's suicide in Sri Lanka. While such violence may not always entail physical abuse, it is often associated with chronic verbal abuse, and its coercive nature is tantamount to psychological abuse. In the case of married women, the precipitating factors surrounding their suicides, as reported by family members, entail a preponderance of gender violence, meaning chronic physical, psychological, and verbal abuse.

Gender Violence and Suicide

A range of descriptors are used in Sinhala to capture violence directed at another, whether physical, verbal, or psychological. These include the terms *vada-hinsa* (harassment and injury), *hirihara* (oppressive harassment), *aravul athikireema* (create strife), *tharavatu kireema* (rebuke/reprimand), *tharjanaya kireema* (threaten), and *randu-dabare veema* (fight/quarrel). These descriptors are used in many of the narrative accounts of suicide causality to capture the nature of interpersonal conflict between married couples. As such, we may argue that suicide among women in Sri Lanka is often a protest against the expressions of gender violence at the hands of husbands or male family members whose aim is to engage in a form of control of the women. Yet the fact that male violence is inevitably associated with alcohol abuse suggests that a crisis of power is manifested in male–female and perhaps intergenerational relationships to the extent that violence becomes deployed as a means of resolving/reconfirming male power and control. Young women's assertions of their choice of marriage partner, for example, becomes perceived as a challenge to the power and authority vested in male family members. Similarly, married women's protests over a husband's work habits, earning power, extramarital sexual liaisons, or excessive use of alcohol can also be perceived as a threat to a husband's power in the relationship. In the past, gender norms that prescribed endurance and long-suffering by women as a passive acceptance of their karmic destiny may have contributed to women's tendency to bear with and accept physical and verbal abuse, whereas in contemporary times, it is possible that these norms and ideals are increasingly being contested. Obeyesekere offers a possible explanation for this transformation in contemporary Sri Lanka: "Owing to the delayed age of marriage and the greater pervasiveness of Buddhist modernism, the control of sex and aggression in socialization and their continuous repression have increased."[21]

Faced with this kind of intensified repression, women as daughters and wives are constantly engaging in efforts to redefine the norms of patriarchal authority structures and their marginality in such configurations, as the narrative accounts of suicides I collected suggest. They do so via verbal protests and by contesting the dictates of male kin, who maintain a surveillance and regulation of their sexuality. While such verbal protests are rarely confrontational, they convey a norm that belies the hierarchies apparent in their lives. Women who resorted to suicide because they simply could not bear the verbal and physical abuse they have been subjected to are making a statement about an ideal of marital relationships free of such conflict. Indeed, many have repeatedly openly expressed their opposition to such abuse, in effect articulating a norm about harmonious marital relationships. As such, I suggest that the preexistence of a norm or an idealized notion of a smoothly functioning marriage is the backdrop against which we need to understand women's resort to suicide as one of protest against a situation they perceive as unacceptable and unbearable.

The extent to which women engage in practices that challenge and contest patriarchal authority suggests that contrary to a set of absolutes regulating gender relationships, there is ample space for disputing the terms of a marriage and negotiating its conditions. Nonetheless, such elasticity does not necessarily lead to the effective transformation of gender systems. The forceful and continued assertion of power by a husband—either in the form of verbal/physical abuse, and/or in his insistence on continuing an extramarital affair, and/or in accusations of infidelity by his wife—has prompted suicide by many women in my research sites. In other words, despite the prevalence of elasticity in gender systems, the various degrees to which males assert power can be perceived as particularly oppressive from the perspective of women.

Regulating Women's Sexuality

Rural Sinhala women's subjectivity is constituted by their understandings of Buddhist notions of womanhood and popular interpretations of such scriptural edicts. Women articulate the condition of womanhood as full of pain and suffering *(dukkha)*, while Sinhala Buddhist gender codes tend to construct woman as impure, the source of "sin" and temptation, both potent and dangerous, as discussed for example by Winslow. [22] The illuminating corpus of ethnography on Sinhala Buddhist culture by Obeyesekere is an excellent source for understanding the complexities of Sinhala Buddhist gender systems. As Obeyesekere has documented for Laggala (an isolated village in the Central province), "The inferior social and ritual status of the women is validated and defined through the concept of *kili,* or impurity."[23] Although exact parallels of the characterizations of female nature that Obeyesekere encountered thirty years ago may not be found in the Dry Zone regions of the country, variations on the traits assigned to females—i.e., seductiveness, untrustworthiness, and ritual impurity *(kili)*[24]—are generally prevalent in the culture.[25] As Obeyesekere has illustrated in his seminal work on the cult of goddess Pattini, the strict enforcement of Brahmanic gender norms pertaining to female sexuality are mediated in rural Sinhala areas by the institution of cross-cousin marriage. The latter permits continued affiliation with the woman's natal family and ample opportunities or a woman's affective needs to be met (unlike a woman entering a completely strange virilocal household). In effect, cross-cousin marriage in rural (non-elite) Sinhala areas means that there is a lower preoccupation with the strict enforcement of Brahmanic values pertaining to female sexuality. As such, we may surmise that the regulation of women's sexuality, the manner in which such regulation is undertaken, and the extent to which it involves actual physical violence directed against women varies from region to region in Sri Lanka.

Obeyesekera has argued that the Brahmanic scale of values as ideals anchored to a religious scheme of values, as it is in India,[26] is absent in Sri Lanka (i.e., the emphasis on virginity and chastity in females, *pativrata* [meaning "complete devotion to the husband"], and its concomitants of unquestioning loyalty and veneration of the husband, unassertiveness and submissiveness, the proscription of sex and aggression drives). Nonetheless, it is his contention that the incorporation of this scale of values as a secular ideology—as a set of practical ethics—and their reinforcement via the edicts of Victorian morality under British colonial rule have meant that "women are expected to be submissive and remain sexually pure until marriage. Parents take care to enforce these ideas, so that females are trained early to rigidly conform to a pattern of submissiveness and sexual modesty."[27]

The characterization of women as fickle and untrustworthy sexual beings subject to the slightest temptation, in a culture that emphasizes sexual moderation, permits the blame for male sexual excess to be transferred to women. The internalization of Buddhist values of moderation as they intersect with notions of women's sexuality permits the scapegoating of women as either suffering from "excess of affect," or vulnerable to sexual indiscretions. In a thought-provoking article exploring the configuration of love and hate in the upsurge of suicide in Sri Lanka, Silva and Pushpakumara (1996) provide an interesting gendered argument as one of the factors implicated in suicide in the impoverished Dry Zone settlement areas.

> By virtue of their poverty, marginality, and lack of opportunities, women from marginal settler or squatter backgrounds in particular are often compelled to enter secret sexual liaisons with men of influence, usually in the form of premarital or extramarital relations. When terminated or exposed, these secret love affairs can become a potent source of stress, social rejection, and disrepute for the parties involved, the women in particular.[28]

While this argument alludes to the gender inequities inherent in the society (albeit while betraying the gender biases of the authors at the same time), it fails to acknowledge the element of coercion in the formation of such liaisons between individuals who are invested with vastly different and gendered forms of power. By placing the blame squarely on the part of women who are "compelled" to enter such sexual liaisons, the authors fail to grapple with the economic forces that might collude in creating such a scenario on one hand—or to grapple with the role of "men of influence" in maintaining or perpetuating such economic conditions, not to mention their complicity in engineering such liaisons. In effect, the agency of all parties is suppressed in an equation that suggests the "law of the jungle" is at work in Dry Zone settlements where raw emotions hold sway over all human interaction. This complex rationalizing serves effectively to regulate and control women's sexuality and perceived violations of the gendered sexual mores, when in reality, these practices speak more to the status concerns of kin groups.

In the next section, I will turn to a consideration of how the characterizations of female sexuality impinge on male suicides. How do we interpret the fact that spousal infidelity by women is a more common reason for suicide by males than the converse? It is my contention that local gender constructions that characterize women as likely to indulge in sexual indiscretions, and the expectation for women to internalize the sexual mores of chastity and fidelity, coexist in a precarious tension where women's extramarital affairs are perceived as an affront to male notions of masculinity, hence, power and identity. Indeed, as Obeyesekere's research has shown for Laggala, the intense suspicion of women by men arose from the construction of women as "unregulated" beings, likely to take sexual license. Instead (and perhaps expressly because of the construction of women as overly sexual beings), male privilege is exercised via a kind of gender surveillance that is carried out by the monitoring of women's dress, attire, conduct, and mobility as markers of sexual freedom. The mere threat of exposure ensures the regulation of gendered norms of conduct, while by contrast, such exposure and the shame and humiliation it entails can lead to suicide, as evidenced in several cases I recorded. A unique kind of double standard is enacted in this scenario with regard to male sexual jealousy—a primary motivator for male aggression against his spouse and often for the internalization of such aggression. Perceived or inferred infidelity by a woman is interpreted as a slight against a man's masculinity, and thus evokes shame and humiliation. As such, it may lead to the direction of aggression against her, or conversely, to self-directed aggression in the form of suicide. Yet given that the use of physical force is not a legitimated or justifiable strategy, it is likely to be condemned under Buddhist ideals of conduct. Despite the subordinate role expected of a wife, it is customary for marital relationships in rural settings to accord certain powers to women. Wives reserve the right to correct *(hada ganna, harigassana)* errant behavior and to express their outrage at excessive practices. Thus, male privilege rarely goes uncontested, except among middle-class households, and wives tend to engage in unhesitant, if not unrelenting, questioning of a husband's behaviors.

Summary: Suicide as Resistance Performance

In closing, my analysis was inspired by James Scott's formulations about resistance practices as hidden transcripts that contest hegemonic authority and power. It soon became evident to me that although suicide is enacted as a private performance of resistance, in effect it becomes very much a public affair, inevitably capturing the imagination of the community/nation. The household/family of the suicider is subject to the scrutinizing gaze of the public/village eye. Although acts of suicide take place within the private domain, without the whisper of a public announcement, the very nature of suicide as a grave, life-threatening matter propels it quickly into a public arena. In this manner, although suicide is purportedly enacted in a private realm, it becomes an expression of protest that transgresses its predetermined boundary of the private/domestic, refusing to be contained and infringing boldly on a public stage. In this kind of double veiling, a private mode of resistance can daringly break through to the public mode without appearing to do so, and without risking the castigation, condemnation, or outright suppression that a more obvious act would invoke. Suicide can thus be seen as a performance predicated on the existence of the family/nation as an audience, and at once as a witness to and arbiter of private grievances. As such, suicide becomes a powerful staging ground for protest against perceived and experienced injustice. The resort to suicide, then, is at once a bold statement, a critique, an appeal, and a protest. It is thus an agentive act, aimed at transforming a woman's life conditions. Implicit in the act of suicide is a claim to autonomy, a refusal to unquestioningly accept the gendered cultural code of passive suffering, premised on a belief in the right to challenge this gender role. In this type of transcript, the articulations that take place "offstage," behind the backs of those who wield power (in this case, patriarchal authority and its representatives), are foregrounded almost innocently, yet in an incredibly powerful manner, since they displace the powerful in an extremely powerful way.

Unraveling Agency and Resistance in Suicide

> *Since speech is identified as self-expression, and silence as self-extinction, they are closely tied into the project of subject-constitution. In a further move, since speech is regarded as a right, and the suppression of speech as a denial of that right in a democratic polity, the access to speech has defined social hegemony, just as its lack has defined subalternity in unequal social structures and situations. 29*

The one vital clue to my exploration of women's suicide as resistance was the overwhelming preponderance of suicidal attempts among women, in comparison to completed suicides. Women's suicides are typically staged for discovery, taking place either in the presence of others or planned in such a way that there would be immediate intervention; this is in contrast to the majority of male suicides, which tend to be carried out in isolated settings. This fact alone bears testimony to the probability that women's suicidal behavior may be prompted more by the need to register a grievance than by the desire to end their lives. Thus—although in many instances suicides are triggered by the inability to bear real, material deprivations and social subordination/oppression—fundamentally, suicides represent the outcome of deep existential predicaments. Although it is impossible to verify whether there is such a conscious intentionality behind the act of suicide, the inevitability of a suicide being hoisted onto a public stage suggests that whether they are cognizant of it or not, the issue of public recognition is central to the expression of suicide by women.

Suicide as Critique

In the hush surrounding suicide as a stigmatized act, private grievances gain public visibility. A silenced being gains center stage as a voice that reverses the scrutinizing gaze of gendered surveillance back upon the conditions of oppression in an inescapably vocal, reflexive indictment. The shroud of invisibility screening privatized gender violence is thus abruptly torn asunder, hurling its bitter details onto a public stage, subjecting the very terms of gender subordination to critique and condemnation. Despite the fact that a life is lost in the act of suicide, the conditions of oppression are unmistakably publicized. As Sunder Rajan suggests, when problematized beyond the binary of speech vs. silence, we may be able to see how women may use silence as a political resource.[30] In this instance, the subjective psychic pain of the subaltern woman is projected on to the body politic as objective spectacle—a loud, accusatory spectacle that confers immense power to the dead subject in a hitherto unimaginable manner.[31] In this manner, an individual suicide assumes a social function in challenging oppressive gendered practices of containment.

Suicide as an Interpellation between Silence and Speech

The construction of Sinhala femininity from the complex of shame/modesty/fear (lajja-baya) that Obeyesekere has discussed extensively (glossed also as "respectability" by de Alwis), calls for silence as a feminine virtue, which is upheld by middle-class Buddhist social circles and those groups emulating such norms. Against this backdrop, suicide becomes an insistent form of resistance that invokes cultural norms of silence while simultaneously using such norms as a political resource. While women's tendency for "oral rage," as characterized by Obeyesekere's Laggala informants, for instance, suggests that compliance to the gender expectation of silence is not entirely complete—silence may also be usurped by women to register subordination rather than subjugation. The power of silence is then in the refusal to speak upon command.

The commentary by a young psychologist training in the North Central province (at the Polonnaruwa base hospital) about a young woman patient's refusal to reveal the intentions behind her attempted suicide betrays the gendered characterization of women's speech as both always and necessarily self-implicating. Describing his efforts to elicit a response from her about what ailed her to the point that she attempted to take her own life, this physician characterized the silence maintained by the young woman as a gesture of stubbornness. Her resistance to his benevolent intervention, predicated on his belief in the power of Western psychiatric tradition to fully "cure" and restore, was perceived as an affront, a subordinate act (the subtext being that she, as the subaltern with little power or recourse to other means of salvation, was arrogant in her denial of the power vested in the Western-trained psychiatrist). This juxtapositioning of the woman as a resisting agent and the psychiatric as the benevolent but hegemonic force reveals the disjunctures of class and gender as hierarchy at the periphery.

Assertions of agency, resistance, and the politics/practices of opposition are all life-embracing social practices. Despite the risks they entail, in general, such expressions of resistance are rarely life-threatening and are certainly not inherently and inevitably fatal, as are practices of suicide. If so, how can we understand suicide as a way to construct and transform unbearable life situations, and as attempts by individuals to reconstitute themselves and their quotidian realities? My inclination is to argue that, from the perspective of suicidal individuals, what is lost in terms of a gamble with one's physical/corporeal existence is gained in terms of the meaning rendered to one's psychic existence. My conjecture is that a blurring of the distinction between life and death occurs at this juncture, where Buddhist concepts of birth and rebirth *(samsara)* intervene to provide assurance of a suicider's existential concerns. In other words, it is possible that the finiteness attributed to death in other social contexts is unfamiliar to Sinhala Buddhist understandings that have acute cognizance of the instability of corporeal existence (the *nama-rupa* distinction), as compared to the infinity of the soul.

Not Too Far from Here
(Reflexiones de Juárez)

Jackie Joice

A t night from Juárez, Mexico, the city lights of El Paso resemble fireflies scattered among the hills. At the border, vendors sell glittery pictures of the Virgen and *elote* (grilled corn) while pushing carts back and forth between vehicles. The air is pervaded with the mixture of car exhaust and *carnitas*. Not too far from here, women are being gutted like fish and discarded into the nearest vacant lot. Since 1993, close to five hundred women have been abducted and brutally murdered in the city of Juárez. The victims are mostly in their late teens and early twenties. The majority of these young women are poor, reside in the countryside, and are employees of the *maquiladoras* (factories). Because of the distance from countryside homes to the *maquiladoras,* some of the women have to leave their homes at twilight morning hours to take the bus to work. Some of these women never make it to work. Instead their bodies are found in the desert among other places . . . decaying. According to a report by Amnesty International, 41.3 percent of the victims were found in sparsely populated areas on the outskirts, 24.6 percent were found in sparsely populated urban areas or the industrial area, 15.9 percent in the city, and 10.1 percent at a home.

When I traveled to Juárez, I was in the company and also a member of a group of artists called Viejaseskandalosas ("the Viejas" for short), founded by filmmaker and photographer Azul Luna. The Viejas consist of male and female visual artists, filmmakers, writers, dancers, and activists that are involved in bringing awareness to this crisis taking place in Juárez. There's no doubt that a woman's safety and welfare is not the first priority of the local government.

We traveled to Juárez for a weekend in February 2002, all of us from different parts of the United States, some as far as New York, to show solidarity with the families of the victims in the form of art and peaceful protests. On the first night of the events in Juárez, I read my poem "Not Too Far from Here" at the INBA (Instituto Nacional Bellas Artes), a contemporary art museum. The INBA was hosting the Viejas exhibit of art and photography on one side of the museum. Ironically, Santo Niño de Atocha was being exhibited on the other side of the museum. Santo Niño de Atocha is the patron saint of travelers and the unjustly imprisoned, and he rescues people in danger. I interpreted the synonymous exhibits as symbolic and significant. After a couple of years of artistic protests, fundraisers, and educating the public in the United States, I traveled to Juárez to verify the rumors of carnage and show solidarity with the families of the victims.

In November 2001, eight bodies were found in an arid cotton field surrounded by busy intersections. We visited this crime scene on a crisp and cold Saturday morning. Three months later, rope still outlined the spaces were the bodies were dumped. Each roped-off section was marked with paper tags that read *Cuerpo #1, Cuerpo #2, Cuerpo #3,* and so forth. The Viejas were briefed by *El Paso Times* reporter Diana Washington Valdez. She informed us that the bodies were severely beaten, some mutilated and raped, and their hands bound behind their backs. The tree branches on the cotton field did the tango with the cold bad breath of Mother Earth. Dried cotton leaves and stems cracked, crumbled, and scattered among the indentations of female corpses. Half-buried liquor bottles, women's panties, and a headless doll were all discarded within the same parameters of the scene. Clumps of stray raw cotton, detached and dirty, blew across the neglected field. I picked up some of the cotton and stuffed it into my pocket.

Although the blood of the bodies has vanished, the memories of the struggle are like epileptic flashes of bruised skin and torn limbs. At one point, I'm sure I looked into a killer's cold-blooded eyes as he pushed a car, drove a bus, or sold a newspaper. Later that Saturday, the Viejas dressed in black and marched to the border in solidarity with reporters, concerned citizens, and families of the victims. We draped a banner across a bridge that commuters leaving Juárez would see. The banner read JUSTICE TO THE WOMEN OF JUÁREZ. Commuters and passersby honked their horns and waved in support.

Señorita Extraviada is a documentary by filmmaker Lourdes Portillo about the murders in Juárez. The film is composed of interviews with law enforcement, government officials, and moving testimonies from some of the victims' family members. Portillo uses footage of the popular bus routes that the women workers utilize and on which some ultimately lose their lives. *Señorita Extraviada* demonstrates the outright carelessness and disregard for human life among some of the officials of Juárez. Another documentary from a more investigative perspective entitled *Border Echoes,* by Fox 11 reporter Lorena Mendez-Quiroga was issued in 2006.

As the city of Juárez sleeps, its women are being yanked from life. The mysogynistic approach to these murders must be addressed and stopped so that carnage will stop too.

Not Too Far from Here

smudged red lipstick
remains on the hands
of two-legged coyotes.
who savor women's flesh.

Not too far from here
piles of parched bones and
burgundy smocks lie in the desert
and names of maquiladoras
are etched on the skull, femur,
somewhere.

Not too far from here
women are expendable
last page news
equivalent to the peso.

Not too far from here
the stench lingers through
barbwire fences

crossing the borders
and tickling our noses.

Not too far from here in Juárez
hundreds go unsolved
meaningless breasts and wombs
strewn across vast amounts of land
decaying.

Not too far from here
an eerie silence
covers unmentionable deaths.
Brujas blancas are working overtime
calling on the Virgen for assistance.

Not too far from here
we can hear whispers of restless souls
crying for peace
crying for justice.

Chapter 3.

Speaking Truth to Power

Pentagon

May Chan

Introduction

How can one not speak about war, poverty, and inequality when people who
suffer from these afflictions don't have a voice to speak?

—Isabel Allende

There are well-documented correlations linking the establishment of military installations and armed conflict with an increase in the physical and sexual exploitation of the women living in such fraught regions of the world. It is a horrific commentary regarding state-sanctioned violence against women and children, particularly those of color, that there is not one continent on earth free of such historical engagement.

This chapter starts with an essay that illustrates how "rape culture" emerges from cultural, political, and economic institutions and is sustained by representations circulated in mainstream media. A brief wrenching poem describes the deadly effect of hypermasculinity on two women—the first killed while working as a peace activist in Palestine, the second killed because her transgender identity threatened her California suburban murderers. Another poem poignantly speaks about the devastating effect of warfare on indigenous Hawaiians and reveals how militarism is the root cause of generational poverty and cultural obliteration in the Islands. A third poem offers a glimpse of the personal pain felt by an Iraqi woman who is surrounded by the desert graves of her family and friends and the ruins of her village. A thoughtful essay draws upon the conditions of women in Palestine and Afghanistan as its point of reference in a discussion that links critiques regarding domestic violence to those concerning global violence. An essay and a poem, each crafted by Guatemalan women, speak eloquently about the trauma that their compatriots have endured during decades-long civil wars. Rufina Amaya was the only surviving eye witness to the infamous Massacre of El Mozote, in which an estimated nine hundred villagers were murdered over three days by U.S.-trained Salvadorian Special Forces. A remarkable essay describes how Amaya's *testimonio* is critical to understanding and halting state-sanctioned violence in all parts of the world. The concluding two works, an essay and a poem, both take for their subjects the Japanese-government sanctioned enslavement of approximately two hundred thousand women as sex workers, before and during World War II. Their focus is on Korean comfort women, and together these writings form a powerful argument and demand for a formal apology from the Japanese and U.S. governments.

Militarism and its attendant acts of rape, murder, and mayhem are not the exclusive problem of particular countries or regions. However, until the militarization and institutionalization of crimes against women of color is recognized, it will not be understood that these are crimes against all people.

The Way We Do Things in America: Rape Culture and the American Military

Alisa Bierria

Remember that bizarre Nike "chainsaw" commercial from a few years back? The commercial featured a menacing fiend, replete in hockey mask, pursuing a half-dressed woman somewhere in the mysterious backwoods. Luckily for her, the terrorized woman is not just any woman, but a superwoman—or to be specific, an Olympic athlete woman—sprinting over broken tree branches. Our heroine makes a dramatically narrow escape (the attacker collapses out of breath, unable to keep up with the potential victim), and our screen is filled with Nike's infamous "swoosh" logo along with an assertion: "Why sport? You'll live longer."

Transforming a Rape Culture, a book published in 1993, defines rape culture as "a complex of beliefs that encourages male sexual aggression and supports violence against women . . . a society where violence is seen as sexy and sexuality as violence, . . . [that] condones physical and emotional terrorism against women *as the norm.*"[1] The Nike "chainsaw" commercial illustrates this definition of rape culture. It exploits the pop culture idea of the male brute, creates an unrealistic construction of what a woman needs to achieve (Olympic-level athletic ability) in order to elude a violent attack, and generally objectifies the idea of violence against women in order to do the most important thing—that is, sell running shoes. After Nike's commercial aired, antiviolence activists rightfully demanded that it be removed from television, and NBC eventually relented to their pressure.

Despite the troubling nature of Nike's "chainsaw commercial," it has always bothered me that antiviolence activists chose this issue as the most pressing one to

147

protest the giant multinational corporation for making. The definition of rape culture does not have to be confined to modes of entertainment such as television, music, or movies. For example, Nike not only makes commercials selling rape culture, but it has also been cited for sexual violence in its Indonesian factories, where women employees have reported being forced to trade sexual favors to gain employment. Why the outrage on the commercial, and not a similar mobilization addressing the sexual and economic exploitation of Nike's Indonesian workers? It could be that, for American women, Nike's commercial represented a direct link to the culture of violence against women, but the issue of worker exploitation in faraway factories suggests seemingly distant issues such as globalization or workers' rights. Alternatively, perhaps they agreed that the sexual coercion of those factory workers is a "violence against women" issue, but one based on economics and not culture, as if the two were independent. Yet the same cultural norms that prevented Nike executives from anticipating the controversial response to their commercial also discourage them from letting workplace sexual violence in Indonesia obscure the bottom line. Just as culture exceeds art to include behavior patterns, belief systems, and values, rape culture is infused in much of our attitudes and institutions here in the West.

Locating Rape Culture

We must create a working definition of rape culture that not only acknowledges the cultural normalization of violence against women, but also incorporates a consciousness of how our institutions operate from a rape culture *paradigm*. A rape culture paradigm includes a set of principles that shape priorities, decisions, and goals that drive individuals and institutions. An institution operating from a rape culture paradigm does not have to specifically name violence against women as a goal or a tool to reach its objective, but it must incorporate those principles that help manifest sexual and domestic violence. We can locate the principles of rape culture by examining the impact of rape on rape survivors. The action of rape signifies much more than physical violence. Rape survivors report experiencing their bodies being reduced to objects, their sense of self erased, their sense of power subjugated, and their ability to connect to others disrupted. The ordeals that survivors describe—*objectification, dehumanization, disempowerment, and isolation*—are all fundamental elements of a rape culture.

These paradigmatic elements of rape culture not only arise in an individual event of sexual assault, but—as we've seen with the Nike example—we can also locate them in our economic and political institutions. For example, workers' bodies are *objectified* and used for economic gain by corporations that exploit prisoners for cheap labor. Afghanis killed in the U.S. war are *dehumanized* by our military when the military identifies the dead as "collateral damage." The Bush Administration's $1.5 billion plan to marry off single mothers on welfare *disempowers* poor women to make decisions that are right for their families without the pressure of the government's judgment on their lives. People with disabilities are *isolated* from communities when they are forced by the state to live in institutions and nursing homes. All of the institutions listed in the above examples (prisons, corporations, the military, welfare, disability institutions) actively exercise the values of rape culture.

Not coincidentally, these institutions are also environments where significant amounts of sexual violence (including rape, sexual coercion, and sexual harassment) occur, reminding us that rape culture produces rampant amounts of sexual violence. However, the above examples not only demonstrate how rape culture produces sexual violence, but how it also produces racism, colonialism, ableism, class bias, and misogyny. *Transforming*'s assertion that rape culture supports violence against women is true but incomplete. Rape culture as a paradigm representing a set of principles shows us how the culture of rape actually supports many types of violence against many groups of people.

Cultural Lessons from Abu Ghraib

"That's not the way we do things in America," asserted President George W. Bush in response to graphic photographs of Iraqi prisoners being sexually abused by American military officers and private security contractors. As the terrible and disturbing images flooded the international media, Bush, presidential candidate John Kerry, and many other supporters of the war on Iraq were quick to clarify that the torture being exhibited in those photos were isolated incidents and that the behavior of a few rogue soldiers should not be generalized as reflecting the character of the American military.

As I write this article, however, there are increasing reports that reveal a widespread endorsement and institutional support of torture and sexual abuse of prisoners captured in our War on Terror. The few bad apples have been revealed to us as a whole ruined and rotted grove. The photographs have accomplished the interesting feat of placing the United States on the defensive in a cultural battle designed to determine which culture (Western, capitalist, Christian vs. Eastern, Muslim, Arab) will be portrayed and understood by the rest of the world as barbaric. After the attacks of September 11, 2001, many Westerners, from white liberal feminists to neoconservative hawks, supported the war on Afghanistan, because a "barbaric" culture needed to be eradicated. The War on Terror rapidly became codified in terms of superior and inferior cultures, good people and evil (or at the very least backward) people—deftly positioning the United States as a "model country" for the world to emulate. Commentators came to define the United States in opposition to Afghanistan: We were civilized, democratic, and respectful of women, unlike *them*.

As if trapped in a house of mirrors, those haunting photographs from Abu Ghraib were distributed widely, everywhere, or so it seemed. Supporters of the war on Iraq did their best to deflect attention away from the embarrassment. Bush expressed his "disgust," hoping to identify with shocked Americans and assure them that those few bad apples would forthrightly be tossed out of our barrels and our barracks. Conservative pundits attempted to minimize the abuse as "fraternity pranks." Still, the images continued to drown out their weak declarations, causing us to question what kind of superior culture uses sadism, humiliation, and sexual violence as institutionalized tools for establishing control over individuals.

Despite our deep grief about the torture reflected in those images, many of us know better than to engage in the indulgence of being surprised. We understand that the culture of the American military is rooted in a legacy of rape culture that continues to manifest itself with each new invasion. Robert White, former U.S. ambassador to Paraguay and El Salvador, remarked,

> *We are living an illusion if we think these practices are unique. What is unique is the graphic pictorial evidence that drives it home. But that the United States has been complicit with torture in Vietnam and Latin America, there can be no doubt. It may be sinking into the public consciousness for the first time, but expressions of shock from people whose business is foreign policy are quite hypocritical.*[2]

Despite President Bush's assertion to the contrary, the Abu Ghraib photographs are all-too-accurate representations of "the way we do things in America," particularly when it comes to the military.

The U.S. military's goal to protect and expand the interests of the United States as the most powerful country in the world is built on a rape culture paradigm. We do not need proof that rape is happening during the course of the War on Terror, because we understand that the principles of objectification, dehumanization, disempowerment, and isolation are the mechanisms with which the military transforms human beings into soldiers, sent to kill and devastate. The military teaches soldiers to objectify and dehumanize an enemy in order to numb their normal human reaction to killing other people and to motivate a hatred for the enemy, thus exciting them into killing other people. Colonization is the most extreme example of collective disempowerment, preventing whole peoples from their right to self-determination with regard to traditions and governance. Isolation is used to keep people from organizing a resistance to war and occupation and also to hide wrongdoings from the rest of the world. As example, the secretary of defense used isolation to hide a prisoner of war in Iraq from the International Committee of the Red Cross to prevent them from monitoring his treatment.[3]

Examining how the U.S. military operates from a rape culture paradigm could have helped us anticipate the tragedy at Abu Ghraib. Torture, particularly *sexual* torture, is a powerful force of the contemporary U.S. military—a fundamental component of military culture—and its application exceeds the events at Abu Ghraib. Rape is consistently used by our military to establish control over prisoners of war, communities of people, or other groups identified as "the enemy." Besides contemporary instances of sexual violence in the context of war, the U.S. military established a legacy of using rape as its most powerful tool with the colonization and genocide of indigenous peoples in North America. Andrea Smith, professor at the University of Michigan, Ann Arbor, and founder of national activist group INCITE! Women of Color against Violence, asserts,

> *Not only were [Native women] killed, but they were routinely raped and sexually mutilated as colonizers tried, both symbolically and literally, to control Native women's reproductive capacities.[4] Although Native men have also been scarred by abuse, Native women have often been the primary focus of sexual*

violence, because of their ability to give birth. Control over reproduction is essential in destroying a people; if the women of a nation are not disproportionately killed, the nation's population can always rebound. This is why colonizers such as Andrew Jackson recommended that, after massacres, troops complete the extermination by systematically killing Indian women and children.[5]

Rape is also wielded internally within the ranks of the military to establish superiority and control over female soldiers or male soldiers identified as weak or gay. The 1991 Navy Tailhook scandal, the reports in 2003 that dozens of female cadets at the United States Air Force Academy had been sexually assaulted by male cadets, and the recent revelations that dozens of women in uniform deployed to Iraq and Kuwait were raped by American soldiers demonstrate the widespread practice of sexual assault of not only the "enemy," but also fellow troops.

Further, rape is transported to American civilians through the abuse of military wives, such as the five domestic violence murders occurring over the course of six weeks at the North Carolina Fort Bragg military base in 2002. Soldiers who had returned from the war in Afghanistan perpetrated most of these murders. The culture of the American military necessitates sexual violence, and, as we can see, sexual violence is deeply infused into the institution as a common practice.

While people who perpetrate sexual violence have obvious moral failings, I do not mean to convey that American soldiers as individuals are inherently bad people, destined to rape because of their participation in an institution founded and sustained by the principles of rape. However, a rigorous examination of how the U.S. military operates from a rape culture paradigm reveals how people recruited into the military (who, because of the exploitive nature of recruitment, tend to be disproportionately working class folks and folks of color) are at risk of adopting the principles of rape culture as normal ways of behaving and of using those principles to make choices to sexually violate those around them.

A Path Out

We must not only target instances in our culture that specifically condone violence against women, but we must also undermine the institutional endorsement and embodiment of the principles of rape culture. It is this work that will ultimately end rape, a project in which I have much faith. Organizing against rape ultimately calls on our responsibility to reject the principles of rape and critique institutions not only for their actions, but also for the values from which their actions were developed.

We must support a values-based paradigm shift, creating a new paradigm that is inconsistent with the principles of rape culture. The Latin origin of the word "survivor" means one that lives over or beyond something else. Ending rape culture is an active process of choosing values that celebrate life over oppressive beliefs and practices. It requires us to participate in a broad-based, multiagenda liberation movement that values peace over violence, humanization over objectification, self-determination over disempowerment, and connection and community over isolation.

Rachel and Gwen

Merle Woo

R achel Corrie

Rachel was 23

In Palestine

Lived her convictions and died
By an Israeli bulldozer.
Brutally slaughtered by its blades

Crushed

Israel primed for apartheid —
Hating the defenders of Palestinians

Rachel stood valiantly with a bullhorn

G wen Araujo

Gwen, 17

In Newark, CA

Lived her convictions and died
By 3 sexist men.
Brutally beat her head in with
shovels

and then crushed again —

Gwen's killers primed for militarism,
Hating that she was a he —

Valiantly dressing like the beautiful
Chicana she was — gorgeous

In a bright red jacket —
A young white college student
Shielding a doctor's home about to
Be destroyed.

Bright red lipstick
She would not wear a mask —
Nor live a lie.

She was just too willful!

She was just too blatant!

Indicting Israel of genocide

A young transgendered male to Female

Lived her convictions and died.

Lived her convictions and died.

Rachel's parents taking up her cause
Publicizing Rachel's last emails about
Israeli genocide. Rachel wrote
"This is the systematic destruction of a
peoples survival."

Gwen's mother who could only call her
"Eddie" in her short life —
Put "Gwen" on her tombstone
forever — and embarks on
demanding civil rights for Queers.

Truth is the weapon of the oppressed
and lives on beyond one's life and death.

Kanaka Maoli 9-11

ku'ualoha ho'omanawanui

*K*anaka Maoli o ka 'āina,
offspring of earth, sky, *kalo:*
This is not our war.
We did not sanction it,

It is like all the others before:
World Wars I and II,
Korea and Vietnam
Desert Storm, and now Iraq, Afganistan.

So many young Hawaiians gone:
Fathers and brothers recruited,
now sisters and mothers, too —
names immortalized in Walls of stone
pōhaku haole — never to return home
Not one more Hawaiian —
What for?

For loss of sovereignty? Theft of land?
For welfare roles and poverty,
the houseless living on shifting sands?
For crack houses, missing children,
domestic violence and — Spam?

Yours is not our dream, America,
nor our destiny,

This is not our war.

We fight for freedom, for our own liberation
from your greed, your violence thrust upon us
We resist your corrupting presence —
It is in our *'āina,* our *mo'olelo,* our *kūpuna* we trust.

We are children of *kalo,* whose backs bend with the winds of resistance
We are *a'ali'i kū kamakani,* whose roots hold fast in the winds of change
We are *nā lālā o ke kumu lā'au,* whose multitude gives voice to the winds of war
We are *ke one, ka pōhaku,* and *ka lepo* whose dust swirls blood red in the wind.

Leo sang our history, about our capture by the guns of the "land of the free" —
Your hypocritical, oppressive and colonial ways have realized better days.
We will persist in our resistance as surely as waves lap our shores,
and agitate for peaceful change and continue *mau a mau* to proclaim:
Yours is not our destiny —
This is not our war.

Glossary

Kanaka Maoli o ka 'āina – Native Hawaiians, indigenous people of the land.

kalo – taro. In Hawaiian mythology, Hawaiians descend from the taro plant, the native staple vegetable crop.

pōhaku haole – foreign stone; it is reference to the Vietnam memorial, and burials of war dead outside of Hawai'i, our *one hānau* or birth sands

'āina – land, literally means "that which feeds"

mo'olelo – history; may also refer to oral traditions

kūpuna – ancestors

'a 'ali'i kū kamakani – *a 'ali'i* is an indigenous plant known to be strong; a traditional saying equates resilient and strong individuals with this plant, as *"a 'ali'i kū kamakani,"* or *'a 'ali'i* plants who stand and resist the strong wind.

nā lālā o ke kumu lā'au – literally means branches of the tree, and refers to our genealogies as native people)

ke one – the sand

ka pōhaku – the stones

ka lepo – the dirt

Leo – a reference to Leo Anderson Akana, who wrote "Song of Sovereignty." Leo also literally means "voice."

mau a mau – for all time

War Story

Sham-e-Ali al-Jamil

I t is her fabric of grieving
freshly washed and
worn at even
fresher gravesites.

Ritual of
hand touching
tomb offering prayer peace
cool marble
against burning fingertips
splintered wood
against calloused palm
new mounds of earth
appearing in
uncountable numbers.

Ritual of tears
they dry like
embroidered stories
war stories
and here,
the truth is told.

Competing Masculinities: Probing Political Disputes as Acts of Violence Against Women from Southern Sudan and Darfur

Rogaia Mustafa Abusharaf

> *Everyone, as a member of society, has the right to social security and is entitled to realization, through national effort and international co-operation and in accordance with the organization and resources of each state, of the economic, social, and cultural rights indispensable for his dignity and the free development of his personality.*
>
> —The Universal Declaration of Human Rights (Article 22)

Introduction

This piece identifies the major forces militating against the promotion of women's rights in the Sudan. These factors are intimately linked to the country's multiple political disputes, including Darfur and southern Sudan. The effects of political violence are elaborated through a detailed examination of women's political, economic, and cultural rights. The article concludes by identifying the promotion of good governance and democratization as fundamental prerequisites for advancing human rights and sustainable peace in the war-torn nation.

The Sudan, Africa's largest country in area, is a territory with incredible historical and political importance. The land and its location at the crossroads of Africa and the Middle East have influenced the course of its history and politics in a dramatic fashion.

The country is the place of birth of numerous ethnolinguistic groups, all with distinctive outlooks on life, culture, faith traditions, cosmology, and experiential knowledge. This remarkable variety is in itself not a cause for clash and fragmentation. However, ethnic differences coupled with widespread competition over scarce resources and systematic marginalization have presented grounds for conflict and hostility rather than providing a basis for concord and tranquility as group differences became increasingly politicized under successive military regimes.

One observer astutely pointed out that the Sudan is a country at war with itself, and in so being, it infringes upon numerous conventions, including the International Covenant on Civil and Political Rights, which declares that "In those states in which ethnic, religious, or linguistic minorities exist, persons belonging to such minorities should not be denied the right, in community with the other members of their group, to enjoy their own culture, to profess and practice their own religion, or to use their own language."[1] Indeed the Sudan's past and present civil wars contradict every feature set forth in the Covenant, working against human rights in general and women's rights in particular, in devastating ways. First, these conflicts violate the rights of indigenous people of southern Sudan and Darfur in general by undermining the functioning of their communities to live in security critical to human welfare. Second, these wars led to substantial population displacement, forcing people to flee to locations where they become subjected to laws and regulations that ignore their rights to culture and self-determination and dismiss the legitimacy and soundness of their indigenous associations and modes of knowing. The Qanoon El-Nizzam El-Amm, or Public Order Law, in Khartoum, for instance, is a case in point. This law has been demoralizing to Sudanese displaced people by restricting their mobility and participation in some labor-force occupations viewed illicit by the Islamic State.

In this article, I comment on the effects of the multiple civil wars in the Sudan on the rights of women from the regions of southern Sudan and Darfur. I will bring into play material gathered in various Sudanese shantytowns in order to illuminate the specificity of gender-based violence in Sudan's political disputes. I will then advance to provide particular examples on the breach of cultural, social, and economic rights in those locations. I end by highlighting the emergent sense of political subjectivity and agency among displaced women as the unintended consequences of these fierce disputes.

It should be stated at the outset, however, that highlighting individual rights and self-determination, in this case, should not be understood as mere advocacy of a liberal tradition that has no roots in Sudanese society. Defenders of the liberal traditions of human rights would argue that, "While we are right to be concerned about the cultural health of minority communities, this gives us insufficient reason to abandon, modify, or reinterpret liberalism. Far from being indifferent to claims of minorities, liberalism puts concern for minorities at the forefront."[2] For the purposes of this commentary, pointing out to the pervasive contraventions of the rights of Sudanese indigenous people problematizes and interrogates the institutionalized state power over minorities, especially defenseless populations such as displaced women from southern Sudan and Darfur.

Case 1: Southern Sudan

Elsewhere I have argued that the Sudan is a perfect illustration of an African country unable to achieve nationhood despite a successful struggle for independence. As a result, the southern Sudanese people in general, and women in particular, have been enduring the wrath of the longest-running civil strife in world's history. A report titled, "Follow the Women and the Cows," by the U.S. Committee on Refugees, stated that the death toll of southern Sudanese is larger than the combined fatalities suffered in recent wars in Bosnia, Kosovo, Chechnya, Somalia, and Algeria.[3] Since the civil war started, an estimated 1.9 million Southerners have died, 2.5 million are famine afflicted, and 350,000 crossed the borders to neighboring countries. This war continues to expose the South to widespread instability, forced capture and slavery, destruction of physical and natural environment, disturbance of cultural life and social cohesiveness, death, and displacement. Approximately four million people have been forced to flee their homes in the Southern provinces of Equatoria, Bahr Elghazal, and Upper Nile. Joyce Yatta, a Christian Fujulu from Yei, explained what war displacement has meant to her:

> I arrived from Juba in 1993. I have very fond memories of pre-war days and before I was forced to move. I am very sad and stressed about the thoughts of what happened to my family back home and in Khartoum. I pray that peace will come back so that we can return to our land and enjoy life in the same way as we did before war displacement.

Yatta's story resonates with the stories of millions of others and speaks forcefully to how war has undermined the rights of Sudan's indigenous peoples to live peacefully in their home villages. Largely cast in religious terms, the conflict has embodied the ideals of Arabization and Islamization of the Sudanese populations, irrespective of their indigenous affiliations. In this regard, the war exemplified an uncompromising effort on the country to manufacture one national identity against the wishes of ethnic and religious minorities. As Michael Ignatieff argues, nationalism in this respect can be seen as "the claim that while men and women have many identities, it is the notion that provides them with their primary form of belonging."[4] According to Ali Mazrui, Arabization and Islamization have been transforming North Africans' identities since the seventeenth century. Although the effort to create one national identity is by no means recent, it was introduced in the Sudanese political scene by former President Jaffar Mohamed Nemeriy and strictly enforced by Omer El-Bashir, another military commander, who came to power in 1989.

This forced assimilation process, deeply embedded in the forging of a monolithic Sudanese national identity, did not go unchallenged. "Faced with the assimilative excesses of the ruling classes in the North," writes Mansour Kahlid, "the South has experimented with the entire spectrum of resistance, from a political crusade to be recognized as having their own authenticity and rights as citizens of the Sudan, to carrying arms."[5]

In diagnosing the root causes of war, some observers have suggested that British colonial policies planted the seeds of disunion in the Sudan, a country with extraordinary ethnic diversity, pitting North against South, Muslims against Christians, and Arabs against Africans. In the process, the policies enhanced the development and security of one group at the expense of another. But upon closer inspection, we find that colonial history, memories of the slave trade, unequal development, and other abuses of political, economic, and cultural rights undermined the trust upon which a peaceful environment could have been founded.

To concentrate on the culpability of history, though important, not only oversimplifies the agency of violators who infringe upon conventions and rules but also absolves them from their responsibility in shaping policies that made Sudan's civil war the longest in world's history. Colonial history notwithstanding, since the country attained its independence from Britain in 1956, millions of southern Sudanese have been left dead or displaced as competing masculinities continue to undercut human security and welfare.

Let us take a look for example at the crimes against humanity that were committed by former President Jaffar Mohamed Nemeriy (1969–1984), whose own military record in southern Sudan in 1965, before his coming to power, not only earned him the derision of many Southerners, but attests to egregious forms of violence against innocent civilians as evidenced in the document released by Anya-nya Movement in 1971, and titled "What Nemeriy did."

It should be noted that Major General Gaffer El Nemeriy was the garrison Commander in Torit. He was responsible for Eastern Equatoria that is Torit and Kapoeta Districts. Before he went to Khartoum to take the government by the usually military coup d'etat, the following villages were burned according to his orders:

- Obira with a population of about 500
- Ilen with a population of 3,000
- Galamini with a population of 300
- Oronyo with the population of about 3,000
- Lohuto with a population of about 700
- Mura-Hatiha with a population of 500
- Tirrangore with a population of 1,500
- Burung with a population of 200[6]

Nemeriy's adoption of Islamic Sharia laws in September 1983 contributed significantly to the reactivation of civil war, which had not only imperiled individual and collective security that has been acknowledged in international conventions as a basic inalienable right, but also has infringed on cultural, economic, and political rights deemed fundamental more than five decades ago by the United Nations in the Universal Declaration of Human Rights. Unquestionably, the devastation of the villages enumerated above should supply strong justification for bringing perpetrators like Nemeriy before an international criminal tribunal. Alas, Nemeriy's crimes against humanity continue to go unpunished after receiving clemency from Khartoum's regime. As a young southern Sudanese student points out, "There is no accountability in the Sudan. If people like Nemeriy are punished, others will be afraid to commit murders and steal the wealth of the country. But it seems that no one cares."

Case 2: Darfur

To the readers of Samantha Power's compelling report "Dying in Darfur: Can Ethnic Cleansing in Sudan Be Stopped?" which appeared in the *New Yorker,* history has repeated itself yet again in the most dreadful and rancorous manner.[7] Examining the Darfur crises through the lenses of a personal story of Amina Abaker Mohammed. Power illuminates the multiple ways in which the Janjaweed "evil horsemen" have perpetrated acts of ethnic violence and genocide against a defenseless, immobilized population.

Notwithstanding, stories like those of Amina Abaker Mohammed were common among a group of recently displaced Darfurian women in Khartoum who reiterated trials and travails markedly similar to those noted in Power's essay among many important reports on the crises like those of Jennifer Leaning, Amnesty International, and other local and international NGOs. For example, in the words of Asha Ali, whom I interviewed in Khartoum on August 14, 2004:

> *Our situation is a real catastrophe. When the fighting started we all tried to run away with our children. The men fled after seeing others get killed and beaten by the Janjaweed. These people acted like devils. They don't have good hearts. They burned villages, attacked and kidnapped women, and caused a lot of pain and misery. We fled on foot. Now we are staying with people from home who came to Khartoum a long time ago. Like us they don't have a lot, but they allowed us to stay with them in these small houses. We don't have money to buy food. We are also very worried about work. We cannot find work since this place is very far. Now the rainy season created added problems because this area is flooded. We depend only on Allah to change our situation. Our children are in danger too. Our situation is extremely terrible. We don't know what had happened to other relatives and neighbors. We hope that they are still alive. We are also worried that we will not be able to go back. We have no hope that we will get assistance. Not in this place anyway.*

These stories, which are originating from the western region of Darfur, bear witness to the worst humanitarian crises in the world today.[8] The total death resulting from these crises is estimated at fifty thousand in the entire region. In the words of Davaid Nabarro, head of crisis operations for the World Health Organization, "These figures are higher than those we had from East Timor, higher than the figures we had from Iraq in 1991, comparable to what we had in Rwanda in the bad times."[9] This conflict exploded in early 2003 when two main rebel groups, the Sudan Liberation Movement/Army and the Justice and Equality Movement, decided to strike military installations with the intention of sending a hard-hitting message of resentment and bitterness toward the region's unremitting sociopolitical and economic exclusion and marginality. The International Crisis Group has also reported that

> [The rebels] also took arms to protect their communities against a twenty-year campaign by government-backed militias recruited among groups of Arab extraction in Darfur and Chad. These "Janjaweed" militias have over the past year received greatly increased government support to clear civilians from areas considered disloyal. Militia attacks and a scorched-earth government offensive have led to massive displacement, indiscriminate killings, looting, and mass rape, all in contravention of Common Article 3 of the 1949 Geneva Conventions that prohibits attacks on civilians."[10]

While peace negotiations are presently underway in Abuja, Nigeria, many Darfurian refugees and internally displaced people are particularly skeptical about the prospect of peace and repatriation. According to a compelling study by Suleiman Hamid, the Islamic movement, which was led by Hassan El-Turabi, perpetuated an ideology of creating an Arab-Muslim State in spite of the country's ethnoreligious differences. The government reinforced this project even after El-Turabi's marginalization by continuing its mission with incredible zeal. Darfur, in light of this analysis, was seen as part of this pervasive project. Therefore, the characterization of the conflict as ethnic cleansing has a particularly strong resonance as far as the targeted groups (Zaghawa, Massaleet, and Fur) are concerned.

Women's Rights to Physical Integrity

Perhaps the biggest concern that plagues women dealing with the civil war in the Sudan, as well as other ethnoreligious antagonisms around the world, is the grueling abuses they face as sexed bodies. Catherine MacKinnon sees the underlying principle behind this glaring lapse as follows:

> What is done to women is either too specific to women to be seen as human or too generic to human beings to be seen as specific to women. Atrocities committed against women are either too human to fit the notion of female or too female to fit the notion of human. "Human" and "female" are mutually exclusive by definition; you cannot be a woman and a human being at the same time.[11]

Although displacement is harrowing for everyone involved, it is far worse for women and girls, who are the most likely victims of sexual violence and torture, as the Darfur crisis makes abundantly clear. Displaced women are confronted with sexual violence experienced before, during, and after flight and arrival in new communities and are left to deal with significant physical and psychological effects of this victimization. Christina Dudu, a Southern displaced woman living in Khartoum, outlined the gendered forms of exploitation that accompanied the mass flight of women and girls but were absent at home in the South before the renewal of the civil war, including sexual abuse, prostitution, and harassment.[12] This wide constellation of sexual abuses contravenes the right to bodily integrity as a fundamental right, which includes sexual and reproductive rights. These rights signify the capability of women and men to exert control over matters concerning their sexuality and reproductive freedom. Alas, these entitlements have proved to be the most widely violated rights during wartime.

Consider the striking similarities in two reports released by Amnesty International on the topic of rape and other violence against women during the civil war in Sudan and during the Darfur Crisis respectively. The first report on South Sudan covered the period of January to December 2000 and stated that

> Violence against women by combatants on all sides, long a feature of the conflict in Sudan, intensified during the year. There were widespread reports of

sexual abuse, including sexual slavery, rape and forced pregnancies. Rape was
used as a tactic of war by both government and opposition forces to dehumanize
and humiliate civilians in the conflict zone. However, because of the taboos
and stigma attached to rape, reports were rare and impunity for the rapist was
the rule.[13]

Contrast this report with a 2004 statement regarding sexual violence against women in Darfur. This statement is based on testimonies from refugee women in Chad in the camps of Goz Amer, Kounoungo, and Mile:

The organization was able to collect the names of 250 women who have been
raped in the context of the conflict in Darfur and to collect information concerning
an estimated 250 further rapes. This information was collected from testimonies of
individuals who represent only a fragment of those displaced by the conflict. Other
human rights that have significantly targeted women and girls are abductions,
sexual slavery, torture, and forced displacement.[14]

The violation of women's rights to bodily and sexual integrity is compounded by the victims' reluctance to report rape in fear of shame and community ostracism.

What makes rape an exceptionally alarming affront is the widely held beliefs toward sex and sexuality. Attitudes toward sexuality and reproduction are positioned at the heart of significant cultural and religious beliefs among the Sudanese. Open discussion of matters pertaining to sexuality is extremely proscribed by these beliefs. To a great extent, this interdiction is intimately linked to how society views sexuality in the first place. As it is largely seen as an ominous threat that looms largely over one's purity and morality if left unchecked, social and physical regulation is aggressively pursued.

Among large segments of Darfur populations, female circumcision is one of the most important vehicles for dulling women's sexuality. Violations of these taboos embody an insult on the community's codes of morality and honor, a factor that produces significant fears of speaking about and reporting rape crimes. A displaced woman echoed this fear when she explained the situation:

Many women who have been attacked and raped are afraid to report the incidents. When we were talking about this issue, some people said el-kalam da aib, *this talk is shameful. That is why many preferred to suffer in silence. We are a religious people and this crime has brought dishonor and humiliation. It could have been better to kill than to rape. Our only hope is that Allah will punish the criminals.*

Closely linked to the abuses of women's bodily integrity are the violations of their rights to health as they become exposed to STDs and HIV/AIDS, among other diseases. It is therefore imperative that the international community should urge state and non-state actors to investigate the full extent of the infringements on women's rights to physical integrity and health.

Cultural Rights

One of the most salient features of Arabization and Islamization is embodied in what came to be known as the Public Order Law, or El-Nizam El-Aam, for Khartoum State of 1996. This law, which is emblematic of the politicization of ethnoreligious identities, is also an authoritative commentary on the status of "minority cultures" of people living under Sharia. This law was passed by the government to curb practices that government officials labeled as "un-Islamic." Those who do not comply with its codes are brought to court. This law, which is extensive in scope, deals with a wide range of issues. It limits the length and duration of wedding parties. It affects women's employment and Islamic dress, or *hijab*. It mandates gender segregation on public transportation.[15] The law even prohibits people from bathing naked or half-naked in the Nile, a practice accepted by previous governments.

To ensure the enforcement of this law, the government expanded the Criminal Procedures Act of 1991 and vested the Supreme Court, Courts of Appeal, General Criminal Courts, and People's Criminal Courts with full authority to imprison, fine, whip, confiscate, and enforce any punishment they see fit on noncompliants. The law was hailed as the right arm of Arabization and Islamization. Indeed its infringement on the rights on religious and ethnic minorities did not seem to warrant its modification. According to a report put out by the Sudan Council of Churches Unit of Advocacy and Communication, "The Public Order Police are not bound by any geographical jurisdiction. Any of the units may make a campaign of searches *kasha* in any place even if it falls within a jurisdiction of another unit. This makes it very difficult to know the jurisdiction to which the arrested persons are taken." The report points out that the targets of the Public Order Police are primarily displaced persons, especially women held by authorities in Omdurman Women Prison for charges ranging from prostitution to alcohol brewing, the latter made a crime under the law. The law also made the Islamic dress *hijab* mandatory among women irrespective of their religious affiliation.

As Susan Sered correctly argues, this imposition reflects the thinking of "[an] authoritarian institution with a large stake in women's bodies."[16] Emelide Kiden, a forty-five-year-old Kuku Christian from Bahr-El-Jebel, told me: "I came to Khartoum in 1995. Ever since I was not able to wear my traditional dress and I felt forced by law to cover my whole body. I am also afraid to brew." Other women echo the same sentiments. For many, alcohol brewing is not only about making a living, but also has many uses in numerous ceremonial practices ranging from birth, to marriage, and death.

Cultural rights as numerous conversations with displaced women have been among the most obvious casualties of war. The link between cultural rights and human rights was strengthened through the 1966 International Covenant on Economic, Social, and Cultural Rights, although the Covenant does not attempt to define cultural rights per se. The Covenant's preamble recognizes that the "ideal of free human beings enjoying freedom from fear and want can only be achieved if conditions are created whereby everyone may enjoy his economic, social, and cultural rights, as well as his civil and political rights." Boutros Boutros-Ghali argued, "By the right of an individual to culture, it is to be understood that every man (or woman) has the right to access to knowledge, to the arts and literatures of all peoples, to take part in scientific advancement and to enjoy its benefits, to make his (or her) contribution towards the enrichment of cultural life."[17]

As can be expected during war, human distress multiplies and takes on different forms of individual and collective trauma. Selfhood and personhood also undergo dramatic shifts. Since personhood is a highly differentiated experience, the systematic destruction of a community's physical safety and cultural life intersected to strike at its foundations in profound ways. The loss of community has meant that people are reconsidered afresh.

Everyday experience, which emerges from dislocation, prompts a serious deliberation of the dialectal relationship between person and community and self and the world in roundabout ways. The sense of solidarity and the fear of losing it were explained in Francis Deng's analysis of attitudes toward moving away from home: "To a Dinka, his country, with all its deprivations and troubles, is the best in the world. Until very recently, going to foreign lands was not only a rarity, but also a shame. For a Dinka, to threaten his relatives of leaving Dinkaland was seen as little short of suicide. What a lot to give up, and for what?"[18] In the context of war, violence, and forced migration, assimilation into the Arabo-Islamic practices of host communities in the North means annihilation of an "unambiguously" African world, though itself far from monolithic.

The effect of war on self-perception and sense of security is distilled in Eisenbrush's notion of "cultural bereavement." This bereavement is attributed to the loss of shelter as well as vanishing security. Eisenbruch's notion of bereavement receives ample validation from the testimony of Theodora Poni, a Kuku Christian from Equatoria, who has lived in Khartoum since 1984. "Sometimes I say to myself, it is better to die rather than live in the conditions I am living in right now," she says. "I desperately want to reunite with my family members from whom I have been separated twenty years ago. I cannot stop thinking about them. I hope to be able to go back to the South so that these feelings could get resolved."

Forced migration, as shown in Poni's story and many others, affects collective and self-perception, representations of self and others, national and ethnic culture, as well as material and economic security. Consider for example the migration biography of Cecilia Joseph Wani (Morawska 2000):

> *Wani, a thirty nine-year-old Christian Nilo-Hamite, moved to Khartoum from Kajokeji in 1979. A widow with five children and one dependent, and whose husband died in Khartoum, Wani now works as a cleaner in St. Phillip Health Center. Wani's husband came to Khartoum to look for work, and before the war, she describes life as "very good," her lifestyle as normal, and the youth as decent. When the war started, life changed in Khartoum. Wani describes an influx of relatives, the changing lifestyle of youth, market changes, and her inability to afford rent for a house, which resulted in her move to a displaced location. During this move, her*

husband died, and she had to sell all her assets to maintain her children. She resides in an area where other relatives live, as they joined her after departure. Aspects of cultural life that she has been able to maintain include her food, and her language, Bari, but she notes that her children refuse to learn it. As a result, she cannot teach, or tell, her children the folktales that she considers to be valuable. She is not able to maintain her folk dances, traditional dress, and folktales. These folk dances are hard to maintain because they are not allowed, and she is prevented from maintaining her traditional dress due to laws requiring the Islamic lawful dress, or tobe. She has no interaction with Northerners, but knows that their cultural practices include "henna," circumcision, the prohibition of young girls from attending the market, dressing "tobe," etc. She is not prepared to embrace any of these practices except for dress, which is required, and is repulsed by female circumcision, which she describes as "dangerous" and wrong. Since her husband has died, she is responsible for the decisions in her household. Life for her, she says, is difficult, and will be more difficult as long as there is a war, both economically and socially. Besides that, her most pressing concern is that her children will forget her culture.

Wani's biography effectively illuminates the ways in which bereavement becomes associated with vulnerability, an emotion that is also powerfully depicted in the story of Nora Mule below:

Mule is sixty years old and has been separated from her husband since she departed Kopoeta in 1989 with her son. She works as a housekeeper, but relies on her grown children for support. She described life before the war as much better, but feels better being in Khartoum, away from the sounds of guns in Kapoeta. She lives far from other friends or relatives, but has been able to maintain her culture through food and occasional folk dances. She has given up alcoholic drinks, however, due to her commitment to Christianity. Since she was separated from her husband, she has maintained decision-making authority in her household, which she feels has given her a better life. She was, as she puts it, "at peace with [her husband]." Although she feels that her life has no pressing conditions, she misses her children who are working in the army, and makes do with the photos she has of them. When asked for an acceptable solution to the problems facing herself and others, she reflected that, although peace would bring some joy, death might be the only solution.

Stories like those of Nora Mule prompt the question, how are loss and bereavement to be understood in the southern Sudanese milieu? In the words of Margaret Mondong, who arrived in Khartoum in 1996:

> *I am concerned that continued residence in Khartoum would lead my people to abandon or lose contact with their culture. Although we try to teach our children our culture, we often find it impossible to compete with Arab and Islamic culture taught to them in school. I feel that my problems are the problems of all displaced people; we are drinking in the same pot. The only acceptable solution to these complicated issues is peace.*

Displaced women's experiences show that as family forms and kinship systems disintegrate as a result of war and violence, identity and belonging take on complex meanings, and new memories are made. One existential condition that prompts the negotiation of self and community is residential patterns. Finding shelter, wherever that may be, is more immediate for displaced people than the need to live among relatives. Also important to note is that the kinship "vacuum" that results from displacement does not go unfilled. Neighbors in the host communities step up to fill the role as fictive kin, both ready and willing to enter into a new chain of exchanges and conversations. In spite of the importance of these new relationships, cultural loss remains a powerful force that contributes to the reshaping of ideas and values.

Loss of cultural rights in both their ideational and phenomenal dimensions are therefore of special importance to non-Muslim Southerners. If we are to assess the meaning of cultural rights in southern Sudanese cosmology, we will be confronted with an impressive overabundance of cultural expressions and rules that govern every aspect of one's existence from the cradle to the grave. The fact that the very foundation of village societies has been blasted to bits has meant that whatever notions and significances people attached to their practices are being shattered. These include many "traditional structures":

age classes, clan classifications, childbirth rituals, kinship rules, betrothal, and marriage, laws regulating inheritance and property ownership, rules of compensation of injury, distribution of resources, totems, magic, oath-taking, rainmaking and sacrifice, Supreme Beings and Guardian Spirits, initiation, burial, and stories told around the evening fire.

Philister Baya, a southern Sudanese woman living in Khartoum, explained the extent to which displacement in Khartoum destabilized their cultural life:

> When we organize for social occasions such as marriages, funerals and rites, which are to continue late at night, we should get permission from the local authorities, namely El-Nizam El-Aam to conduct such occasions. In most cases El-Nizam El-Aam go into houses and interrupt the occasions without good reasons. Christians are ordered to close their shops on Fridays during Jumma prayers by the same governmental body. On refusal, the Southern displaced women are struggling to maintain their living, are dragged to the Public Order Court to be fined.[19]

In Sudanese shantytowns and camps for the internally displaced, people repeat analogous concerns, showing the enormous pressure of the Public Order Law on their economic rights, to which I turn next.

Economic Rights

Contraventions of cultural rights, notwithstanding the consequences of the Public Order Law outlined above have been immeasurable in the economic realm as they restricted women's involvement in certain occupations. Susie Pito, a Mikaya Christian who arrived at Khartoum in 1996, said: "I am no longer able to make alcoholic drinks because of Sharia law. I am troubled by being viewed as an infidel under Sharia." Since little work is available for women who struggle against urban poverty, in desperation they turn to sex work and alcohol brewing. Yahya el-Hassan, a PANA correspondent, described the forbidding reality:

> Once in the north, [women] are forced to live in cramped camps around the big cities that lack all conditions of a decent living. This situation forces women

to compete for the very limited opportunity available, such as washers and maids. The rest opt for the brewing of local gin (araqi), *or prostitution, two lucrative but dangerous businesses if the police catch the women. If convicted, the women are moved to an all-female prison. A recent UN research has found that over 80 percent of the inmates of Omdurman women prison in Khartoum were women from the South convicted of trafficking in* araqi *or prostitution.*

Obviously, the Public Order Law has deleterious effects on southern Sudanese displaced women's economic rights by abrogating their right to work and earn a living in a secure environment. This problem was addressed by Christina Dudu:

> *The other major problem facing Southern displaced women is unequal job opportunities. If one makes a survey, one will find that there are many Southern women and men who are highly educated graduates but are jobless. Southern women in government and nongovernment institutions are accommodated within the domestic labor force. They are sweepers, cleaners, or messengers. Southern women have to accept, as they had no other options for survival.*[20]

As for women from Darfur who do not necessarily engage in beer brewing for religious considerations, displacement violated their economic rights by undercutting their access to adequate standards of living, which "encompasses several more rights, including the right to food, the right to health, the right to water, the right to necessary social services, the right to clothing, and the right to housing."[21] Khadijia Yagoub, who arrived at Khartoum in May 2004, explains:

> *We used to farm back home in our village. We did not extend our hands or beg for food or anything else. The poverty and want we saw in Khartoum is causing us a lot of worries and stress. We have to think about the little children because at least the adults are strong enough to bear hunger. Our life in the village was merciful. Here in Khartoum there is no assistance. We are here in this faraway place where we cannot move to find work, especially the majority of women who have little children. There is no food and our hosts are struggling and are themselves*

in trouble. This fighting destroyed our life there and caused us humiliation and hunger here. I don't know what the future holds. Now, I have no hope.

Political Futures

In this article, I tried to demonstrate the ways in which Sudan's multiple conflicts have led to serious violations of economic, social, and cultural rights. These infringements have certainly far more damaging effects on women and girls since they are denied the opportunity to live in an environment in which they could take part in decisions vital to their safety and well-being. The perpetuation of gender-based violence before, during, and after the conflicts has positively sharpened women's consciousness about themselves as first and foremost political subjects. Furthermore, it refined their views on their political futures as they ponder new roles in peacemaking and the reconstitution of communities. In contemplating the role of women in southern Sudan and Darfur as the major stakeholders in peaceful settlements in their respective communities, we have to take into consideration their experiences as displaced women. Without romanticizing forced migration, we can concede that it created avenues for women to express agency and create avenues for self-empowerment in ways previously unknown.

Nowhere has this been so powerfully demonstrated than in Mary Hillary Wani's compelling paper "Women's Agenda for Peace" that she delivered at the Sudanese Women's Peace Forum held on October 29, 2001. Relying on indigenous conceptualization of peace, Wani writes:

> *For the purposes of drawing a women's agenda for peace I have opted to consider the definition as projected by the majority of the displaced women. In simple terms they defined peace to mean having security; peace means the right to move without restrictions; peace means love, unity and solidarity; peace is justice, freedom and absence of all forms of discrimination; peace means having a house, a job and land to cultivate, having enough food and being free from diseases; peace means the right to education for our children; peace means freedom of worship; peace means the right to our historical heritage, peace means participation in decisions and plans that affect our lives.[22]*

As much as gender-based violence, war, and displacement have combined to create a legion of challenges and struggles, they generate new spaces within which women can participate on equal footing with men in decisions vital to their lives. The renegotiation of these roles was made clear in two accounts from a Southerner and a Darfurian respectively. In the words of Olga Odera, a Christian Acholi who moved to Khartoum from Torit in 1993:

> *Men are used to making decisions in my community of origin. Women accepted that as a natural thing. Since I came here alone, I feel free to make my own decisions. A long time ago, I used to ask my husband to tell me what to do about many things. Now I am in control of my life and I support myself. This situation gave me the chance to have a say on many issues. I no longer think that women should follow men obediently. They can use their experience in Khartoum to influence decisions outside the home as well.*

Views like those of Olga Odera abound, as becomes obvious from the narrative of Sakina Adam from Darfur:

> *When the fighting started in my village, all the women started to run all over. We fled to Kas before coming to Khartoum. The journey with the children took us very long days. It was the most difficult journey. We started to talk about why the men were preying on us. What did we do to them? We understood that after they burned villages, looted animals from many people including Haboba [a woman who was sitting next to Sakina during the interview], that men were using us to hurt the men in our family and village. They wanted to cause a lot of pain by attacking the women. The whole village fled fearing for their lives. Some beautiful women were abducted and others were beaten and humiliated. Now we understand that we are here because the men wanted to degrade the community. For this reason we cannot go back until we are assured that we will not be hurt again. We need security and we need everyone outside to know that without providing safety we cannot take this big risk. We will remain in Khartoum and see about peace. Peace will help but the*

damage has been done. We need women to be able to protect themselves, because some back home did their best to protect their families.

This view corroborates Amartya Sen's most commanding observations on women's agency:

> *The active agency of women cannot, in any serious way, ignore the urgency of rectifying many inequities that blight the well-being of women and subject them to unequal treatment. Thus the agency role must be much concerned with women's well-being also. Similarly, coming from the other end, any practical attempt at enhancing the well-being of women cannot but draw on the agency of women themselves in bringing about such change.*[23]

Drawing on the experiences of Sudanese women from the South and Darfur will help formulate strategies for gender equity in post-conflict Sudan. This approach will depend fundamentally, however, on the state and state-actors' capability to uphold peace and fortify security measures so that war-displaced women can help rebuild their shattered lives. In light of this political context, women, as the main stakeholders in the reconstitution of their communities, have undoubtedly earned their right to equitable participation. In the meantime, for those women who still live in shantytowns and camps, fulfillment of the Guiding Principles on Internal Displacement as has been brilliantly articulated by Sergi Vieira de Mello is fundamental. According to de Mello, "Internally displaced persons shall enjoy in full equality, the same rights and freedoms under international and domestic law as do other persons in their country. They shall not be discriminated against in the enjoyment of any rights and freedoms on the ground that they are internally displaced."[24]

I would like to acknowledge the RAI support of my ethnographic research in the Sudan. I also want to thank Leni Silverstein and Sheila Dauer for inviting me to the Northwestern University workshop on human rights in Africa.

Layered Violence, Imperialism, Occupation, and Religious Fundamentalism: The Cases of Afghanistan and Palestine

Shahin Gerami

Discourses of violence against women need to move beyond the dichotomy of men-to-women violence and consider the global context. The separation of domestic violence from public and global violence creates artificial boundaries, reducing our analytical frame of reference. Global capitalism entails forms of oppression exerting both direct and indirect harm to women, and at times more harmful and sinister than individual harm.

The reach of globalism has spread and incorporated new territories, both peacefully and by force. Women's bodies and roles are the contested terrain of political domination and military victory. Forces of global violence harm women directly as victims of war, but also as victims of internal factional and political struggles. Whether the imperial powers invade directly, as in the case of Iraq, or empower liaison groups inside the nation states, like the Taliban in Afghanistan, the consequences for women are equally harmful. Iraqi women are killed in U.S. air raids, house searches, and are harmed by the factional struggle in street bombings and suicide attacks. Additionally, women's bodies and roles are used to construct national identity, cultural authenticity, and/or religious authority by both occupying forces and the warring factions. Consider Mrs. Laura Bush's radio address in November 2001, in which she said, "The fight against terrorism is also a fight for the rights and dignity of women."

Global violence gives impetus to nationalistic or fundamentalist impulses to preserve their authenticity, often at a cost to women's or an ethnic group's demands for equal treatment. Additionally, it may give one group more ammunition—as in the case of the Taliban—to overcome the enemy of global capitalism. Similarly, the Palestinian women have paid dearly as a result of occupation, house demolition, closures of territories, and bombing. Moreover they have been victims of factional fighting among their own men. The impacts of the financial blockage by the Western powers since the election of the Hamas have intensified the infighting since the spring of 2007. As a consequence, women are killed or left as heads of household to care for their dependents under occupation.

Locating the violence against women in the global context does not diminish the responsibility of the local, cultural, and indigenous forces; rather, it gives them further ammunition and hampers women's agency in securing their own and their families' safety. During the Indo-Pakistani war, women were raped by the opposing factions, killed, and displaced; they became single heads of households; and as refugees, they were responsible for themselves and their dependents. At times of foreign occupation and imperialist attacks, women's issues become secondary and lose their prominence. Women are induced, forced, or led to choose between domestic struggles for gender equality or the larger battles for national autonomy or ethnic identity. Since 9/11, Muslim women in the West are placed in a tenuous position of siding with their faith and ethnic identity or choosing to spend their energies on gendered issues. President George W. Bush's State of the Union Address in 2002 amplifies this premise: "The women and children of Afghanistan have suffered long enough. This great nation will work hard to bring them hope and help." Thus, the contested terrains of national or ethnic identity impose a double burden on women to choose between their community and their agenda for equality. The demarcation between the private domain of home and the public domain of polity and economy become mutually exclusive instead of overlapping. Hatem talks about the "condescending construction" that the war on terrorism has on "objectified Arab and Muslim women as victims that needed the U.S. to liberate them."[1]

As global violence has encroached more on civilians, the size of displaced populations has increased. Postcolonial Asia and Africa have witnessed massive population dislocation, creating both refugees and internally displaced people. The largest of the refugee groups is the Palestinians. Amnesty International reports increased occurrence of domestic abuse as a side effect of postwar trauma.[2] Women and their dependents are victims of layered forms of violence in their communities and their homes.

Palestine: The Violence of Occupation and Dislocation

As stated by a refugee woman in the West Bank,

> *The root cause of women's problems in this society is the political situation—the continuing occupation and the economic situation. No one, men or women, has freedom here. There are no jobs for men or women. Poverty is women's greatest oppressor. . . . Even women's lack of freedom is a consequence of the occupation; families rightly fear for their daughter's safety and honor when they must confront foreign soldiers whenever they leave home.[3]*

With regard to displaced refugees, the most significant in terms of raw numbers is the case of the Palestinians. It is estimated that there were seven million Palestinian refugee and displaced persons in 2003.[4] The process that began in 1948 with the establishment of the state of Israel has continued though several major upheavals. "In 1948, 85 percent of the Palestinians living in the areas that became the state of Israel became refugees."[5] The case of Palestinians is unique, since they are not covered by the mandate of the United Nations High Commission for Refugees (UNHCR); rather, they are receiving assistance from the UN Relief and Works Agency (UNRWA). Therefore they are denied all the legal protections and assistance that the UNHCR can afford a refugee population, among them "refugee rights" and "durable solutions" as prescribed in the UNHCR's mandate.

Palestinian women in general, and those in occupied Palestinian territories or camps in particular, suffer direct and indirect consequences of the occupation. They have been killed in crossfire while traveling to work, walking children to school, or being stopped at checkpoints. They are imprisoned, "held in solitary confinement, forced to give birth in their prison cells, tortured, verbally and sexually abused and threatened."[6] With the first (1987–1991) and the second Intifadas (2000–2005), women were killed during the Israeli assassination of Palestinian leaders, when access to ambulances were denied, or when homes were demolished. From 2000 to 2004, 3,334 Palestinians were killed; 132 were women. Of these, 74 were girls under the age of eighteen. According to Amnesty International, targeted assassinations carried out in densely populated areas kill and injure civilians.[7]

Indirectly, Palestinian women have lost family members, resulting in 50 percent of refugee families being female-headed households. This is one of the most impoverished populations in the world. Closure and curfews, sometimes for days, are tantamount to home detention, where women are denied basic necessities due to their inability to leave their homes. Israeli checkpoints, permit systems, roadblocks, road demolitions, and bypass roads—as well as the activities of Israeli settlers in the occupied territories—make mobility for all Palestinians difficult and at times impossible. When homes are demolished, men are arrested, and women, girls, and the elderly are left homeless.

In June 2002, Israel began construction of a wall between Israel and the Palestinian territory. This wall separates and isolates communities from each other and from their economic means of support, from children's schools, from clinics, and/or from other family members. These practices affect women's domestic responsibilities and agricultural work and have adverse physical and psychological effects for women and girls. A study by the Palestinian Central Bureau of Statistics (PCBS) on the effects of the wall specifically highlighted the long-term effects on women and the gendered roles of girls and their education.

The case of Palestine is a prime example of global violence that has evolved through its history from colonial domination to anticolonial liberation, to multistate regional war, and to urban guerrilla war. And even this last metamorphosis does not indicate an endpoint. Through it all, more than one generation of women has suffered physical violence and psychological trauma due to the disruption of their social roles. Clearly, women are doubly harmed by international violence. They are victims of occupation directly, and indirectly they pay for the gendered construction of their national identity. Women's roles and lives are integral to the social construction of political identity. Palestinian national identity incorporates mother/martyr; therefore, Palestinian women deal with systematic impositions on their daily lives through their culture.

Afghanistan: The Violence of Fundamentalism and Dislocation

The modern history of Afghani women is marked by periods of collective harassment at the hands of foreign forces or native men. Women's lives and rights have been an ingredient of Afghanistan's struggle for statehood and an excuse for armed conflicts among warring factions. In 1919 the Afghans defeated the British efforts at colonial domination, and the 1921 Anglo-Afghan Treaty recognized Afghanistan's autonomy. In 1923, Afghanistan adopted its first constitution, which gave Afghans civil rights and declared all Afghans—men and women—as equal.

Tribal customs and Islamic tradition were the basis of the social construction of family and individual life. From the 1950s to the 1970s, Zaher Shah initiated several reforms to register marriages and establish a minimum age of marriage, as well as to promote female literacy. Most of these reforms were limited to large urban areas. Tribal patriarchy remained entrenched, and the conflict between the central government and tribal leaders derailed the state-building initiatives, leading to a series of uprisings in the 1970s called the Saur Revolution.

A social democratic group under the leadership of the People's Democratic Party of Afghanistan (PDPA) came to power. The PDPA moved to transform Afghanistan from a feudal tribal society to a secular industrial one. Tribal disputes and factional conflicts in the ruling party led to Soviet intervention in 1979. An armed opposition of a loose federation of resistance groups—called the Mujahidin and assisted by the United States, Saudi Arabia, and Pakistan—resisted the Soviet forces. In 1989, the Soviet army left Afghanistan, and in 1992, several Mujahidin factions entered Kabul and removed President Mohammad Najibullah. Between 1992 and 1994, power changed hands in violent clashes between Mujahidin factions, with an estimated fifty thousand civilians dead. This was a period of direct assaults on women, from rape and murder to the slavery of young girls. The unrest and lack of security created an alarming increase in the rate of both refugee and internally displaced populations. This societal disruption created a political vacuum filled by a little-known faction of the Mujahidin called the Taliban. Taliban, a word meaning "students of Islamic seminaries," took control of 90 percent of Afghanistan in 1994 and came to full power by 1996.

At that time, they officially rescinded all previous reforms and launched a campaign of terror against ethnic minorities, especially Shiite Hazarahs and some Tajiks. From 1994 to 2001, the Taliban established order at great cost to many segments of the population, especially women. The Afghani women—who had already suffered direct and indirect harm as a result of a protracted civil war, refugee status, and extreme economic conditions—now had to deal with the Taliban's imposition of Shari'at.

The Taliban took the engendering of their power quite literally. A reign of terror based on strict gender segregation and ethnic suppression exacerbated the plight of women. Their policies to establish order clearly marked women's bodies and their social roles as problematic. To rid society, especially the public domain, of women's bodies, they were removed from the social institutions of education, from the labor market, and from civil polity. When in public, all women were required to wear burka and to be accompanied outside their homes with male guardians.

The Taliban's rule in Afghanistan had several characteristics that directly or indirectly affected women's lives. To begin with, the Taliban's ideology and the experiences of its leaders lacked any foundation for state-building. Their simplistic notion of an Islamic state disallowed any basic rudiment of bureaucratization necessary for state formation. Their regional sponsors, such as Pakistan and Saudi Arabia, were more interested in their own agenda than the stability of Afghanistan. Secondly, their objectives of public morality and the eradication of vice led to intense scrutiny of citizens' lives in both public and private domains. Thirdly, their ethnic and social backgrounds emphasized supremacy of Pashtun tribal identity, Sunni Islam, and traditional patriarchy. Added to this mixture were a long and devastating civil war and drought that left the countryside in ruin (except for poppy cultivation) and destroyed most urban structures. The result was a devastated economy controlled by misogynistic and ethnocentric rulers, which led to an increased refugee influx into Iran and Pakistan and further economic destruction.

Initially, the UN and NGOs, supporters of the Mujahidin, ignored women's conditions in the country and in the refugee camps in Pakistan. Claiming cultural sensitivity, they focused on aid distribution to male heads of household or leaders of the camps. The Taliban's policies received world attention; governments and NGOs duly condemned these policies. Unfortunately, condemnation focused on the Islamic fundamentalism of the Taliban and overlooked tribal identity and women's place in it.

Taliban forces were Pushtun boys trained by conservative mullahs in madrasses, or Islamic seminaries, in Pakistan. There, they absorbed a potent revolutionary ideology constructed of Pushtun's notions of tribal superiority and hypermasculinity. In *madaris,* this ethnic and gender supremacy was cast into conservative Islamic theology to create the Taliban's notion of a pure society.

There are similar states and political entities that, like the Taliban, cast their legitimating rhetoric in gender discourse. They measure decadence and morality based on shifts in women's gender roles. An individual man's honor is transferred to the state, which in turn becomes guardian of a whole society's shame and honor by controlling dangerous female sexuality. They impose or reinforce *hijab* (Islamic dress code) to impede women's presence in public, and they invariably ban women from certain public arenas or activities, such as driving, working in a mixed environment, and entering sport stadiums. This is true to some extent of Pakistan, Saudi Arabia, the Islamic Republic of Iran, and in the most extreme case, Afghanistan.

From 1979 to 2002, the Afghani population lived with unending foreign intervention, a fractured government, and Islamic extremism. Women have paid heavily for the instability and violence of war. There are estimates of 1.5 million internally displaced persons and 5 million refugees. Women and girls have been denied education, employment, and basic healthcare. The result is one of the lowest standards of female well-being in the world. Female literacy rates and life expectancy for Afghani women are some of the lowest, while fertility and maternal mortality are among the highest. A survey of a small sample of women living in Afghan and Pakistan refugee camps showed that women living in both countries had numerous displacement hardships, as well as high rates of depression and other health-related problems.[8] Both groups have been or knew of people who have been subjected to harassments and human rights abuses at the hands of the Taliban.

Women, along with men and children, have suffered indiscriminate bombings, burnings of their cities and their fields, ethnic cleansing, and other atrocities. Women additionally have endured gender-specific costs of the war as victims of rape, sexual assault, abduction, forced marriages, and prostitution. These specific costs are the result of marauding soldiers, who assault and rape women of other ethnic groups to shame and dishonor their men. The status of Afghani women during the civil war and under the Taliban is an example of women being harmed by the social construction of the masculinity, ethnicity, and nationalism of their own society during times of global violence. Women's bodies and roles are often used to construct ethnic identity, national unity, and even territorial hegemony.

Conclusion

The gendered aspect of global violence is assumed by political leaders and taken for granted by military commanders. Deconstructing the men-to-women binary modes and codes of behavior uncovers the role of global forces and their impact on gender relations at local and domestic levels. The Cold War policies of the two superpowers led to the West's support of fundamentalist groups in places like Afghanistan and Pakistan. These beneficiary groups, like the Taliban, received direct and indirect support from their international sponsors, and they have wreaked havoc on the women of Afghanistan. The Western countries' policies toward the Palestine–Israel conflict have direct and immediate consequences for Palestinian women's daily lives.

Furthermore, a global framework of gender allows us to move beyond the abuser/abused dichotomy and permits an exploration of the complexity of gendered arrangements in diverse and dynamic family structures. It is then that we can see that most cases of violence are committed by men against men, and we uncover women's multiple layers of agency and rescue strategies. The construction of masculinity in relation to violence, and men's agency in liberating themselves and others from violence, are other aspects of this gendered narrative. Binary arrangements of "soldier-prostitute, soldier-wife, or soldier-mother overlook the multifaceted roles that women perform in international violence."[9]

Simplistic dichotomies overshadow women's agency as individuals or collectivities. Algerian women broke many barriers and became the true comrades in the revolution, but they failed to capitalize on their heroism and translate it into political rights. Indian women effectively used their newfound freedom of action, as did Lebanese women, and as are the Palestinian women, who are working to increase their rights. In cases where women are harmed or restricted by their community, like the Islamic Revolution of Iran or the Hamas operation in the occupied Palestinian territories, women individually and collectively challenge the restrictions imposed on them. As gendered oppression is multifaceted, so are women's and men's construction of agency, strategies of rescue, and alternative gender relations.

Why Speak of Femicide?

Ana Silvia Monzón

Every day we wage the battle against hatred
We dodge its demented tricks
We break its codes
Only breaking the silences
Is the spell undone.
—Gisela López (2006)

For Guatemalan women, the words gender and violence immediately bring to mind the violent deaths of so many of us. As the statistics regarding violence against women relentlessly grow in number, images of tortured, mutilated bodies cross our vision—their grotesque descriptions in the media "normalized" by their frequency and amplified by the comments made by family members, neighbors, coworkers, or people on the bus. Comments we hear, "Poor thing, see what they did to her," are followed by "Who knows what she was into? Maybe she was messed up in something? She liked partying. She would walk alone at night. She would dress inappropriately, provocatively," and the voice trails off with an unspoken answer left in the air.

We associate gender and violence with danger, vulnerability, and risk, generally suffered by women at the hands of men, as demonstrated by the available statistics. The social conditions underlying these statistics refer to the condition of gender relations as constructed within a patriarchy. The international ruling patriarchy overvalues that which is masculine and devalues that which is feminine. The conditions that emerge from patriarchy explain, in part, the existence of violence against women. This violence is at the core of concerns for women's movements around the world, particularly during the last three decades. However, the existence, identification, analysis, and condemnation of this violence date from much earlier times.

It is important to acknowledge that it is the feminists' and the women's movements that have placed the violent deaths of women in the public sphere and that have emphasized this social problem. In the process, these activists have also presented new parameters for analysis and new concepts that were unknown at the beginning of the modern movements. These new concepts now have gained meaning, because they bring forth a reality that was obscured for a long time. It is important to note that it has been more than twenty years, coinciding with the emergence of feminist groups in Guatemala, since it was revealed that striking a woman is not "normal" in a relationship. Thus the saying "You always hurt the one you love" loses its value as popular wisdom and becomes a questionable and unacceptable phrase.

In this process of labeling, conceptualizing, and categorizing the pervasive reality of violence against women—a reality that, because it was so obvious, remained invisible— concepts were created such as "violence against women," "gender violence," and more recently, *femicidio* or *feminicidio* (femicide). These public definitions are the result of the observation, confirmation, analysis, and conclusion that violence against women is any "violent act against the female sex that can result in injury, physical, sexual, or psychological injury, including the threat of these acts as well as coercion or arbitrary limiting of freedom in either the public or private spheres."[1]

This statement, based in the InterAmerican Convention for the Prevention, Sanction and Eradication of Violence against Women, signed in 1994, summarizes hundreds of studies and debates that can no longer be ignored. As intellectuals, civil servants, teachers, fathers and mothers, and responsible adults, we cannot plead ignorance in the face of the existence of abuse, its frequency, and above all, the negative impacts on the lives of people who have been affected by fear, mistrust, and lack of self-esteem, which originated in the first blow that a child received.

On the other hand, now that the market dictates social life, violence in gender relations can now be seen to result in economic loss. Even without considering the ethical imperative, there is a solid economic argument that should serve as a pretext for nations to take action to eradicate violence against women and, therefore, to avoid the loss of workdays, medical expenses, and the utilization of public safety resources. Violence against women is not just the business of women. These horrific conditions affect all of society: men, children, the elderly. Such violence crosses class boundaries, ethnic groups, religious beliefs, and age. No one is safe from the negative effects of violence that, as we already know, is not limited to blows (its most visible sign), but extends to economic, sexual, working, political, symbolic, and cultural relationships. Studies regarding violence and its effects have become more in-depth and extensive, particularly regarding the identification of the many forms that violence can take. There are, for instance, sexual, psychological, patrimonial, and, as Venezuelan women have recently denounced, obstetric and media forms of violence.[2]

These facts lead us to conclude that we live in a world of hierarchical relationships that resort to violence as a mechanism of subjection and dissuasion to prevent any possibility of questionings, and to ensure that these relationships are forever reproduced. Las Moiras, a group of women who work toward encouraging more women to think about women's issues, point out in their 2002 annual feminist Women's Agenda (Madrid, Spain: Horas y Horas, 2002), "It is not because she is rich or poor, or because she is illiterate or educated; it is not because she walks alone on the street, or because she wears a short skirt, or because she is a prostitute. It is because of all this and nothing. It is because I am a woman and they want me quiet, silent, and in fear." Fear—the fear of losing privilege—and weakness—weakness that is expressed with aggression—are aspects of violence against women. This fear and this weakness were learned by women during centuries-long oppression and subordination. Fortunately, more and more women are unlearning and challenging these norms.

Between 2000 and 2006, more than two thousand women—young women and girls alike—have been murdered in Guatemala. Women's groups, in solidarity with the victims' families, continue to challenge the notion that it is the norm for women to be passive and silent. They strongly demand that the authorities properly investigate and solve the murders of these women who had a name: Flor de María, Orquídea, María Isabel, Marleny, Ileana, Santos, Claudina, Bernarda, Evelyn. . . . They all had a face, a history, and an identity. We shall not forget them!

We Know Violence

Lucía Morán

Translation by Ingrid Martinez-Rico and María Ochoa

When it is said
To name that which is female is ridiculous
We know violence

When it is written
Female literature is vaginal / male literature is cerebral
We know violence

When it is asked
Why investigate the killing of women / if more men are killed than women
We know violence

When women prisoners
Wear the overalls of men / are deprived of family visits
We know violence

When police extort / rape / execute sex workers
We know violence

When schools teach women the perfection of domestic work
For a future in an unpaid job
We know violence

When the need to measure / investigate sexual violence
Against women involved in solidarity movements is questioned
We know violence

We, Guatemalan women
Unveil our secret pain
Question the world
Confront the rules
Imposed on us

Every day we must speak
In an unconquered voice
So that violence abates
Because simply put
We do not want any more violence

Rufina Amaya: Remembering El Mozote[I]

Ana Patricia Rodríguez

Maybe if everyone sees these things clearly, they will have to do justice. The Government cannot see all of these children and not want to do justice.[2]

On March 6, 2007, two days before International Women's Day, Rufina Amaya Márquez died at the age of sixty-four from the effects of a cerebral stroke in her homeland of El Salvador. Amaya was the only eyewitness survivor of the Massacre at El Mozote, which took place on December 11, 1981, during the early phase of the Salvadoran Civil War (1979–1992). Registering a death count of over eight hundred children, women, and men at the hands of U.S.-trained Salvadoran Special Forces, the Massacre at El Mozote and its outlying communities is recognized today as "the single largest massacre to take place in [the Western] hemisphere in modern times."[3] Among the slain figured Amaya's husband and four young children (the youngest was eight months old), as well as the villagers and neighbors of El Mozote. Amaya escaped her own death only by hiding in the bushes, within earshot and view of the killing that took place in the village, and by coming out of her hellhole eight days after the massacre. Among the first U.S. journalists to reach El Mozote and to interview shell-shocked Amaya following the massacre were Alma Guillermoprieto (then a reporter for *The Washington Post*) and Raymond Bonner of *The New York Times*. Guillermoprieto recalls that "[i]n precise detail [Amaya] told the same story she would repeat throughout the years and that forensic evidence would confirm a decade later."[4]

In an article titled "Shedding Light on Humanity's Dark Side: The Outspoken Survivor of Slaughter," published, in all poetic justice, in *The Washington Post* on March 14, 2007, only days after Amaya's death, Guillermoprieto invoked the unresolved legacy of the Massacre at El Mozote and the historical relevance of Amaya's *testimonio*, explaining that "[w]hat was at stake in believing Rufina Amaya's testimony, along with Susan Meiselas's photographs and our first-hand reports, was the Reagan administration's continued support for the Salvadoran government." During and after the Salvadoran Civil War, Amaya was "for years . . . called a liar," and Guillermoprieto and other journalists' accounts of the massacre were thoroughly discredited by U.S. government officials and the U.S. media industry.[5] Until her death, however, Amaya continued to give her *testimonio* of a massacre that purportedly did not happen and certainly was not supposed to have happened. But it did, and for many years, the U.S. government denied its role in it. Finally, on October 22, 1992, Tim Golden, in an article appearing in *The New York Times,* declared that, indeed, "bones have emerged as stark evidence that the claims of peasant survivors and the reports of a couple of American journalists were true."[6]

After her death, Amaya's body was returned to El Mozote and buried near her loved ones, whose massacre is commemorated by a popular memorial site at the village center, as well as in multimedia texts that include Internet sites, YouTube testimonial videos, performances, audio recordings, film documentaries, journalistic reports, and a range of print texts, including Mark Danner's *The Massacre at El Mozote* (1994) and *Luciérnagas en el Mozote* (1996).[7] In several obituaries following her death, Amaya was remembered as possessing "a clear memory of what took place"[8] and as dedicating "her life to telling about it."[9] It is fitting, then, that a proliferation of print, visual, audio, and electronic texts memorialize Amaya's life and *testimonio*. Indeed, Amaya was repeatedly quoted as saying that she was spared because someone had "to tell the story of what happened" in El Mozote.[10] Her living *testimonio* and memorial to the massacred at El Mozote continue to challenge what historian Jeffrey L. Gould calls "the politics of amnesia that the Salvadoran governing elites [have] promoted."[11] At the twenty-fifth anniversary commemoration of the Massacre at El Mozote, on December 11, 2006, Rufina Amaya retold her *testimonio* one last time: "Once again—as so many times before—she recounted the events, how the soldiers dragged her children away and placed her with another group of women, and how she snuck away and heard the soldiers execute her children. Her repetition was part of her fight against amnesia at this moment, twenty-five years after the atrocity."[12] In this essay of remembrance, I explore how Amaya's *testimonio* and the memory of El Mozote beg us to revisit the story of how one woman refused to forget recent history and to be silenced.

Through (re)telling her *testimonio* up until her death, Rufina Amaya insisted that we hear her story of the massacred in the hope of preventing state violence of the magnitude of the Massacre at El Mozote from ever occurring again. However, in 2005, the George W. Bush administration proposed the "Salvador Option" as a solution to control the "Iraqi counterinsurgency," by way of using U.S. Special Forces to train Iraqi paramilitary squads, much like the Reagan administration had done in El Salvador and Central America in the 1980s.[13] This method of clandestine warfare and special-force deployment was first implemented and tested in El Salvador, and with it were trained death squads that killed, tortured, and/or disappeared more than eighty thousand civilians and produced large-scale massacres like the one at El Mozote. Rufina Amaya was one of the few massacre survivors who lived to tell of the very methods of war used in El Salvador. As proposed by the Bush administration, the "Salvador Option" of state violence and death squads gives even greater credence to Amaya's testimonial voice today. This essay, thus, also explores how Amaya, even in death, continues to speak to, to "shout out" against, or in Alicia Partnoy's words, "to make a fuss"[14] about the Massacre at El Mozote, so that violence of that magnitude will not be repeated, and so that other testimonial truths may be known.

Testimonial Truths and Consequences

Like many scholars, the feminist, cultural critic, social activist, and testimonial writer Alicia Partnoy suggests that "*testimonio* is *not* about truth. Rather, the form serves as a tool for building a discourse of solidarity with victims of state terrorism."[15] It is a practice whereby the testimonial subject may be empowered or silenced. In *testimonio*, the stakes are always extremely high, for the potential always exists that "little will be heard in academia of what survivors have to say."[16] Indeed, as a consequence of the "Rigoberta Menchú controversy,"[17] scholars lined up on contentious sides of the "truth debate" enshrouding the genre and discourse of *testimonio*. In heated discussions, scholars, journalists, and others critics of *testimonio* interrogated the veracity of the "subaltern" voice, the credibility of her/his truth(s), and ultimately, the (im)possibility of the testimonial subject to speak, especially when, in Menchú's case, the anthropologist "[David] Stoll ha[d] been able to show that *some* rather than 'much' of Menchú's story is not true."[18] In his book *Rigoberta Menchú and the Story of All Poor Guatemalans* (1999), Stoll exposed various "inaccuracies, omissions, or misrepresentations" in Rigoberta Menchú's *testimonio, Me llamo Rigoberta Menchú y así me nació la conciencia* (1983; *I, Rigoberta Menchú: An Indian Woman in Guatemala,* 1984),[19] questioning thus Menchú's reliability as an "eye/I" witness, interrogating her validity as a representative of her community, and finally, casting "verifiable" doubt on her narrative.[20] In the end, as John Beverley reminds us, "[t]he argument between Menchú and Stoll [and perhaps those engaged in the so-called controversy] is not so much about *what* really happened as it is about *who has the authority to narrate*."[21] If Menchú could speak so out-of-line and in her right, with purpose, intention, and authority, then there would be no place for anthropologists, academicians, and "authorities" to speak for Menchú and others, and they (like Stoll) would "feel compelled to listen to" them on equal footing and not as "subalterns."[22]

Along these lines, Alicia Partnoy insists that survivors of state violence like herself, Menchú, Amaya, and others must be heard not as "native informants" of their tortured experiences, but as "authoritative narrators" posing critical interventions. According to Partnoy, "[t]o listen to and respect survivors' contributions . . . does not always mean to understand their words,"[23] but to engage them in dialogical discourse and equal exchange. Likewise, Rufina Amaya made claims that, as a sole surviving "eye/I" witness of the Massacre at El Mozote, she had "the authority to narrate" her story of the massacre in light of official discourses that sought to deny, forget, and erase that episode of Salvadoran history.

After her death, Amaya has left many of us asking in her absence: Who will tell other stories of the Massacre at El Mozote and of the ongoing methods of state violence, besides governmental agents and their corroborators? Who will continue to challenge state impunity in El Salvador and the Américas with their voices? How can we ensure that Amaya's *testimonio* and those of so many victims and survivors are not dismissed and forgotten? Indeed, how does Amaya's *testimonio* speak to us today?

Rufina Amaya's Testimonio

On December 11, 1981, the U.S.-trained Atlacatl Battalion (an elite special unit in the Salvadoran military) carried out Operation Rescue, killing more than eight hundred people in the village of El Mozote and its surrounding areas in the northern department of Morazán. Only one person—Rufina Amaya—survived to tell the story of the massacre to whoever would listen, in and outside of El Salvador. Amaya's account of the violent destruction of El Mozote circulated in *The Washington Post* and *The New York Times* as early as January 1982, although the U.S. government vehemently denied and discredited early news leakages of the event.[24] Despite the immediate cover-up of the massacre,[25] the story of El Mozote quickly slipped through the channels of disinformation, prompting the international community to take note. In her newspaper article of January 27, 2002, Alma Guillermoprieto, a correspondent for *The Washington Post* and one of the first international journalists to reach El Mozote, wrote about the macabre scene she found at El Mozote. Guillermoprieto described walking into a village "looted of all contents" and reeking "of the sweet smell of decomposing bodies. This was El Mozote."[26] All that was left of the people were "countless bits of bones—skulls, rib cages, femurs, a spinal column—[that] poked out of the rubble."[27] In an article published around the same time in *The New York Times,* Raymond Bonner reported that "it is clear that a massacre of major proportions occurred here last month."[28] Both reporters, however, were accused by U.S. government officials of producing "propaganda" in their stories. After El Mozote, a silent uneasiness would permeate U.S. news reporting on human rights violations in El Salvador until the end of the civil war in 1992.

From the start, Guillermoprieto's and Bonner's articles drew firsthand details from Rufina Amaya's *testimonio,* as did Mark Danner's feature article published in *The New Yorker* on December 6, 1993, and his spectacular book-length exposé titled *The Massacre of El Mozote: A Parable of the Cold War* (1994). Amaya's testimonial narrative served as primary evidence pointing to the Salvadoran government's human rights violations, which were much later reported in the UN Truth Commission's publication, *De la Locura a la Esperanza: La guerra de 12 años en El Salvador* (1993). Various other print documents and visual documentaries such as Bill Moyers's *Portraits of a Revolution* (PBS, 1992) and *Denial* (1994) also called on the eyewitness, Amaya, to (re)tell her story. In the United States, a traveling musical theater piece written by Chilean feminist writer, scholar, and professor Marjorie Agosín, titled *Tres Vidas* (Three Lives), weaved Rufina Amaya's story into the larger narrative of Latino American women's resistance, setting it parallel to the stories of Mexican painter Frida Kahlo (1907–1954) and Argentine poet Alfonsina Storni (1892–1938).[29] The short independent film *Homeland* (1999), the electronic musical composition *La masacre del Mozote* (1999), and the OnRamp Arts video game *Tropical America* (2002) offered other media representations of Rufina Amaya's *testimonio*.[30]

At the heart of all these texts lies Amaya's chilling hour-by-hour account of how government soldiers killed men, women, and children as she hid nearby in the bushes for eight nights.[31] Only Amaya was left to answer the question *¿Cómo fue, Rufina?* (What happened, Rufina?) She recalled how:

> *A las doce del mediodía, terminaron de matar a todos los hombres y fueron a sacar a las muchachas para llevárselas a los cerros. Las madres lloraban y gritaban que no les quitaran a sus hijas, pero las botaban a culatazos. A los niños que lloraban más duro y que hacían más bulla eran los que primero sacaban y ya no regresaban. (At noon, they [the soldiers] finished killing all the men and then they took the girls to the hills. The mothers cried and screamed not to take their daughters, but they knocked them down with the butts of their guns. The children who cried the loudest and made the most noise were the first taken, and they did not return.)[32]*

Amaya describes waiting in the bushes, crawling on hands and knees through pasturing cattle, and hearing the children's cries: "Mamá, they are killing us; Mamá, they are choking us, Mamá, they are stabbing us!" She recalls telling herself, "If I die, there will be no one to tell this story. There is no one but me." She would begin telling her story to the passersby who gave her shelter and the "international people" who interviewed her fifteen days after the massacre. In an attempt to escape the war, Amaya fled to and lived for seven years in the refugee camp of Colomoncagua, in Honduras, which housed up to eight thousand Salvadorans during the war. Through it all, Amaya reminded herself, "What they did was a reality, and we must be strong to tell it."

Interpolated into other texts, Amaya's story of what happened to her family, friends, and community at El Mozote recovers primary memories of war for Salvadoran nationals, exiles, immigrants, and diasporic communities, as well as a wide range of international spectators. The story of El Mozote, and by extension the story of the countless nameless disappeared in El Salvador, form the referential corpus (the missing but not forgotten bodies) in many texts. Together, these texts function as symbolic and discursive memorial sites that represent unresolved social trauma such as that experienced by Salvadorans as a consequence of the civil war and the multiple forms of state violence. Examining the recuperation of traumatized memory in Chile after the Augusto Pinochet regime, Alexander Wilde identifies various memorializing public acts, symbols, and performances, such as "official ceremonies, national holidays, book publications, discovery of the remains of disappeared persons, [and] the trial of an official of the dictatorship—which remind the political class and citizens alike of the unforgotten past."[33] In the context of postdictatorship Chile, Wilde cites "a series of expressive ceremonies" sponsored by Chilean authorities, public institutions, and grassroots organizations and made public by the media to denounce Pinochet's reign of terror and to commemorate the lives of those who were killed or disappeared during his dictatorship. In contradistinction to the case of Chile, in El Salvador there have been few, *if any,* state-sponsored memorializing public texts, acts, and events, forcing Salvadorans thus to deal with postwar social and personal trauma on their own, on superficial levels, or not at all.

Public and Popular Acts of Memory in El Salvador

Since the signing of the Salvadoran Peace Accords on January 16, 1992, state-sponsored public acts recognizing and memorializing the civil war have been few and far between in El Salvador. Immediately after the war ended, the official postwar agenda of the Salvadoran state was to move the nation toward "reconciliation" and "reconstruction" and to produce of a "culture of peace" through disarmament and the formation of a new National Civilian Police force (the PNC), consisting of former military personnel and leftist guerrilla combatants.[34] From the start, few provisions were made and carried out for the institutionalization of public acts memorializing the dead, disappeared, and victimized during the war and other periods of repression, such as La Matanza of 1932, in which more than thirty thousand peasants and indigenous people were massacred by the military dictatorship of General Maximiliano Hernández Martínez. The massacre of 1932 set in motion a cycle of repression that only intensified with the civil war of the 1980s. As part of the postwar national reconstruction plan, in 1991, the National Republican

Alliance (ARENA) Ministry of Education founded a cultural entity called Concultura, whose primary directive was to develop cultural politics and projects that would promote the image of a reunified and pacified Salvadoran national identity. At its inception, the main objectives of Concultura were to *"investigar, fomentar, promover y difundir la cultura y valorar las artes* (research, foment, promote, and disseminate culture and valorize the arts)" according to the postwar agenda. Material cultural projects involved preserving folk culture, restoring the arts and traditional cultural expressions, and building innocuous monuments. Further, Concultura's mandate was to assist in the reconstruction of "national patrimony," the promotion of cultural heritage, and the recuperation of Salvadoran folk traditions.[35]

While the Salvadoran government, through Concultura, sought to preserve Salvadoran folklore, costumes, customs, and traditions—in essence, the "local color" of El Salvador—it did not in any significant way, in my opinion, recognize, memorialize, and represent the greater losses of the war, that is, the lives and ways of life of all those who had been killed, massacred, disappeared, and displaced. By executing postwar, state-mandated cultural policies, Concultura aided in the construction of a postwar cultural industry and imagination that capitalized on diffused memories of the war and nostalgic images of the country. Rather than produce cultural spaces for mourning, recovery, and recuperation, programs sought speedy cultural recovery by sponsoring Casa de Cultura events, publishing the works of the Salvadoran literary canon, and producing modern icons such as that of "El hermano lejano." Under the auspices of Concultura, the monument dedicated to "El hermano lejano," or the Salvadoran emigrant, materialized as a public works project aligned with the imperative of economic recovery: It was a tribute to the emigrants who routinely send generous remittances to their families and communities in El Salvador, valued in 2006 to be over $3 billion. Following a material rather than ethical imperative, the government to date has not memorialized the victims and survivors of the civil war, a task that has been taken up by religious, grassroots, and nongovernmental organizations, as well as by the Salvadoran people themselves.

Thanks to the tireless efforts of relatives of victims, survivors, and various nongovernmental organizations under the umbrella group Comité Pro Monumento de las Víctimas Civiles de Violaciones de Derechos Humanos,[36] a public monument dedicated to the victims of the Salvadoran civil war was finally built and opened to the public in San Salvador on December 6, 2003, more than a decade after the end of the civil war. Notably, the Salvadoran government did not support or contribute funds for the building of the only mass-scale public monument dedicated to the memory of victims of war in El Salvador, although the Truth Commission investigating war crimes and human rights violations that were committed during the civil war had directed the government to recognize the dead and disappeared through public memorial acts, monument, and symbols. Located in Parque Cuscatlán in San Salvador, the *Monumento a la Memoria y la Verdad* (Monument to Memory and Truth) is an eighty-five-meter black granite wall inscribed with the names of more than twenty-five thousand identified civilians killed and/or disappeared. The text on the national monument reads: *Un espacio para la esperanza, para seguir soñando y construir una sociedad más justa, humana y equitativa* (A space of hope, to keep on dreaming and constructing a more just, humane, and equitable society).[37]

In the village of El Mozote, a memorial consisting of the black metal silhouettes of a family stands before wooden plaques engraved with the names of more than eight hundred people. It pays homage to those massacred in 1981. Since the end of the civil war, many Salvadorans and international people have made their pilgrimage to this site to pay their respects to those killed en masse. An article titled "Salvadoreños conmemoran 15 años de la masacre de 1.000 campesinos" (Salvadorans commemorate 15 years of the massacre of 1,000 *campesinos*), which was published on December 9, 1996, in *La Prensa* of San Pedro Sula, Honduras, reported on the popular commemoration ceremony that took place in El Mozote fifteen years after the massacre.[38] The writer described how *"Cientos de salvadoreños observaron ayer con actos culturales y religiosos el décimo-quinto aniversario de la masacre de 1.000 campesinos, llevada a cabo por un batallón del ejército entre el 11 y 13 diciembre de 1981* (Yesterday, hundreds of Salvadorans commemorated, with cultural and religious acts, the fifteenth anniversary of the massacre of 1,000 *campesinos,* carried out by a government battalion between December 11 and 13 of 1982)."[39] In 2006, on the twenty-fifth anniversary of the massacre, another commemoration was held in El Mozote, where speakers identified El Mozote as "the Capital of Salvadoran memory."[40] They reminded spectators that historical memory in El Salvador would quickly be eroding were it not for individuals like Rufina Amaya and other unofficial recorders of history, who struggle to tell their (hi)stories.

Seeking to bury the past, to grant general amnesty to offending government officials, and to rebuild the economy after the signing of the Peace Accords in 1992, Salvadoran authorities have left the remembrance of the war to civil sectors such as nongovernmental organizations such as the Museo de la Palabra y la Imagen (MUPI; the Museum of the Word and Image). Since its founding, the MUPI has dedicated itself to preserving the cultural memory and material texts of the war, and to fighting *contra el caos de la desmemoria* (against the chaos of memory loss)."[41] Since its founding, the museum has amassed a collection of photographs, *testimonios,* posters, recordings, videos, print texts, testimonies, literature, and other objects of material culture that document the popular historical memory of El Salvador and its wars. The museum has digitized much of its collections, while its virtual galleries are open for viewing at the museum's website. Beginning with the publication of its inaugural book, *Luciérnagas en El Mozote,*[42] the museum has produced texts on themes of vital importance to the history and memory of the civil war, has organized traveling installations throughout El Salvador, and has opened a permanent exhibition site with library and archival space in San Salvador, where visitors and researchers are welcome. According to the museum's founder and director, Carlos Henríquez Consalvi,

> *Hemos lanzado nuestra primera publicación: Luciérnagas en El Mozote (Testimonio), que integra testimonio e investigación periodística sobre la mencionada masacre ejecutada en 1981, y que fuerzas poderosas trataron de borrar de la memoria latinoamericana, primero negando su existencia, luego obstaculizando su investigación. Nuestra intención era dejar memoria escrita sobre hechos que no deben olvidarse, precisamente para que jamás se repitan. (We have launched our first publication, Luciérnagas en El Mozote (Testimonio), which includes testimonials and journalistic research about the massacre executed in 1981, and that powerful forces tried to erase from Latin American memory, first by denying its existence, then by preventing research on it. Our intention is to leave written memory over deeds that should not be forgotten, precisely so that they are never repeated.)[43]*

For Argentine scholars of memory construction, Elizabeth Jelin and Susana G. Kaufman, the MUPI might represent a "public memory site" or location of "memory struggle," where negotiations occur in the construction of collective memory.[44] In "Layers of Memories: Twenty Years After in Argentina," Jelin and Kaufman suggest that spaces consecrated to memory, such as museums, are also "attempts to make statements and affirmations; they are facts and gestures, a materiality with a political, collective, public meaning."[45] In El Salvador, unofficial cultural and political memorial spaces challenging state-sanctioned programs of forgetting include not only the MUPI, but also the Archbishop Romero Center and the memorial to the massacred Jesuit priests, their housekeeper, and her daughter on the grounds of the University of Central America José Simeón Cañas (UCA) in San Salvador; the Museum of the Salvadoran War in Perquín, Morazán, founded and run by former guerrilla combatants; and the monuments and walls of names in Parque Cuscatlán and El Mozote, dedicated to the victims and survivors of war. These memorial sites challenge the ongoing context of impunity in El Salvador through the recollection of unresolved human rights violations and current crises.

Connecting past and present impunities, Rufina Amaya's first-person collective narrative appropriately serves as the core of MUPI's inaugural publication, titled *Luciérnagas en El Mozote,* as well as the core of other sites dedicated to the remembrance of those who did not survive the atrocities and those guilty of the violence, who nonetheless were never tried for it because of a general amnesty law passed in 1993. As the journalist Alma Guillermoprieto explains, "[t]he events at El Mozote are no longer in dispute, but after a quarter of a century, they are also no longer even a memory for the majority of Salvadorans, most of whom had not been born on the day when young girls were dragged screaming to the hills to be raped, and children cried out to their mothers as they were murdered."[46] Amaya's testimonial account of the Massacre at El Mozote is the kernel of "truth" that lies at the center of postwar memory and history in El Salvador, which unless preserved will be lost to the larger imperative of impunity and forgetting.

Testimonial Afterlives

Although Rufina Amaya may have died, her *testimonio* of the Massacre at El Mozote circulates by way of journalists, human rights organizations, truth commissions, word-of-mouth, and multimedia texts such as audio and visual recordings, musical and dance compositions, and videos featuring Amaya posted at YouTube in early 2007. Amaya is "now part of [El Salvador's] history" and "the history of this [U.S.] country, too."[47] The postwar historical irony in Amaya's case and for El Salvador, however, is that "people who once argued passionately over El Salvador would be hard pressed to remember when they last talked—or cared—about the fate of that tiny country."[48] Under the cloud of historical forgetting, the mantle of generalized impunity, and the cover-up of U.S. intervention in Central America, Amaya's struggle to keep alive the memory of El Mozote becomes an even more pressing issue after her passing, for how will we remember Rufina Amaya and the disappeared at El Mozote now that she is no longer living to "tell about it"? How will her *testimonio*—*her* truth, and not the government's truth of what happened at El Mozote, which she struggled so hard to live to tell—not be dismissed now that she is gone?

Alicia Partnoy—herself a torture survivor of the Argentinean Dirty War, whose *testimonio* is told in *The Little School: Tales of Disappearance and Survival* (1986)—offers insight to the significance of *testimonio* in a post-*testimonio* era following the so-called "Rigoberta Menchú controversy." Indeed, the *testimonio* genre cannot be read as trustingly, transparently, and truthfully as it might have been read before the controversy. Instead, Partnoy suggests that we embrace the double-valence and contradictions of *testimonio*—most vividly its impossibility to tell the whole truth, to represent an entire community, and to provide an "unquestionable" first-person story. Recognizing the limits of *testimonio*, moreover, we need not dismiss *testimonio* as *untrue, unreal,* and *useless.* Rufina Amaya and other testimonial subjects would not submit their "narrative authority" to that type of dismissal, silencing, and cynicism. Instead, Partnoy, along with Amaya and others, would challenge readers, scholars, and critics of *testimonio* to look still to the discursive potential of *testimonio* "to engender and regenerate a discourse of solidarity" and to empower survivors of violence.[49] Partnoy asserts that

> [t]hrough the act of testifying, through the creation of testimonio, the survivors of horrendous abuse are empowered. They are no longer tortured bodies to be pitied or patronized; they became the central force in a process that makes a difference in their own personal lives and also helps to further their personal agendas.[50]

The "personal" truths and testimonies of survivors of (state) violence, understood here as critical public texts and interventions, can help us thus to challenge new and revamped forms of institutional violence such as that proposed by the "Salvador Option."

Finally, Partnoy asks readers, scholars, and others to liberate *testimonio* from "the leash of truth,"[51] whether it be attached to notions of personal experience, morality, scholarship, or authority on all levels. Like Partnoy, who takes issue with the dismissal of testimonial genres and discourses on the heels of the "Rigoberta Menchú controversy," I continue to believe that "[w]e must focus on what testimonial texts *do* and how they do it to understand their empowering potential."[52] In other words, although Rufina Amaya may be gone, her *testimonio* still has a crucial story to tell in a society that not only is quickly "forgetting" the massacre of a village and people but moreover is being subjected to the violence of the "Salvador Option" in the twenty-first century. Rufina Amaya's *testimonio* of the Massacre at El Mozote reminds us that, although state violence may be an option for some, it is not the solution for those who are crushed under its weight.

"Comfort Women" Want Justice, Not Comfort

Dai Sil Kim-Gibson

During the Asia/Pacific War between 1931 and 1945, Japan officially institutionalized sexual slavery on a massive scale. Unlike countless military rape cases stretching back to antiquity, it was not just random violence. It was a systematic and carefully designed system ordered and executed by the Japanese military. The Imperial Government of Japan established "comfort houses" and shipped girls and women like military supplies, roughly two hundred thousand of them, euphemistically calling them "comfort women." Many advocate replacing the term with "military sex slaves" (MSS), but I prefer the term comfort women, because "comfort" more accurately depicts how the sexual servitude was committed with a chilling casualness and dehumanizing brutality.

Japan denied direct responsibility and/or involvement in the comfort women system as long as they could, until the early 1990s. They maintained that there was no forced recruitment. The girls and women came through private traders and/or family members who sold their sisters and daughters. However, reluctantly and bit by bit, as undeniable evidence was discovered, the Japanese government had to admit its involvement. The first such evidence came from Japanese historian Yoshimi Yoshiaki. In December 1991, he discovered a military document, issued by the Japanese Army on March 4, 1938. On camera, Professor Yoshimi Yoshiaki explained it to me in his book-lined, cluttered office on the outskirts of Tokyo in April 1997, pointing to a document,

This document is a notice addressed to the chief of staff at the Japanese Army in China—North and Mid Region. The war broke out in China, and the Army had started to establish "comfort facilities." The army chose purveyors and sent them to

205

Japan, Korea, and Taiwan to recruit women. The notice said that an expeditionary army should control the recruitment of comfort women to avoid problems with the purveyors working with military and civilian police. The Japanese government approved government involvement with the comfort women system.

Prompted by Yoshimi Yoshiaki's discovery, the Japanese government admitted on January 13, 1992, that the Japanese Army forced tens of thousands of women, the majority of them Korean, to have sex with Japanese soldiers. Since then, the Japanese government has admitted its complicity in this sexual slavery, including its forced recruitment, though it has continued to deny legal responsibility and has not offered an official apology.

On March 1, 2007, Prime Minister Shinzo Abe "denied that Japan's military had forced foreign women into sexual slavery during World War II, contradicting the Japanese government's longtime official position."[1] Abe, age fifty-two, hails from the most conservative wing of his Liberal Democratic Party, and with his ratings sagging, I am sure he went insane, eager to woo his conservative base ahead of a July upper house election.

The entire comfort women issue is so heartbreaking that every time I think of it, my intestines coil with sharp pain and sorrow. I manage, however, to continue my fight for these women, to help them get justice, not comfort. With so many urgent crises of gigantic magnitude unfolding before our eyes now—the senseless war in Iraq, genocide in Africa, and nuclear threats that can destroy humanity in a massive scale—many ask "Why drag up this history? Why not leave the past alone and move forward?"

Czech writer Milan Kundera addressed this question eloquently in his conversations with Philip Roth in March 1980 after his novel *The Book of Laughter and Forgetting* was published. To him, forgetting is the great private problem of the individual, since death is the loss of self, "the sum total of everything we remember." Thus death is not the loss of the future but the loss of the past. He applies this definition to nations as well and discusses how a big power uses "the method of organized forgetting" when it wants to deprive a small country of its national consciousness.[2] This is what Japan did to Korea during its colonial rule for thirty-six years. And this is what the powerful do to the powerless, the oppressor to the oppressed. An individual or a nation that does not face its past is not ready for the present, not to mention the future.

I spent many years of my adult life in the United States trying to forget Korea's colonial past with Japan and move on. Forgetting was a willful act for me to create a present and envision a better future. In November 1992, all that determination and effort evaporated. I was asked by a group of Korean Americans in the Washington, D.C., area to translate for one of the surviving comfort women for television, radio, and print media. Her name was Hwang Keum Ju, and as she talked, I saw the tremors going through her body, caused by the pain from her past, so remote yet so close. Then the tremors stopped, and her voice, tainted with a regional Korean accent, shook, drawing my attention even closer. She said, "This Japanese officer took his thing out and wanted me to lick it like a dog. I yelled, 'I would rather die than do that, you son of a dog!' When they were on top of us, shamelessly exploding like animals, we were simply imprisoned sex machines put to use. . . . " Her breathing became rough, her body literally shaking, as she concluded, "He took away the last shred of human dignity from me." Hwang Keum Ju gave me voice to go out and shout about this horrendous crime committed long ago and silenced for over half a century. Wartime rapes and everyday rapes are still rampant. If we bury this past, we cannot move on.

In April 1997 I went to the outskirts of Seoul to visit Grandma Kim Hak Soon, the first public witness of Japanese sex slavery. I brought a film crew with me to talk with her on camera, but I found her coughing constantly and short of breath. I offered to come back, but she said, "Stay. I am rarely free of this kind of ailment. This is *han* [a complex Korean concept, but simplified, it means long-accumulated sorrow and resentment]. From the time when I was little, what the Japanese did to me, to my family—that's what made knots in my chest. This knotted *han,* how can it be untied?" Her breathing stopped when she passed on December 16, 1997.

By the end of the war, only about 25 percent of the more than two hundred thousand girls and women forced into sexual slavery had survived. We have no idea how many died after the war's end while en route to their homelands. In South Korea, since Grandma Kim Hak Soon gave public testimony in August 1991, roughly two hundred women have come forward. Of them, more than forty have passed away with their knotted *han* untied. Japan still seems determined to send all these grandmas to the land of no return with their knotted *han* untied. As late as March 2007, Japan is still failing to admit its moral as well as legal involvement.

From December 7 to December 12, 2000, I attended the Women's International War Crimes Tribunal for the Trial of Japan's Military Sexual Slavery. It was organized and convened by the Japanese-based NGO Violence against Women in War Network, as well as by people from six victimized countries—South Korea, North Korea, the Philippines, Taiwan, Indonesia, and China. Each day, sitting among the crowd of more than a thousand people at any given time, I heard presentations by a distinguished international team of prosecutors, headed by Patricia Viseur-Sellers, an American legal advisor to the International Criminal Tribunal for the Former Yugoslavia; Ustinia Dolgopol, an Australian legal scholar; and other prosecutorial teams from North and South Korea, China, Taiwan, the Philippines, Indonesia, East Timor, Malaysia, and the Netherlands.

Chief Judge Gabrielle Kirk MacDonald, an American who had served as president of the Yugoslavia War Crimes Tribunal, declared Emperor Hirohito guilty at the height of the tribunal when she said, "Hirohito knew or should have known about the establishment of the system of 'comfort stations,' but he took no action to respond."

However, nothing matched the power of the testimony given by the women themselves. Many of them, in public and private, told how they came forward from a long silence. One South Korean woman, Grandma Kim Hak Soon, had inspired all, and the group's courageous efforts to seek justice were seen as nothing less than pioneering the entire movement to define sexual slavery and wartime rapes in the context of international law. It would not be far-fetched to say that Grandma Kim and the other comfort women who came forward helped to bring about a *New York Times* editorial called "A Landmark Ruling on Rape," which said, in part,

> *The conviction this week by the Hague war crimes court of three Bosnian Serbs for rape and sexual enslavement marks the first time an international tribunal has convicted defendants exclusively for sexual violence or prosecuted sexual slavery at all. The decision shows the progress that women's issues have made in international justice, which routinely ignored mass rape, considering it a natural occurrence in war. The tribunal's verdict should also encourage individual nations to treat sexual violence more seriously.[3]*

When asked, as part of the oath prior to testimony, if they would tell nothing but the truth, two women from East Timor said in voices almost defiant, "Would we have come all this way to tell lies? Of course, we will tell nothing but the truth!" The truth they told was indeed tragic, but the spirit that rang out was so strong that I wanted to stand up and dance. When a grandma from China, Wan Aihua, couldn't bear her sixty-year-old pain any longer while relaying her experience about how she was enslaved by the Japanese soldiers when she was only eleven, and how she witnessed her parents being killed, she collapsed on the stage and was taken away for emergency hospitalization.

Then there were the grandmas from South Korea with whom I had spent countless hours—Grandma Hwang Keum Ju, who had given me the voice to fight and threatened to kill me if I did not depict her story accurately in my film and book, and Grandma Chung Seo Woon, whom I met at the Fourth World Conference on Women in Beijing in 1995 and who made my chest burst with pride when I translated her words in the packed auditorium. She said, "You can do whatever you wish with my body, but you cannot take my spirit away!" There was also Grandma Lee, who advised me to comb my hair like a lady. I could go on with a long list of grandmas who were so brave. To hold their hands and share a giggle or two in the midst of solemn speeches warmed our hearts and helped us tackle a variety of emotions ready to explode—sorrow that choked the pit of our stomachs, inspiration by the sheer fact that persons could survive such unspeakable crimes by fellow human beings (let alone with resilient spirits intact), and fury at those who committed crimes beyond any human imagination.

Then I spotted a face among the crowd that I had first seen at a small airport in Wuhan, China, in 1995. While I was attending the Fourth World Conference, I was able to contact a former Korean comfort woman living in Wuhan and managed to fly there. I still remember how I felt, looking down a long stretch of the Yangtze River from the plane, how overwhelmed I was by a historic sense of sorrow. Wearing sneakers, with a brown knapsack on my back, I walked among people, greeting those who came on the flight with me. Then I spotted a face among the crowd that I had first seen in 1995, grandma in a navy blue dress, her face brown and lined but with a smile so full of compassion that it could have come only from absorbing human suffering as wide as the Yangtze River. Before I opened my mouth, she grabbed my hand and asked in halting Korean, "You are a Chosun person, aren't you?" She still called Korea "Chosun," the land of morning calm, the much-cherished name of her motherland when she was taken by the Japanese at the age of seventeen. "Yes! You must be Grandma Ha Gun Ja," I replied. She nodded, wiping her eyes with a handkerchief. Her small hand, enclosed in mine, was chapped, but it sent such soft warmth through my body that I was mystified. Standing in almost tropical heat, I shivered with the connection that I felt with this stranger. It was Grandma Ha whom I recognized with a few other Chinese women at the Tokyo Tribunal. We both started walking toward each other with our mouths open. "Oh, my, who could have dreamed that I would see you here!" she said, again wiping away her tears.

The South Korean team had invited Grandma Ha—one of many former comfort women who never made it back home to Korea and lived all these years in Wuhan, China—to the tribunal. When I went to her room, which she shared with three Chinese women, she said, "You remember Grandma Hong, don't you? She died. Remember how she wanted to go see her younger brother in Korea and take care of him? But she died." As if to rescue me from the choked silence brought by the news about Grandma Hong's death, she continued, "Remember how you were almost thrown into a jail by the Chinese police because we were caught talking to each other when they had said no?" (At that point, China was still reluctant to challenge Japan for its war crimes for fear of hurting its trade relationship.) "How can I forget?" I said.

After we sat down on the floor, she urgently looked for something in her purse. What she showed me was a letter I had sent to her. "Recognize this? I carry this around wherever I go. I told you people like you were my only connection to the motherland from where I was forcibly taken such a long time ago. If only Grandma Hong were here with me—but she is gone, gone to the land of no return."

The comfort women issue was silenced for half a century. People have attributed and continue to attribute this long silence to the women themselves. They were too ashamed of their pasts and too fearful of society's condemnation of themselves and of their families. There is some truth in that, but it is by all means not the primary reason for the long silence. Further, contrary to this persistent view, many women did not feel ashamed. Grandma Chung Seo Woon, a graceful woman who speaks in even tones, raised her voice one octave when I asked if she felt ashamed of her past. She replied firmly,

No way! Why should I be ashamed? When I returned home, I told everything
openly to all my friends and neighbors. Those who think it is shameful I consider
strange. Why is it our shame? Those who dragged us and treated us like slaves, as
sex slaves, the Japanese government; they should feel shame, not us. Why us?

Actually, their wish to tell the story was similar to Viktor Frankl's *Man's Search for Meaning*. It helped them to survive the most inhuman existence. They wanted to talk. It was their families, neighbors, and politicians who did not want to hear them.

What, then, were the real reasons for the decades of silence? Firstly, Japan didn't want to reveal this horrendous atrocity. Japan burned most of the relevant documents immediately after the war. Secondly, the Allied Forces, especially the United States, did little to seek justice for Asian atrocities committed by Japan. After Japan signed the Instrument of Surrender on September 2, 1945, the United States spearheaded the Far Eastern war crimes operation. General Douglas MacArthur was appointed Supreme Commander of the Allied Powers (SCAP), and the International Military Tribunal for the Far East (IMTFE)—the so-called Tokyo Tribunal—was convened on January 19, 1946. At this tribunal, the predominant charges focused on waging the war. The cases of gross human rights violations were largely neglected. If any cases were considered, they were heavily focused on Western victims; little justice was meted out for the crimes committed against Asians.

The Allies knew about the comfort women; they repatriated many and conducted studies about them. In addition to finding several such documents in the U.S. archives, I interviewed retired U.S. Sergeant Grant Hirabayashi, a Japanese American who interrogated Korean comfort women in Burma immediately after the fall of Myitkyina on August 3, 1944. Only the Dutch held trials about interned Dutch women who were forced to become sex slaves for the Japanese soldiers. In Batavia, known as Jakarta now, Dutch women's cases were prosecuted and the offenders sentenced. By now, it is an undeniable fact that the United States knowingly neglected Asian war crimes of the highest order—including comfort women, the infamous Nanjing massacre in 1937, and the gruesome biological warfare program conducted by Unit 731.

While the Allies did not punish those responsible for the crimes committed against fellow Asians by Japan under the banner of "Asia for Asians," they convicted some

178 Taiwanese and 148 Koreans, who were mostly working as prison guards for the Allied prisoners of war. The 1951 Peace Treaty of San Francisco, which recognized the sovereignty of Japan, showed remarkably little interest in justice for peoples of Asian origin. The South Korean government failed to articulate any issues regarding comfort women at the time of the 1965 Treaty with Japan, which settled the damages of the war and colonialism.

Actually, the more I deal with this topic, the stronger my feelings become, particularly regarding how the United States failed to deal with postwar Japan and other Asian countries. While the United States carried out its sense of righteous mission and Manifest Destiny as the sole occupying force of Japan, transforming the Japanese people "from a bestial people fit to be annihilated into receptive exotics to be handled and enjoyed,"[4] the United States was oblivious to the condition of other Asians that might have been harmed by the warfare of the region.

If the case of comfort women was ignored because the United States had little interest in Asian women, it is also because this was a sensitive topic for the United States. As early as August 18, 1945, a secret wireless message was sent to regional police officials throughout Japan, instructing them to prepare special and exclusive "comfort facilities" for the occupation army.[5] By August 27, 1945, "1,360 women in Tokyo had enlisted in what soon would become known in English as the RAA [Recreation and Amusement Association.]"[6] RAA women engaged between fifteen and sixty GIs a day. Such recreation and amusement centers expanded rapidly in Tokyo—soon numbering at thirty-three by one count—and spread to some twenty other cities. In January 1946, occupation authorities ordered the abolition of all "public" prostitution, declaring it undemocratic and in violation of women's human rights. The real reason was probably the rapid spread of venereal disease.[7]

Clearly, the United States government chose political expediency because the Cold War agenda overwhelmed any concerns regarding the violations of fundamental human rights. The government of Japan was not held accountable, and it was given a helpful hand so that it could flourish economically—all for the sake of the Cold War. The neglect of comfort women, then, was an expression of a triple discrimination in effect—gender, race, and class, as most of those women came from poverty-stricken families. It is difficult to imagine how the U.S. government might have dismissed the enslavement of more than two hundred thousand girls and women had they been white. Worse still, the racial discrimination continues. As opposed to the countless reckonings of the Holocaust in Europe, the case of the Holocaust in Asia, e.g., comfort women, warrants no serious attention. It is time to express the equality of all human beings not only in recognizing human rights, but also in recognizing human suffering.

The Tokyo Tribunal of 2000 carried enough emotional power to move mountains but had no legal authority. Japan should be punished for its crimes against women and girls. It's time for the Allied Forces, especially the United States, to accept responsibility for not using their legal authority to put Japan on trial for this crime immediately after World War II.

We should recognize some efforts made to redress this issue in the United States. From the California State Assembly to the U.S. House of Representatives, some bills have been presented that urge the Japanese government to extend a formal apology for its aggression against women and girls during World War II and to pay reparations to the survivors of Japanese war crimes. Tucked among "other" victims were comfort women. Until his retirement from Congress in 2006, Congressman Lane Evans was a tireless supporter for rendering justice to comfort women. Most recently, Congressman Mike Honda introduced a nonbinding resolution calling on Japan to acknowledge and apologize for forcing women into sexual slavery. The controversy prompted by Prime Minister Abe's denial came as the U.S. House of Representatives considered Honda's resolution. Japanese Prime Minister Abe's denial (March 2007) of the forced sexual slavery stirred up a flurry of articles in a variety of press, but not one of them mentions the responsibility of the United States for its long silence and delayed struggle for justice. The United States should take responsibility for silencing this brutal crime for more than half a century, not just blame the nation of Japan.

In the struggle for comfort women to obtain long-delayed justice and not comfort, I think of the ongoing wartime rapes in Kosovo, Rwanda, Indonesia, and Darfur. The list is long. Ultimately, wartime rapes are not just the problems of some countries or regions. They are our problem—crimes against humanity, against us. We have to join forces together—all women, all men—to fight against this common foe, brutal rapes so enormous and so timeless that we might render it as part of war and human nature. It shouldn't be part of war and it shouldn't be part of human nature. It is our common foe, against which we have to fight. The justice that comfort women are seeking is a human issue—not just theirs, women's, or those belonging only to specific countries. The silence was broken by the voices of these courageous women. They should not fall silent again until the knotted *han* of the living and dead can be untied; until justice is given to them, not comfort.

House of Sharing/ Comfort Women

Ishle Yi Park

I can forget everything when I sing, when the blood is burnt up

Drunk from pots filled with rice wine, she pulled a quilt
over her mouth to cover her smell,
listened to Nam Insoo through
the blanket, stack of songbooks piled
by the foot of her *yoh.*
I was 14.

Flash flood melts the road into a river.

3 pine trees. my parents thought they sent me to a good place.
my hands like rubber gloves.
my heart bleeding.

This *halmoni,* silver streaked
hair marcelled down her neck, in a *hanbok* of 5 layers like a white lotus.
She wipes red pepper stains
from the concrete windowsill, thin
tissue shredding in her fingers.

215

At the sill, she tells me to keep secrets from my man, even if he is good. No one should open

all your contents. You don't even know the word contents? She sucks her teeth and closes

the window.

They cut her open because she was too small.

With rusted scissors. Virgin. Doctor first

to enter her after the operation.

She ate rice balls prone on stone bed,

thin mattress, one washcloth to rinse between soldiers. Beheaded if she bit down.

I can forget everything when I paint, when the blood is burnt up

I cannot reconcile this *halmoni* with a girl 50 years ago, lips like a pressed heart,

neck long as reed, who never learned to write

her own name, this *halmoni,* bundled thick in 2 wool coats, bus ticket clenched tightly in

gloved fist to attend her 882nd rally,

pushing the glass-covered policemen young enough to be her grandsons, to be in spitting distance

of the Japanese embassy.

She draws a painting larger than herself

of a soldier in mustard green, wrapped to a cherry blossom tree with black barbed wire,

guns pointed at his chest from 3 directions,

white doves taking flight from its branches

white doves taking flight, and she danced like this,

hands flicking, hip jut, wrinkles filling her eyes

ash falling from her cigarette, cup of *macculi* splashing upraised, she danced like this.

Chapter 4.

Messages of Pain

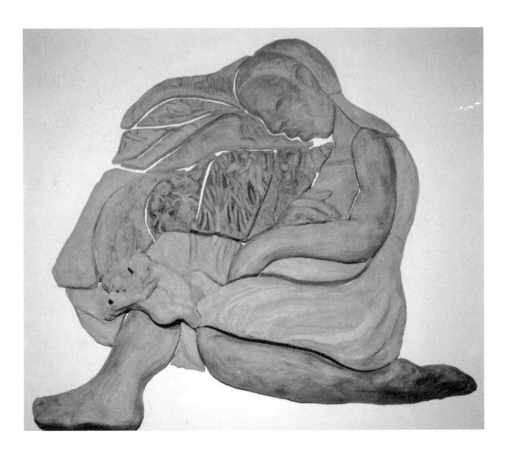

Colonization and Rape

Darrell Ann Gane-McCalla

Introduction

My painting carries with it the message of pain.

—Frida Kahlo

Speaking up is an act that resides at the core of all agencies. Silences, too, have a role for survival in a dangerous world. Each work in this chapter examines the outcomes that result from loudly articulating resistance and strategically remaining quiet.

All that we know comes from our ancestors; in keeping with the acknowledgement of this fact, the chapter starts with a poem whose inspiration derives from the cultural work of Toni Cade Bambara. Do expect not a paean; this work is a piercing cry of rage about the centuries-long denigration of black women. In an essay that is both a pedagogical discussion and poetic discourse analysis, a university professor describes how she taught her students about violence against women of color by applying the poetry of Janice Mirikitani and the prose of Audre Lorde. A colleague, who urged her not to raise such issues "for the good of the community," did not dissuade her. Following this essay, there is a poem written by Mirikitani that speaks to the liberating and healing qualities resultant from identifying the sources of psychic and physical pain. Another poem demonstrates how silence is an essential strategy for surviving hostile environments, especially when the threat of physical violence is close. For the American Indian lesbian narrator of the poem, her quiet exacts a high psychic price after the threat of harm has passed. Through a fusion of poetry and prose, a woman tells the story about how her Chinese American family responded to a frightening, hate-crime-inspired fire, set outside their home. A work of historical fiction that is based in part on the true-life experiences of two generations of Korean woman during the 19th and 20th centuries is crafted by their great-granddaughter, who also reflects on how these family stories have affected her identity as a Korean American woman and her relationship to her father. This chapter concludes with two vibrant essays that offer critical analyses regarding literary discourses, race theories, and the circulation of such ideas as applied to African and African American women during the 18th, 19th, and 20th centuries. The first work directs its attention to

Algerian women and touches on matters such as arranged marriage, colonialism, rape as a site of political agency, a reworking of the veil, and the voice of the "obstinate woman," as described by Frantz Fanon in his germinal work *The Wretched of the Earth*. The second paper concentrates on the little-acknowledged and little-discussed insurgency among enslaved communities of the 18th and 19th centuries in the Americas. Through a contemporary analysis of historical publications and other primary documents, the author demonstrates how the "unnatural" acts of resistance by African and African American women served as ringing testaments against slavery as an institution.

As stated earlier, Gloria Anzaldúa influences the sum of this book. This chapter stands as the one whose genealogy is directly traced to her work as poet, essayist, intellect, and editor. The writings in this chapter are exemplary in their presentation of ideas and critiques that surprise the reader with a hybridization of form and content that disrupts a familiar reading.

A State of Rage

Aishah Shahidah Simmons

for Toni Cade Bambara

Throughout U.S. history Black[1] women have been sexually stereotyped as immoral, insatiable, perverse, the initiators in all sexual contacts—abusive or otherwise. The common assumption in legal proceedings as well as in the larger society has been that Black women cannot be raped or otherwise sexually abused.[2]

This is NOT an objective piece.

I said . . . This is NOT an objective piece.

I am in a STATE OF RAGE

I said. I am. I am. I am.

I AM IN A STATE OF RAGE ABOUT THE RAPE AND SEXUAL ABUSE OF WOMEN OF AFRICAN DESCENT IN THE united states of ameri-kkk-a.

I am tired of the silences that have been imposed on us. *Shhhhh. Black women and girls.*

I am tired of the silences that we Black women have imposed on ourselves and on our daughters.

I am angry that when a Black woman says that she has been raped by a Black man that many Black people view it.

The Black woman's charge

As an act of betrayal against the Black community.

As if the Black woman's rape ain't an act of betrayal against the Black community.

I am angry that the very same people . . .
Particularly those designated Blackmaleleaders. Y'know the ones who supported Tawana Brawley and yet charged Desiree Washington with treason against the Black community.

I am angry that the rapist is more important than the woman who is raped.
I am angry that the fate of women who have been raped is judged by the race and class of their rapist.

This is a meditation peace.
A peace that is uncompromising.

A peace that is Black woman identified.
Black woman identified
Black woman identified
Blackwomanidentified

A peace that doesn't hold back for the sake of community.

A peace that vehemently rejects the notion that Black women have to sacrifice our bodies and silence our tongues for the sake of the community.

A peace that will include the diversity of women of African descent, regardless of class, physical ability, sexual orientation, and/or religion.

From the time we were brought over here in SHACKLES

This is a meditation peace

We have been under physical, emotional, and spiritual attack.

OUR ABUSE HAS BEEN IN THE DUNGEONS IN WEST AFRICA, WHERE
ENSLAVED AFRICANS WERE HELD CAPTIVE.

*Through The Middle Passage. Through The Middle Passage. Obatala. Through the
Middle Passage. Oshun. Through the Middle Passage. Yemenja. Through the Middle
Passage. Oludumare. THROUGH THE MIDDLE PASSAGE. Mohammed. Through
the MIDDLE PASSAGE. Isis. THROUGH THE MIDDLE PASSAGE. Jesus
throughthemiddlepassage Mary throughthemiddlepassage Osiris throughthemiddlepassage
Elegba throughtheMAMABABADADAmiddlepassage Ya Allah throughthemiddlepassage
God throughthemiddlepassage MAMA throughMAMAthemiddleBABApassage
DADAthroughthemiddlepassageMAMA throughtheDADAmiddlepassage
BABA throughthemiddlepassage throughthemiddlepassageMAMA
throughthemiddlepassageMAMA throughthemiddlepassage throughthemiddlepassage
DADA throughthemiddlepassageBABA throughthemiddlepassage
throughthemiddlepassage throughthemiddlepassage throughthemiddlepassage
throughthemiddlepassage throughthemiddlepassage . . . Ase.*

A healing peace
On the auction blocks

A meditation peace
In the fields

A healing peace
In the homes we cooked for and cleaned in

A meditation peace
In the factories we worked

A healing peace
In the homes we lived

A meditation peace
In the schools we founded and attended

A healing peace
In the churches, mosques, and temples where we worshiped

A meditation peace
In the movements we led

Given this history. Given Black women's her story. Given all of our his/her story, will someone please tell me what the HELL is rape?

Well . . .

Is it enough for a woman to say NO!
Ask the question?

Or does she have to prove that she fought
Almost to her death

To protect her virtue, her womanhood . . .
As defined by a heterosexual patriarchal point of view.

Does a woman's behavior, attire and/or poor judgment justify her rape . . . her sexual assault, physical or verbal?
No

Did you hear me?
Ask it again sistah; we don't think they heard you.

I said, does a woman's behavior, attire, and/or poor judgment, ever, ever, EVER justify her rape, her sexual assault, physical and/or verbal

HELL NO!

This is a meditation peace.
This is a healing peace
A meditation peace
A healing peace
Meditation peace
Healing peace.

Rage
Meditation
Action
Healing
Ase.

Maintaining the Casualties of Silence: "For the Good of the Community"[1]

Barbara K. Ige

The strongest prisons are built
With walls of silence.

—Janice Mirikitani[2]

Liberation is a praxis: the action and reflection of men
upon their world in order to transform it.

—Paulo Freire[3]

Paper after paper was turned in, depicting violence against women. One student described her memories as an eight-year-old, when she watched, helpless to protect her mother, as she was being beaten with a golf club by her stepfather. Another student described holding and crying with a friend she was helping to hide from an abusive husband. The stories were different, but all were about violence against women and survival.

These were some of the stories my students shared with me at the University of Hawai'i, Manoa, where I was teaching in the '90s. My literature classes were not very traditional, as I attended graduate school at the University of California, Santa Cruz (where grades were once eschewed for personalized narrative evaluations and the beloved mascot is a banana slug). Being different, teaching different, was a good thing. At UCSC, I learned how to unify the literature and teach with the powerful writings of authors like Janice Mirikitani and Audre Lorde. These women poets, writers, activists of color put their power into language, and their language into action that inspires my pedagogical approach. Another source that informs my teaching is Paulo Freire, the revolutionary Brazilian activist and teacher of literacy to the poor, and his liberation pedagogy. As a woman of Uchinanchu ancestry, born and raised in the diverse city of Los Angeles, the works of those writers motivate me to teach about oppression and the individuals'/students' abilities to use their education to become critical thinkers, active learners, and empowered citizens. Even though the student populations were very different (UCSC consisted predominately of Caucasian, upper-middle-class students often from privileged backgrounds, and my UH students were mostly first-generation, low- to medium-income students of color), the violence against women knew no boundaries, crossing land and sea, class and race. I saw the teaching of literature as more than plot summaries and narrative arches. In choosing which multicultural books I would teach, I looked to Lorde's belief in the power of poetry and its potential role in the writers' and readers' lives as a guide:

> *For women, then, poetry is not a luxury. It is a vital necessity of our existence.*
> *It forms the quality of the light within which we predicate our hopes and dreams*
> *toward survival and change, first made into language, then into idea, then into*
> *more tangible action. Poetry is the way we help give name to the nameless, so it can*
> *be thought.*[4]

When I was teaching Ethnic American Literature at UH, I was taken aback, but not surprised, when a colleague knocked on my door, entered with an apprehensive smile, and said, "Some of my students told me you're teaching Janice Mirikitani's collection of poetry." She, a Japanese American faculty member, chatted superficially for a bit and then, with purported good intentions, she questioned my choice of readings. "Here, in Hawai'i [where she was a local, someone born and raised in Hawai'i, and I was not], we don't talk about certain things; it isn't good for the community. I know you're not from here and not used to the way things are here, but this isn't Los Angeles. L.A. is a big city where people can disappear."

As my colleague continued, I wondered who was this woman of color in my office telling me how to teach my course? It was obvious that she thought we had some connection, both of us being Asian American women; however, this superficiality did not make us fast friends. Her comments quickly ventured beyond the realm of advice into censorship and the disturbing terrain of consensual silence. "You must think about the students," she continued. Choosing Mirikitani's work, which includes topics such as domestic and sexual violence, from this faculty member's perspective, indicated that I selfishly had not thought enough about my students. She was positioning herself as the students' guardian—an intellectual gatekeeper—and said that, due to geography and culture, people in Hawai'i simply "do not make waves."

> *I swore*
> *it would not devour me*
> *I swore*
> *it would not humble me*
> *I swore*
> *it would not break me.*[5]

Incredulous, I asked, "Does this mean you would prefer I protect the abuser instead of helping the victim?" Awkwardly, she explained this was not what she meant, but that sometimes it was "better to let things go." Her points were not about literary style, form, or semiotics, but purely base content. I could not help but wonder whether she thought the students uncritical or unsophisticated. Also, how was I supposed to teach students to be judicious in discussing literature, to base their analysis on quality and content and not the fear of upsetting the status quo? My colleague assumed that because I was not from Hawai'i, I was unaware of the island politics or that I was a novice in the classroom. She was wrong on both counts.

In this "paradise" (a euphemism that obscures another type of violence: decades of colonialism), was I to believe that there was only a statistically insignificant number of women and children being hurt, or that the overall number of people involved was negligible? The facts and figures in the 1990s told another story:

The Hawaii Crime Brief issued by the Attorney General in April 1996 found that nearly 30% of all homicides from 1985–1994 in the state were the results of domestic violence. A study conducted by the Hawai'i State Commission on the Status of Women (1993) estimated that nearly 50,000 women in this state between the ages of 18 and 64 have been victims of domestic violence. The Department of Health's Plan for Prevention of Injuries in Hawai'i (June 1995) reported that between 1989 and 1994 almost 100 women were killed by men in Hawai'i. Most of the killers were partners, boyfriends, husbands, or acquaintances.[6]

What was most disturbing was that at the time of our conversation, these statistics were current, accessible via the Internet and daily newspapers, and seemingly unknown or unrecognized by a local. Her reaction implied that there was a level of acquiescence—something akin to accepting a pervasive and unheeded epidemic of violence—masked by the paradisical phrase "aloha spirit." While she might have been ignorant of this information, I was not. My father was born on Maui, and my parents come from a small prefecture in Okinawa, an island very much like Hawai'i—one that is also overwhelmed by the U.S. military. I am only too familiar with the sexual violence perpetrated by the military on the Okinawan women and girls, such as the horrific rape of a twelve-year-old girl by three U.S. servicemen in 1995. Having grown up in Los Angeles, I have always been keenly aware of violence, and frankly, I was tired of the endless cycles and sense of helplessness.

"For the good of the community" this colleague suggested I teach something less inflammatory and less upsetting. But how could I ignore these statistics, Mirikitani's stunning control of language and topics, or the fact I had already ordered a lot of books? Being party to a purposeful act of societal make-believe, I told her, would be to commit a different type of damage, one that not only offers up the survivors as sacrifices to a veneer of superficial, social tranquility, but reaffirms a status quo of violence. Freire describes educational protectionism in this way: "Any attempt to 'soften' the power of the oppressor in deference to the weakness of the oppressed almost always manifests itself in the form of false generosity; indeed, the attempt never goes beyond this."[7] I explained to my colleague that my intent was to not teach safe or sanitized literature, but to provide the students the access to a skilled Japanese American poet who addresses challenging topics, from the Japanese American internment to images of beauty. Mirikitani's poetic power lies in her ability to address a mundane act, such as preparing fish, and transforms it into an act of intense personal and political rebellion—as her title "Why Is Preparing Fish a Political Act?" asks. The poem interchanges from the point of view of the grandmother to the granddaughter and is infused with references to the food the grandmother is making for the Oshogatsu, Japanese New Year. However, in Mirikitani's skilled hands, after she eloquently describes the grandmother's movements, like a dance, the granddaughter resituates the scene by rewording the poem's title and closes with it. However, this time it is not a question, but a statement, "Preparing fish / is a political act." It is the political nature of Mirikitani's work that inspired me not only to teach it, but to interweave her poems throughout my essay to act as transitional bridges. Her words gave voice to my collegial frustration and kept me moving forward, determined to resist the safe path of erasure.

Even before my run-in with my colleague, throughout my years in the classroom, I repeatedly witnessed how "false generosity" lulled survivors into an unsettling complacency. I began to see a composite student profile that endemic violence had trained them—in particular, the women—to disappear. Violence had conditioned "her"[8] to hide within a crowd, to be rendered indistinguishable and invisible. She sits quietly in classrooms, fulfills her assignments, and silently matriculates, unnoticed. If her bruises are covered with clothing or makeup, then her teachers and peers need never know anything is wrong. Yet no matter how adept she is at covering up, there are times when she is unable to continue to conceal her psychological and physical scars, and she begins failing her classes and quietly disappears.

The personal pain was evident and began to emerge in many of my students' essays after they read authors such as Mirikitani and Malcolm X. I began to notice how some of the papers were disjointed, uneven, yet obviously not written at the eleventh hour. The papers were written as if the writers were at once emptying their pain in a blurred but a cathartic exhalation of ideas. The papers' structures, while rough in presentation, contained a brilliant intensity that reflected an astonishing amount of analytical depth.

Upon encountering these papers, I knew I had to take a different pedagogical approach. Instead of issuing a grade, I would ask the student to come to my office hours to discuss her papers. I would tell her that we needed to tease out her ideas and organize her thoughts. I let her know that I was there to help her work on content and style, and together we would unravel and trace her writing process. We would begin to explore her writing history, which was inexorably entangled with an anguished past. As we discussed and organized different topics, we would simultaneously distill emotions, experiences, ideas, and analysis inspired by the readings. Writing is an intensely personal and oftentimes messy process. To believe a student could or should shut out a visceral response limits the potential for intellectual development. Sadly, many teachers only want the perfect student, someone who ironically does not need to be taught. If not in college, where and when do we expect a student to grow?

Modeled after Peter Elbow's pedagogical approaches to writing, I individualized the student's grade and assignment. I asked her to keep an informal or creative journal focused on the readings. In these pages, we would find the most viable topics and develop them into a formal essay. Along with turning in her informal journal (which is not read in detail but scanned) and formal writing, she must include a reflection piece about her writing process. Based upon these writings, it was apparent that for the first time in the writer's life, the literature provided her with a vehicle to convey previously incomprehensible experiences that had overwhelming and unrecognized effects upon her life. As her emotions cleared, so did her writing. More often than not, the students would willingly write two papers, one creative and one analytical.

> *What are the words you do not yet have?*
> *What do you need to say?*
> *What are the tyrannies you swallow day by day*
> *and attempt to make your own,*
> *until you will sicken and die of them, still in silence.*[9]

From paper to paper, the students grew, first struggling to control their ideas, then finding their writerly voices and finally learning how to separate out the personal from the analytical.

Stripped of polite blinders and informed by the literature, what if, along with the survivors, the students and general population became aware of the means, the language by which they could confront the abusers? What would it mean for an island community, one predominately of color, that violence against women would not be tolerated? The oppressed are conditioned to fear freedom and unknowingly maintain a dictum of self-silencing, preventing their liberation. Given the negligible societal and institutional support available to survivors in many communities, changing the legal system, society, or culture seems impossible, and so fear is too often tolerated. It becomes pervasive and overwhelms a culture already held in the grip of a colonial mindset and by its geographic insularity.

In order to make apparent, to concretize something as obtuse as fear, I preface Mirikitani's poems by assigning Audre Lorde's essays, in particular "The Transformation of Silence into Language and Action." Writing a few months after she was diagnosed with breast cancer (a long-taboo subject), Lorde—an African American lesbian poet and activist—confronted old and new fears about speaking out and being seen. She acknowledged her personal "priorities and omissions," which included regretting her "silences. Of what had I *ever* been afraid of."[10] She realized that, ultimately, regardless of social or personal pressures, "Your silence will not protect you."[11] That "[i]n the cause of silence, each of us draws the face of her own fear—fear of contempt, of censure, or some judgment, or recognition, of challenge, of annihilation. But most of all, I think, we fear the visibility without which we cannot truly live."[12] Lorde's articulation of the paradox of fear, that it is simultaneously powerful and mundane, is quite stunning. She takes this a step further and explains that African American women inhabit another deadly paradox: "Within this country, where racial difference creates a constant, if unspoken, distortion of vision, Black women have on one hand been highly visible, and so, on the other hand, have been rendered invisible through the depersonalization of racism."[13]

I then asked my class: What will be lost if they—women of color, an island paradise, and survivors of violence—are no longer silent? What if they make visible the distortions of racial discrimination, colonialism, and abuse? What will be lost? What will be gained? Lorde's article serves as an essential guide to my teaching of Mirikitani's poetry. After linking the works, I give the students the option to write a personal response and/or to delve into the paradox of in/visibility: What is to be gained by being and not being seen?

For survivors of violence, "silence" is a double-edged sword. Understandably, out of mortal fear, some women actively conceal themselves from their abusers. For these women, their greatest enemy is the social climate:

Victims are sent opposing, mixed messages. They are blamed for provoking violence on the one hand, yet chastised for failing to defend themselves and flee on the other. Instead of public outrage, victims of domestic violence routinely encounter silence, indifference and blame.[14]

Fueled by these "mixed messages," and by Hawai'i's weak penal system, the abusers, whose mandatory minimum was as little as forty-eight hours in detention, were able to maintain their control over the survivors and society. I did understand that coupled with this, on an island with limited economic support, running might not be an option. Yet how long is one expected to continue to live in fear before she is caught, either by the abuser or her own psyche? How many women and girls will die at the hands of a family member before someone fights back? What would it take to change the cultural climate, where "letting things go" is no longer tolerated?

If you speak of this,
you will kill your mother.[15]

Controlling the survivors—controlling the literature—is facilitated, "for the good of the community," if they are taught not to make waves. But when those doors close the violence does not end. Instead of prosecuting the offenders, the survivors turn upon themselves or the defenseless. The young abused narrator of Mirikitani's poem "Insect Collection" thinks of the beating wings of the "beetles, / crickets, / butterflies" that she has killed. Like the insects, she too died when she was molested, "I think I hear / butterflies / scream. / He peeled back my skin, / pierced my flesh / with the dull blades / of his hands, slowly pulled off my wings, / impaled me, writhing."[16] All too often, victims become the abusers, and the cycle continues.

As with many of Mirikitani's narrators, one of my students, "Grace," had also maintained her silence and shame.[17] With each passing day, she was dying within and had no language with which to describe her anguish. In a prior class I taught, she struggled, her papers revealing flashes of extremely sharp and critical insights, juxtaposed with the dissonance of uncontrolled torrents of emotion presented in a stream-of-consciousness narrative. Initially I thought her writing problems were due to English being her second language, but that was only part of the story. Then, right before the semester ended, Grace disappeared without completing her final paper. She returned the next year to apologize for having left abruptly. I asked her what had happened, and, looking nervously at the floor, she said she could not tell me, but hoped that I would trust her and allow her to enroll in my current course. I consented.

I, along with the entire class, learned why Grace had left the previous year. When it was her turn to present her analysis of Lorde's articles and Mirikitani's poetry, the once very formal student began by grabbing the edges of the podium and staring down in silence at her notes. After a few moments, she looked up at the ceiling, as if collecting her courage, then finally looked out at the students. She then began in a slightly quavering voice, which grew stronger as she continued to speak, to tell us her story. As the emotional floodgates opened, the class and I sat riveted as she took to heart Lorde's and Mirikitani's messages. One of Lorde's passages remains vivid, as I remember Grace reading, "And I began to recognize a source of power within myself that comes from the knowledge that while it is most desirable not to be afraid, learning to put fear into perspective gave me great strength."[18] Like Lorde, Grace remained silent no longer.

Grace went on ardently, however awkwardly, to explain how she found strength in the readings, particularly because the authors were women of color. She empathized with the authors because they addressed what it was like to be violated, abused, and stereotyped because of the way they looked, because of who they were. She then described how her Asian culture teaches and trains girls to be submissive to male dominance. She acknowledged that being away from her home country, culture, and family enabled her to see how little she knew about human rights and personal dignity. With each self-revelation uttered, her fear melted away, and she wove into her presentation the horrific experiences Korean girls and women—such as the comfort women, who were enslaved for sex by the Japanese Army during World War II— had suffered at the hands of many occupying armies. But the list did not end there; she described how the women suffered at the hands of their own men, and then she revealed that she too had been raped.

As an obedient Asian daughter and proper girl, Grace had not known she could have fought off a trusted family friend. She did not struggle, believing that to do so was not proper; or, she thought, maybe she had led him on—asked for it. Her Asian culture taught her it was her fault, she told the class. She had never heard of the term "date rape," and until she had read Lorde's and Mirikitani's works, she had not known she could say "NO!" She had never read political writings of U.S. women of color, and she now found strength in every word.

In front of the class, Grace transformed. With tears streaming down her face, she no longer called herself a victim, but an activist. She stopped blaming herself and her country, and she defied the men who abused their power and who took away her dignity.

> *They hear. All hear.*
> *The men who assault women hear:*
> *Not tonight.*
> *Our children will not comfort soldiers this night.*
> *Not any night.*[19]

As Grace closed her presentation, she looked into the captivated faces and she asked everyone, especially all the men, to help stop the violence, and said that she too would begin this process. She swore that wherever she ended up after graduation, she would not remain silent. And yet, even as her confidence grew, throughout her presentation and afterward she held her hand over her mouth, would bow slightly, and apologize for her comments and tears. Her inability to stop apologizing exemplified the power of her cultural conditioning of silence and shame. All we could do was to hug her and tell her she was incredibly brave for having shared so much of herself with us.

Silent no more, Grace was not the only one in the class who was transformed by Lorde's and Mirikitani's works. She, however, was the one who brought their words to life. Many of the students—female and male, local, mainland, and international— recognized and acknowledged their responsibility to resist being silently complicit. Her courageous act to speak out set in motion a radical social and personal change, not only for herself but for others. The classroom's walls dissolved as she united and interconnected the literature to herself, the class, and hopefully the world. Not every student will respond this way, but being exposed to this information will at least allow them the opportunity to face a side of human nature that we often choose to ignore. Most importantly, it will show them the resilience and resistance of those who survive. Some students may not want to take such a personal approach; for them, I always allow for more-traditional papers. Similarly, I never force a student to reveal personal information; it is always voluntary. They have the option of not sharing their work with the other students. While I can never be sure how the students will react to the readings or presentations, it is my hope that they leave the class with a broader understanding of society—one that they are able to challenge and critique—and become engaged citizens.

Hiroshima

Vietnam

Tule Lake

And yet we were not devoured.
And yet we were not humbled.
And yet we are not broken.[20]

Violence knows no geographical or emotional boundaries; from date rape to incest, my office hours were filled with endless conversations about the pain, self-mutilation, anger, and healing. The students, the casualities, wanted to stop running, to stop hiding, and to stop being ashamed. As I passed out crisis hotline numbers, I knew that this was not enough. I continued to spend hours talking with these women, making sure they felt safe, making sure they met with professional counselors. Theirs would be a long journey until they, like Grace, an exceptionally brave student, began healing themselves.

We give testimony.
Our noise is dangerous.
We beat our hands
like wings healed.

We soar

from these walls of silence.[21]

As the hours passed and the sky changed from a royal blue to the darkest of night, I sat and thought about that colleague who had come into my office only a few weeks into the semester to try to steer me away from Mirikitani's deceptively slim book of poetry. I wondered how many lives had been silenced, how many souls and minds had been lost, in the pursuit of maintaining the facade of a paradisical community. If that is the world some choose to inhabit, then that is their decision, but it need not be mine. Instead, I choose another path—one where poetry frees the writer and reader, and also liberates the student and teacher.

Invocation

Janice Mirikitani

L ight breaks
Around our faces,
Not bruises—
Clear eyes see ourselves
New, rising up from our bones
Not broken bones
Strong bones dancing
In the music of our words,
In the light
Of broken silence.
We dance
like a samba's birth
in our thighs
powerful as tides,
we rise up and exorcise
demons of violence from our lives.
We are free, a woman
Who feels worthy
Of cold lemonade,
a warm loving man or woman
and a gentle blue sky . . .

When I Lived by the River

Janice Gould

"**F**ucking queer," he said.
   "I ought to beat the shit out of you.
Your kind would be better off dead!"
We were driving around the back woods
in the state of Washington
at night.
It was winter.
The cold stars
shone in the dense sky,
so many stars
in their strange unearthly hues:
purple, magenta, some
the color of honey,
some like blood-red lava.
The snow lay on the meadows,
tranquil pastures
bordered by willows
and dark Douglas fir.

In the car were six of us,
maybe seven,
and a case of beer
half drunk.

I was twenty-one,
the one who delivered
that cold frothy liquid,
placing it in the back seat of the car.

"You almost killed that one guy," said Jeanie.
She was my coworker.
"They found him in a ditch
with his ribs crushed
and his face shoved in."
"Yeah," replied Tom,
"and that's why I can't
cross the state line,
that's why me and Billy
are hiding out
on this side of the river.
Ain't that right, Billy?"
Billy mumbled, gave a sleepy nod.

The river looked ominous,
huge and wide, that green water
full of suckholes so large
they could swallow a car
if you were unlucky enough
to skid off the road
on the black ice.
You'd plunge
through the guardrails,
the willows, the patterns of ice
that had formed on the chilly
lip of the river.

I wondered if the boys were lying.
Not six hours before
all of us had gone to a tavern
on the south end of town—
we were in Oregon, across the river—
and shared at least
two pitchers.
It was after work,
after the long shift
in the fishing-lure factory
where all that snowy afternoon
we women assembled
L'il Chief Smokers.

At work it was me, Jeanie,
Dee, and the others:
the old woman who smelled bad,
the mother-daughter teams,
the sexy redhead,
the quiet little blonde
with the pink parka.
And of course there were Okies—
that's what the redhead called them—
a girl who lived in a Quonset hut
in the muddy apple orchard,
a woman who lived at the south end
of the green Hood River valley.
One day she'd said to me,
"Aren't you an Indian?
You look like my relatives
in Oklahoma.
Just like," she said.

And she mused on my features
till I got embarrassed.
She was pretty, a loner.
I was afraid
I'd fall for her.

Earlier, at the tavern,
I was squeezed behind the table
with Jeanie on one side
and a wall on the other.
And Tom, or Billy,
or whoever,
was already bleary-eyed,
muttering to himself,
viciously berating Jeanie
in a monotonous chant:
"Cunt, cunt, cunt, cunt!"
"Stop that!" said Jeanie.
"Don't call me that."
"You shit," she said.
"Who do you think you are?"
He just kept chanting,
his lips turned down
like a fish's mouth.

"Don't worry," said Jeanie—
this was much later—
"he won't beat you.
He's too drunk."
I remember they had made love,
her and Tom,
in her apartment.

We'd gone there after the tavern
to continue our drinking.
I was dozing in front of the TV
when I was awakened
by Tom's fierce grunts
and Jeanie moaning, writhing so hard
her wig popped off her head.
A wig! I was surprised. I thought
I'd never seen anything
less romantic.

Again in the car
somewhere back of the river,
on a ridge above the woods
and frozen meadows,
we turned towards town,
headed back towards the river.
"I will too beat her up,"
said Tom, "soon as I find a place
to pull over.
I'll beat the shit
out of her,
fucking little queer,
thinks she's some kind of man!"

"Just let him talk," whispered Jeanie.
"Don't answer.
It's all just talk."

And pretty soon he shut up.
For a time we were silent
driving through the wild

lonely night
with snow all around,
the stars gleaming like amber.
I wanted to go home,
back to my solitary existence.

Finally on the highway,
near the lane near my trailer,
Tom stopped the car, and,
almost courteously,
let me out by the side of the road.
Then off they sped,
without a word.

I stood for a moment,
wavering. A mist
had formed along the river,
had rolled up over the highway,
the pastures.
I wanted to walk into it,
to walk forever.
I wanted to disappear.

Fire

Sharline Chiang

Fire. An ocean of fire, a forest of fire.
Flames so hot and close
I can hear them calling out to me
like the voices of children begging me to play.
Wake up. Wake up.
I wake up. Outside it looks like daylight but it's only 1:00 AM
It's Mischief Night. 1980. New Jersey.
I am ten.

My parents never liked Mischief Night. They didn't understand it. Every year, the night before Halloween, kids covered trees with toilet paper and smeared car windows with soap and shaving cream. I always looked forward to waking up in the morning, like waking up to the remnants of an all-night fiesta, toilet paper flapping like party streamers, like crazed voyagers on a cruise ship, waving farewell.

As the fire rages I am still stirring from the kind of dream
I will never quite have again—
A dream of spinning around in a
Snow White costume,
the sticky clay taste of lipstick on my lips,
and pillow sacks full of B-B Bats, Mary Janes,
and Pixie Sticks.

I was always so excited before Halloween that it was hard to fall asleep. Halloween was my favorite holiday, because it didn't belong to anyone. It wasn't like Christmas or Easter, which my parents said really belonged to Christians, which we weren't. It wasn't like Thanksgiving, which they said belonged to real Americans, which apparently we also weren't. But mostly we didn't celebrate Thanksgiving because my mother thought turkey was a total waste of money, the world's most worthless meat.

"So *gan*. That's why they make gravy, to mask the dryness and the no-flavor," she always said. "We Chinese would never try to get away with that. That's not cooking. That's cheating."

Halloween was a time for all kids. For one day I could be anything I wanted.

Almost everyone in my class that year said they were too old to dress up and go trick-or-treating, but I was going anyway. *So what if they see me and make fun of me,* I thought. They already do. Halloween fell on a Saturday, and that meant I had the whole day to get candy, which I recognized as a once-in-a-lifetime opportunity. Besides, trick-or-treating was a special ritual for me and my father, even though I was starting to feel too old to go out with him, where all the other kids in the neighborhood could see us together—see my father dancing his funny dance in the street, see him holding my hand.

The week before, my mother and I had worked on my witch costume. She cut up a piece of black fabric and turned it into a cape. My father made a tall hat for me out of stiff construction paper and glued it together with a special paste he made from rice. I was so excited to wear it. On Halloween morning, my mother was going to draw scary green lines all over my face. I could hardly wait.

> *When my mother starts screaming,*
> *"The trees are on fire!"*
> *I think she must be talking to herself*
> *in her sleep.*

Even though she was so short that from the back she looked like a little girl (I was almost taller than her), my mother's voice could pierce through the house, cutting like a light saber. That night I heard something I wasn't used to hearing in her voice—fear—a shaky, verge-of-tears sound in the voice of a woman I thought feared nothing. My father flung open the bedroom door, eyes wide, bewildered, his thick black hair sticking up at all angles like antennae. He mumbled, *"Okay, okay,"* grabbed his robe, and ran out.

My eyelids were still heavy and sticky with sleep. *Fire? Where?* It didn't make any sense. Outside my window, edges of flames illuminated my dresser in the corner. The soft glow brightened, casting flickering streaks of gold across my ceiling, onto the bright blue rug, my sad-faced harlequin poster, my white canopy bed, my pink Holly Hobby duvet, my stuffed unicorn with the purple velvet collar. On the other side of the wall, the fire lit up my parents' bedroom like a lantern. I could hear our dog Charlie outside barking loudly. My breath quickened. I wasn't dreaming anymore.

A loud squeak of brass on brass echoed beneath the floorboards, making the hair on my arms stand up. My father was frantically opening the valve of the garden hose on the front lawn. I already knew that the hose would not be long enough.

I stepped outside and felt my skin tighten against the crisp, clean air. A few stars quivered in the black sky like children huddling together for warmth. I could smell the salty ocean mist of Sandy Hook Bay wafting in with the tide. My breath floated in tiny white puffs. I stepped gingerly as the rough gravel on the street scratched my bare feet. The entire line of pine trees on the side of our house was ablaze. The heat from the flames warmed my skin; my cheeks started to burn. A breeze stirred, filling the air with the smell of roasting pine needles.

> From the neighbor's yard I watch flames lick the sky.
> My mother stands quiet and pale with her hands on her thin hips.
> The earth feels cold and wet on my feet.

"Xiao Lin, don't stand so close," my mother said to me in Chinese, pushing me away. "Go over there."

I watched from our neighbor George's sticky asphalt driveway. A gust of wind brushed up against my neck. I shivered. George, who had already called the fire department, was pounding at the flames in a bed of rust-colored needles with a heavy shovel. I barely recognized him without his fuzzy toupee on. He seemed angry, maybe because he already knew what we didn't: that this was no accident.

My mother stared hard at the fire, assessing the situation with her small, hard eyes, so shiny they looked metallic. Her pajama top was missing a top button, and it flapped open in the draft.

"Aim higher! You'll never get it that way. Do it this way," she shouted at my father. She waved her hands up and down, left to right, as if she were writing Chinese with a giant calligraphy brush. I knew how much she loved those trees. They were one of the main reasons she had decided to buy that house—our first home—when we moved out of the Newark projects four years earlier.

My father whipped the hose around. Water spewed out in a steep arc, but it couldn't reach the flames that were inching toward the treetops, lapping at the roof, the telephone wires. Pinecones hissed, popped, and then exploded, spraying shards of cones and seeds everywhere like brown confetti. He grabbed another shovel as my mother took over the hose. She shook her head.

"Maybe someone was smoking a cigarette and accidentally got careless," she said.

Slowly the lights of each house on Lonely Oak Road flickered on. Neighbors stepped out to watch, cupping hands over mouths, wondering out loud if the Chinese family's fire would travel to their homes. From windows and lawns, paper and plastic witches, scarecrows, zombies, Frankensteins, and mummies seemed to watch too—a long line of mute, immobile witnesses.

My eyes watered from the smoke. I could taste the melting resin from the pinecones, a bitterness that made my mouth pucker and my nose burn.

> *I will remember the rich smell of crackling pine needles.*
> *I will remember thinking*
> *This is the most beautiful thing I've ever seen,*
> *as I listen to the rhythm of a shovel*
> *and my father's breath*
> *beating back the fire.*

The flames danced faster, soared higher. My father was no match for this beauty. He was sweating; his calloused and scarred hands gripped tightly around the shovel's wooden handle. A light stubble mottled his face like black sand. He licked his lips, the skin over his throat pulsating with fear. His dark eyes widened. Embers fell softly from above, burning holes into the pockets of his green flannel robe. The tips of his hair, always styled in an Elvis pompadour, singed into white powder, the raw acrid smell mingling with the smoke. To cool down and work faster, he had peeled off his robe. I was embarrassed that people could see him in his sagging white underwear and BVD undershirt covered in soy sauce and other cooking stains. My father, who usually looked so tall and strong to me, seemed small and weak. I wanted him to look tougher, to put out the fire and show everyone that he could be a hero.

Sirens wailed. A fire engine screamed toward our house, splashing red light across the front of every yard. An American flag waved from its hood. I had never seen a fire truck on our street before. It almost felt like an honor. A few kids gathered outside and their parents urged them back into their homes. I felt so grateful that the firemen had arrived so quickly. They were so alert, awake. Stomping the ground with their heavy boots, they surrounded the back yard, yelling out for more hose, more water.

Finally, the fire was out. All that was left behind was a soggy, steaming mess. The trees looked like sad black skeletons, water dripping like rain from their limbs.

My mother thanked the firefighters, patted them on the back as if they were boys who just helped shovel the snow. My father smiled and shook their hands, his lungs still wheezing from the smoke. One fireman rooted through the area one last time. He stepped out with something white in his hands and showed it to my parents. It was a roll of toilet paper.

"There were probably more like this one. It was soaked in gasoline," the man said.

> Last week the boys at school chased me home again.
> "Go home, Chink. Go back to China," they said.
> But I've never been to China.

I could tell that my parents were surprised to see this mushy white ball; it looked so harmless.

The next day, my parents told me that it was all an accident, a prank gone wrong.

For a long time, I believed them. I ignored the voice inside my head that said: "You already knew that being Chinese could get you hurt at school. Now you know it can hurt you at home too. They can hurt you, not just you, but your mother and father as well."

> When it is over, our back yard is completely exposed.
> The sunlight now
> shines through my window
> where the trees once stood.

Three Curses

Yvonne S. Lee

I decided to write this story as a way of embracing my family history and as a way of acknowledging its importance to my own identity. As I entered adulthood, I realized how important my Korean heritage is. Unfortunately, distance and cultural misunderstandings prevented me from questioning my grandparents about their lives before they died. I regret not recording their stories on tape. I know very little about them, especially on my mother's side. My maternal grandmother graduated from the prestigious Ei-hwa women's university in Seoul. It was founded by Christian missionaries. My maternal grandfather went to a university in Tokyo—a product of the Japanese occupation. He got a master's degree in sociology from Boston University, which allowed him to bring his family to the United States. The story centers on the paternal side of my family, because through my father's stories, I have more knowledge about them.

This story is not a memoir, but incorporates events from my childhood and family history. Fog is a theme, because much of the information I have about my family is fuzzy and unclear. Many of the holes in my history come from my mother. Either she was too traumatized by her childhood to remember, or she has made a conscious decision to leave the past behind. Most of the knowledge I have about her comes from relatives or from spontaneous recollections of her youth. The part in the story where the family burns pine needles comes from one of those outbursts. My mother and I were hiking at Stone Mountain Park, in Atlanta. The ground was covered with pine needles. My mother said that during the war, many families were camped out in the back yard of their home. She said they used to burn pine needles to make fires. I didn't learn until I lived in Seoul for three months that my mother was a very accomplished pianist. Her aunt told me that she

250

was written about in newspapers, and that she had graduated valedictorian in her major from Yonsei University, considered the Yale of Korea.

I fictionalized parts of the story where I had no details about the events that took place. For example, I knew that my father's family had escaped to Manchuria, but I don't know exactly what was said and done during the journey. My father was born in Manchuria on December 21, 1941, during the Japanese occupation. He was fed rice water instead of milk, because his mother was sick when he was born. My father recently told me that his great-grandmother is buried there, in Manchuria. She died before he was born. It is also true that she had been considered to be a powerful *mudang* in her village in Korea. My paternal grandmother, according to my father, was very superstitious. He said that she predicted three tragedies would occur in 1978. Two of them came true: My baby brother died, and she herself died later that year from lung cancer. While my mother was in labor, my father became sick with pneumonia. He sat in the hospital waiting room, sweating profusely, barely able to keep his head upright; meanwhile, the nurses taunted him, telling him his baby would have "slanty eyes." Had my father died, his death would have been the third tragedy my grandmother predicted.

My father told these stories to us matter-of-factly, as he did the horrors of the Korean War. I obviously don't have exact quotes from these nurses or the doctor. All the quotes in this story are made up, more of what I imagined they said. Other parts of the story come from events in my father's childhood, like the water drills, and being put in the cellar so the lepers wouldn't get him. As far as I know, none of his aunts were taken as comfort women. That part was added as a nod to the brutal history of the Japanese occupation.

When I was younger, my father would constantly tell us stories about the Korean War and his childhood. We were resistant to those stories, because they made us uncomfortable, and we wanted independence from the long and laborious way he would narrate these tales. As I entered adulthood, the stories stopped. I found that I missed them. I started to become interested in my family history as a way of discovering my own identity. The more I asked about my father's circumstances during his childhood, the less willing he became to share them. At times he couldn't help himself. Telling stories is part of who my father is. From the time he was a teenager, saying the elegant prayers I mention in my story, to the time of his ordination as a minister, he has always had the gift of speech.

Growing up Christian was painful. I constantly rebelled against the patriarchy and manipulation of the Korean church. The first time I felt a sense of loss over the Buddhist faith that was abandoned by both sides of my family is when I read a play by Henry David Hwang, where the main character talks about the faces of his ancestors, and how they were Asian, not white. I always felt alienated from the "white" Jesus, as depicted in most paintings of him. Korea has embraced Christianity in way that is unique from other nations. Other Koreans did some of the original proselytizing. In the 19th century, Christians were persecuted and tortured, which is why I added the part about a great-uncle who was burned to death. This didn't actually happen to my family, but it certainly did to many people. South Korea is now home to the largest Presbyterian church in the world. The zealousness by which this religion has been embraced disturbs me at times. I am afraid that thousands of years of history are being pushed aside in favor of Western traditions. Most of my family remains Christian, except for myself and cousins on my father's side.

Finally, some of the other events, such as the meeting about Korean immigration, are taken from events in my life. I had a friend in Atlanta who attended a meeting organized by the late black council member Hosea Williams in the late 1980s. The comments that "Koreans smell like onions" and "Why should a Korean drive a better car than me" were actually said. I remember feeling enraged and frustrated by the lack of understanding between the two communities. I added the incident as a way of showing how many immigrants, including my father, struggled to assimilate in the United States.

The First Curse

Ahnee Lee was four when her grandmother said three curses would befall their family that year. Wavy black hair topped her solid, graceful body, but weak, wispy roots struggled to find a place to anchor themselves in the white fog that surrounded her. Silence was the only history she knew. Her family's past was a mist that covered her with choking moisture. It granted no stories to water her parched skin. She felt like a ghost wandering the halls of Queens Hospital in Culver City, California. All she could see through the mist were nurses in white uniforms walking in wide arcs around her family. They seemed to be afraid of something, their round eyes glaring at them as they whispered.

"Look at those slanty eyes. That baby is going to have slits stretched from ear to ear."

Ahnee's mom had just given birth to their family legacy . . . the twentieth son of the last great general of the Lee Dynasty. The nineteenth was her father, who survived starvation, the Japanese occupation, the insult of being born in Manchuria, and the years of exile from his Korean homeland. The baby lived two days. The white doctor had waited too long. Four days of labor following the water break did not concern him.

"Maybe Chinese babies like to break the dam and crawl back in their holes. They are yellow-bellied, after all," the doctor chuckled.

Ahnee's mother nearly bled to death from the delivery, her red blood staining crisp, white sheets. Ahnee was left in her mother's room while the family huddled over the baby's incubator. Her mother looked beautiful, achieving the paleness she so often imitated with Covergirl Transparent foundation. Ahnee got close to her face, gently touching the epicanthic folds that creased her mother's lids. She desperately wished she were born with those folds so her eyes would be rounder, and she would be pretty.

No one asked about her mother after the newborn, James Jr., died. The family wailed and screamed as they buried their faces in the purple body. They were beating their chests with closed fists, keeping the nurses from taking the body.

"They sound like goddamn animals," a nurse said. "Those crazy chinks."

Grandma Lee had warned that six hundred years of family history would die if they left Kwangju for America. She said their ancestors would punish them for converting to the white man's faith. Ahnee's father began this chain of events when he converted to Catholicism. He latched onto the missionaries from America as surely as he took gum from their soldiers. The first curse had arrived. A six-pound, five-ounce baby boy—who looked exactly like Ahnee's elder sister, Vera—sputtered into hostile territory, and died.

Ahnee's parents had picked Vera's name carefully, poring over Latin books, looking for a name befitting a firstborn.

"Truth," her father said. "She will be called Truth."

Ahnee was an afterthought. Born slimy in red afterbirth, nothing between her legs, she was given a name without meaning, a word that literally translates in Korean to as "no, or nothing, or nothingness."

The death of James Jr. left a void so big that Ahnee's father fell in it and never reappeared to love them. The twentieth heir took her father's spirit with him, the great general's legacy going into the grave with its last and final son. Women were all that remained.

The spirit of Ahnee's great-grandmother was so strong that she stirred inside the forgotten one. She was a powerful shaman, or *mudang* in a village in Kwangju. Her power would draw men to her, heads bowed, asking for a chant to bring good crops. Every person in the village feared her, revered her. She wore a simple white headcloth, and a white *hanbok,* the color of death, every day. She was mourning the loss of land to the island invaders, the loss of language to the Japanese tongue, the loss of purity to the savage samurai rapes.

She ended her days in a foreign land making food for Chinese bachelors who were so desperate for sex that they looked hungrily at her aging body. She was buried in Manchuria. All her powers and love for Korea were unable to bring her home to the land she'd caressed and loved with brittle hands since childhood.

Great-grandmother Chu married Soo Hwang Lee when she was sixteen and he was nine. The spring harvest was coming, and the family needed labor. She was content to marry as a first wife into a good family. She didn't lie with Great-grandfather until he was fourteen. Until then, she entered the earth, split it with her bare hands, wet it with her spit, fertilized it with her shit, and banged it into submission, until her fields were the shiniest, wettest rice paddies in the entire village.

Soo Hwang was fourteen when he realized that he must put his seeds into her body to produce an heir. He grabbed her in the fields as she was bending over tiny stalks, her backside a round, white mound. She fought him in the stagnant water, ruining hundreds of rice stalks, their rootlets too short to hold on to the dirt. Grandmother Chu grabbed fistfuls of stems, trying to pull herself away from him, as he fell on top of her.

His seeds entered unwelcome terrain, a passage so hot with fury that it almost melted his progeny. After repeated violations in the fields, Soo Hwang's seeds reached their destination, and the eighteenth heir was secured. It was 1901, before the island people who burned its proud legacies defiled the hermit kingdom, noble in its solitude. These silk-covered books encompassed hundreds of years of family histories, knowledge as necessary to the honor of an individual family as to an entire nation.

The Second Curse

Ahnee's father was born in Manchuria in 1941. He was named Young Gwang, or "Glory," because everyone knew he would be great someday. The nineteenth heir was fed rice water instead of milk from his sickly mother, Young Ju. She had traveled while pregnant through the mountains of North Korea, determined for her child to speak Korean, not the clipped grunts of Japanese. He would call her *um-mah,* and she would coo to him *oo-rhee-ehh-gee,* "our baby."

Great-grandmother Chu made the journey with them, tied to the eighteenth heir's back with blankets. She was leaking black bile from her lips, her sides as swollen as her daughter-in-law's belly. Years of eating rations of saccharin handed out by Japanese soldiers had corrupted her stomach. She never got used to the bitter residue left on the beef they seasoned with it, mixing it with more soy sauce than usual to mask the insincere taste.

She didn't want to die in China. Worse was the thought of dying alone, without her family to mourn over her. She convulsed at the thought of being used for medical experiments by visiting doctors, eager to point out the doglike features of Korean women.

Young Gwang's mother was afraid for her child. She had seen lepers in their village—skin blistered by bloody lesions—chase small children into the woods. They were never seen again. Remnants of their bodies were left in smoking pits of fire. The lepers, said *mudangdul* like Great-grandmother Chu, thought that the organs of pure children would drive the evil blackness from their bodies, and ate their hearts, lungs, and livers. Young Ju fled these lepers as sure as she fled the island invaders.

She was tired of oppressors in her land. The white missionaries didn't understand their customs or beliefs. They were responsible for filling the souls of the weak with visions of a white god, draped in white robes, living on a shining white city on the hill. They were the color of death. She watched how her Christian brother was captured by soldiers and forced to walk on nails. He spent that evening in jail, blessing fellow prisoners with a white cloth, touching their heads, and saying "Glory to God." She watched as he was tied to a chair, ropes twisted around his legs and burning through flesh, as guards pulled them back and forth like a knife sharpening on stone. They didn't stop until the ropes touched bones. He screamed and begged for Jesus to save him. But she knew a white god would never hear him. She watched as Catholics were beheaded, their heads stacked like pyramids before Buddha's belly. She watched as the faces of ancestors rose above the burning body of her brother, telling him only they heard his prayers.

Young Ju would never forget her ancestors, never forget the land that filled her with so much pride. In any other country, she was a nobody, a foreign invader like those she despised so much. As she crossed the bridge into China, she vowed that if she ever returned to Korea, she would never leave.

The family walked all the way to Manchuria. Along the way, they ate grass, shaped into patties and fried with black beetles. The precious rice was saved for Great-grandmother Chu. It was cooked for hours until it was burned on the bottom. The crunchy husks were stirred in to make a soupy *jook*. Her son Dae Young cradled her head as he spoon-fed her the precious mixture. The black bile continued to ooze out, even as she slept.

The family stopped when they saw purple smoke rising in the distance. Great-grandmother said it was a sign from the spirits, telling them to stop. The Japanese soldiers burned villages, killing everyone who lived there, taking only young women to comfort the soldiers at night.

Young Ju's sisters had been taken while they were doing a water drill at the well. The soldiers ordered the women into line and told them to pass buckets from the well to a waiting jeep. The commander walked up and down the line, pulling every girl under seventeen into the jeep. He stripped off their aprons and headscarves. The mothers who screamed and pulled on their daughters were stabbed with bayonets. The commander took a five-year-old girl and ripped her bloomers off. He unzipped his pants and tried to push himself into her, but her small body would not yield. So he took out a curved sword, and cut her from vagina to rectum. She died while he violently entered into her body, blood spurting onto his pants.

The family crept into the woods to set up camp under a grove of pine trees. They used the fallen needles to make a weak fire. In the morning, Young Ju went into labor. She grabbed at the loose pine needles while she screamed. Great-grandmother chanted to their ancestors on her son's back, flicking a white cloth up and down as they walked in a circle. After two days, Ahnee's father slid out onto the loose, shifting ground. The twentieth heir did not cry, but whimpered.

Great-grandmother had allowed her eldest son to marry Young Ju after examining her hands. She was no great beauty—skinny eyes, bowed legs, and tanned skin. But on her hand she bore the mark of a *mudang*. Five intersecting lines making an M on her palm. She wouldn't be powerful like Great-grandmother, but would have the gift of second sight. The mark on her left hand would leave her with a stifling superstition, believing to the end that their family is doomed.

In 1978, the year of the three curses, Young Ju had a dream about a young woman whose husband was so ill she became desperate for a cure. Only ginseng, found at the highest point of Mount Kumgangsan, would save him. Ghosts haunted the mountain. No one who climbed the mountain ever returned. If her husband died, they would starve. So she strapped her baby boy to her back with a sheet, took a sword for protection, and started climbing the mountain. Her terror at hearing the howling ghosts paralyzed her limbs. She felt as if a demon were squeezing the breath out of her lungs. Several times, the woman fainted and woke to find that she could not move. Fully conscious, she would try to get up, but felt a weight on her chest so strong that she would stop breathing. When she reached the final passage before the peak, the fog began to encircle her like a tornado. The howling grew louder and turned into screams. She grabbed the sword and began swirling it around her in wild panic. Around and around, slicing anything that was solid. She heard a scream and felt something fall to the ground. The screams were gone. She looked around and saw her baby's head on the ground.

Young Ju knew that this dream was about her. She was going to die. Her son, Ahnee's father, told his mother she should pray, that her dreams were punishments for not accepting Jesus into her heart.

"Satan is powerful *um-mah,*" he said. "If you die without God, you will burn in hell forever. The fear that you felt, you will feel for all eternity. That is what you should learn from that dream."

It only took two months for Young Gwang to see his mother had been right. The cold he thought was responsible for her coughing turned into bloody phlegm. X-rays showed a dark mass that looked like swirling fog in her right lung. She refused surgery to remove it and spent her last days sleeping with oxygen canisters tied to the bed. While she lay dying, she remembered the hunger that stabbed her during the war, like the breaths that were piercing her chest now. She used to pick up the packets of cigarettes the American GIs threw at them. "Smoke 'em if you got 'em," they would yell. She found that smoking quelled her raging hunger. It became a comfort to her, after her sisters were gone, after her country was split in two like the girl at the water drill. It made her forget the family she would never see again above the 38th parallel, her memories too painful to fill with anything but the white-hot smoke.

The Third Curse

Young Gwang buried his son in March, and now he was burying his mother. He tied a white scarf around his forehead and fell to the ground.

"*Um-mahhhh,*" he cried, thinking about the breasts he never got to suckle. If mother had nursed him, she would have given him some of her strength. Instead, he was a small, weak man, constantly sick from headaches and stomach pains.

"*Joo-Yoh,*" he called to God.

He knew that she was not with his Lord. She never accepted Him. Even as the priest wove a rosary through her fingers, he knew it was too late. He approached the coffin in a black suit, relatives staring openly at his disrespect. All five hundred mourners were dressed in white, a sign of the fear she enforced in all who knew her. Young Gwang looked at the black hair she had been so proud of in her youth. It was a luminous blue-black, so thick she could loop elastic around it only once. During the war, she sold her hair for $30 and a pack of cigarettes. She would never grow it long again. After moving to Los Angeles, she kept a perpetual perm. The tight little curls were dyed black for the funeral.

Mother had always been his protector. When she was called to water drills in their village, she would place him in the cellar. It was full of pickled cabbage, cucumbers, salted pork soaking in sesame oil, eggs floating in jars of vinegar and soy sauce. If she didn't come back from the water drill and became a "Japanese whore" like his aunts, he would have enough to live until winter, when the water froze and the drills stopped.

Young Gwang used to sneak out of the cellar when the house was quiet. He was afraid of the lepers but had never seen one and wanted desperately to know if they really had black skin. One Friday, after a hot, tiring week of school, Young Gwang was thrust into the cellar upon returning home.

"No *um-mah!*" he said. "I want to swim today. Please, it's so hot."

He let his rear fall to the ground, crouching in a *kimchee* squat. Village elders would make this pickled cabbage with knees spread wide over their feet, butts on their heels. It was an indelicate pose, more disposed to giving birth, but it allowed them to work all day without losing feeling in the legs.

"Stop fooling around, you animal!" Mother yelled. "The foreign doctors are here. The lepers will be seen rounded up. Do you want them to eat you?"

He watched through a crack in the door as she put on her white apron, blue cotton dress, and nurse's hat. The foreign governor thought that a shaman should learn how to practice real medicine and ordered her to work in the infirmary. He tried to be good, but thought he would go crazy inside the dark cellar. So he snuck out. He started hopping on the road singing, "Hill bunny, bunny-one. Where are you coming from?" The road was quiet and empty, no bicyclers or women on porches. He looked behind him and saw a group of people, noses gone, bloody blackened stubs for fingers. They were walking toward him, chained together, and led by his mother. He screamed and ran back to the house. Never again did he sneak out of the cellar.

Mother wasn't always his protector; she was also his tormentor. Young Gwang often wet his bed. If mother found out, he was forced to remain in the soiled underwear and beg for salt. Begging for salt was a traditional form of punishment for wetting your bed. With his head bowed, he would go to their neighbors, holding a bowl out in front of him. They would laugh and throw salt in his face.

"Oh the little baby is still wetting his bed?" they said. "What a shame you are to your parents."

On his twelfth birthday, Young Gwang thought he had conquered this weakness. But he awoke to find a sticky wetness clinging to his skin. Mother found him examining this substance when she walked into his room. Instead of salt, she poured scalding water in the bowl and threw it over his head. The blisters that formed never truly healed. Every summer, he would get heat sores on his scalp, exactly where she had burned him. When he was older, his daughter Ahnee would rub aloe on the itchy scabs, always wondering why there were so many.

Young Gwang wanted to escape mother's cruelty. Every other relative treated him like a prince, even grandfather's second wife. Only mother didn't love him. He despised her superstitions. She predicted that he would be nobody, that he would eventually betray her. So when the Catholic mission came to Kwangju, he embraced their community. Father Thomas told him what a charismatic speaker he was, "a miniature Pope Pius XII."

Young Gwang was baptized and given the name James. He especially liked the "Amens" that were shouted when he said an eloquent prayer.

"Heavenly Father, you are the way, the truth, and the light," he said. "Your mercy instills us with a purity that cleanses our hearts from Satan's evil darkness."

He wasn't sure he believed in God, but he felt a spiritual high when he saw the girls looking up at him as he led Bible study. It wasn't hard for him to prostrate himself before the cross and convert when he turned sixteen. Young Gwang's mother remembered her brother—how he turned his back on Korea and their traditions and became a pawn for the white man. She said their ancestors would punish them all for his trespass.

"Your God was made in the white man's image," she said. "He sees us as he sees an insect, just part of the landscape he created for his chosen ones. He will forsake you, just as he did my brother."

Young Gwang's yearning for acceptance from his mother didn't end. It just transferred to the church. In this too, he would remain unfulfilled. His life became an addict's hunt for spiritual highs. After his conversion, he was convinced that to truly serve God, he had to move to America. In the midst of a Christian nation, he would surely be loved unconditionally.

All the favoritism he received from their relatives did not prepare him for the hatred he encountered upon arriving to California. Only five thousand Koreans were living there in 1969. Endless white faces taunted him and told him to "Go back to yer own country!"

While looking for a job, he saw a flyer for a meeting about the problem of Korean immigration. He thought he could use his elegant speaking skills to convince his neighbors they were all brothers in Christ. He introduced himself as James.

"Well, Jaaaames. Koreans smell like onions," a black council member said. "They come here and take money from *our* government and open businesses in our hood. Why should a slanty-eyed, noodle-eatin', yellow nigger gook drive a better car than me?"

James rushed out of the meeting feeling light-headed and drunk with anger. They were no better than the Japanese.

"Ignorant savages!" he yelled.

He could not go back to Korea. He left illegally on an expired passport, with a limited visa to the United States. He borrowed money from relatives who were certain he would find greatness in America. He traveled alone to Central America—Costa Rica and Nicaragua—to try to renew his visa to the United States. Everyone but his mother wept when he got on the plane.

His salvation came when he found a Korean church in Long Beach. The pastor noticed his powerful voice and asked him to lead hymns on Sunday. Eventually, he was promoted to choir director, and met Ahnee's mother, Jin Myung Kim. She accompanied the singers on piano, having trained at the prestigious Yonsei University in Seoul.

They became engaged after only a month. Jin Myung made James feel needed. She went to him for counseling about her father. He was an embarrassment to her, constantly standing up in church and arguing with the pastor. He would dig in garbage for cans and take them in a wheelbarrow for redemption at Ralph's grocery store. They didn't need the money. Her father was studying for his PhD at UCLA. He used to dig in garbage cans, covering his arms in filth just so he could get extra change, which he would then give to beggars. She hated him for bringing them to Los Angeles. Jin Myung had imagined a city bigger than Seoul, with lovers dancing in the streets and concert halls filled with clapping at her energetic piano playing. Instead, she found a sprawling, concrete desert without sidewalks or cafés, so unlike the neon lights and crowded intimacy of Seoul. Meeting James gave her hope that she could escape from the gray sky and desiccated brown canyons.

James felt he couldn't have found a better wife. She was educated and came from a distinguished Pusan family that had been Christian for two generations. Her naiveté about the evils of the world made her seem pure.

"James, father walked into the room without pants on," she said. "Can you imagine anything worse than that? I have endured so much suffering because of him."

Innocence gave way to bewilderment the first time he yelled at her after they married. She had never been addressed with such abuse before, having been raised by parents who didn't believe in striking children.

"You can't do anything for yourself!" James screamed. "I feel like I'm taking care of a child. If I knew what a burden you would be, I would have never married you, stupid woman. You can't even cook!"

When their first child, Vera, was born in 1972, he vowed to change, holding her as tightly as the baby chicks he found when he was five. The chicks suffocated to death, but Vera just looked into his eyes and gurgled. It took a week for him to break his promise. He stood over her crib yelling at her to stop crying. He shoved a finger in her mouth, threatening to sew it shut. Jin Myung moved to her mother's house for the summer, returning when she discovered she was pregnant again.

On Halloween night, she was busy giving candy to trick-or-treaters when the contractions started. "Oh God, don't let her be born on Halloween!" she prayed. Ahnee was born at 2:00 AM on November 1. She was burning hot, missing the devil's holiday by only two hours, and had to be thrown into ice water immediately. The baby wailed in agony, and Jin Myung thought she would die of heartbreak. But Ahnee would turn out to be the strongest of them all, the icy water unable to drive her great-grandmother's spirit from her body.

Young Gwang was disappointed at having a second daughter. He didn't have money or prestige, but at least he could try to be responsible for continuing the family line. Everyone would understand if he returned to Korea because he wanted to raise his son there. No one would look at him as a failure.

He was careful not to upset his wife when she became pregnant again. He watched as Ahnee pushed hard against her mother's stomach, playing patty cake on the growing belly. When James Jr. died, he blamed Ahnee for hurting the baby with her games.

"You were jealous of him," he said. "So you hurt him on purpose. You wanted him to die, you son of a bitch. I hope you die instead. We never wanted you. You were supposed to be a son. Your evil spirit took his life."

That fall, Young Gwang become ill with pneumonia, and he was certain the second curse had arrived. Ahnee wasn't allowed to visit him in the hospital. She looked too much like his mother's reproachful face. His elder sisters brought him *jook* and ginseng tea. The nurses cringed when they gave him a sponge bath, staring at his hairless chest. He had no purpose in life. Raising girls was not worth his effort. He begged God to take him away from this hell.

"Lord, I don't deserve this," he prayed. "I am your suffering servant. I don't deserve the life I've had. Please take me to my son."

God didn't grant his wish. He bit the pillow when the fever broke and sobbed. Ahnee came to him at the hospital and placed her small hand on his face.

"It's okay, Daddy," she said. "Grandma told me that I will carry the family name. She said I am a *mudang* like her. I won't ever change my last name. I promise."

He slapped her.

"*Mudang* are evil," he said. "Your grandmother's superstitions are evil. And you are evil."

Mother told him at the hospital that two more curses would come to pass that year: her own death and his.

"*Um-mah.* I'm still alive. There are no curses," he said. "What do you mean only two more curses will come to pass? Nothing has happened!"

James believed his mother's sorcery was evil and somehow caused the tragedies in their family in 1978. So when she died, he thought the curses would end with her, even though one more curse had yet to be fulfilled.

At the funeral, he touched his mother's hands, and was surprised by their frigid coldness. She left him knowing that he had failed her. The difficult birth of his only son had left his wife barren. He could not take a second wife here. No one would have him. No one cares about the honor of marrying a firstborn son, especially if he is a "yellow monkey," as the customers in his grocery store would call him. No one wants a man who is so poor he has to buy makeup for his wife at Pick and Save. The Kwangju Lees would die with him, a son unworthy to end their legacy. He watched mourners lay white carnations on her coffin, and wished he had died with his son, realizing only then that the third curse his mother predicted is that he lives.

The Rape of an Obstinate Woman: Frantz Fanon's Wretched of the Earth

Tiffany Willoughby-Herard

Preface

Given what we know about the status of women in Algeria since the 1984 Family Code Act has been enacted;[1] given what we know about the role of the National Liberation Front (FLN) in trying to hold onto power unsuccessfully against the Islamic Salvation Front (FIS) by coopting their deployment of religious orthodoxy;[2] given what we know of the disastrous impact of economic development strategies that have since 1830 deployed female identity in various ways; given what we know about the way women in the Arab world, Muslim world, Africa, South Asia, and the rest of the Third World have reworked the veil yet again to inspire feminist anticolonialist revolt;[3] given the profound level of Islamaphobia marketed in global consumer culture that encourages United States and British women to wear bindis, saris, and burkas while their "sisters" in the rest of the world must be read as enslaved for the same things: I would like to focus my remarks on the haunting spectral voice of the obstinate woman, Case 1 of Series A, in Frantz Fanon's first case study in *Wretched of the Earth*.[4] I came to this text having taught *Wretched of the Earth* as part of a U.S. Foreign Policy course in 2001 in the Black Studies Department at the University of California, Santa Barbara. Students were saddened by the events of rape and torture of a woman, described by her husband while he was in Fanon's care. But my students' responses perplexed me, because while I wove a gender analysis into each text, they found so much more sympathy with the man's loss—his sexual dysfunction—not the loss of the woman or the loss of the relationship between them, fostered by the patriarchy that was part of Algerian society, onto which the French mapped colonialism. I want to spend some time using a third world feminist lens to talk about the relationship between the couple and to think through the impact of her silence for the text and for the revolution. My central question is how this haunting voice can help make sense of work still to be done by the anticolonial revolution. This is not work that comes without precedent, as Algerian women during the 1960s and today continue to articulate the most radical notions of anticolonial feminism for their context.[5] One major part of this work is the undoing of the sexualized, racialized gaze that is deployed against women of color. I will focus on arranged marriage, colonialism, and rape as sites that can be appropriated for political agency; reworking the veil and the voice of this particular woman have rendered her an invisible or silenced victim to some first world readers.

Introduction

Beginning with Cedric Robinson's 1990 charge that Fanon scholarship must move beyond the "he said, she said" of postcolonial theory and engage with Fanon's works in their specific historical context, my intervention begins with a methodology that requires that Robinson be taken seriously from a third world feminist perspective. This paper is a close reading of one of Fanon's case studies, Case 1 of Series A, in *Wretched of the Earth*. My goals are to read the case of the obstinate woman through the lens of third world feminism in order to place the voice of one of Fanon's patients in its historical context of Algerian women's insistence on their political agency. Why does this close reading function differently from other postcolonial attempts to read Fanon? Ultimately, my close reading uses Fanon's own psychology to speak to issues of concern related to mental health and liberation that were Fanon's key goals.[6] However, Fanon also hopes to usher in a new domain for women, not the domain that would result in instilling coverture-type protection for women on college campuses as has occurred in the 1980s and '90s in Algeria. This response to Islamist men's political organizing witnessed the unintended outcome of the Women's Dormitories at the University of Blida being surrounded by Muslim Brotherhood members in 1989 to enforce female curfews.[7] Rather, Fanon's new era for women suggests that the female subject is possible, and that Algerian women did experience changes during the political emancipation that Fanon participated in—changes that affirmed their humanity *against* their conditions.[8] Fanon's text must be read closely to hear the straining voice of the women, but their voices are there, and their role in liberating themselves *and* their society can be heard.

Fanon's revolutionary psychology hoped to create a "New Man" that would be able to undo the ways that Algerian masculinity and access to political power had been diminished. This New Man also had to be able to respond to the characterizations of Algerian masculinity as prehistoric, premodern, and primitive. Meanwhile, multiple forces besides colonialism, particularly economic forces, betrayed Algerian men's ability to represent themselves as (or to literally function as) so-called "modern" economic men. Algerian men who utilized a wide range of ways to survive colonial devastation, landlessness, urbanization, or the effects of patriarchy on men were cloaked, while a particular type of masculinity was hailed by Fanon as *the* revolutionized Algerian man.

Yet phallic masculinity, as it was deployed through war or moments of intense political mobilization, sustained the construction of a fearless, courageous masculinity. The images and stories linked to heroic masculinity tended to hide the more complex ways through which colonized men answered to the colonial hegemonic discourse. The heroic soldier and the fearless leader were tropes that set up as their opposite the unheroic, weak man who implicitly belonged to the colonial past.[9]

Similarly, the modest and chaste Algerian woman of the new era would replace the silent voice of the Algerian woman, who was either a measure of French domination or a measure of Algerian self-sufficiency.[10] The New Woman was only yielded a thin role to play if she were to take part in the revolution of the self and the revolution of gender identity. Multiple causes of alienation brought Fanon's patients to the hospital at University of Blida-Joinville, but in all his compassionate care as a healer, which I truly believe he was, he offered a single type of one-size-fits-all revolutionary self-consciousness as remedy. These other revolutions of poverty, physical ailments, gendered discrimination—though transformed forever by the unequivocal rejection of colonization—remained as haunting signifiers of changes yet to come.

Theoretical Framework and Third World Feminist Methodology

The silenced voice of Algerian women under colonization and anticolonial struggle is precisely why my methodology considers third world feminist scholarship as the most appropriate means to think through the complex presence of Algerian women in this historical moment of liberatory promise. Rather than perpetuate the "feminist critique of Fanon" that replicates the dismissive division that Robinson warns of ("he said, she said"), third world feminists have drawn on Fanon and utilized his theory of revolutionary self-consciousness to propel new movements to address their political concerns. My task, then, is to trace the lineage of a feminism that brings together the best that Fanon offers and the best that feminism offers. Fanon offers this insight: The stakes for Algerian women are not simply whether they will be coopted by the French or by the nationalists. The stakes are whether Algerian women's identity will be the basis for subjectivity and liberation.[11]

Third world feminist scholarship, like other liberatory philosophies, reflects the need to reconcile revolution with the possibility for cultural renewal through gendered critiques of the economic relations with colonial and military power.[12] Moreover, third world feminism hinges on the recognition of multiple types of, or "intersectional," injury (and therefore multiple sites of agency) and the need for more-complex types of redress.[13] Lastly, though the most controversial and perhaps least important aspect of third world feminism is that it differs from "Western feminism," which has been used to reproduce, rationalize, and naturalize biological categories, third world feminism in its most useful manifestations recognizes the ways that gender violence engenders not only biology-based discrimination but also colonialism, imperialism, and militarism. For example, much "Western feminism" focuses on the way that decolonizing nationalisms used women to resolve the contradiction of their own claims on post-Enlightenment European political tropes.[14] However, many third world feminists acknowledge Fanon and hold close to his work because he does not try to resolve the contradictions and oppositions that pepper the experience of revolutionary nationalism. Third world feminism acknowledges that the study of gender is not simply the study of women's bodies and the manipulations that are acted upon them, but also the study of deepening social inequality and resistance to this, no matter what face a systematic type of inequality takes.

Thus, third world feminism as a methodology is not simply hearing from the silent, but more a methodology concerned with how Algerian anticolonial struggle was waged. Those silenced in the history of the anticolonial struggle affected the way the struggle was understood, as well as which priorities were granted and which priorities got lost in the shuffle. The stories of the successes and failures of political emancipation are gendered stories, and the history of this struggle is incomplete and partial until we can think through the problems caused by, *and* the opportunities made available by, deploying gender identity in the movement. As Fanon instructs, "technicians for advancement of retarded societies would do well to understand the sterile and harmful character of any endeavor which illuminates preferentially a given element of the colonized society. Even within the framework of a newly independent nation, one cannot attack this or that segment of the cultural whole without endangering the work undertaken. . . . "[15] Third world feminism in this project is intended to aid the larger goal of giving greater insight to the cultural whole in Algeria that fomented dramatic and enduring social change through revolution and the rejection of one type of French power. Perhaps the ultimate question would be then: What changes were wrought in France as a result of Algerian women defining feminist consciousness against that which was offered to them as feminism—a helpmeet to colonial power?

Fanon and Political Emancipation

Francoise Verges argues that Fanon inaugurated a new era in colonial psychology in much the same way that Philippe Pinel introduced a new psychiatry in the context of the French Revolution. While metropolitan psychiatry continued to evidence great concern for the changes that had to occur in society for the alienated mental patient to recover, colonial psychiatry remained in the throes of a colonizing project that both supplanted and interlocked religious difference and racial otherness. By ignoring the power relations between France and Algeria, the French national myth of cultural superiority was allowed to flourish. Whatever national self-analysis that could have been possible through psychiatry and other social sciences was neglected in the colonial practice of psychology prior to Fanon. Colonial psychiatry hyperracialized Algerians and did not see political emancipation as central to their cure. "Fanon broke with the colonial-racial notion of madness" and suggested that modernization and all that it reflected were the cause of mental illness among Algerians.[16]

This intertwined aim of mental health and liberation are central to third world feminist philosophy, as they were for Fanon. Like Fanon, a great deal of third world feminist philosophy considers the linkage between mental health and liberation as a natural site for discussing the difficulty of negotiating with culture, traditions, nationalism, gendered political agency, manhood and masculinity, and femininity. As Marnia Lazreg insists, religion in Algeria stands in for a larger nexus of power and culture because it is more easily diminished as irrational and perplexing and bound by the insider status of one's culture or territorial authenticity. This stand-in, religion, represents femininity as mysterious in order to deflect attention from struggles between masculinist political parties. Fanon shared this conclusion about Algeria, suggesting that "what is in fact the assertion of a distinct identity, concern with keeping intact a few shreds of national existence, is attributed to religious, magical fantastical behavior."[17] The veil, for instance, and its religious connotations, represented both a rejection of French colonial power and patriarchy in Algeria—like the double-edged sword, the *labrys,* the veil cut in two directions at once.

I also take seriously the conclusion of radical women of color and third world feminisms that feminist analysis must not be placed above or be devoid of critical race analysis. Rather, the intertwining of race and gender, and class and nation, must occur for Fanon scholarship to avoid the imperialism of Western humanists posing as the feminist liberators of Algerian women.[18] This aim cannot be met as long as Western women's feminism rests on its supposed progress in comparison to third world women—or in other words, its colonial impulses[19]—just as the aim of mental health could not be imagined by a French colonial system of psychiatry working from presumptive racialized hierarchies of civilization.

Does It Matter That It Was an Arranged Marriage?

How are we to interpret the husband's claim that he shares some guilt with his wife's tormentor(s) because he ignored her in their arranged marriage? In Fanon's Case 1 of Series A, the case of the obstinate woman, the husband felt guilty because he did not love his wife. The admission that he intended to marry another person, for Fanon, is part of the husband's coming to terms with his wife and her experience in the war.

The husband was ashamed because he had not loved his wife in their arranged marriage. I find this admission—the first in a series—to be a disingenuous one, because it is part of a series of moments when the husband seeks to absolve his wife. In the second moment, he states: "Oh, well, there's not much harm done; she wasn't killed."[20] This husband is attempting to minimize the harm done to his wife, not simply out of remorse but as a way to diminish the impact to himself. The husband introduces this diminished harm in three places on that same page. Somehow through 1) not loving her, 2) saying he is grateful for her life, and 3) saying, "She's tasted the French," this man can reclaim his dignity.[21] He can reckon with the fear that his wife betrayed him 1) by her very surviving, 2) by being raped, and 3) by telling him the truth. In the most telling revelation, "She's tasted the French," the sad patient reconfigures his wife as a connoisseur, as if her experience was one of cultural appreciation, appropriation, or tourism. However, she did not in fact fancy or wander toward her own victimhood. Long before the revolution proper, she, like him, was a moving target of colonial power. This metaphor is problematic on many levels that, unfortunately, are not problematized by Fanon. It places a special burden on Algerian women to be especially responsible for resisting colonization when men in fact had greater access to "tasting the French." In fact, we see the obstinate woman's husband visits Fanon only after he fails to have consensual sexual relations with a French woman.

> *Every rejected veil disclosed to the eyes of the colonialists . . . revealed piece by piece, the flesh of Algeria laid bare . . . announced to the occupier an Algerian society whose systems of defense were in the process of dislocation, open, breached. Every veil that fell, every body that became liberated from the traditional embrace of the haik [everyday outer apparel worn in North Africa], every face that offered itself to the bold and impatient glance of the occupier was a negative expression of the fact that Algeria was . . . accepting the rape of the colonizer.[22]*

This conflation makes Algerian women automatically pornographic. It does not see Algerian women as the site of creative authority or empowerment, but always the automatic site of dishonor. Algeria, the nation, was already figured in this position, and the analogy to women, though evocative, does not illumine the political relations that have led to Algerian women being perceived as betrayers. No woman "accepts" rape. Women survive, repel, and reject rape. But the assumption of the "emasculation thesis" of French colonization views the real damage done by colonization as a diminished male capacity. Algerian women are left either in the position of being more vulnerable to sexual abuse—because as women they are more in need of protection than men—or as the betrayers of Algerian men themselves. Neither of these two roles is adequate to explain the work that Algerian women in fact performed in the revolution, or the multiple ways they did resist colonization. Fanon's essay "Algeria Unveiled" represents the psychic experience of colonialism but configures a place of blame for Algerian women in that experience. In the dreams that Fanon relays in his case studies, Europeans dream of raping Algerian women, but Algerian women never consent or speak in these dreams. They are simply humiliated in these dreams.[23]

From my own reading of Case 1 Series A, I am not sure that I trust this husband's admissions. It is a disingenuous recognition/resignation that this approach to healing his sexual dysfunction will not give him greater compassion for his wife. While understandably overwhelmed by the burden of her survival, he does not make sense of it in a way that renders her a complete being—simply a being of his imagination. Sadly, his admissions of not loving her cannot take away what she endured. Nothing changes, and she is still a survivor of rape and torture.

So many women were raped and tortured by the French police and military that "his personal misfortunes and his dignity as an injured husband remained in the background."[24] And yet he could not help the anxiety, mistrust, pain, and misery that accompanied the personal loss of his wife's dignity and bodily integrity and wholeness— thus the desire to absolve her. He would not have become impotent had a child been raped and tortured. But in this marriage that *he did not want,* the raped and tortured wife speaks to his shame and his dreams of his rotten daughter. He cannot get rid of the fear of their complicity—his own failed sexual attempts with French women notwithstanding— he cannot bring himself to see this wife as she is. She must be a patriotic heroine *and* a whore to make sense of the violation. Who else might she have been? If it had not been for the context of colonization, we might hear her voice more distinctly.

Arranged Marriages and Colonialism

Some scholars insist that Fanon is neither a feminist nor sensitive enough to the culture and struggles over the meanings of the female and gendered political agency. My concern, however, was that, arranged marriage notwithstanding, colonialism exacerbated and reinforced hierarchies that people in Algeria were experiencing in their intimate and public relations. Colonialism, like development policies that follow in their stead, rigidified social inequalities like gender discrimination to such a degree that an indictment of religion or culture—or even Fanon's failed attempt to read religion and culture—is quite an inadequate explanations for patriarchy. Certainly, colonialism succeeded because it was able to map itself onto preexisting patriarchal relations that were hierarchical and exploitative. But colonialism heightens these tensions and this level of hierarchy. Colonialism goes even further: It attempts to learn about the preexisting hierarchies and tries to utilize them to justify further exploiting, deepening the exploitation. Moreover, colonialism tries to offer new symbolic meanings for dichotomies like "public and private," or "modern and traditional." The work of the anticolonial struggle, then, is to reveal that "public and private," for example, have multiple meanings: Both can be sites for transformation and repression, and both can be sites to wage major social change.

Some would argue that the husband's shame is based in his nonrecognition of his wife before he became part of the resistance and the revolutionary activities. However, I insist that when he accepts his wife and tries to see her as a heroine of the revolution (as Fanon suggests at the closure of his retelling of this case), that is not a resolution. Here, the patient idealizes his wife and perpetuates an act of nonrecognition that is as "dangerous" in its misreading as was the reading forced on him in the arranged marriage. He still does not see the multifaceted person that has survived this attempt at dishonor. He still does not see the woman of profound dignity and profound pain that endured his absence, and he attempts to ignore and minimize their relationship.

This husband's nonrecognition of his wife, while it is a consequence of an arranged marriage, is also a consequence of the nonnational but territorial status of Algeria during the war. The husband's dismissive tone is central to the French manipulation of gender identity and femininity and thus is an outcome of it. His failure to be a companion is part of colonialism, because colonialism does not nurture companionship or camaraderie. It does not nurture personhood in relationships—it nurtures personhood that exists radically separate from others. Relationships under colonialism are vastly different from relationships under revolution. The sort of relationships that were nurtured among combatants in the revolution were critical to the liberation and freedom that Fanon imagined and theorized and envisioned. They were critical relationships, because they taught people not only how to assert their liberal humanity but how to assert their humanity in the context of a communal notion of the good; so that "individuality is not divorced from culture."[25] These wartime relations flew in the face of the individual notions of emancipation that were central to French notions of liberty and personal rights. Fanon stresses that a community emancipation is possible even through the confines of psychology, the science of the individual. In his Pinelian work to reconnect people suffering from mental illnesses to the society that has ejected/rejected them, Fanon insisted that the society must change in order for their cure to occur. The cure is a social cure.

But these companionships, these lessons in survival through acknowledgment of those who reflect your same situation, have to also cross gender boundaries.[26] Companionship must be able to hold the energy created by people who are located differently in the world because of prescriptions of gender and because of patriarchal domination. This social cure, then, must extend to the relations that ascribe power according to one's gender. Though Fanon signals this in his essays in *A Dying Colonialism,* the myth that this can occur while Algerian women are silent confuses and strangles his analysis. Men must not simply feel a sense of sympathy for women's trials and tribulations, but their work as revolutionists must be learning to follow progressive leadership from Algerian women and utilize passive resistance not simply as a response to the state or constabulary, but in their relations with Algerian women.

In the United States, a social movement has organized around women of color and violence; this movement challenges racist notions about violence that ignore the experiences of men and women of color and the ways that violence affects them. They insist that colonization is a feminist concern and put it on the agenda right next to issues like women's educational access and women's access to reproductive choice. But the question for me that I direct toward Fanon's work is whether decolonization struggles figure out that feminism, defined as autonomous definitions of gender and sexual identity, is part of the anticontemporary colonial agenda. I ask this question in this way, because the struggle for global justice demonstrates that colonial relations have ended only to be reframed in more-hidden financial relations and more mystified patterns of consumption of "world culture." So perhaps the great need of decolonization struggles to attend to feminism is most critical right now. I wonder whether Fanon's understandings of liberation and relationships that have to be created in order for that liberation to render the whole society humane—including the insight that decolonization was an incomplete process as long as patriarchy was allowed to endure. It is not simply that women waited until the nationalist struggle was over, expecting to get their part of the new national pie, but simply that decolonizing nationalisms often ignored patriarchy and thus were prevented from seeing their own masculinist tendencies.

Rape Is Political Warfare

Rape is political warfare, and this is the place that we must begin to take hold of the experience of the woman whose story is told through her husband's impotence in Fanon's Case 1 of Series A. Colonialism is about making war on people and seeing as a "combatant" everybody who does not concede all authority to the colonial power brokers; the choice that this woman makes to survive was a social but primarily political act. The best example of this is the commander in the same set of case studies who requests Fanon's help to keep torturing. He explains the stakes for the French is in the information they get from torturing Algerians. The stakes for Algerians are of course their lives as survivors and witnesses of torture.

Whether this wisdom that rape is political warfare is part of the oral history of the virgin whore myth/legend or whether it is recited by liberatory psychologist Frantz Fanon, it must be understood like dropping bombs and other sorts of torture. It must be understood in this way, or there is nothing to prevent it from being construed as a private act of vengeance or humiliation; or simply a gendered act that targets unique biological characteristics and social categories rather than something with long-range harm to entire communities. Rape in the context in which Fanon was treating patients at Blida-Joinville was most certainly an act of war. It repressed the sexual autonomy and violated the bodily integrity of the persons that experienced it. It caused irreparable personal and communal and social harm. It functioned to keep women and men away from the battlefield, away from the consciousness and resistance that were central to the work of the nationalist struggle. Rape was an attempt to stifle women's participation in any type of revolutionary movement to improve their life conditions. Women were targeted not because they were weaker or because their victimization caused more social harm, but because women as caretakers of major networks of political action could interrupt colonial attempts to wreak an even wider degree of harm and social control. Women were targeted to suppress their own activism, to punish their partners, to preempt their resistance. Moreover, rape functioned for colonial France in ways quite like other types of torture in that it made, to use Fanon's term, "depersonalized people" know themselves only through the shame and horror with which they were seen by their oppressors. When scholars insist that rape is political, they are granting this crime the same status as other violations, not to insist on a hierarchy of oppressions but to demonstrate the interlocking nature of oppressions.

> [I]t was the rape of an obstinate woman, who was ready to put up with everything rather than sell her husband. And the husband in question, it was me. This woman had saved my life and had protected the organization. It was because of me that she had been dishonored. And yet she didn't say to me: "Look at all I've had to bear for you." On the contrary, she said: "Forget about me; begin your life over again, for I have been dishonored.[27]

Though in *Wretched of the Earth* and *A Dying Colonialism* Fanon recognizes that rape is political, in *Black Skin, White Masks* he concludes that rape is not the major concern of anticolonial struggle; rather, prostitution and sexual commodification are. In this contradiction, Fanon demonstrates ambivalence about gender violence by implying that rape is the result of force, while prostitution and sexual commodification are the result of women's complicity with colonialism.[28] In writing about Capecia, Fanon relates that this Martinican woman commodifies her antiblack ideology to titillate a French male gaze embodied in both male and female novel readers.[29] This is particularly disturbing as a reading of Capecia, because Fanon overlooks his own inability to be sympathetic with black women's desire to distance themselves from blackness if blackness represents sexual vulnerability and being targeted for emotional disdain. While some have championed Capecia and called her work a tome on "sexual autonomy," I disagree and conclude instead that her deep desire for assimilation is a cause for sympathy, because it speaks to the depth of her degradation and oppression as a sexually vulnerable black woman and a sexually vulnerable black person. The criticism of Capecia reflects Fanon's inability to see this black women's attempts to reject the French gaze as a type of passive resistance against the antiblack stereotypes that are the currency of racism spoken by both blacks and whites in the French colonies. Capecia is held to a higher standard of morality, a higher standard that the sexual vulnerability of black women makes almost impossible to maintain. If black femininity represents the "pit of niggerhood," as Fanon claims is the cornerstone of Capecia's *La Négresse Blanche,* then it is little wonder that black female subjectivity has had to be recast as moral, underexposed, and private in order to be recuperated. Fanon concludes that modesty will yield the requisite political sophistication necessary to protect black women from the Eurocentric male gaze. But this modesty, while self-edifying, is not going to change as much about the experience of sexism and patriarchy as an anticolonial struggle that embraces antisexism as its goal.

Fanon is not alone in trying to correct the misrepresentations provided by the Eurocentric sexual gaze. Much 19th-century women's organizing by black female conventions focused on removing them from the realm of public commentary and scrutiny. At the core of essentially every activity of the National Association of Colored Women's Clubs, founded in 1896—what many have called the most enduring Afro-American protest organization—was a concern with creating positive images of black women's sexuality. To counter negative stereotypes, many black women felt compelled to downplay, even deny, sexual expression.[30]

Clearly the only sexual autonomy that women of color could claim was that which denied and downplayed them as having any sexuality at all. Other examples of this abound in one case, documented by George Sanchez, the Americanization programs directed toward Mexican American women had to be resisted because of their attempts to force assimilation to correct the stereotypic problems of hyperfertility and joblessness. Mexican women were the targets of such programs because they were seen as the key to the cultural transformation in Mexican American society. Chicana feminists document this process of removing the "taint" of Mexican identity in order to replace it with "American" culture. Ultimately, it was a white supremacist and colonialist political process, masked in the dominant social science and public health discourses of the day. Fanon's assessment of Capecia is correct; she is more interested in synthesizing images that enthrone racist and sexist justifications for the French gaze of women of color.

However, the question that Fanon fails to answer is this: How were women of color to claim sexual autonomy—when they were the victims of sexual violation, both physical and representational—through the perverse gaze referenced in both the work of the French and of the French subjects?[31] Nevertheless, Fanon's ability to critique Capecia does not make him a feminist (of the antiporn or prosex variety). But there is a voice haunting the *Wretched of the Earth* that suggests something about how to make this liberatory text speak to the feminist task of liberation from colonial and patriarchal violence. That voice is the voice of the "obstinate woman."

The Western Veil

In "Algeria Unveiled," Fanon intimates that the veil provides this needed modesty and self-protection for Algerian women and for Algeria. Not only will this modesty protect Algeria's national, cultural, and sexual identity from colonial invasion, war, impotence, and exploitation, but the modesty of women will guarantee liberation for Algerians as subjects of French domination and Algerian women. He grounds this insight on the findings that the veil, though an artifact of culture, has come to signify "backwardness" and "restraints on women" that supposedly more-modern French society could correct. European women, social workers, charitable women's organizations, and experts in native affairs, as well as ethnographers and anthropologists serving the colonial regime, suggested that the veil was the key to Algerian national identity.[32] French colonialism posed itself as the solution to the problem of Algerian women.

Fanon draws attention to the falsehood inherent in a colonial power's seeking to emancipate women while asking for their collaboration with the suppression and exploitation of the national aspect of their identities. Fanon finds this desire to "unfetter" the Algerian woman using French liberalism to be untenable. The French endorse liberal traditions in Algeria inasmuch as they subjugate Algerians.

He even indicts the French woman's vanity and fear of the Algerian woman. Thus he intimates that what the French offer as female liberation is a ruse, because French women's freedom is dependent on the exploitation of Algerian women. Moreover, French women are not free as women while they are addicted to the perverse gaze—a hypersexualized, exoticized gaze—that confirms white supremacy and degrades Algerian, Martinican, and any black women. Europeans, says Fanon, confronted with the veil, react in an aggressive fashion, because it signifies a limitation of their perception. European rationality is supposed to give Europeans access to understanding, knowing, and measuring everything about Algerian women—as another curious object in the natural world.[33] French women go much further by saying that the Algerian woman is both a shameless competitor when unveiled as well as a seductress hiding imperfections when veiled.[34] French women were unfree, and not because they did not wear the veil, but because they took their identity from brutalizing people weaker than they in international discourses of public authority.

Fanon demystifies the Eurocentric fetish with the veil but reinstates another appropriation of the veil. "For the French, the veil was the key to justifying their liberatory role in Algeria, and for the Algerian revolutionary movement [as represented by Fanon], the veil was also a key metaphor in the liberation struggle. This appropriation of female clothing and female sexuality happens throughout the history of French colonial intervention in Algeria."[35]

Specter of the Obstinate Woman

There is a voice that is central to this story that haunts what Fanon teaches us and that reveals the limits of his gender analysis. This voice is the voice of the woman who reports to her husband, "Forget about me; begin your life over again, for I have been dishonored."[36] A number of ways have been suggested about how to explain her circumstances and how to understand what she is doing through this announcement. One possibility is that her admission, her recounting of her experience, forces her husband to carry the burden of the manifestation of the French gaze onto Algerian women's bodies. Another possibility is that she has exceeded and defied the "desire of the French to make Algerian women accomplices in the cultural destruction reinforced on cultural traditions."[37]

This "obstinate woman" was moving for me for several different reasons: 1) we still have the prevailing image of the woman as betrayer with the colonizer, 2) men still need to learn how the practice of relinquishing male privilege enables them to create a more sustainable revolution, 3) women are always given the "choice" to utilize the location of rape as a site for political agency by viewing it as a structural occurrence and by viewing their survival as the ultimate goal.

The political agency that this woman demonstrates is hard to make sense of. Her survival and refusal to provide information to her torturers condemns her, because she commits her husband to impotence. It means that she remained a combatant in a war of men where her sexuality was the currency for national independence. It means that French are dishonored for experiencing their freedom through the perverse misrepresentation and fascination with Algerian women that they claimed to liberate. It means that patriarchy and misogyny can only be replaced if she becomes a martyr. Lastly it means her body and her experience is at stake, while she is forced to stand in for a complex set of ideas about power and identity.

Conclusion

Ultimately, for Fanon, the healing occurs in the life of this obstinate woman and others like her when their husbands and communities take them back and realize that they were victims of French colonialist masculinity, Western feminism, or heroines of the revolution. Moreover, when Algerian men accept their long-suffering wives again, these men achieve a type of saintliness, because they do not see their wives as dishonored or dirty for having gone outside the marriage. When this patient could express sympathy for his wife, remorse for not treating her well, and remorse for seeing her and their child as betrayers and as rotten, his healing had occurred. I find this to be an inadequate type of healing, an inadequate type of resolution, because Algerian men and women continued to have to deal with these sexual assaults and an internal feeling of betrayal. Perhaps, one could argue that Fanon's case studies represent tragic incidents and not resolution of any sort, because none could be possible until the French quit Algeria. I would disagree, because there are resolutions other than the end of French colonial power. This case illustrates that the ultimate work to be done in Algeria was not simply the return of people who had been tortured to their communities, or the ability to reclaim them and to forgive them for having survived, or the ability to forgive them for having revealed the weakness of men to "protect *their* women," or the ability to forgive them for telling what they suffered. This case illustrates that the ultimate revolutionary work to be done in Algeria to recover from the losses of colonialism was to see each other anew—not as patriots or as beneficiaries of the nation—but to see each other without the lens of the French gaze blinding them. The task of decolonization that would bring freedom required Algerian men and women not to see the war in sexual terms at all. The war was about conquering and the desire to conquer. This colonial ideology perverted the relationships between Algerians. The real anticolonial revolutionary must choose not to reenact the colonial through social and gender hierarchy. The work of the revolutionary has to be to pay attention to those more vulnerable than you are and to help those persons work to change their own condition. I take very seriously Albert Memmi's insight that a "pyramid of petty tyrants" does harm to movements to destabilize colonial power.[38] Audre Lorde called this "Oppression Olympics" or the "hierarchy of oppressions."[39] It is a losing battle all around. Taking our anger as oppressed people out on those more vulnerable than ourselves is not an "outlet for our spirits" but simply makes those weaker people into containers, storage units for our own suppressed resistance—this takes away our agency. But building up the weakest among us challenges any systems that seek to oppress. In analysis of African American women who were subject to sexual violence as part of the internal colonialism of the post–Civil War era, Darlene Clark Hine insists that although "these women were sexual hostages and domestic violence victims . . . [that] did not reduce their determination to acquire power to protect themselves and to become agents of social change."[40]

"I Will Do a Deed for Freedom": Enslaved Women, Proslavery Theorists, and the Contested Discourse of Black Womanhood

Alexandra Cornelius-Diallo

> *Then said the mournful mother,*
> *If Ohio cannot save,*
> *I will do a deed for freedom*
> *Shalt find each child a grave.*
> —Frances E. W. Harper, "The Slave Mother, A Tale of Ohio"

In 1856, Margaret Garner and her husband John decided that their family no longer would live as slaves. This decision was not made on the day that Garner murdered her daughter, the haunting event that became the subject of Toni Morrison's novel *Beloved*. Liberation had become the couple's primary objective upon making the bold, albeit perilous decision to take their family on the dangerous journey across the frozen Ohio River to "free" country. According to an editorial in Canada's *Provincial Freedmen*, the family successfully reached the free state of Ohio but were pursued and soon surrounded by eleven armed men that included Kentucky slave hunters and a U.S. Marshall.

In desperation, the Garners resisted recapture with a will for freedom that would be praised and sanctioned by black and white abolitionists across the nation. Their demonstrated resolve to be free contradicted proslavery theorists such as Sidney Fisher, who argued that "the internal evidence of the negro's nature" indicated that enslaved Africans were "in all ages, contented and submissive in slavery."[1] In an effort to stop the encroaching men from seizing his family, John Garner fired at and wounded two "slave hunters." In an equally determined effort to evade certain reenslavement, Margaret Garner turned to her children, killed one, and wounded two others before she was stopped.[2]

In response to the Garner case and other reported and rumored demonstrations of defiant acts of self-defense, defenders of slavery—and more specifically, men who asserted that slavery complemented the "natural condition" of black men and women—searched for ways to explain these revolutionary moments. The defense of the institution of slavery rested on two notions: that blacks were savage, inferior, weak, and therefore dependent, and that accordingly, slavery was a benign institution.[3] To acknowledge insurgency among enslaved communities would attribute courage, selfhood, and independence to slaves, qualities of which they were supposedly inherently bereft. These "unnatural" acts of resistance served as ringing testaments against slavery as an institution. During the 19th century, incidents of black women's resistance were continually documented by the press and made public by abolitionists. Africana women's decisions to resist slavery at all costs, exemplified by Garner's act of infanticide, countered the image of "docile," "subservient" slaves such as those portrayed in proslavery pamphlets. In this paper, I argue that slavery's justifiers were compelled to use and develop theories that negated the rumored and reported accounts of black women's "rage and resistance" as it manifested itself in costly personal rebellions, as well as in moments of publicly humiliating subjugation.

Reports of black women's resistance posed a particularly threatening psychological challenge to white men, whose patriarchy rested not only on the subjugation of all nonwhites, but also on the social, economic, and political subordination of all women. Of the psychological challenge that enslaved women's resistance presented, Darlene Clark Hine observes:

> A woman who elected not to have children—or, to put it another way, engaged in sexual abstinence, abortion, or infanticide—negated through individual or group action her role in the maintenance of the slave pool. To the extent that in doing so she redefined her role in the system, she introduced a unit of psychological heterogeneity into a worldview, which depended, for its survival, on homogeneity, at least with respect to the assumption of its ideology.[4]

Hine's keen analysis is valuable in that it illuminates the ways contested accounts of black women's experiences could influence the development of ideologies specific to citizenship, independence, and racial character.[5]

A careful reading of the discourse surrounding slavery reveals the ways in which African American women's rage and resistance permeated the public's imagination and haunted the American mind. In his seminal work *The Black Image in the White Mind: The Debate on Afro-American Character and Destiny, 1817–1914,* George Fredrickson asserts, "My principal concern has been with the relationship of racial doctrines and images to general social and intellectual developments, and especially to the great historical conflicts involving the status of the Black man in the United States." In a reassessment of his own work, Fredrickson admits that his discussion of racial ideology is crippled by his failure to address African American intellectual thought regarding racial differences. He concedes that African Americans did in fact contribute to this debate.[6] In a successful effort to delineate African American contributions to scientific racial thought, Mia Elisabeth Bay's important book *The White Image in the Black Mind: African American Ideas about White People* examines the beliefs that African American intellectuals held about white racial character and destiny in the 19th and early 20th centuries. In response to Fredrickson's assertion that future historians should try to track dialogues between blacks and whites, Bay determines the extent to which African Americans accepted or rejected 19th-century notions about innate racial characteristics. Using the writings of black intellectuals and novelists, as well as the narratives and testimony of unlettered African American enslaved and free persons, Bay synthesizes African American contributions to racial discourse.[7] In addition, her examination, analysis, and use of primary source materials such as the Works Progress Administration (WPA) narratives have expanded the realm from which historians can gather information specific to "study of ideas" as it relates to 19th-century African American history.[8]

I seek to provide a more deliberately gendered analysis of the ways in which the presence and resistance of enslaved black women influenced the development of discussions regarding race that were informed by the "science" of ethnology.[9] More commonly discussed as a reaction to abolitionism, the development and subject matter specific to scientific racial discourse also was shaped in reaction to the threat of black men's and— more specifically for the purpose of this paper—black women's unrelenting insurgency.

I begin with a brief discussion that will illuminate the way that ideological frameworks, political rhetoric, and scientific theories were shaped and are shaped by black women's experiences. I show that a close reading of the ethnological theories produced by scientist of race Josiah Nott and proslavery pamphleteer Sidney Fisher actually were quite "bloody." I then explore the Margaret Garner case as a means of illustrating the ways in which her use of violent resistance informed the work of proslavery theorist John Van Evrie.

Enslaved women endured unthinkable hardships in their struggle for daily survival. At times, however, the desire to live gave way to the recognition that "survival" demanded a price that they no longer were willing to pay. Such recognition served as a catalyst to armed resistance, murder, or suicide. In this state of mind, black women acted not as the allegedly grateful and compliant wards and seducers of slaveholders, but as warriors in the fight to end slavery. At times, as in Margaret Garner's case, black women fought alongside black men. At other times, black women who struggled against sexual abuse sought healing, support, and strategies of resistance from other black women who had been subjected to similar experiences. Still, on other occasions, black women were horribly alone in their attempts to end sexual violence. In all of these cases, black women's determination moved them beyond resistance, toward the total destruction of the master slave relationship in which they always had been unwilling participants. In solidarity to their enslaved sisters and to free black women who also were subjected to violence, black female abolitionists continually publicized reports of black female abuse that simultaneously drew and repelled white audiences.

Unable to ignore these reports, slaveholders also were forced to speculate on the incendiary potential of enslaved women who could be driven to embrace murder, death, and even suicide in efforts to regain ownership of their bodies even as they liberated their spirits. Pushed to the limit, black women's bodies could be "made strong with madness."[10] I employ the term "madness" to convey not only black women's fury as it manifested itself physically, but also the psychological space black women entered when they challenged with appropriate fanaticism the functionally "sane" and "normal" world that expected compliance to sexual exploitation and domination.

Efforts to delineate the tortured conditions under which enslaved women labored and the defamation of black womanhood during the 19th century are not extraneous to the development of scientific racial discourse. The prospect of recovering enslaved black women's harrowing experiences with ideological, political, and physical "domination," however, is an uncomfortable one. Scholars including Angela Davis, Deborah Gray White, and Darlene Clark Hine have cautiously sought appropriate language and theoretical frameworks to explore the political, economic, and cultural ramifications of black women's sexual exploitation. I find particularly useful efforts to understand black women's exploitation as it was complemented and reinforced by laboring conditions and economics. In her work, for example, Adrienne Davis uses the term "sexual economy," in an effort to use language that underscores the extent to which rape and sexual abuse were functions of black women's work. She writes,

> *The political economy of slavery systematically expropriated Black women's sexuality and reproductive capacity for white pleasure and profit. Yet what discourse has confronted and accused this national horror? What documents record its effects on enslaved women? In the face of this unspeakable work, chroniclers of American history have all but erased its existence.*[11]

Research into the way enslaved women's experiences intersect and complement economic and political systems of oppression have led to a better appreciation of what Davis describes so appropriately as "this national horror."[12] Enslaved women's use of violent resistance should be neither romanticized nor simplified as supernatural manifestations of anger, or impulsive decisions to resist. Rather, violent resistance was one of many natural reactions to perpetual assault and the dehumanization processes associated with enslavement. This characterization of the culture of enslavement was ideologically and psychologically threatening to slaveholders, who tried instead to deem these acts as unnatural. In this context, ethnologists and proslavery theorists who, based on their "scientific observations," promoted theories that justified and pardoned the physical and sexual abuse of black women, found a ready audience for their work. Thus enslaved women's experiences, in turn, also shed light on the development of racial scientific discourse.

Analyses of the sexual exploitation of black persons can very easily be reduced to descriptions of the sexual use of black *bodies*. Scholars fear that bringing ostensibly "objective" attention to the violation of black women will unwittingly provide more material that objectifies, and thus victimizes further the arguably overexposed, sexualized, black female body of the American public imagination. In reference to her decision not to include Frederick Douglass's description of the brutal beating of Aunt Hester, Saidiya V. Hartman offers a thoughtful and compelling consideration of the problem,

> *Only more obscene than the brutality unleashed at the whipping post is the demand that this suffering be materialized and evidenced by the display of the tortured body or endless recitations of the ghastly and the terrible. In light of this, how does one give expression to these outrages without exacerbating the indifference to suffering that is the consequence of the benumbing spectacle or contend with the narcissistic identification that obliterates the other or the prurience that too often is the response to such displays.*[13]

As an alternative, Hartman interrogates the "terror of the mundane." In doing so, she illuminates the extent to which slavery as a dehumanizing project permeated disparate aspects of everyday living. Hartman and Evelyn Hammonds also indicate that contemporary scholars share many of the same qualms about unveiling the black women's experiences with which many 19th-century advocates grappled.[14] Contemporary scholars (in their choice of subject matter specific to the interrogation of rape and violence) and black female abolitionists of the 19th century have employed "the culture of dissemblance." Darlene Clark Hine uses the term effectively to describe "behavior and attitudes that created the appearance of openness and disclosure but actually shielded the truth of their inner lives and selves from their oppressors, and often from Black men and Black children."[15] According to Hine, "secrecy" and subsequent "self-imposed invisibility" enabled women to secure the "psychic space" needed to exist and resist.[16] In like manner, Deborah Gray White notes "slave women understood the value of silence and secrecy."[17] Evidence that black women embraced the culture of dissemblance can be found in both slave narratives as well as in primary source material culled from black women of the late 19th and early 20th centuries.

Yet it is important to remember that dissemblance offers a relative luxury—a luxury of which enslaved women were bereft. While former slaves, including Linda Brent and

Elizabeth Keckly, could ostensibly protect some privacy, they earned this option only after they had secured their freedom. As a slave, however, the household of slaves knew Brent's impending doom. According to Brent, "Many of them pitied me; but none dared to ask the cause. They had no need to inquire. They knew too well the guilty practices under that roof; and they were aware that to speak of them was an offense that never went unpunished."[18] Similarly, Keckly asserts that her valiant efforts to resist to the death the brutal beatings and sexualized violence to which she was subjected were widely known in her community. Of the violence, and the failed attempts to "subdue [her] proud and rebellious spirit," she writes, "These revolting scenes created a great sensation at the time, were the talk of the town and neighborhood, and I flatter myself that the actions of those who had conspired against me were not viewed in a light to reflect much credit upon them."[19]

The violation of enslaved women often was very public. Consider for example the following description of enslaved women's work environment.

> *Ma mama said that nigger 'oman couldn't help herself, fo' she had to do what de marster say. Ef he come to de field whar de women workin' and he tell gal to come on, she had to go. He would take one down in de woods an' use her all de time he wanted to, den send her on back to work. Times nigger'oman had chillun for marster an' his sons and some times it was fo' de ovah seer.*[20]

During the course of a day at work, black women on this plantation were chosen randomly to perform sexual acts with slave owners, their sons, and overseers. Such conditions rendered the "terror" of rape to the realm of the ostensibly "mundane."

Rendered mundane, the merciless violation of black women on slave plantations provided the context in which racial theorists could casually refer to the sexual domination of black women. In their defense of slavery, proslavery theorists and ethnologists pitted their "scientific observations" against factual accounts of the daily experiences of black women. Black women vigorously and, at times, violently defended their children and their persons from slave masters, overseers, and other men. Nonetheless, slave owners portrayed the master slave relationship as a mutually beneficial domestic arrangement under which enslaved men, women, and children were cared for and protected. Nott, for example, argued that blacks were similar to "the canine species," in their devotion to and dependence on slave owners. In his postemancipation portrayal of the system of slavery, Nott asserted that blacks failed to care for each other in sickness, and that children of the enslaved died "from neglect of their parents." He claimed that in contrast, enslaved Africans were "untiring in their kindness and attentions to the members of their master's families in sickness." He continued, "They watch night after night by the bedside of the whites, as if prompted by an instinct like the canine species. Their devotion in this respect is incredible to those who have not witnessed it; and their history shows the race is a dependent one."[21]

An analysis of the evolution of Nott's theory of racial inferiority makes clear the ways that an ethos of racial and gender oppression complemented each other and left little room for the consideration of black women as anything other than a dominated subject. While studying at the Museum d'Historie Naturelle, Nott became particularly intrigued by his colleague Dr. L. A. Grose's suggestion that there "existed on the earth passive races prior to the active races, and that the primitive races had multiplied considerably before the apparition of the latter."[22] Alluding to the fact that the concept may have been new to "readers of English," Nott sought to make the application of the theory clear by supplanting "passive" and "active" with the terms "inferior" and "superior." With this in mind, he also asked his readers to consider M. d'Eichthal's opinion that "the African negro race has attained its present civilization through the influence of the white race." He inferred from d'Eichthal that blacks were "civilizable" if not "domesticable," but that Africana people were not able to initiate civilized lifestyles. Thus, Nott reasoned, the state of "normal relations" between blacks and whites was one in which "the one is passive, the other active in respect to it." In fact, he claimed,

> *Thus in the most intimate of their associations [sexual intercourse between white males and black females], these two races preserve the character which we have recognized the ensemble of their destinies. The white race is Man; the black race is Woman. No formula can so well express the reciprocal characteristics and the law of association between the two races. It suffices moreover to explain how one of these races has been able to be initiator, the other initiated; the one active,*

and the other passive; without its following that this relationship carries with it, as has been maintained at least for the future, on the one side superiority, on the other inferiority.[23]

In making this claim, he clearly argues that the sexual domination of black women by white men personifies and realizes the past and continual relationship between the races. Because, according to Nott, domination also has a "civilizing" effect, political and sexual domination is positioned as "a positive good."[24] In addition, by assigning "the white race" a masculine, active identity, black men and women all are feminized, rendered passive, and thus unworthy of the rights of men. The idea of black manhood is erased, invisible, and nonexistent; black men are emasculated and dominated. In theory and in practice, black women become an object and medium through which the domination of the "inferior" race is perpetuated and continued. In this manner, even the unspoken reality and necessary violence associated with "active" white male sexual domination over "passive" black women is accepted as a component of the "normal relations" that exist between white men and black women. Rendered passive, black women's "intimate associations" with white men function symbolically to preserve the social "law of association" that rests on Africana inferiority.

In their attempts to assign political relevance to notions of biological and racial differences, proslavery theorists fueled efforts to belittle black womanhood and, more generally, to publicly desecrate "conquered" women's sexuality. Sidney Fisher, for example, melded the rhetoric of political expansion with that of an aggressive language of romantic pursuit, passion, and conquest. In doing so, he maintains the alleged superiority of the Anglo-Saxon race vis-à-vis both Africana and Mexican people. In his estimation, further annexation of "tropical territories" and the revival of the slave trade

> *[A]ppeal directly to the ruling passions and marking traits of the Saxon; his love of conquest, his love of colonizing and founding, his love of material prosperity and profitable industry, his love of supremacy and control. These qualities have sent him all over the world in quest of land to subdue and cultivate and possess, and have encircled the earth with his drumbeat and his canvas, his language, his laws, and his arts. Tempting, indeed, are the fertile regions in and around the Gulf of Mexico, rich*

in the productions for which the markets of the world open their hungry mouths, and occupied now by a weak, effete, mongrel, withered race who cannot govern them, or cultivate them, or bring out of their soil a tithe of wealth, or defend them against an invader.

Although "effete, mongrel, and withered," the Mexican race of which Fisher spoke was "tempting" nonetheless. In fact, Fisher declared that while they were not able to "defend" themselves from "invaders," they welcomed subjugation. He wrote, "They invite us by their alluring looks, by their syren smiles, by their bewitching beauty, and say to our valor, our enterprise, our daring mounting ambition—come and take us and our delights; we belong not to the weak, but to the strong and bold." According to Fisher, conquest was an urge that white Americans simply could not resist; the erotic lure of adventures involved with consorting with those who offered themselves, ostensibly, so freely would not be denied.[25] The effort to conquer these willing, albeit dangerous, seductresses would be ensured with the generosity of "Africa who offers her dusky millions of docile laborers, feebly and inefficiently protected now, by repealable laws."[26] Nott and Fisher provide useful examples about ways the domination of conquered women infused the rhetoric of white superiority.

ᴍ

In a speech to the New York City Anti-Slavery Society, Sojourner Truth proclaimed, "I could not speak English 'til I was ten years old, and I can't read now, but I can feel! I heard many people say that we're a species of monkeys or baboons; and as I had never seen any of those animals, I didn't know but they were right."[27] Although illiterate, Truth addresses disparaging allusions to black women's alleged link to orangutans, allusions that were expressed by Thomas Jefferson and legitimized further by scientific theories that purported that blacks were, in fact, a separate species of animals. Although she could not read, she was able to engage popularized theories about Africana humanity as they permeated the public sphere.

In the reference to the publication of the second edition of his text *Thoughts on the Original Unity of the Human Race,* Charles Caldwell pointedly appealed to "enlightened readers and ingenuous thinkers, to whom alone it is addressed," and not to "readers enthralled by an opposite condition of mind, who never, in the true sense of the term, think at all, but are the slaves of sightless feeling and passion."[28] Similarly Henry S. Patterson castigated those who "embraced or rejected with violence or heat" ethnological arguments of racial differences as they intersected with religious beliefs. To illustrate his point, Patterson cited Payne Knight's assertion that "Men think they *know* [sic] because they are sure they *feel,* and are firmly convinced because strongly agitated."[29] In Patterson's view, such feelings were inconsequential and in no way relevant to the study of racial differences.

In contrast, Truth maintained that while she could not read, it was important to note that she could "feel." To a certain extent Truth's and other black female slave narratives were powerful because they had experienced, resisted, and survived the "sightless feeling and passion" of others. Thus she questions the assumption that literacy should be a marker of humanity and that one could not use "feelings" to challenge those who would label her an animal. In doing so, Truth raises the fundamental question: In what ways did black women who were not privy to either scientific language or to the written word engage, inform, provoke, and provide ammunition against theories of racial inferiority that assaulted not only Africana humanity, but also, in specific terms, black womanhood?

Slave society relied on the complete reversal of social mores that respected Africana humanity. George Fitzhugh, for example, claimed that free society was "a monstrous abortion," while slavery was "the healthy, beautiful, and natural state of being."[30] Because black women were routinely publicly violated, it is understandable that in their efforts to resist, they were willing to reclaim, at all costs, their always already publicly exposed, publicly abused bodies. In one example, an ex-slave recalled, "I knew a woman who could not be conquered by her mistress, and so her master threatened to sell her to New Orleans Negro traders. She took her right hand, laid it down on a meat block and cut off three fingers, and thus made the sale impossible."[31] While the woman in this account was made bereft of the full use of her right hand for the rest of her life, she did seize ownership of her own body. The horrific and perverted circumstances provided a context in which self-mutilation could become an act of resistance. Significantly, however, it is important to note that continual resistance to the mistress's attempts to "conquer" her preceded this rash act.

In addition, our understanding of black women's resistance cannot be fully grasped without a complete appreciation of the extent to which their perpetual violation could lead to ostensibly "irrational" forms of resistance. In his recollection of black women's activities during the Haitian Revolution, William Wells Brown provided his readers with a context for black women's insurrectionary, albeit unconventional, behavior so that it would make sense. He recalled,

> *While white women were cheering on the French, who had imported bloodhounds as their auxiliaries, the Black women were using all their powers of persuasion to rouse the Blacks to the combat. Many of these women walked from camp to camp, and from battalion to battalion, exhibiting their naked bodies, showing their lacerated and scourged persons; these were the marks of slavery, made many years before, but now used for the cause of human freedom.[32]*

As Brown asserts, in an effort to remind men of the complete horrors of enslavement, women uncovered their bodies, pointing to the "evidence" of their scars. In doing so, both Haitian men and women were forced to recall the sights and sounds of slavery that they had muffled during decades of enslavement. Full recognition of the lasting impression that slavery had left on their persons, these women reasoned, could serve as the needed catalyst necessary to propel formerly enslaved Haitian people toward full revolution. Brown's 1885 interpretation implicitly argues that women who survive the dehumanization process can become quite dangerous provocateurs and participants in revolutionary violence.

Proslavery theorists, however, rejected this "unit of psychological heterogeneity" and willfully misinterpreted the ability of black women to survive the daily threat of sexual abuse as complicity with forced sexual labor. Even in the eyes of many abolitionists, blacks grew desensitized to the sight and sound of sexualized abuse. After describing the whipping assault of a naked young woman tied to the ground in a prison, abolitionist James Redpath observed,

> *A shocking part of this horrid punishment was its publicity. As I have said, it was in a courtyard, surrounded by galleries which were filled with colored persons*

of all sexes: runaway slaves, slaves committed for crime, or slaves up for sale. You would naturally suppose they crowded forward, and gazed, horror stricken, at the brutal spectacle below. But they did not; many of them hardly noticed it, and some were entirely indifferent to it. They went on in their childish pursuits, and some were laughing.

Yet Redpath also placed the blame for black female exploitation squarely on black women, asserting that mulatto women were "gratified by the criminal advances of Saxons."[33] Such observations reveal the extent to which such sexualized scenes of terror could be simultaneously acknowledged and dismissed.

Slavery's apologists were hard-pressed to defend a system that so traumatized Africana people, that in desperation, rage, and defiance some enslaved Africans would runaway, mutilate themselves, murder, and, at times, actively decide to take not only their own lives but also the lives of their children. The Garner case provides a particularly useful example of the influence black female resistance had on the development of ethnological, proslavery arguments. Over the course of the 1850s and 1860s, the Garner case became the subject of numerous newspaper articles, poems, essays, and speeches. According to her biographer, Steven Weisenburger, Margaret Garner's contemporary importance as a symbol of the antislavery cause rivaled that of Anthony Burns's and Dred Scott's.[34] Yet Margaret Garner's story disappeared until resolutely, beautifully, and lovingly resurrected over a century later by Toni Morrison.

As Morrison's novel intuits and historical accounts confirm, Garner's decisions—and similar acts of women's insurgency—were preceded by lifetimes of resistance to the soul-wrenching day-to-day experiences and unspeakable horrors to women. Black and white abolitionists inundated the abolitionist and national presses with accounts of these revolutionary moments. Incidents involving enslaved women were especially compelling to the reading public.[35]

Particular attention focused on enslaved women who elected death over slavery, as they made conscious decisions that their lives—as they were constrained, manipulated, and devalued by slaveholders—were no longer worth living. The Africana press lauded, for example, the Garners' actions. An editorial printed in the *Provincial Freedmen* (see note 36) asserted that the press received daily accounts of men, women, and children who managed to escape "the land of oppression." Margaret Garner's resolve to kill her daughter rather than allow her to be reenslaved, the writer claimed, was a particularly notable example of "utter abhorrence of the fiendish system manifested." Rather than criticize her, the author proclaimed, "may her spirit be fostered wherever the land is polluted with the unhallowed feet of those accursed beings, namely, Slaveholders." Moreover, he stated that her efforts embodied Patrick Henry's revolutionary call, "Give me liberty or give me death." In doing so, the writer affirmed Garner's claim to democratic principles that had been denied to all men who were not white and all women. Defiantly, the writer advised his readers, "all endeavors should have been made to cut the throats of the lawless pursuers, which would have been in compliance with the Sacred Scriptures, which say 'Resistance to tyranny is obedience to God.'"[36]

Reports of women who killed their slave owners, overseers, themselves, or their children forced readers to speculate on the everyday experiences that would drive them to take such rebellious, albeit desperate measures. In reference to the Garner case, for example, the public speculated on the paternity of Garner's youngest three children, all of whom were described as light mulatto children. It is plausible that her owner, Archibald K. Gaines, as the only white male adult on the plantation, could have fathered the children during the frequent occasions when her husband, Robert, had been hired out on distant plantations. The possibility that Margaret and Robert were fleeing not only their owner but also a man who took full advantage of the access he had to Margaret during her husband's absence fuels and could explain further their desperation at the time that they decided to flee the plantation.

Using a term coined by T. Denean Sharpley-Whiting, Garner's attempts to wrest sovereignty over children who had been "conceived violently" further complicated her roles as mother in economic and social terms that bound them to, and yet challenged, slaveholders.[37] The disturbing presence of children born out of violent conceptions—often spoken of in black and white women's accounts of plantation life and gingerly alluded to in both antislavery and proslavery publications— simultaneously challenged both the myth of the "benign institution" and the assumption that blacks and whites were separate, distinct species.[38] In her actions, Garner attempted to wrest "black motherhood" from the power of slaveholders.

During the mid-19th century, many black women defended their natural right to mother their children and to define the conditions under which they would become mothers. Black women, at times, could not prevent rape. They were unable to will their raped bodies not to conceive; but they could attempt to control the body's efforts to bring new life into the world, thus thwarting the legacy of the rape. Garner's choice to kill her children may be read as a desperate attempt to wrest control over her children from her slave owner.

For solace, many slaveholders could turn to scientists of race and antiblack pamphleteers, who constructed empirical ways not only to deny the existence of black female insurgency but also to justify the everyday atrocities on slave plantations. John Van Evrie, for example, provided his readers with an alternative narration of the Garner case. In the process of being "taken back to her home," he asserted, Garner "cut the throat of her child, whom she had carried off in her flight."

Van Evrie's description of the plantation as a "home" complemented proslavery theorists' attempts to depict with domestic harmony what was, in fact, a site for the perpetual commodification and inhumane abuse of Africana people for the purposes of profit.[39] He maintained that the enslaved woman "has always control and direction of her offspring at the South so long as that is needed by the latter." Of course, the slave owner determined the black child's need for a mother. Conveniently for slaveholders, Van Evrie asserted, "the negro child, with its vastly greater approximation to the animal, is also less dependent at a certain age than the white child."[40] Moreover, he argued that as the child aged, mothers often cared little for their children, and children lost affection for their mothers. "A few years later," he wrote, "and she forgets it altogether, for her affections corresponding with her intellectual nature, there is no basis, or material, or space for such things."[41] Such ethnologically derived presumptions implicitly made the trauma associated with the separation of enslaved mothers from their children trifling and inconsequential.

In addition, his emphasis on the fact that the child had been "carried off" implies that Garner did not have a right to "take" her own child. Yet, in the same text, he described slave masters as "the supreme ruler, the guide director, the common father." The "simple and subordinate" people under the master's charge were protected. According to Van Evrie, "the relations of mother and child are rarely interfered with, for both the interests of the master and the happiness of the mother demand that she should have the care and enjoy the affection of her own offspring."[42]

He went on to ridicule abolitionists, who "of course, admired and praised this bloody deed, and declared that, rather than her child should live as a slave, she with Roman sternness and French exaltation, herself destroyed its life."[43] Yet in his effort to provide an explanation for her decision, Van Evrie could not bring himself to condemn the act itself; instead he attributed her valor to the fact that Garner was a "mulatto"; presumably, any courage could be attributed to the "white blood" coursing through her veins. According to Van Evrie, such acts were "scarcely possible to the negress, whose imperative maternal instinct, as has been observed, shields her from such atrocity."[44] In placing an emphasis on black women's "instincts," as opposed to the more-complex emotion of "love," Van Evrie sought to emphasize in the reader's mind the alleged animal-like qualities of black women. In reference to black women, he maintained, "her maternal instincts are more imperative, more closely approximate to the animal."[45]

Van Evrie simultaneously justified and scientifically "naturalized" the continual sexual, economical, and political exploitation of black women. In doing so, his work actively sought to distinguish white womanhood from black womanhood. According to Van Evrie, black women were unable to blush with "maiden modesty." While he did not go so far as to deny that black women were wholly without a sense of morality, he underscored the fact that "she has not the moral nature of the white woman."[46]

In addition, his description of black women's hands denied black women the femininity and the ability to do skilled work. According to Nott, black women's hands were "incompatible with delicate manipulation." He described black women's fingers as "coarse," "blunt," "webbed," and "lacking in a sense of touch." He maintained, however, that blacks' sense of touch became more sensitive on the surface of their bodies. This sensitivity, in his mind, explained the exaggerated, pained reactions to whippings.[47]

Van Evrie challenged directly abolitionists' rhetoric regarding the abuse of slaves. He ridiculed abolitionist conventions in which ex-slaves were "expected, of course, to horrify the crowd with awful tales of his suffering." Van Evrie downplayed slaves' testimonies, comparing them to the normal level of discipline a parent would give a child. "Those who can remember being flogged in childhood will also remember the great pain that it gave them; tough now in their adult age, they would laugh at such a thing. The negro is a child forever, a child in many respects in his physical as well as in his mental nature, and the flogging of a negro of fifty does not differ much, if any, from the flogging of a child of ten."[48]

At every turn, it seems, Van Evrie's ethnological work served only to denounce, defend, or deny the grisly torture and sexualized violence to which Africana men and women continually were subjected.

By exploring theories specific to alleged Africana women's inferiority, I reveal the extent to which their scientific conclusions were informed by regional, economically driven expectations of the role black women should play in Northern and Southern societies. In their work, Josiah Nott, Sidney Fisher, and John Van Evrie attempted to shape, control, and define the public's image of black womanhood. I argue that they used scientific language to exonerate slave masters and, in fact, "objectively" dehumanized black people, thus allowing whites to distance themselves from any impulse to respect Africana humanity and—more specifically for the purposes of my line of inquiry—black womanhood. An analysis of their work illuminates the extent to which the aforementioned scientists and pamphleteers attempted to deny and/or justify the conditions under which black women were expected to live.

As I consider black women's insurgency during the 19th century, I acknowledge that, in the perpetual effort to resist complete dehumanization, resistance manifested itself not only in physical and intellectual struggles and confrontations but also in the formation of families and in efforts to love freely. However, responsible consideration of the historical records of black women's experiences—read against the effrontery of ethnological efforts to discount them—also will serve to bring us to the unflinching realization that, for some women, "resistance to tyranny" as "obedience to God" assumed the forms of abortions, infanticides, suicides, murder, and death.

Chapter 5.

Defining a Principled Peace

Homenaje a Francesca Woodman

Consuelo Méndez

Introduction

Reconciliation should be accompanied by justice, otherwise it will not last. While we all hope for peace, it shouldn't be peace at any cost, but peace based on principle, on justice.

—Corazon Aquino

Peace. The word emerges from lightly pursed lips, that next open to permit vowels to emerge, followed by teeth and tongue that form a sibilant sound and concludes its utterance. If this is how we speak of a compassionate world, how do we articulate the reality of violence? As we have read, we do so by naming in a loud voice those histories, institutions, behaviors, and experiences that oppress and steal the humanity from women and girls of color.

A walking meditation enacted by a queer Korean woman describes how she heals from the physical and mental abuse of homophobia as she journeys the streets of her neighborhood. She does not dismiss the violence she has suffered, but tries to find compassion for those who harmed her, and by doing so, hopes not to replicate the anger and physical threat wreaked upon her. Young African American women walking the mean streets of Chicago find safety and courage in one another: The Rogers Park Young Women's Action Team offers adolescent girls and teens the opportunity to collectively create brave and heartfelt written responses—poems and spoken word performances—to the public onslaught of demeaning and threatening behavior directed toward them. Two domestic violence counselors working in Houston offer their experiences in crafting poetry as a method of reducing the shame of abuse. By offering bilingual, crosscultural examples of prose and poetry to Chicana and African American survivors of violence, they assist clients in acquiring the voice of self-worth and empowerment. Mothers imagine a better life for their children and endure much to create that reality for their offspring. In a poem, we read of a Japanese mother working in a sweatshop, laboring on article after article of clothing, and dreaming of a better life for her children. It is well known that generational violence in families occurs. What is less known is how different generations of families might heal, together, from the abuse. A work of creative nonfiction, inspired by the domestic violence in the author's family, ends up providing her and her father the space for rapprochement. Dawn brings the promise of a new day, and with it comes the hope for a better life. A blessing poem that evokes the many nations of American Indians chants the promise of hope, represented by the morning star. Healing happens in its fullest circumstance when an individual is surrounded by those who love and support her—family, friends, community. A choreopoem rooted in the many cultural traditions of African American women ritualizes the healing process. The visual arts provide another modality of healing. In an essay we hear from a Chinese American artist who works not only in Philadelphia but also in South America, Africa, and Asia, applying the balm of collective creative expression. Honoring the Four Directions is an indigenous tradition; a poem illustrates how the elements of the spiritual world can center us, who dwell in the material world. It is impossible to predict when or whether we can ever come to personal or collective resolve regarding the violence that we experience in the everyday. What we can do, however, is reflect on its effect. The book concludes with a personal tribute by a Chicana whose murdered cousin's memory caused her to work on this volume.

Chinaman in Brooklyn

YK Hong

Over the past few years I have been living in Bedford Stuyvesant and Crown Heights in Brooklyn, New York. These are two neighborhoods that I have truly grown to love and struggle in. As someone who has organized in communities around gentrification, I have always examined my own space and role in gentrification. I am a thirtysomething Korean living and surviving in a predominantly black neighborhood, with folks from a rich diversity of African descent. These neighborhoods get gentrified and regentrified, both by people of color and white people, by people of African descent and those not, by young families and new professionals. When I walk down the street in Brooklyn, I feel a sense of understanding that this community has undergone many generations of transformation to get to this current moment.

I have made many friends along the way—some who were born and raised here, and others who are newly relocated. This is the community I have found and that has been found for me. Among queer, trans, and intersex people of color, in particular, I have talked with individuals around the country and world who have been ostracized from their families, alienated, or perhaps simply cannot keep as close to them as they would like. This is when one's community is even more important, and when community truly becomes family and home.

It makes sense that the composition of those who have brought violence against me are from the neighborhood, hence predominantly black. Some believe I am a bit overly optimistic in my hopes of building with a community I am obviously not a part of originally. Friends and family have encouraged me to move to different neighborhoods, different cities even. My entire life I have moved around the country and around the world, and at this moment, I feel that my home is here in Brooklyn.

I would not say that violence here is any more extraordinary than other places I have lived. Violence comes in so many forms, but is often only documented when it is physical. I have been punched, slapped, mugged, hit with a pipe/rocks/bricks, verbally harassed, stabbed, grabbed, fondled, touched, and sexually violated. Even so, I can honestly say that I do not feel more oppressed here than I do anywhere else. Cuts on my body heal quicker by far than injury to my passion.

The reasons for this violence seem to range from questions of my sexual identity, gender identity, from being Asian, to general ambiguity. I am told very clearly what they see me as: "Hey, Chinaman," "faggot," "batty boy," "chinky," "dyke," so many things. Though I do not identify as any of these, sometimes how one is perceived is such an entirely intrinsic part of one's being that it must also be embraced critically.

I actually have tried to have conversations—sometimes successfully, usually not, perhaps at not the most strategic of moments—with those who initially come to me with violence. The times I have had successful conversations, people have listened with curiosity, confusion, and genuine thirst, and I have been able to defuse what could have been a violent interaction. It is at these rare opportunities I have been able to communicate with the very people that have expressed their violence through me. We typically have discussions that I have had hundreds of times; people want to know who I am, what I am, and what I'm doing here. These passing conversations serve a multitude of purposes: They may save my life, they may allow me to build personally with individuals, and they may take down some inhibitions that exist historically between Asian and black communities.

The most I have done legally, in response to the violent incidents, is have conversations with other community organizers and organizations and make sure I have people with me when I walk home late at night. I haven't made reports to the police for this violence primarily because I do not want the police going after my community. In addition to this reason, from past experience, I have found that I am often the one interrogated when I come into contact with the authorities. Who am I, what am I, and what was I doing there? Even though these are the same questions my neighbors ask me, when I am asked by the authorities, it does not seem to yield potential for building in the same way.

There was a time, after a particularly tough rash of getting roughed up, that I was afraid to walk alone. After a couple of weeks of refocusing, I talked myself through this fear and exercised my confidence to understand that I needed to be who I am and still be able to survive. So I overcame that fear and took a long stroll down the street, and I fell in love with this city again.

There is something that happens to many of us—I call it "one in ten days"—where nine days out of ten, I can handle the violence without a problem, without thinking it is affecting me. However, on that tenth day, I know it has been building, because that is the day, regardless of how big or small the violence, that I am deeply wounded and saddened.

If one could capture the expression on my face in slow motion when a fist is coming at me in these situations, it might portray what I feel accurately. My face reflects the utter sadness I feel; with tears in my eyes, my body probably stands with awareness of the world being fucked up and certain events having to happen, but asks *why?* at the same time.

As long as I have been talking to thousands and thousands of people around the country about internalized oppression, antioppression, and oppression in general, I still feel the hurt when I see it as strongly as I did the first time I remember being called a "chink" as a small kid. I am physically fit, have extensive martial arts defense experience, and am quick on my feet. Nevertheless, I am not at war with my people, and unless it is life threatening, I do not strike back.

I feel sadness that people I am trying to build with are feeling so much pain that it manifests in violence. My sadness centers around the fact that what people don't know creates fear, which creates violence. My sadness centers around the fact that our internalized oppression is so deep; that we have been carrying a fear of the unfamiliar with us from the days of colonization—destroying that which we are unfamiliar with is the historical basis for the founding of the United States.

For many years there have been community programs, neighborhood block association initiatives, and community organizing efforts to curb violence within our communities. When we hurt, we hurt each other. I think of this violence, as many of us do, in the larger context of how everyday survival to us often leads to acting out our anger. It seems the most basic and elementary of reactions, acting out on others when we are angry, and it is so fundamentally a part of our conditioning.

Of course violence increases when gentrification happens. Families that have been struggling to hold onto their abodes for years are pushed out in days. Of course there is tension between Asian business owners and the mostly black folks who make up this community. This hostility and violence are what we are taught to have internally and externally. We are taught to destroy our bodies, to be unhealthy. This leads to addictive, abusive, hurtful behavior to those in our own families and communities. We know all of this. In addition, this is where we need to stop killing ourselves.

My entire life's work is based on the knowledge that we, as oppressed beings, are working toward something much larger than us. This is simply the way that I personally have been venturing through these challenges. I am, with many beside me, working to radically change the world and how things work. I truly believe in revolution, and I work to have that vision every day. I struggle with keeping sight of this vision and the larger picture, with keeping myself afloat, and with building with a community in which people need one another to survive. This is the street I walk down every day, these are the people that may feel the need to fight me today, but that will fight beside me another day soon.

Dedicated to all those who walk down the streets and experience
emotional, physical, and sexual violence every day.

In Our Own Words: What the YWAT Is All About

Rogers Park Young Women's Action Team

Two B-girls are walking down the street on their way home from school. A group of young men is standing in front of the local drug store smoking cigarettes.

Boy 1: Hey ma was'up?

Girl 1: (talking to her friend) Who is he talking to?

Girl 2: I don't know.

Boy 1: Hey girl in the black jacket (talking to Girl 1), let me holla at you for a minute. (walking up to her)

Girl 1: What?

Boy 1: So was'up lil'ma?

Girl 1: I don't see your mother out here so who is you talking to?

Friends of Boy 1: Oooh she treated you!!

Boy 1: I'm talking to you. Can I get yo' number?

Girl 1: Umm, no!

Boy 1: Girl you know you want this. (grabbing his crotch)

Girl 1: No, correction, you want this, bye. (and starts to walk away)

Boy 1: (grabs her arm) Wait!

Girl 1: Look you betta get yo' hands off me! I said I don't want you, so bye!

Boy 1: You feisty just like I like 'em.

Girl 1: Well you'll just be liking 'cause you ain't getting me. (turns to her friend) Let's roll, ain't nothing poppin' over here. (they walk off)

Boy 1: Ooh you playin' hard to get that's alright cause I ain't want yo ugly
ass anyway.

Girl 1: Yeah, I couldn't tell, whatever. (the girls walk off)

This scene plays out every day in a hundred ways in our community.

We, the Rogers Park Young Women's Action Team (YWAT), came together to address the very serious problem of street harassment in our community. We started in July 2003 by conducting some research. We asked girls who were our ages, between thirteen and nineteen, about whether they felt that street harassment was a problem for them. We surveyed 168 girls between the ages of ten and nineteen. We also interviewed 34 other teen girls. Of the girls surveyed, 86 percent said that they had been catcalled on the street; 58 percent said that they had been harassed by men or boys; 54 percent said that they never responded to the catcaller or harasser. The finding that was the most surprising to us was that 53 percent of the girls that we surveyed said that there was *nothing they could do to stop the street harassment.*

We were fourteen teenage girls who disagreed with the idea that there was nothing we could do about street harassment. Although we don't believe that we will be able to *stop* street harassment, we do believe that we can do something to lessen it and to educate people about its negative effects on girls. We do this work as a team. We get support from each other and we believe that we are already making a difference in our community. We have met with our elected officials to share with them the results of our research and our recommendations, we have organized community forums, and we have launched a successful Respect Campaign in Rogers Park. The Respect Campaign enlisted the support of more than 150 local businesses to post our signs in their windows. We organized a citywide day of action against street harassment on May 4, 2006, and were able to encourage more than 140 individual and collective actions across Chicago.

Since 2003, we've addressed other forms of violence (mainly teen relationship abuse) that affect the lives of teen girls like ourselves. We sponsored a poetry contest about teen dating violence and hosted a poetry slam for the winners in May 2004. Many of us in the YWAT consider ourselves to be poets. We've included some of the poetry that members have written about how we see violence in our world. We worked together to create the following visual poem. It captures what we experience as girls in our community and how we confront the everyday violence that we face.

Who's Afraid of the "Big, Bad, Wolf" in the HOOD

Sometimes walking down the STREET
Feels like an OBSTACLE COURSE.
We are constantly trying to avoid DANGER.
It's like Lil' Red Riding Hood
Who was sent into the WOODS
To take food to her sick old grandma and
Was attacked instead by the BIG BAD WOLF.
For us,
the STREETS sometimes seem filled with
BIG BAD WOLVES.
In our neighborhood, which is THE HOOD,
The WOODS are streets with names like
Morse, Howard, Touhy, and Clark.
In our neighborhood, which is THE HOOD,
The wolf WHISTLES
And CALLS like a CAT.
He says:
"Oh what nice LEGS you have."
"Oh what a beautiful BODY you have."
He calls us lovely, FAT ASS, sexy, SKANK,
thick, STUCK UP, all that, BITCH, on fire, HO!
We hear the INSULTS—they are like claps of THUNDER.
In our neighborhood, which is THE HOOD,
The wolf INVITES us to "come kick it with him."

He asks for the DIGITS.

When we say NO, he SPITS OUT

"You ain't SHIT anyway!"

He offers us a smoke and maybe a drink.

He doesn't care if we're 12 or 18.

This wolf is an equal-opportunity HARASSER.

In our neighborhood, which is THE HOOD,

The wolf makes us believe that

We are being HARASSED

Because of the way we LOOK or DRESS or just

Because "BOYS WILL BE BOYS."

Whatever the case, he makes us BELIEVE it is

OUR FAULT.

We take the BLAME—what did YOU do?

In our neighborhood, which is THE HOOD,

Lil' Red FIGHTS BACK.

She refuses to be SWALLOWED whole by the

BIG BAD WOLF.

She STANDS on the corner of Morse Ave. and

Demands R-E-S-P-E-C-T.

She

Demands an END TO STREET HARASSMENT.

She prints up thousands of posters with these words

And HANGS them everywhere in the H-O-O-D.

In our neighborhood, which is THE HOOD,

Lil' Red is

Tan and Mocha

Caramel and Coffee

Brown and Black.

Her name is Shannon and Shauniece,

Crystal and Christine,

Renee and Ronnett,

Jonnae and Jackquette,

Jasmine and Joyce,

Emilya and Daphne,

Karia and Geri.

In our neighborhood, which is THE HOOD,

Lil' Red is

NOT afraid

of the BIG BAD WOLF.

When people ask us what the YWAT is, we tell them that YWAT is about helping our community. We discuss various problems in our community (specifically having to do with violence) and create solutions for these problems. We have researched street harassment, made a movie about violence, and have organized a poetry slam about teen dating violence. We hope that all of these things will reach teens in our community. We are glad to make a difference.

Using Poetry to Reduce Shame

Leticia Manzano and Deborah Okrina

Introduction

We use poetry for our own healing. Some years ago, after counseling sessions with teens that had been raped, molested, or beat up by their partners, we talked about how difficult it was to hear story after story. Working as sexual and domestic violence counselors, we often experienced secondary trauma, which included feelings of anger, powerlessness, and shame. Ultimately, when we'd get that out of our system, we talked about our personal experiences and how we coped with them. We found that both of us used writing as a way to process our feelings and as a way to sort out our thoughts. Moreover, we both discovered the power that writing had to help us feel differently about our lives and about our perceptions of women's realities. It made perfect sense to incorporate poetry into our work when we discovered that many of our clients at the Houston Area Women's Center were closet poets.

We began incorporating poetry into our counseling program. We started with individual clients, most of whom were young inner-city women of color who had experienced sexual or domestic violence. As our confidence grew, we used poetry in our group sessions. We continued to search for new and better ways to inspire and encourage our clients to tell their stories about how violence had affected their lives.

We learned that in order to create a safe place for survivors to write, we had to praise the work that was shared. We made it a point to let people know that spelling and grammar were not important. We also explained to our clients that poetry did not have to rhyme or even follow rules. Sometimes it felt like there was an unlearning process that we had to help them through in order to set their creativity free. Out of that, our clients began to produce true poetry. They expressed real, raw emotions, including pain, anger, shame, rage, and sometimes even hope. Often, with tears in our eyes, we listened to women share their secrets and tell their stories through poetry. We had the privilege of watching our clients, who had been victims, walk out of a reading with their heads held high, as strong, confident survivors.

This success led us to create monthly poetry readings at the women's center. We were inclusive in our invitations to survivors, friends and families of survivors, advocates, and any community members who supported an end to violence. Some readings were small, some large, but we always worked hard to maintain a safe, supportive environment. Our poetry readings are usually bilingual Spanish/English, because it enriches communication, not inhibits it. We made it a point to translate all poems and group writing activities. Finally, we decided to share our ideas with other counselors so they could use this in their work. The work that follows is an outline of what we learned about using poetry to address violence in the lives of women and teens.

Shame

One of the consequences of domestic violence and sexual assault is the shaming of victims. The perpetrator humiliates and degrades the victim by the act of violence. Friends and family may discredit the victim. Finally, shame can be a product of the way institutions in our society treat victims. The very label, victim, can produce feelings of shame.

According to feminist psychiatrist Judith Jordan, "A powerful social function of shaming people is to silence them. This is an insidious, pervasive mode of oppression, in many ways more effective than physical oppression." (Jordan, 1989) All women experience oppression. Whether or not they are survivors of violence, the prevalence of its existence in our society results in some degree of shame and silencing. Women of color experience oppression in the form of racism as well. One of the goals of healing is to reduce this shame. We believe that poetry can be a significant and meaningful shame-reducing intervention.

Poetry

Survivors have long used writing as a healing technique. Writing allows the survivor to express her thoughts and feelings. The next step in the process, perhaps the most significant for reducing shame, is for the survivor to read her work aloud and to realize that she can be honest and still accepted by her listeners.

Poetry lends itself to writing about trauma, because it does not have rules. Poetry does not have to be linear or make chronological sense; therefore, it can encompass any survivor's reality, even if some of her memories are unclear. Poetry allows survivors to use metaphors instead of directly retelling the details, which permits a safe measure of distance, yet keeps the ability to retell precise feelings. Poetry permits the survivor to collect her strength and give voice to something that has not been expressed.

Poetry is also useful for women who have not experienced domestic violence or sexual assault. It allows them to express feelings about violence against women. Shame is often an underlying feeling for these women. Poetry, read aloud, serves to facilitate dialogue with other women on how to address these issues.

Using Published Poems

For educational purposes, published poems about domestic violence or sexual assault can be an interesting way to open a dialogue that will allow you to facilitate an enlightening discussion. Before you use a poem, read the poem yourself. Ask yourself how it makes you feel. Published poems can also demonstrate that poetry does not have to follow rules. For example, spelling and grammar do not have to be proper. To encourage women to write, it may be important to shatter the myths about poetry that they have learned from being required to read classic poetry in English classes (which is often written by white males). In counseling, it is important to match the feeling of the poem with where the client is. If you keep a notebook of poems that you are familiar with, you can pull out a poem that may speak to the client during that particular session.

Some Questions That Facilitate Discussion of a Poem

- What is your reaction to the poem?
- Is there a theme or message in the poem?
- What is the mood of this poem? What do you think the narrator was feeling?
- Is there a particular line that has special significance to you?
- If you could say something to the poet, what would you say?
- For counseling sessions: How does this poem relate to what is going on in your life?

Encouraging Clients to Write Poetry

Poetry helps clients identify and express feelings; it may be used in individual or group settings, and it may be created during sessions or as homework. Poetry allows the use of images and metaphors, and as a result, it permits the client some distance through the use of a third-person narrator. Fuzzy or unclear memories are sometimes easier to express in poetry than in journals or other forms of writing. Clients are sometimes resistant to the idea of writing poetry. Therefore, encouragement is important. Keep telling clients they can do it. Eventually, most clients will try writing. Those slow to engage in the work sometimes feel the most empowered by and proud of their writing after some time.

Some Suggested Writing Exercises

- Write a poem about how difficult it was to keep the abuse a secret.
- Write a poem in the form of a letter to the abuser.
- Write a poem in the form of a letter to another survivor, offering encouragement and support.
- Choose one feeling that for you has been more frequent and more intense since the abuse. Write a poem describing that feeling.
- Write a poem about how the world might be many years from now, when violence against women is no longer a problem. Try to include what it took to get to that point in history.
- Freestyle: Write about anything.
- Select at least one of the following openings or invent one, and write a list of fifteen sentences, each beginning with the same opening clause. It can be about any subject. "I have known" . . . "I have seen" . . . "I am listening for" . . . "I am waiting" . . . "Let there be" . . . "I have desired" . . . "I have felt."
- Imagine two sides of yourself as distinct characters, each with reasons to be angry at and to love or need the other parts. Write a poem in the form of a letter, where one part of you writes to the other.
- Group poem: Each participant goes up to a flip chart that everyone can see and writes one line. Then another client goes up and writes another, and so on, until the group feels the poem is done. The facilitator can read the poem out loud and confidently, as if it were a published poem, to demonstrate how the poem is coming along. The

facilitator can read it in its entirety upon completion. Additionally, the facilitator can then type up the poem and give copies to the attendees the following week.

Sharing Poetry with Others

This is the most important aspect for shame reduction. The space for sharing needs to be a safe, controlled environment. Teach the "audience" not to critique poetry, but to listen to the feelings behind the words. This will happen naturally, but you can facilitate it. Ask the audience to make positive comments on the work. Some will read very quietly. Listen closely. Comment on what you could hear. A soft-voiced woman will get louder as her personal power increases.

Poetry and You

Secondary trauma may include feelings of shame. Other aspects of working with survivors can also lead to shame and frustration. Some examples: In our work with survivors, we cannot always see immediate results; many of our skills are difficult to define and evaluate; people on the outside may admire our work, but few understand or even know what we do. These and other aspects of our work can take us to places of vulnerability that we did not know existed. Poetry is a useful self-care tool for those of us who work with survivors. Be careful with self-disclosure if you read in a group that includes clients. You may need to find another place to read your work. Start your own group, or read at a staff meeting. Make an effort to share your work in a supportive environment.

Poems

The poems listed below were chosen for different reasons. They are a variety of poems written by women about women's experiences. Some of them are empowering, some of them might serve to validate a woman's experience with violence or the feelings that she may be having after that experience.

Maya Angelou, "Phenomenal Woman," *Phenomenal women: Four poems celebrating women.* New York: Random House, 1994. Empowering; celebrates being a woman who is beautiful for who she is, not how she looks.

Sandra Cisneros, "Loose Woman," *Loose Woman*. New York: Vintage Books, 1995. Defiantly addresses the names women are called, and how independent women are seen as a threat in our society.

Lucha Corpi, "Romance Negro" / "Dark Romance," *In Other Words: Literature by Latinas of the United States,* Roberta Fernandez ed. Houston: Arte Publico Press, 1994. A young girl is sexually assaulted, her offender offers a mare to her father as a marriage proposal, and the girl commits suicide to avoid the marriage. This poem is available in English and Spanish.

Nikki Giovanni, "Hands: For Mother's Day," *The selected poems of Nikki Giovanni (1968 1995)*. New York: Morrow, William & Co., 1995. Explores how women use their hands to nourish, and how this is our history, and how we evolved as womankind. "Woman." Describes a woman trying to be herself in a relationship with a man who is not supportive, and coming to accept that the problem is with him, not her.

Marge Piercy, "The Ordinary Gauntlet," *The Moon Is Always Female*. New York: Alfred A. Knopf, Inc., 1980. Addresses sexual harassment.

Carolina Monsivais, "Somewhere between Houston and El Paso," *Somewhere between Houston and El Paso: Testimonies of a Poet*. San Antonio: Wings Press, 2000. Beautifully describes the overwhelming feelings of a woman who works with teens who have experienced violent relationships and sexual assault.

Ntozake Shange, "With No Immediate Cause," *nappy edges*. New York: St. Martin's Press, 1978. Addresses the frequency of domestic violence, sexual assault, and child sexual abuse; also addresses the fate of women who defend themselves.

Mariahadessa Ekere Tallie, "Forced Entry," *Listen up! Spoken Word Poetry*, ed. Zoe Anglesey. New York: One World/Ballantine, 1999. About a teen survivor's reaction to acquaintance rape, connecting her experience to violence against women.

Sojourner Truth, "Ain't I a Woman?" *Ain't I a woman! A Book of Women's Poetry from around the World.* New York: Random House, 1987. Addresses issue of women of status being treated differently than poor and/or minority women. Also expresses the belief that women are stronger than men are.

Alice Walker, "Be Nobody's Darling," *Anything we love can be saved: A writer's activism.* New York: Ballantine Books, 1998. Be yourself, don't listen to "them," great to use with adolescents. "A Woman Is Not a Potted Plant." A woman is not to be confined or taken care of, but is to be free.

Useful Books

These are a few of the books that have helped us use poetry and writing with our counseling clients. There are many more books that you can find about writing and the healing process.

Rosemary Daniell. *The Woman Who Spilled Words All Over Herself: Writing and Living the Zona Rosa Way.* London: Faber & Faber, 1998. In this book, Ms. Daniell tells about her experiences of teaching poetry in prisons, and in low-income schools. She also tells about her writing groups that were created for people who want to become writers but are very much like support groups. She provides many writing exercises and as a bonus, some great recipes of the food shared by group members.

Nicholas Mazza. *Poetry Therapy: Interface of the Arts and Psychology.* London: CRC Press, 1999. This book is a clinical look at the use of poetry in therapy. Mr. Mazza gives a practice model for individuals, families, and groups. He also addresses special populations, one of which is battered women.

Brene Brown. *I Thought It Was Just Me: Women Reclaiming Power and Courage in a Culture of Shame.* New York: Gotham, 2007. We have been influenced by Brene Brown's research on shame and have used her shame resiliency work with our sexual and domestic violence clients for years. Her newest book is helpful for anyone dealing with the issue of shame.

so

Barbara K. Ige

the whirring of the sewing machines
lulls the little one to sleep

   maybe the hum will sink into her bones
         naturally,
         she will know how to sew
         without me teaching her
         how to create beauty out of scraps
   this one will be an artist
   i know
   i can tell
         her hands move like my mother's

                        haha's[1]
                        with grace
                        with determination
   maybe the sound of the machines will tell her
   i want your life to be better
         she will have strong, clear eyes
         not eyes that fail her at night
         she will have beautiful, scarless hands
         not fingers that were sewn
                  with thick black thread
                        when she was tired

319

i dream of her

i dream for me

i work for us

her body

their bodies

fabric

upon which they sew

finding the patterns

in the texture of life

nestled next to my feet

baby

akachan[2]

sewing aunties

obasan[3]

caring for you

teaching you

loving you

believing in you

your aunties

your sisters

your family

sewing machines

time clock

imprison the women who create

beauty out of cloth

3 cents a piece

the whirring of the sewing machines

lulls the little one to sleep

gentle comfort

but not enough

piece of heart
piece of hand
shoulders hunched over

     cannot stop

     cannot fall behind

     feed the children

       we must

not

miss a stitch

we will ruin the pattern

       of their ways of keeping us in

line

       Them

       those who never sewed

       clock/us/watch/us/control/us

       They

       who speak our language

       know our fears

       know our religion

       know how to humiliate us

          they know

            Us

       but they will never own

            Us

    zigzagging

over-lacking

     bodies fray under the stress

as oil eases the pain of the machine

     bodies break

     minds splinter

a new girl

next generation

     using two feet

we are all beginners

as we struggle

     to regain our lives

     our dignity

     we will teach her

     we are your *okasan / obasan / onesan*[4]

     kazoku[5]

     familia[6]

     jya ren[7]

     family

baby beneath my pedals

you will be free

This poem is dedicated to my mother, "aunties," and all of the workers around the world who have worked and continue to work in sweatshops.

Spitting Images . . . or Luck, Accident, and Truth: Breaking the Cycle of Domestic Violence

Teresia Teaiwa

I am the spitting image of my father. There is no mistaking our relationship. I am the eldest of three daughters. Unlike my sisters, I have his skin color and hair color. I have his eyes; I have his bone structure. I am clearly his daughter.

It's very strange when you look so much like your father and so little like your mother. You can feel a little bit distant from the parent you don't look like. And you can feel a little bit doomed by the parent that you resemble. And here I am, the spitting image of my father.

But what I have inherited from my father is not as clear-cut as if I had been a son. As his daughter, I am not a twin, or a mirror image, or a "mini-me" of my father. I am he—as a woman. How weird and wonderful for fathers of daughters—for men to see what their lives might have been as girls and women. It's like surrogate crossdressing. But the results can be unpleasantly edifying.

My relationship with my father was forever changed by three conversations.

This is not exactly how the conversations went. My memory is a bit hazy. I think if things had turned out differently I would have remembered the details more clearly.

CHARACTERS

Me: twenty years old, at home on vacation after graduating college

Dad: approximately forty-five years old

Mom: approximately forty-five years old

SCENE 1: LIVING ROOM

Me: (groaning and writhing on the couch)

Dad: (leaning over the couch, concerned) What's wrong with you?

Mom: (alarmed) Darling?

Me: (feverishly delirious—the combined effects of drunkenness and coral poisoning—words slurred and garbled) Police . . . came . . . scared . . . he scared me . . . hurt me . . . rough . . .

Dad: (confused) What are you talking about?

Me: Rough . . . breaking things . . . choking . . . pushing . . . I fell . . . out of car . . .

Dad: What?

Me: Scared . . . too scared . . . to fight . . . back . . .

Dad: What's wrong with you? Damit! I didn't work my guts out for you to get a good education only to let you let some jerk rough you up!!

Me: You . . . hurt . . . Mom . . . he . . . hurt . . . me . . .

Mom: Oh, darling!

Dad: What?

Me: You . . . hurt . . . Mom . . . he . . . hurt . . . me . . .

Dad: (choked with silence)

Mom: (looks defeated)

Me: (loses consciousness)

SCENE 2: BREAKFAST TABLE, A FEW DAYS LATER

Dad: I've got to travel to ——— for work. Do you want to come with me?

Me: Okay. Why not?

Dad: Since we'll be out that way I thought we could go to the island. Visit your grandfather and great-grandfather.

Me: Cool! That would be great!

SCENE 3: HOTEL ROOM, A FEW DAYS LATER

Dad: You feel like having a beer?

Me: Yeah!

Dad: (picking up the phone) Room service? Can you bring six bottles of ——— to room ———? Thank you.

FIVE OR TEN MINUTES LATER

Me: (sucking on a cold beer bottle) Oh that tastes good.

Dad: I think we need to talk.

Me: (hesitant) Okay . . .

Dad: You know what you told your mother and me the other day?

Me: Oh, I was pretty out of it! (laughs nervously)

Dad: I want to tell you about the two old men we went to visit yesterday.

Me: Yeah?

Dad: Well, let's start with your great-grandfather.

Me: Oh, man. He's amazing! How old is he? Ninety? That was so cool meeting him!

Dad: Yes, well let me tell you about that man: I grew up watching him kick my grandmother around. In the front yard—where all the neighbors could see. He'd kick her while she lay on the ground.

Me: Oh, shit.

Dad: And your grandfather? I grew up watching him hit and kick my mother as well.

Me: Oh, my god.

Dad: That's what I grew up with.

Me: Oh, wow.

(We sit and drink our beers in silence.)

So this is not exactly how the conversations went. But it's close enough. My father and I have never talked about these things again, either. We haven't had to. My dad never hit my mother again. And I've never let another man choke me, or push me, or try to run over me with a car. Four generations of domestic violence ended after three conversations.

I could never have imagined these conversations prior to them happening. Words were beyond me.

It was images that were overpowering me. I grew up watching my father go into drunken rages against my mother. One morning when he had come home from a drinking binge, I saw him rip the dressing gown she was wearing from neck to waist. I was eight years old. I ran to the neighbors' house in panic and in tears, to get help. The neighbors' father had been drinking with my dad. I was a bit doubtful about his unbuttoned shirt and beer breath, but he came to my mother's rescue. The next day I noticed she had a cut lip.

There were a few more images like that before and after, but most of all, I wasn't seeing violence, I was hearing it. I was hearing glass and plates breaking, pots and pans banging, doors slamming, yelling, swearing, whimpering, pleading. I hated it.

I wanted to storm outside and say to my dad, "Stop it!! Just stop it!!! Stop scaring us!! Stop hurting Mom!" But those words were beyond me, so I stayed silent. And prayed that I could become someone else—be adopted by a larger, loving family. My friends became my life. Not my family.

Sometimes my mother would come to me and ask me what to do. I had the answer when I was a teenager: "Leave him." My mother couldn't do it. And I thought to myself, "If this ever happened to me, I'd leave him just like that!" with a snap of my fingers.

Yet those words were beyond me the first time my boyfriend raised his voice at me and pushed me hard. They were still beyond me the first time he put his hands around my throat and held me up against the wall. They were even further beyond me when he took a club to his den and smashed up everything he could. They were way beyond me as I stood shaking behind the locked kitchen door with his grandmother, praying that he wouldn't try to come in to get us.

"If this ever happened to me, I'd leave him just like that!" If you've ever thought those words, they do come back to haunt you. Tease you. Taunt you. It's not as easy as that snap of your fingers. It's pretty damn complicated. Because the more strong you thought you were, the harder it might actually be to get out of it.

I was lucky. It was luck. I had to leave—geography made me do it. I had to go home, and home was far away from where he was. So I got out, in one sense. But I was going home to the same thing. And how was I going to get out of that? How were any of us going to get out of it?

Well, the truth: It sets you free. The truth came out accidentally. I was drunk. I had coral poisoning. I had gone to the beach with some friends, and while drinking, I had fallen over in the water, cutting myself on live coral. (Live coral in your bloodstream is not good.) I wasn't planning on telling my parents what had happened with my boyfriend. I wasn't planning on talking to my parents about their fucked-up marriage.

It just came out. The result could have been my death—the combination of alcohol and coral poisoning can be lethal. The alternative was to carry on lying for all our lives. The truth: It sets you free.

What made my father change? What made my father choke on my drunken poisoned words? What made him swallow them? What made him digest them? What made him regurgitate them over bottles of beer?

They say that violence dehumanizes the perpetrator as much as it dehumanizes the victim. Violence can dehumanize the witness as much as the participants. My father sought to be human again. He sought to be freed from his dehumanizing witness to his father's and grandfather's violence. He sought to be freed from his dehumanizing actions toward my mother. He sought to free my mother from his dehumanizing actions. He sought to free me from my dehumanizing witness to his actions. He sought to free me as a victim of dehumanizing violence. It was simple, really. He changed because an opportunity was presented to him to change.

Why didn't he change sooner? Why didn't my mother stand up to him earlier? Why didn't I or any of the other witnesses do something before? That does not matter now. And blame does not provide any answers.

The cycle of domestic violence was broken by truth. Now I'm proud to say, "I am my father's daughter."

Postscript

CHARACTERS
Me: approximately forty years old
Dad: approximately sixty-five years old

SCENE: A CONVERSATION WITH MY FATHER OVER THE PHONE
Me: So, Dad, did you read my piece?
Dad: Yes, girl.
Me: What did you think?
Dad: Gee, I didn't realize I was such a monster. I guess I don't remember things quite the same way.

Me: Of course, I'm remembering it from the point of view of a little girl. So it would be much scarier from that point of view.

Dad: True. (silence)

Me: Oh, Dad, but the point is, you've changed!

Dad: Yeah. (silence)

Me: The point is you've changed, and others could really really benefit from reading our story.

Dad: Of course. (silence) If this can help others, I'm happy. (silence) Some of it is a bit strong, though. I don't know how your mother would feel about it. (silence) I do remember that time in ——— , though. When the neighbor had to come over. It sort of haunts me.

Me: Yeah?

Dad: Yeah. Maybe you can change that bit about the dressing gown. Make it not so bad. Your mother would probably want you to lighten that bit up.

Me: You're right. Mom needs to read this too.

Dad: Yes, give your mother a chance to read it. I've told her about it over the phone, but I couldn't describe to her how strong it was. It really hits you. She has to read it for herself. When she gets home she can read it.

Me: Okay, I'll wait for that.

Dad: You know, that time when you told your mother and me about what was going on? I didn't know what was wrong with you. I thought you had been possessed or something! (laughs)

Me: You thought I was possessed?! (laughs)

Dad: Yeah! I couldn't figure out what had gotten into you!! Now you tell me it was coral poisoning!! (laughs) You're right, girl. The truth does set us free.

Me: I love you, Dad.

Dad: Love you, girl.

Morning Star Children

Suzan Shown Harjo

Morning Star radiates blessings

      for Mother Earth

      and all the worlds

            Her brilliance is

            a gift of the Spirit

Maheo sent Morning Star Woman

      with Corn and Squash

      and Beans and Tobacco

            to nourish the People

            to feed the Spirit

      She delighted the People

            as a shining Star Child

      She inspired the People

            as an Enlightened Elder

      She encouraged the People

            as an Everyday Woman sparkling

            with hope

Maheo told the Cheyenne People:

      "The Nation will be strong

      So long as the hearts of the Women

      Are not on the ground"

Dakota and Osage People sing a song, and it is Wakan:

> "We are not defeated
>
> While the Women are strong"

Messages of Creation

> for all Peoples
>
> for all Time

Messages in the hearts of Women from Arawak and Acoma

> as they turned away from hairy faces
>
> and fixed their eyes on severed hands
>
> and fixed their eyes, and fixed their eyes

Messages in the hearts of Women from Washita and Palo Duro Canyon

> as they were stampeded and invaded
>
> to the sound of ponies screaming in the sunset
>
> to the sound of screams, to the sound of screams

Messages in the hearts of Women from Bosque Redondo and the Crazy Horse Bar

> as they traded themselves for their children
>
> as they sold themselves for food and drinks
>
> as they gave nothing away, as they gave nothing away

Messages in the hearts of Women from Warm Springs to Siletz

> as they end a century of missing memory
>
> as they once again dance in emergence dresses
>
> as they sing their lost and found song:
>
> "They Never Touched Me"
>
> "They Never Touched You"

Messages in the hearts of Native Women

> for all who are touched in unkind ways
>
> for all who pray to end unholy days
>
> for all who shelter the disheartened in loving ways
>
> "They Never Touched You"
>
> "You Are Blessed By The Morning Star Woman
>
> And Your Heart Is Not On The Ground"
>
> "You Are Blessed By The Morning Star Woman
>
> And The People Are Strong"

"You Are Blessed By The Morning Star Woman"

"You Are Blessed By The Morning Star"

"You Are A Blessed Star Child"

"You Are Blessed"

"No Fault": A Story of Personal Pain and Healing

Akasha Hull

T he years 1979 and 1980 inaugurated for me a cycle of conscious spiritual activity that synchronized with the accelerated changes taking place both for other African American women and throughout the world. A second personal-growth spurt occurred about seven years later, when I wrote the following poem. The topic of the poem is the sexual abuse of little girls. It starts in an oppressive, accusatory voice intended to mirror the falsely internalized guilt of girls and women, but this perspective is ultimately vanquished by a ceremonial enactment of collective healing. Here is the poem.

NO FAULT
(for the Circle)

It's your fault, sister
You danced in front of your uncle
when you were three
with just your panties on
So, it's your fault, baby

All your fault—
that your father needed a second wife
      who looked just like your mother

that your mother only had
        her daughter to love
that your grownup brother
            took you for a toy
            when he was drunk

That Satan's family
            wanted a ritual victim
the neighbor next door
            a backyard thrill
that your stepfather really believed
            he wasn't any kin to you

That the deacon said God commanded you
            to be his little angel
that the people at the daycare
                played mommy-and-daddy
                played a nasty pattycake with you

Remember, it was you who danced
in your baby-pink panties
It's all your fault
that they fondled and patted
            fingered and poked
            rubbed, sucked
            diddled, daddled, and fucked
on you

It's your fault, sister
your fault
It's your fault
The voices, the internal tape
            droning on and on

It's your fault
You know that you did it
So, it's all your fault,
the tapes and the voices
staining deeper and deeper
It's your fault
It's your fault
It's your fault

Sister, woman
Sit down lotus here
in front of me
Lay your hot palms
in my own two hands
Head to head, heart to heart
look me in the eye
and say out loud,
however softly:
"It wasn't my fault."

I give it back to you,
the anger and blessing mingling:
"No, it wasn't your fault,
it was never, ever your fault,
it was not your fault."

You were just a child
(It wasn't your fault)
You're such a beautiful woman now
with so much good in you
to give the world
(No, it wasn't your fault)

They always try to say we did it
always place the blame on us
It wasn't my fault, either
I was just a little girl, too
another sweet spirit filled with joy
like you

It wasn't your fault
It wasn't my fault
No, it wasn't your fault,
it was never, ever my fault,
it was not your fault

Another sister's hands
join this circle of healing
She adds her voice
to the growing song:
"It wasn't your fault,
I love you,
Love yourself,
Forgive the awful nothing
that you did,
Love yourself,
Love yourself."

Look me, mirror, in the eye
and speak out loud and free:
It wasn't my fault
Goddamn the liars
It was not my fault
It was never, ever my fault
It was not my fault

It was not my fault
(sense the note of surprise)
It was not my fault
(hear the real conviction)
It wasn't my fault
(let the newfound knowledge sink through)

Now, say it with a smile:
It wasn't my fault
(I am laughing here with you,
helping to fan the sparkle inside)
It wasn't my fault
It wasn't my fault
(she's up now, dancing,
pulling a chain of feet
to shout with her):

It wasn't our fault
It wasn't our fault
It wasn't your fault
It wasn't my fault
It wasn't our fault
It isn't our fault
It isn't our fault
It wasn't our fault . . .

(Chant this until you know
that it is true.)

My Story

Lily Yeh

The story I am telling is a very personal journey made public. It is about my search for meaning, involvement, authenticity, and a personal voice. My life unfolded through the work I did in North Philadelphia and subsequently in Africa, China, and other places in the world. My story is a look into how personal endeavors can become a catalyst for community actions, and how an inward journey can manifest in social change.

It is important to say that I did not start out to create a detailed system for doing my work, nor did I originally intend to create an organization to sustain my work and the work of others for eighteen years. Instead, I managed to rise to the opportunity placed in front of me, albeit with apprehension and fear. I followed my heart and took action. The process of community-based work certainly felt messy and chaotic much of the time. Yet something was working, and what began as a simple project grew into a complex nonprofit organization with multidimensional programs and activities. Looking back (although I acted intuitively), I was guided by strong principles. In my story, I want to share the pivotal moments and events in my life that shaped my sensitivity and thinking and gave me courage to walk my own path. I hope it will help you to find your own voice and authenticity, and that your life will unfold through your brave actions.

A Complicated Journey Reveals a Simple Path

Somehow destiny has a way of unfolding itself through people in certain circumstances. The creation and the growth of the Village of Arts and Humanities (the Village) have turned out to be my life's work up to this point. The fact that it came into being, flourished, and became successful was a surprise to me. Eighteen years ago, when I first started a humble summer project to convert an abandoned lot in inner city North Philadelphia into a modest art park, I could not have dreamed of such a possibility. However, despite the improbability of its existence, the Village came into being.

My experience as cofounder and executive director of the Village has been difficult and challenging, yet at the same time exhilarating and enlightening. I described it as being in the battlefield, which demanded my constant attention and energy. People often asked me how I was able to work with such intensity for so long without being consumed and spent. Most of the time I did not sense such a problem. I felt connected and charged. I felt that I stood at an energy center, and that the meaning of my life manifested through the work I was doing in North Philadelphia. That work became the Village, an entity and force that has been creating itself for the past eighteen years and is continuing to evolve into the future.

The irony in life is that to accomplish something simple, it often requires one to go through a complicated process. For me, it was a twenty-year journey after my arrival to this country in the 1960s to find my passion and light. I studied a lot, traveled a lot, nurtured a family, and tried to understand the real meaning of things. I was exploring to find a way to become a contributing citizen living in contemporary America, yet still keep my personal values and integrity that were shaped by a different world and era. It was a difficult journey. There were times I would suffer panic attacks, fearing that somehow life was passing me by and I was not living it. Gradually, through this patient search, clouds began to lift, and clarity revealed itself. That was when I stepped into the light and began to live the life of an artist.

Taking Action on a Small Park Building Project

The Village had a very humble beginning, both in intention and scale. Arthur Hall, founder and director of Ile-Ife Black Humanitarian Center and Arthur Hall's African American Dance Ensemble, was the person who invited me to create a park on the lot next to his building. I intended to do a short summer project aimed at converting an abandoned lot into a community park with $2,500 from the Pennsylvania Council on the Arts. The team of workers consisted of myself (an eager artist with few skills), a local resident willing to help, and a bunch of kids from the street. No one felt that it could be done. People told me, "Do a feasibility plan and forget about the building part." Or "Kids will destroy everything you build." It seemed really undoable. Then the city leveled the ten dilapidated houses next to the lot. This left me a huge vacant site with eleven adjacent lots. Then I became fearful and wanted a way out.

As I was struggling to make a decision, I heard a little voice in me saying, *Rise to the occasion, otherwise the best in you will die and the rest will not amount to anything.* I decided to gather my wits and start the project. I engaged children, figuring they would not destroy something they helped to build. Then I found Jojo (Joseph Williams), at Arthur Hall's suggestion. Living in a rundown house next to the lot, Jojo (a jack-of-all-trades and a man of fiery spirit) embraced the idea and became my guardian and partner. Because of him, the park-building project became rooted in the community.

One thing led to the next: first the children came, and then adults drifted in. Then we got plant materials and trees from Philadelphia Green. Then came the volunteers. When the warehouse next to the park, the old Ile-Ife Center headquarters, was abandoned, Stephen Sayer, who knew how to do renovation work, joined forces with us. A lawyer by training, a writer, educator, and builder, Sayer understood the enormous potential in the modest park-building project. With the help of neighborhood adults, he took on the renovation of the vacant three-story warehouse and incorporated our projects into a nonprofit organization. We became cofounders of this new entity, which we named the Village of Arts and Humanities.

Upon completion of the building, we launched our year-round after-school program, which was followed by theater productions, crafts productions, publications, a Core Leadership Program, festivals, and a community health program. In the meantime, we continued to convert more trash-strewn lots into parks and gardens, and we renovated several abandoned buildings into education facilities and offices. In 2000 we converted a two-acre industrial brown field into a lush tree farm, with a meadow filled with wild flowers. The tree farm had sixty-five permanent trees, a hundred trees in containers, and the capacity of holding more than fifteen thousand seedlings. We conducted many job-training sessions and created employment for teens and adults in areas of tree-tending and urban gardening. We were contracted to grow native tree seedlings for Fairmont Park and Awbury Arboretum. The proudest thing I can proclaim is that our tree farm has no fence! Everything is in the open. Yet we have very little vandalism, because the community watches over and protects it.

In addition to all these activities, the Village now assists and collaborates with various community groups, nationally and internationally. All of these activities of the Village have resulted from the little park-building project that I launched some years ago. The ultimate intention is to build a new kind of urban village in which people are reconnected with their families, sheltered in descent housing, sustained by meaningful work, and nurtured by the care from one another, and thus can protect and raise their children together.

Local Becomes International

At this point I want to share with you another momentous time in my life that impacted me in a profound way: my experience in Korogocho, Kenya. Korogocho is a shantytown outside Nairobi with one hundred thousand residents. The town hovers around a huge city dump. Thousands of children and adults enter the dump daily, competing with hundreds of menacing storks, to scratch out their daily bread. It is a living hell, with horrid odor everywhere and thick dark smoke rising from various trash piles spontaneously combusting. It is a place where industrial, medical, and food wastes and animal carcasses are dumped. Yes, this is hell, a vast land of total destitution and despair.

I had the good fortune of meeting Father Alex Zamotelli, a man with a gentle yet fierce spirit and unfaltering faith. He established the St. John's Catholic Church in the midst of Korogocho. He lives there with the poor so he can best help them. With the assistance of my hosts, Phillda and Elimoa Njau, of Paa Ya Paa Art Center, and Father Alex, I was able to mobilize children and adults in the community to transform a barren and bleak churchyard into a jubilant environment filled with painted flowers, guardian angels, and colorful patterns. Here, I witnessed the power of art in transforming environment, to bring hope, joy, and beauty to people. The day of dedication brought together government officials, international guests, and hundreds of community residents. On that day, the heavy door of Korogocho opened and sunlight and hope came in. The jubilance of the people made me realize that our presence from the outside was very important in Korogocho, because it made residents feel that they were not forgotten and that their sufferings were not in vain.

Following the Light Inside

How was it possible for a woman with few skills in park-building, and even fewer skills in community-building, to become a catalyst for such creative energy and rebuild a whole community? The answer is simple. I followed my passion and was guided by the light inside of me. That light does not belong to me alone. It is innate in all of us. Everyone has it. But more often than not, we choose not to see it.

I have often been given credit for helping people transform their lives. However, it was I who felt isolated and separated. It was I who longed to make contact with that which is essential and real in myself and in others. In short, I think I longed for love and a real sense of belonging through reconnection. I did not know where to find it. So the only thing I could do was to be quiet, to listen, to wait, to observe, to understand, to get ready, and finally, to become involved. I traveled everywhere to look for that, and I found it in the inner city of North Philadelphia and the trash land of Korogocho, Kenya. I found it in the hearts of many people who also long to belong and reconnect.

Finding Opportunity on the Flip Side

Back in 1986 I went to North Philadelphia to build a park on an abandoned lot. I was not well equipped with knowledge or resources. I was well equipped with something essential—the desire to take action and the understanding of the power of embracing. The experience of growing up in China and years of studying Taoism and Buddhism made me understand that the world is made up of two conflicting and yet complimentary forces, which the Chinese named the Yin and the Yang. The Yin and the Yang are, for instance, the shady and the sunny side of a mountain or an object. They must appear simultaneously and always in the company of each other. Nothing is ever still. These two forces or elements are constantly moving to become each other. Each element contains the seed of its opposite and will eventually become its opposite. This understanding makes me see things differently. When I see the brokenness, poverty, and crime in inner cities, I also see the enormous potential and readiness for transformation and rebirth. When I see deficits, I see resources on the other side of the coin. When I stepped into the project, I was lacking in every way. This weakness became my most powerful tool in realizing the project. Because I was lacking, I needed help. It provided opportunities for people to meaningfully join the project, helping me to realize my goal. It helped people realize their strength and provided people opportunities to reconnect with each other through working together. Through this process, our separate and individual selves were made whole. Empowering and healing in people began to take place. This was the first step toward community rebuilding.

Becoming a Leader

I did not know how to lead. It was the children who taught me how, the children who came into my project some eighteen years ago. It was a project from which most of the adults stayed away. The children—through their innocence, curiosity, joy, and willingness to take part—showed me the power and source of their creative energy. Their participation forced me to figure out a different way of doing things. It was a way that was not taught in my school, not in my family life, nor in the talk of our society. That was when I learned how to be a leader. A real leader understands the art of following. To lead, one must follow the feeling that comes from the heart and the energy that surges forth directly from life itself.

Embracing Action

I have dedicated myself to making art since my high school years. Then, beginning in 1986, I chose to create art with people in poor communities, such as inner city North Philadelphia; the old town in Accra, Ghana; the trash-filled land outside of Nairobi, in Kenya; and very remote villages in Ecuador, China, Ivory Coast, and the Republic of Georgia. For me, it has been a special gift to work with people in these dire circumstances, to make a real contribution and a difference in people's lives. These difficult and compelling situations make life more real for me. They help me to better understand who I am and why we live, and to see the complexity of human nature in its light and dark manifestations. By looking at challenges face-to-face and by acting with compassion and creativity, we can find hope and new solutions.

For me being an artist is not just about making art, it is a way of life. It is about delivering the vision one is given, about sharing one's gifts freely, and about doing the right thing without sparing oneself. If one does all that, one can eventually become truly free. In May and early June of 1989, I visited Beijing and witnessed the unfolding of the Students' Movement at Tiananmen Square. It was like being in the eye of an immense storm, which revealed history in the making. Quietly sitting in the middle of the enormous square, the students who went on the hunger strike triggered a powerful force, arousing the whole country and the world to support and rally behind their actions. In Beijing at that time, everyone became an artist, expressing their feelings through action: writing poetry and prose, creating paintings and sculptures, participating in marches of people, motorcycles, and trucks. The country was on fire with new hopes, dreams, and intense emotions. The hunger strikers were students from Beijing and Qing Hwa Universities, the equivalent of Harvard and Yale in China. They were the cream of the crop and the chosen leaders of the future. Yet in deciding to do the right thing, they did not spare themselves. That was where their power lay. They did not ask to change others. They simply took action themselves. That left an indelible mark in me.

The most powerful action is to embrace our fear. Wonders happen through that action. Yet most of the time, we lack courage to do it. I almost did not do it. Fortunately in a moment of strength I stepped forward. In this one step, the mystery of my life unfolded in thousands of ways, and my life has forever been changed.

Three Steps Forward . . .

In my most recent trip to Medellín, Colombia, to attend an international conference on Centros y Ciudades Competitivas (Competitive Centers and Cities), I realized that the work I have been doing is not only about an individual artist working with disfranchised people in an isolated situation. It is a part of the global movement to make the world a better place through grassroots efforts. Government, professionals, and the private sector can build powerful systems, such as transportation, utilities, communication, and other infrastructure. They can construct physical buildings, highways, and technology complexes. But they cannot solve all the problems caused by the enormous growth of urban centers all over the world—particularly problems caused by poverty and population displacement. While good systems can bring physical, social, and economic improvement for people, they rarely can address the emotional, mental, and spiritual needs of the people. Although intangible, these needs are critical to people's well-being. We need to focus on building compassionate communities where people have a strong relationship with each other and are genuinely concerned for the welfare of all. Art and culture can function as powerful tools to connect people, to strengthen family ties, to preserve cultural heritage, and to build community.

Scientists explore the mystery of the universe through science, philosophers through philosophy, and artists through art. When we create art that comes from the heart, it heals and transforms. The art we create with community residents flows out of their experiences and deep concerns. It reveals the pain and sorrow and celebrates the hope and joy of the people in the community. Its process is open and inclusive. Through this creative process, participants become reconnected with each other and with their innate creative power and imagination. This creative power and imagination is the light within each one of us.

Through doing projects together, we intend to pass on this light within us to illuminate it within others. Together we unite and shine. This light cuts through the darkness of our ignorance, greed, politics, and social blight. It connects us with compassion, generosity, and kindness. Here, I believe, lies the hope for the future.

Community-building is challenging and often without glory. It is three steps forward, two steps back. It is trench work filled with sloppy and mundane details. Then why do I do it? I do it because it fulfills my deepest longing to be connected with others and to become whole. Despite the endless failings, in that one step, the world begins to change.

Glossary of Lily's Metaphors

The Village of Arts and Humanities works like cultural ecology. It reminds me of the work of ecologist William Niering. He turned bad soil to good soil through cultivating the land. At the Village, we turn bad stuff into good stuff through art and culture. I call this process of turning dark and destructive materials (lead) into positive, nurturing substance and into beauty and joy (gold) "urban ecology." It is magical and very doable. There are steps and structures to this process. It is the essence of my methodology. When I think of the Village and how it functions, I think of the following images in nature.

THE PLANTING OF A SEED

A seed, though small, is potent. It contains all the growth patterns and qualities of a plant, be it a small bush or a huge tree. I see that a seed is like an inspired idea. It has authenticity because it contains life in its small but potent form. Inspiration comes not from our head; it is given from the source of life. It is from an energy source that makes our heart beat fast. It is like our inner light; it guides us. It knows when and how to make things grow. It comes from our heart, which is connected to the divine source of energy, of feeling, and of love. If one is connected to one's heart, one is connected to the primal energy source. Ideas that come from there have immense power for growth and impact. An artist's work is to realize those ideas so that they blossom, come to fruition, and are not wasted.

THE GROWTH OF A TREE

I see that community evolves in the way that a tree grows. As the seed of a tree breaks ground (reaching downward), its stem reaches up toward the sun, the source of light and energy. As the seedling grows stronger, it begins to sprout leaves and branches. The deeper the roots grow, the taller and stronger the tree grows. As the tree grows downward and upward, its branches reach simultaneously in all directions. With the rain and dew in the night, the tree puts out flowers. It begins to attract insects, birds, animals, and people because of the resources it offers: the shelter, shade, cool breezes, nourishment, and beauty. This is the way I see that the Village has become a community. It grew organically and naturally. It emerged and is still in the process of creating itself through many people's hard work and dedication. The deeper the roots grow, the more the tree can open up, reach out, survive stormy weather, and realize its full power and potential.

DEEP OCEAN KELP

Deep ocean kelp is securely rooted in a small and fixed place. Although the plant is pliant, it is tremendously strong. Riding and responding to the ocean current, it can reach everywhere to gather food and look for new opportunities. The Village works this way. It takes root in a particular community in inner city North Philadelphia. It has regional, national, and global impacts due to the clarity of its mission, its values and artistic sensitivity, the simplicity of its primary structure, the flexibility of its methods, and its openness to people's participation.

A SCHOOL OF FISH

Schools of fish are interconnected, in tune with each other, sensitive and responsive to the environment and quick to reorganize. They move in unison and are dynamic.

SHEDDING AND FROGGING

In lean times, plants shed leaves and even branches. A certain kind of frog burrows underground in the dry season. When rain comes, the leaves and the frogs surface and take action. At the Village, we burst into full bloom when resources are plentiful. In lean times, we frog some of our programs. Whatever we have learned and begun is not lost. We simply frog the activities until the resources (rains) arrive.

THE DRIFTING OF A COCONUT FRUIT

Imagine a coconut in a river or on the ocean shore. The coconut drops into the water and gets carried away according to the force of the current and the formation of the land. If the new environment is supportive, the coconut will take roots and begin to propagate. Although the original coconut tree grows only in one fixed place, its impact can have infinite possibilities. This is how the Village can have a local and regional influence and, at the same time, a national and global impact.

THROWING A PEBBLE INTO A POND

The pebble is thrown and touches the water at a particular place. From this place, the center ripples push outward toward the edge of the pond. This reflects the impact of the Village on a local level, then regional, national, and international. The physical center is the Village and, particularly, the circle in the center of Ile-Ife, the first park. When I started, I drew a circle in the middle of the vacant land with a stick I picked up from the ground. I announced that from here, we would build. Looking back, I see that circle was the physical manifestation of my own center, through which I came in contact with the primary energy source that makes the earth go round and the stars rotate. What connected me with that energy source is that I listened and took action in order to realize the inspired idea I received as a vision.

Remember Her Name

Remember her name. This is a beginning. A fog of untold history must not conceal the story. I must remember her name aloud so that her memory is honored, and in the hope that accounts such as hers will one day no longer need to be told.

✒

My *prima* Virginia was murdered on the evening of August 24, 1980. It was hot and humid in the Bay Area. A leaden breeze carried the ponderous news of her death, communicated at dawn's murky light. Her murderer hunted and killed a series of gay men before he pointed a deadly gun at Virginia. An attorney opined that his predator's behavior was "homosexual rage," that he had "an irresistible impulse springing from fear that he was in fact homosexual." Blame the prey. Spare the predator. Save the patriarchy. However, no such defense was articulated in her murder. For what was to be said? She was a woman and had it coming?

✒

Virginia was a musician, vocalist, and excellent student as a youth. I knew her best when we were teens, she a scant three years older. The chains of my adolescence confined me, and I desired her liberty. Her young adulthood beckoned to me as a light from high above the deep well of my girlhood. My ability to survive adolescence was due in large measure to Virginia's encouragement. She was both conscious and intuitive in her efforts to sustain me during my youth.

Virginia's love of color was apparent as she walked through the house—before she left for a rendezvous with her latest boyfriend—going from room to room as though searching for something. Sometimes her meandering resulted in an important color emphasis to her ensemble: a red silk scarf, which whispered sweet nothings into her ear as it swirled around her neck, or brown leather gloves, whose squeak foretold the kisses shared later in the evening. I especially remember her face as it shined a contrast of lights and darks: black eyes, made inky with the liberal application of Maybelline products, blinked in a walnut-colored face made bright with the flash of her large white teeth, outlined by an iridescent pink lip color on her full mouth.

On those evenings when she had dates, I was left in the misery of my own company. Wandering into Virginia's bedroom, I saw the bed covered in a chaotic heap of colors and textures of clothes, and I inhaled the air filled with her odor: Wind Song, Aqua Net, and sweat. A dressing table beckoned to me from the other side of the room. There was a mystic allure of the sticks and pencils scattered about and with names like "Cherries in the Snow," "Passionate Petals," "Parisian Pink," and "Black Midnight." I could only stare, because for as much as my *prima* loved me, she made it clear that her makeup was off-limits to my experimentation.

Sympathetic to my desire for makeup, Virginia occasionally slipped me an Avon sample of some forbidden cosmetic. Eventually, I left the world of clandestine makeup rites and openly spent my allowance and time in the pursuit of my newfound rituals. My leave-taking of the small-scale blackmarket economy in makeup and entrance into the largest consumer market for women was due to the start of my monthly bloods, whose flow made me eligible for certain sacraments.

Time passed. On the day I was confirmed in the Catholic Church as a "soldier in Christ," I came to understand that if I acted out my desires regarding the adornment of my body,

I was sure to deal with a set of consequences. My first lesson came when I arrived at the church with my family. They went to their pews as proud celebrants and I went off to find *mis amigas,* my girlfriends, also being drafted into the Army of God.

Sister M— saw me first. With one glance, she ordered me to remove my lip color. "Honey Red" it was called. People would not consider me "pure in thought, word, and deed," unless I was of "clean" appearance. I hid out in a bathroom until the time to form the processional arrived. Quickly moving into line with lip color intact, I knew that my days in the Church were dwindling. I went AWOL from God's Army soon after.

A second moment of insight came as *mis amigas* and I stood clustered outside the back of the church. We wanted to spend more time gossiping about boys, hairdos, and the tyranny of parents; however, families moved off into cars headed for home, and we said goodbye with *besos y abrazos.* Walking to the car, Elena and I were deep in an exchange of *chisme.* Her brother Bobby joined us, trotting slightly ahead, and said, "Your lips." He made a move to plant his kiss. He missed, but managed to smear the lipstick. Two cars of waiting families exploded with laughter. I was ready to die on the spot. How dare Bobby ruin my colors!

It was not until many years later that I understood how self-adornment was an invitation to critique/colonize/capture my body, and to tame the wildness projected onto me.

Virginia loved colors, especially when she was able to use her body as a palette for the display of her joy in all that was bright. Did these colors attract her murderer? Maybe if she had been more demure? Her laugh was loud and full. Was there something about her self-assured walk that provoked the hateful attack? She clacked her heels on concrete with a certainty of self. Or maybe it was that smart mouth of hers? Always at the ready with a quick parry that could sting. The lists I conjure are limitless because they contain all the possible descriptions of a vibrant, young, brown woman who met life on her terms. The litany of reasons for her murder written/memorized/evaluated/burnished over many years always returns to the speculation that she came upon a 20th-century conquistador who wanted to tame the colors that he could not otherwise claim.

m

In May 2003 a young girl was murdered in Castro Valley, California. Her body was wrapped in a plastic bag and tossed in the back lot of a restaurant. She was suffocated, a rag shoved down her throat. No name, no identity, no family to claim her, no one to give her a history. Authorities thought she might be Latina. In the absence of any family who might bury her properly, people came forward with contributions. "Jane Doe" was laid to rest in a hillside patch of cemetery. Her brutally anonymous death hearkened back to those of the approximately five hundred women butchered near Ciudad Juárez and El Paso.

Four years passed before the identity of "Jane Doe" was known. Her name is Yesenia Nungaray Becerra. Yesenia was sixteen years old when she was murdered. She left her Mexican village, much to her mother's concern, a scant two months before her death. Yesenia was trying to make a better life for herself and her family. Her killer is still at large.

Remember her name.

Glossary

prima: cousin

besos y abrazos: kisses and hugs

chisme: gossip

Daily Mask

Blue Wade

Acknowledgements

Barbara K. Ige, whose passionate involvement as co-editor caused this project to live and emerge as it is today, is a tremendously brave comadre for whom I have the highest regard. My family continually gives me love and encouragement. Mike Sweeney, my hubby, offers compassion and critique. My mother CVO, sisters CiCi and Sue, and brother Joe provide me a space to be vulnerable and open to their caring. Mr. B, Rosie, and Baby offer support as members of the tribe. Colleagues at San José State University in the Department of Social Science and Women's Studies Program deserve a special mention for their inspirational work.

—M.O.

Without the support of friends and family, this work would not have come to fruition. My amazing and tireless co-editor and friend María Ochoa brought me into this important project, and together we hope this collection helps in the understanding of the strength of women of color around the world. M.R. Daniel who never waivers in her support of my dreams. Ana Patricia Rodríguez, brilliant, talented, and uncompromising. Nandini Gunewardena, when there seems to be no light, she is always steadfast and true. Anna Sandoval for nourishing my heart, mind, and soul. Teresia Kieuea Teaiwa and J. Kehaulani Kauanui, *me ke aloha pau'ole*. Beatriz López-Flóres: warrior, ally, and friend. My teachers and mentors, Louis Owens, Judy Yung, Ann Lane and Donna Haraway, whose patience and guidance provide me with the tools to survive and succeed. Colleagues who have supported me on my journey from under the redwoods and palm trees, then back to the Golden State, Shirley Hune, Glenn Man, Christine Mergozzi, Chela Sandoval, Linus Yamane, David Yoo and Ming-Bao Yue. The countless unsung heroes of student support at the University of California, University of Hawai'i, and the Claremont Colleges. My students, you are our future and our hope. My family who gives me sustenance, support, and love, Richard, Janet, Helene, Yoshi and Tatsuo Ikehara, Ana and Jeff Teodorovich. My *inuchans*, the endless source of my joy, Anabelle and Puck. My partner, my best friend, my love, Stephan Teodorovich. *Ippe nifee deebiru.*

—B.K.I.

There are many who deserve thanks for their support, but perhaps none so much as the many contributors and our publisher, Seal Press. Most of the writers and artists in this anthology have witnessed the many cycles that occurred while the book was in process over four long years. Their patience, understanding, and commitment to the project are remarkable. Seal Press and Brooke Warner, in particular, deserve special recognition for understanding the importance of this material. Thank you to Laura Mazer for her visionary leadership as managing editor, Susan Koski Zucker and Tabitha Lahr for their inspired design work, Wendy Taylor for her keen eye and sharp pencil, and Andie East and Wendy Honett for their enthusiastic public relations talents. We especially appreciate that the Seal Press staff always welcomed, understood, and supported the decision to aggregate the different writing genres and the visual art found in this collection. We give a heartfelt thanks to Gloria Anzaldúa, a sojourner taken too quickly from us, who inspired this work. Where there were none, Gloria bravely pointed out the path of social justice for women of color. She had a voice that shattered walls, a fire that made us powerfully wicked, and a belief in humanity to rise above our ignorance and prejudice to create a better world.

—M.O. and B.K.I.

Notes

Chapter 1. Strength in the Service of Vision
THE EVOLUTION OF DOMESTIC VIOLENCE AND
REFORM EFFORTS ACROSS INDIAN COUNTRY

1. Paula Gunn Allen, *The Sacred Hoop: Recovering the Feminine in American Indian Traditions* (Beacon Press, 1992).

2. Lauren Elizabeth Wolk, "Minnesota's American Indian Battered Women: The Cycle of Oppression," *A Cultural Awareness Training Manual for Non-Indian Professionals* (Battered Women's Project, St. Paul American Indian Center, 1982).

3. Paula Gunn Allen, "Violence and the American Indian Woman," *Center for Prevention of Sexual and Domestic Violence Newsletter* 5, no. 4 (1985): 5–7.

4. "History of Victimization in Native Communities by the Center for Child Abuse & Neglect," University of Oklahoma Health Sciences Center (UOHSC) Grant number 97-VI-GX-0002, Office of Victims of Crime (OVC), United States Department of Justice, March 2000, 3–4.

5. Arlene Hirschfelder and Martha Kreipe de Montaño, *The Native American Almanac: A Portrait of Native America Today* (New York: Macmillan, 1993), 19–25.

6. Allen, *Violence and the American Indian Woman,* 5–7.

7. M. Annette Jaimes, ed., *The State of Native American: Genocide, Colonization and Resistance* (Boston: South End Press, 1992), 311–44.

8. Alex Tallchief Skibine, "Troublesome Aspects of Western Influences on Tribal Justice Systems and Laws," University of New Mexico School of Law *Tribal and Law Journal* 1 (2000/2001).

9. American Indian Policy Center, "Traditional American Indian Leadership: A Comparison with U.S. Governance," www.airpi.org/tdsystems.html.

10. Jaimes, *The State of Native American.*

11. UOHSC Grant number 97-VI-GX-0002, 6–8.

12. Sally Roesch Wagner, *The Untold Story of the Iroquois on Early Feminists* (Aberdeen, SD: Sky Carrier Press, 1996).

13. Ibid.

14. "The Role of Indian Courts in the Justice System," the Center on Child Abuse and Neglect (CAAN), UOHSC Grant #97-VI-GX-0002, March 2000.

15. Skibine, "Troublesome Aspects of Western Influences."

16. Hirschfelder and de Montaño, *The Native American Almanac.*

17. "Sexual Assault in Indian Country: Confronting Sexual Violence," National Sexual Violence Resource Center (NSVRC), 2000.

18. Loretta M. Frederick, "The Evolution of Domestic Violence Theory and Law Reform Efforts in the United States," Battered Women's Justice Project.

19. B. J. Jones, "The Indian Child Welfare Act: The Need for a Separate Law," *The Indian Child Welfare Act Handbook,* ABA Family Law Section, 1995.

20. Michael Sullivan, "A History of Governmentally Coerced Sterilization: the Plight of Native American Women," University of Maine Law School, 1997.

21. Ibid.

22. See www.ncadv.org; much of this information was from conversations with members of the NCADV who were participating at the time.

23. Carol Maicki, *Why There Are Two Coalitions in South Dakota.*

24. Vicki Ybañez, "Cangleska: Working against Domestic Violence on the Pine Ridge Reservation," Praxis International, 2001.

25. UOHSC, 16.

26. UOHSC, 17.

27. President's Memorandum on Relations with Tribal Governments, April 29, 1994, 59 Fed. Reg. 22951 (1995); Consultation and Coordination with Indian Tribal Governments, Exec. Order No. 13175, 65 Fed. Reg. 67,249 (2000); and Department of Justice Policy on Indian Sovereignty and Government-to-Government Relations, 61 Fed. Reg. 29424 (June 10, 1996).

28. NSVRC, "Sexual Assault in Indian Country."

29. Allen, *The Sacred Hoop.*

30. Jeremy Nevilles. "Developing Men's Nonviolence Programs," Mending the Sacred Hoop STOP Violence against Indian Women Technical Assistance Project, 2003.

31. Tina Olson, "Sexual Assault in Native Communities," Mending the Sacred Hoop STOP Violence against Indian Women Technical Assistance Project, 2003.

32. Rebecca St. George, "Stalking," Mending the Sacred Hoop STOP Violence against Indian Women Technical Assistance Project, 2003.

33. Valencia-Weber, G., and C. P. Zuni, *Domestic Violence and Tribal Protection of Indigenous Women in the United States, St. John's Law Review* 69 (1995): 76.

34. CAAN, "The Role of Indian Courts."

35. Mary Crnkovich, "The Role of the Victim in the Criminal Justice—Circle Sentencing in Inuit Communities," prepared for the Canadian Institute for the Administration of Justice Conference in Banff, Alberta, October 11–14, 1995.

VOICES OF THE PIONEERS

1. Jyotsna Vaid, "Beyond a Space of Our Own: South Asian Women's Groups in the U.S," *Amerasia Journal* 25 (1999/2000): 112.

2. Maxine P. Fisher, "Creating Ethnic Identity: Asian Indians in New York City Area," *Urban Anthropology* 7 (1978): 277.

3. Margaret Abraham, "Ethnicity, Gender, and Marital Violence: South Asian Women's Organizations in the United States," *Gender & Society* 9 (1995): 456.

4. Mike Tolson, "When Hope Dies," *Houston Chronicle,* July 7, 1996: 1A+

5. Ibid., 17A.

6. Ibid., 16A, 17A.

7. Ibid., 17A.

8. Sudha Prathikanti, "East Indian American Families," *Working with Asian Americans* (New York: Guilford Press, 1997), 81.

9. Margaret Abraham, "Speaking the Unspeakable: Marital Violence against South Asian Immigrant Women in the United States," *Indian Journal of Gender Studies* 5 (1998): 225.

10. Tolson, 16A.

11. Shamita Das Dasgupta, "Charting the Course: An Overview of Domestic Violence in the South Asian Community in the United States," *Journal of Social Distress and the Homeless* 9 (2000): 175.

12. Tolson, 17A.

13. Vaid, "Beyond a Space of Our Own," 119.

14. Abraham, "Ethnicity, Gender, and Marital Violence," 465.

15. Tolson, 17A.

16. Jyotsna Vaid, "Seeking a Voice: South Asian Women's Groups in North America," *Making Waves: An anthology of writings by and about Asian American women (Boston:* Beacon Press, 1989), 403.

17. Vaid, "Seeking a Voice," 402.

THE PREVALENCE OF DOMESTIC VIOLENCE IN AFGHAN HOUSEHOLDS

1. Michele Bogard, "Strengthening Domestic Violence Theories: Intersections of Race, Class, Sexual Orientation, and Gender." *Domestic Violence at the Margins.* ed. Natalie Skoloff (New Jersey: Rutgers University Press, 2005).

2. Firoza Dabby. "Violence Against Women: A Lifetime Spiral, A Tightly Coiled Spring." Domestic Violence in Asian and Pacific Islander Communities National Summit 2002 Proceedings.

3. Bogard, ii.

4. Joy Osofsky. "The Effects of Exposure to Violence on Young Children." *American Psychologist,* 50 (1995).

5. Albert Roberts. *Helping Battered Women: New Perspectives and Remedies* (New York: Oxford University Press, 1996).

6. Shamita Dasgupta. "Women's Realities: Defining Violence against Women by Immigration, Race, and Class." *Domestic Violence at the Margins*. ed. Natalie Skoloff (New Jersey: Rutgers University Press, 2005).

7. Bella Liang, Lisa Goodman, Pratyusha Tummala-Narra, and Sarah Weintraub. "A Theoretical Framework for Understanding Help-Seeking Processes Among Survivors of Intimate Partner Violence." American Journal of Community Psychology 36:1/2 (2005); Ahmad, Farah, Sarah Riaz, Paula Barata, and Donna Stewart. "Patriarchal Beliefs and Perception of Abuse Among South Asian Immigrant Women." *Violence Against Women* 10:3 (2004).

8. Ghuman, Sharon. "Women's Autonomy and Child Survival: A Comparison of Muslims and Non-Muslims in Four Asian Countries" *Demography* 40:3 (2003).

9. Ibid.

10. Moghadam, Valentine. "Modernizing Women: Gender and Social Change in the Middle East." *Gender and Society* 8:4 (1994).

11. Ibid.

12. Central Intelligence Agency. *The World Factbook* 22 July 2006, found online at www.cia.gov.

13. Dasgupta.

14. Ibid.

15. Ibid.

16. Carter, Lucy, Lois Weithorn, and Richard Behrman. "Domestic Violence and Children: Analysis and Recommendations." *The Future of Children*. 9:3 (1999).

17. Carter; Osofsky.

18. Malley-Morrison, Kathleen and Denise Hines. *Family Violence in a Cultural Perspective: Defining, Understanding, and Confronting Abuse* (Thousand Oaks, CA: Sage Publications, 2004).

19. Rachel Latta and Lisa Goodman. "Considering the Interplay of Cultural Context and Service Provision in Intimate Partner Violence." *Violence Against Women,* 11:X (2005).

Chapter 2. Articulating a Global Ethic

SPIRITS IN TRAFFIC

1. Kevin Bales, *The New Slavery* (California: University of California Press, 2001), 11.

2. Neferti Tadiar, *Fantasy Production: Sexual Economies and Other Philippine Consequences for the New World Order* (Hong Kong: Hong Kong University Press, 2003), 116.

3. Siriporn Skrobanek and Nattaya Boonpakdi, *The Traffic in Women: Human Realities of the International Sex Trade* (London: Zed Books, 1997), 102.

4. Lean Lim Lin, *The Sex Sector: The Economic and Social Bases of Prostitution in Southeast Asias* (Geneva: Industrial Labour Office, 1998), 4.

5. Kemala Kempadoo and Jo Doezema, *Global Sex Workers: Rights, Resistance and Redefinition* (New York: Routledge, 1998), 47.

6. Kevin Bales, *Disposable People: New Slavery in the Global Economy* (California: University of California Press, 1999), 88.

7. Skrobanek and Boonpakdi, 8.

8. Ryan Bishop and Lillian Robinson, *Night Market* (New York: Routledge Press, 1998), 17.

9. U.S. Department of State, "Trafficking in Persons Report," June 2003, 79.

10. U.S. Department of State, "Trafficking in Persons Report," Office to Combat and Monitor Trafficking in Persons, June 2006.

11. Tanja Radovic, "One Night in Bangkok," *The United,* http://nasron.dynu.com/united/3-5/articles/radakovic2.html.

12. Ibid.

13. Bishop and Robinson, 7.

14. Minh T. Ha Trinh, *Woman, Native, Other: Writing Postcoloniality and Feminism* (Indiana: Indiana University Press, 1989), 89.

15. Kevin Bales, *The New Slavery* (California: University of California Press, 2001), 34.

16. United States Immigration and Naturalization Services, "International Matchmaking Organizations: A Report to Congress," www.wtw.org/mob/mobrelease.htm.

17. Ibid.

18. Michael Penn and Rachel Nardos, *Overcoming Violence against Women and Girls* (USA: Rowman Littlefield Publishers, Inc., 2003), 48.

19. Kathryn McMahon and Jennifer Stranger, *Speaking Out: Three Narratives of Women Trafficked to the United States* (California: The Coalition the Abolish Slavery and Trafficking, 2002).

20. Siettske Altink, *Stolen Lives: Trading Women into Sex and Slavery* (London: Harrington Park Press, 1995), 46.

21. Sergeant Marcus Frank, "Asian Criminal Enterprises and Prostitution," Westminster Police Department, 2002.

22. Human Rights Watch, *Owed Justice: Thai Women Trafficked into Debt Bondage in Japan* (USA: Human Rights Watch, 2000), 59.

23. McMahon and Stranger, *Speaking Out,* 24.

24. Ibid, 25.

25. John Frederick, "Deconstructing Gita," *Himal Magazine,* October 1998, vol. 11, no. 10.

26. Altink, *Stolen Lives,* 47.

27. McMahon and Stranger, *Speaking Out,* 12.

28. Penn and Nardos, 43.

29. Penn and Nardos, 48.

30. Kempadoo and Doezema, *Global Sex Workers,* 16.

31. Aihwa Ong, *Flexible Citizenship: The Cultural Logics of Transnationality* (USA: Duke University Press, 1999), 6.

32. Sallie Westwood, & Annie Phizacklea, *Transnationalism and the Politics of Belonging* (New York: Routledge, 2000), 145.

33. Satoko Watenabe, "From Thailand to Japan: Migrant Sex Workers As Autonomous Subjects," *Global Sex Workers: Rights Resistance and Redefinition,* Kempadoo and Doezema, eds. (New York: Routledge, 1998), 122.

34. Ibid.,122.

35. Ibid., 121.

36. Pasuk Phongpaichit, "Trafficking in People in Thailand," *Illegal Immigration and Commercial Sex: The New Slave Trade,* Phil Williams, ed. (London: Frank Cass Publishers, 1999), 88.

37. McMahon and Stranger, *Speaking Out,* 65.

38. "The Masala Project: Empowering Victims of Sex Trafficking," http://innerlens.com /masalaproject/index.html.

39. Swapna Gayen, "The Sonagachi Project," *The Communication Initiative,* January 12, 2004, www .comminit.com/pds12004/sld-9486.html.

CULTURE AND TRUTH

1. In total, we have provided support and services to eight women and one man as a result of this one case.

2. According to a press release put out by the U.S. Department of Justice, United States Attorney, Northern District of California, June 21, 2001.

3. Velvadum is a small village, three hundred kilometers from the Andhra Pradesh capital twin cities of Hyderabad–Secunderabad. Velvadam has a population of around 8,500. Its main local economy is agriculture. The Reddy community (by trade a land-owning community) has a strong hold on this village. Velvadum houses Reddy's ancestral mansion and other family homes. His uncles, brother, and other kinsmen live there. Every year, the Berkeley landlord spent millions of rupees to celebrate Hindu and Christian festivals in Velvadam and the nearby villages and to fund educational institutions and hospitals.

4. Alexis Chiu, Putsata Reang, and Brandon Bailey, "Landlord denies importing girls for sex: Authorities say probe expanding in case involving Berkeley man," *San Jose Mercury News,* January 21, 2000.

SELECTIVE STORYTELLING

1. Sue Hutchinson, "Again, Abuse Masquerades as Love and a Woman Dies," *San Jose Mercury News,* August 1, 2003.

2. Julie Patel, "When Culture Rejects Divorce: For Indo-Americans, Breakup Can Be Risky," *San Jose Mercury News,* August 3, 2003; Roxanne Stites, "Milpitas Husband Kills Estranged Wife, Self; Man Distraught Over Breakup of Arranged Marriage," *San Jose Mercury News,* July 22, 2003.

3. Christiane Amanpour, *For Love of Money,* CBSNews.com, October 5, 2003, www.cbsnews.com /stories/2003/10/03/60minutes/main576466.shtml.

4. "Lisa Ling Investigates Dowry Deaths," *The Oprah Winfrey Show.* ABC, January 16, 2004.

5. Ibid.

6. Uma Narayan, *Dislocating Cultures: Identities, Traditions, and Third World Feminism, Thinking Gender* (New York: Routledge, 1997); Veena Talwar Oldenburg, *Dowry Murder: The Imperial Origins of a Cultural Crime* (Oxford/New York: Oxford University Press, 2002); Radhika Parameswaran, "Coverage of 'Bride Burning' in the Dallas Observer: A Cultural Analysis of the 'Other,'" *Frontiers: A Journal of Women Studies* 16.2/3 (1996).

7. Narayan, *Dislocating Cultures;* Sonia N. Lawrence, "Cultural (in)Sensitivity: The Dangers of a Simplistic Approach to Culture in the Courtroom," *CJWL/RFD* 13 (2001); Leti Volpp, "Symposium: On Culture, Difference, and Domestic Violence," *American University Journal of Gender, Social Policy and the Law* 11 (2003).

8. Oldenburg, *Dowry Murder;* Flavia Agnes, "Violence against Women: A Review of Recent Enactments," *In the Name of Justice: Women and Law in Society*, Swapna Mukhopadhyay, ed. (New Delhi: Manohar Publishers, 1998), 81–116; Vineeta Palkar, "Failing Gender Justice in Anti-Dowry Law," *South Asia Research* 23.2 (2003): 181–200; Bhavani Sitaraman, "Law as Ideology: Women, Courts and 'Dowry Deaths' in India," *International Journal of the Sociology of Law* 27.3 (1999): 287–316.

9. Chandra Talpade Mohanty, *Feminism without Borders: Decolonizing Theory, Practicing Solidarity* (Durham: Duke University Press, 2003).

10. Parameswaran, "Coverage of 'Bride Burning.'"

11. Leti Volpp, "Essay: Blaming Culture for Bad Behavior," *Yale Journal of Law & the Humanities* 12 (2000); Parameswaran, "Coverage of Bride Burning."

12. Inderpal Grewal and Caren Kaplan, "Warrior Marks: Global Womanism's Neo-Colonial Discourse in a Multicultural Context," *Camera Obscura* 39 (1996); Mohanty, *Feminism without Borders*; Ratna Kapur, "The Tragedy of Victimization Rhetoric: Resurrecting the 'Native' Subject in International/Postcolonial Feminist Legal Politics," *Harvard Human Rights Journal* 15 (2002).

13. Narayan, *Dislocating Cultures,* 100-17.

14. Ibid.

15. Ibid., 14–5.

16. Lata Mani, *Contentious Traditions: The Debate on* Sati *in Colonial India* (Berkeley: University of California Press, 1998).

17. Oldenburg, *Dowry Murder.*

18. Kapur, "The Tragedy of Victimization Rhetoric," 6.

19. Narayan, *Dislocating Cultures.*

20. Ibid., 95.

21. Ibid., 101–2.

22. Narayan, *Dislocating Cultures;* Oldenburg, *Dowry Murder.*

23. "Intimate Partner Violence 1993–2001," Bureau of Justice Statistics, U.S. Department of Justice, 2003, vol. NCJ 197838.

24. U.S. Department of Justice, Bureau of Justice Statistics. "Supplementary Homicide Reports, 1976–2004," Federal Bureau of Intelligence.

25. U.S. Department of Justice, Bureau of Justice Statistics, Special Report, Intimate Partner Violence, NCJ 178247, May 2000.

26. I. Horon and D. Cheng, "Enhanced Surveillance for Pregnancy-Associated Mortality— Maryland, 1993–1998," *Journal of the American Medical Association,* 11 (2001).

27. Patricia Tjaden and Nancy Thoennes, "Full Report of the Prevalence, Incidence and Consequences of Violence against Women: Findings from the National Violence against Women Survey" Pub. No. NCJ 183781, Washington: Department of Justice, 2000.

28. Patricia Tjaden and Nancy Thoennes, "Extent, Nature, and Consequences of Intimate Partner Violence: Findings from the National Violence against Women Survey" Pub. No. NCJ 181867, Washington: Department of Justice, 2000.

29. Volpp, "Essay: Blaming Culture for Bad Behavior," 89.

30. Ibid., 90.

31. Agnes, "Violence against Women: A Review of Recent Enactments;" Anjali Dave and Gopika Solanki, "Journey from Violence to Crime: A Study of Domestic Violence in the City of Mumbai," Department of Family and Child Welfare, Tata Institute of Social Sciences, 2001.

32. Paras Diwan and Peeyushi Diwan, *Law Relating to Dowry, Dowry Deaths, Bride Burning, Rape, and Related Offences* (Delhi: Universal Law Pulishing Company, 1997).

33. Judith G. Greenberg, "Symposium: Criminalizing Dowry Deaths: The Indian Experience," *American University Journal of Gender, Social Policy and the Law* 11 (2003): 803.

34. Ibid., 824.

35. Ibid., 803.

36. Nishi Mitra and Tata Institute of Social Sciences, Women's Studies Unit, *Domestic Violence as a Public Issue: A Review of Responses* (Mumbai, India: Unit for Women's Studies, Tata Institute of Social Sciences, 2002).

37. Oldenburg, *Dowry Murder,* 219.

38. Leela Visaria, Nishi Mitra, Veena Poonacha, and Divya Pandey, "Domestic Violence in India a Summary Report of Three Studies," International Center for Research on Women, 1999: 1–52.

39. Surinder Jaswal, et al., "Domestic Violence in India a Summary Report of Four Records Studies," International Center for Research on Women, 2 (2000).

40. R. C. Ahuja et al., "Domestic Violence in India: A Summary Report of a Multisite Household Survey," International Center for Research on Women (2000).

41. Ibid., 12.

42. Ibid., 4.

43. *The Protection of Women from Domestic Violence Act,* No. 43 (2005).

44. Mangai Natarajan, "Women's Police Stations as a Dispute Processing System: The Tamil Nadu in Experience in Dealing with Dowry-related Domestic Violence Cases," *Women and Criminal Justice* 16.1/2 (2005).

45. Visaria, et al., "Domestic Violence in India: A Summary Report of Three Studies," 36.

HIDDEN TRANSCRIPTS

1. It is important also to make a distinction between suicide terrorists and those who attempt/ commit suicide as self-inflicted harm in the trajectory of emotions and planning that precede the act. Unlike the spontaneous expression of emotion that self-harm represents, suicide terror is a more organized, orchestrated (to ensure maximum physical damage and public attention), and deliberated act with political intentionality. Yet the range of psychological processes and emotions associated with suicide—i.e., rage and/or depression about injustice— whether against sociocultural/familial or political oppression, may still be the same. For the most part, suicide is an act that registers a protest against unbearable life circumstances, and the extent of premeditation between self-inflicted harm and suicide terror may only be a matter of degree.

2. See Council on Foreign Relations article "Terrorism: Questions and Answers," at www.terrorism answers.com/terrorism/suicide2.html.

3. See Radhika Coomaraswamy, "Women of the LTTE," *Frontline,* January 10, 1997, for a discussion of the LTTE's stance on women cadre and a critical examination of the potential for women's autonomy and empowerment via their military roles.

4. Sri Lanka, Sahanaya, Psychological Health Intervention Center, unpublished 1999 data.

5. Tilak Ratnayake and L. Siyambalagoda, *A Guide to Prevention of Teen Suicide* (Sri Lanka: Department of Health Services, North Central Province, 1998).

6. The underreporting of suicidal deaths stem from the fact that they tend to be grouped as "accidental deaths" or as "deaths from undetermined causes," as noted by Ratnayake and Siyambalagoda.

7. Robert N. Kearney and Barbara D. Miller, "The Spiral of Suicide and Social Change in Sri Lanka," *Journal of Asian Studies* 2.1 (1985): 81–101; Robert N. Kearney and Barbara D. Miller, *Internal Migration in Sri Lanka and Its Social Consequences,* (Boulder: Westview Press, 1987); Kalinga Silva and W. D. N. R. Pushpakumara, "Love, Hate, and the Upsurge in Youth Suicide in Sri Lanka: Suicide Trends in a Mahaweli Settlement," *Sri Lanka Journal of Social Sciences* 19.1-2 (1996): 73–92.

8. Miller and Kearney, 1988.

9. According to Miller and Kearney (1988), "male suicides have outnumbered female suicides annually by about 2.4 to 2.5 to one. In the late 1970s, however, the rate dipped slightly below 2.0 male suicides for every female suicide." Miller and Kearney, "Women's Suicide in Sri Lanka," 116.

10. Miller and Kearney (1988) report that 30 percent of female suicides in 1980 were concentrated in the fifteen to-nineteen-year age group, while nearly 60 percent were concentrated in the fifteen-to twenty-four-year age group. My research shows a similar concentration, with 45 percent of female suicides taking place among women aged fifteen to twenty-four years. Women's Suicide in Sri Lanka; Nandini Gunewardena, unpublished 2000 research data sets.

11. I refer to the term "organic" as the range of psychological and physical illnesses, since the latter are also known to lead to suicide, for example, by elderly individuals suffering from dementia or other illnesses.

12. As argued, for example, by Li Zhang, "Migration and Privatization of Space," *American Ethnologist* 28, no. 1 (2001) 181.

13. Also alluded to by Ravina Agarwal, "At the Margins of Death: Ritual Space and the Politics of Location in an Indo-Himalayan Border Village," *American Ethnologist* 28.3 (2001): 549–74.

14. The colonization of the Dry Zone, in an effort to end land scarcity in the Wet Zone, dates back to the early postindependence years (1950s), beginning with pioneering schemes in Polonnaruwa district, initiated by former Prime Minister Dudley Senanayake. Since then, voluntary and involuntary out-migration from the densely populated Wet Zone has resulted in loosely demarcated village areas dotting the sparse landscape of the Dry Zone. More recent large-scale state-development schemes like the Accelerated Mahaweli Irrigation Development program in Polonnaruwa, and its predecessor in Anuradhapura in the North-Central province (dating back to the 1980s), Gal Oya (1960s), Pelwatte and Sevanagala in the Southeast (1980s) have helped establish settlement schemes throughout the Dry Zone.

15. The paradox of relocation as a national development strategy is that there is a disjuncture between the promise of prosperity implicit in resettling land-hungry populations and the reality of their further impoverishment as relocating households find it difficult to eke out a living from their new resource base. This incongruity might well be at the root of the disillusionment with the resettlement process that often leads to more-severe outcomes. It should be noted, however,

that not all relocation schemes have had the same negative outcomes, nor have all relocating households met with/experienced misfortune and despair.

16. I refer to the causality as "associated," because in the absence of direct interviews with individuals who have completed suicides, only inferences may be made about causality. As such, my attempt has been to list all associated reasons reported by family members of the deceased individuals.

17. Since multiple causality is reported/associated with many suicides, the total reasons exceed the sum of the cases.

18. Ritual impurity that is vested upon a woman at puberty with the commencement of her first menstruation confers an ascription of *jara* (dirty) because menstrual blood is considered to cause *kili,* as does childbirth and death, as per Obeyesekere (1963).

19. Differences in sexual morality seen in various regions of Sri Lanka are discussed by Obeyesekere, *The Fire-Walkers of Kataragama*, 475, as "Puritanical morality and repression of sexuality are not characteristic of the population as a whole. However, though originating as the typical prevailing ethic of the "middle classes" and those who emulate them, it is widely prevalent today among Sri Lankans—except urban proletarians and the more traditional villagers."

Chapter 3. Speaking Truth to Power

THE WAY WE DO THINGS IN AMERICA

1. Buchwald, Emilie, Pamela Fletcher, and Martha Roth, eds. *Transforming a Rape Culture,* (Minneapolis, MN: Milkweed Editions, 1991).

2. Kinzer, Stephen, "Feels Like the First Time," *The American Prospect Online,* June 11, 2004.

3. Schmitt, Eric and Thom Shanker, "Rumsfeld Issued an Order to Hide Detainee in Iraq," *The New York Times,* June 17, 2004.

4. Smith, Andrea, "Colors of Violence," *Colorlines Magazine* 3(1), Winter 2000–2001.

5. Smith, Andrea, "Violence against Women of Color," INCITE! Women of Color Against Violence, www.incite-national.org/issues/warinfo/violence.html, June 21, 2004.

COMPETING MASCULINITES

1. UNESCO. *Cultural Rights as Human Rights.* Paris: UNESCO. 1970.

2. Chandran Kukathas. "Are There Any Cultural Rights?" *Political Theory* 20 no. 1. (1992):105-139.

3. U.S. Committee on Refugees. *Follow the Women and the Crows: Personal Stories of Sudan's Uprooted People.* Washington, D.C., 2000.

4. Michael Ignatieff. *Blood and Belonging.* (New York: Farr Straus and Giroux, 1994).

5. Khalid Mansour. *War and Peace in Sudan: The Tale of Two Countries*. (London: Kegan Paul, 2003).

6. Mario C-Lye-Labu, Anya-Nya (1971:3).

7. August 30, 2004.

8. August 25 was designated by the Committee on Consciousness of the United States Holocaust Memorial Museum a national day of conscience for Darfur (July 26, 2004).

9. Associated Press, Boston Edition (Sept. 14, 2004) 1.

10. International Crisis Group. Crisis in Dafur. www.crisisweb.org. 2004.

11. Catherine MacKinnon. "Rape, Genocide, and Women's Human Rights." In *Violence Against Women: Philosophical Perspectives*. Eds. Stanley French et al. (Ithaca: Cornell University Press, 1998): 43-57.

12. C. Dudu "Southern Sudanese Displaced Women: Losses and Gains." In *The Tragedy of Reality: Southern Sudanese Women Appeal for Peace*. Ed. M. Elsanosi. (Khartoum: Sudan Open Learning Organization,1999).

13. Amnesty International. Sudan Report. 2001. Accessed at www.amnesty.org.

14. Amnesty International. Sudan, Darfur. *Rape as a Weapon of War: Sexual Violence and its Consequences*. (New York: Amnesty International, 2004).

15. Recent months have witnessed a relaxation of this law. Strong economic realities mitigated against the implementation of law as far as sexual segregation is concerned.

16. Susan Sared. *What Makes Women Sick? Maternity, Modesty and Militarism in Israeli Society* (Hanover: University Press of New England, 2000).

17. UNESCO. *Cultural Rights as Human Rights* (Paris: UNESCO, 1970).

18. Francis Deng. *The Dinka of the Sudan* (Illinois: Waveland, 1972): 6.

19. Baya, Philister. "Seeking a Refuge or Being a Displaced: Analysis of a Southern Woman's Personal Experience." In Ed. M. Elsanousi. *The Tragedy of Reality: Southern Sudanese Women Appeal for Peace*. (Khartoum: Open Learning Organization, 1999).

20. C. Dudu.

21. See website at www.cesr.org.

22. Mary Hillary Wani. "Women's Agenda for Peace." Paper presented at the Sudanese Women's Peace Forum, Khartoum (October 29, 2001): 2.

23. Amartya Sen. *Development as Freedom* (New York: Knopf, 1999).

24. Posted on United Nations Office for the Coordinator of Humanitarian Affairs. Accessed at www.reliefweb.int.

LAYERED VIOLENCE, IMPERIALISM, OCCUPATION, AND RELIGIOUS FUNDAMENTALISM

1. Hatem, M. "Arab Americans and Arab American." *The MIT Electronic Journal of Middle East Studies* 5 (2005): 39.

2. Amnesty International, 2002.

3. Rubenberg, 119.

4. BADIL Resource Center, 2004.

5. Ibid.

6. UNIFEM, 2001.

7. Amnesty International, 2003.

8. Zohra Rasekh, 1998.

9. Gerami and Lehnerer, 2006, 1887.

WHY SPEAK OF FEMICIDE?

1. The concept of violence is basically defined as "the use of force, be it physical, psychological, or sexual, or the threat of the use of force over another person who is the victim." It is to force someone to do something against their will, or that goes against their integrity or interests.

2. The Right of Women to a Life Free of Violence Act was passed in November 2006 in Venezuela; this law represents significant progress, as it identifies as a crime the following types of violence: work-related, obstetric, patrimonial, sexual, domestic, psychological, and physical.

RUFINA AMAYA

1. A testament to the power of Rufina Amaya's words, this essay has taken an afterlife from its first iterations. Early versions of this essay were published by the Smithsonian Institution, in November 2002. http://latino.si.edu/researchandmuseums/presentations/rodriguez_paper.html, and in *Istmo* 13 (July/Dec 2006) www.denison.edu/collaborations/istmo/n13/articulos/mozote.html.

2. Rufina Amaya quoted in Tim Golden's article, "Salvadoran Skeletons Confirm Reports of Massacre in 1981," *The New York Times,* October 22, 1992: A1:4; May 20, 2007, www.newslinx.org/articles/10-22-1992ElMozote.htm.

3. Alma Guillermoprieto, "Shedding Light on Humanity's Dark Side: The Outspoken Survivor of Slaughter," *The Washington Post* March 14, 2007: C01; May 20, 2007, www.washingtonpost.com/wp-dyn/content/article/2007/03/13/AR2007031301826.html.

4. Ibid.

5. See editorial, "The Media's War," *The Wall Street Journal,* Feb. 10, 1982, republished in Mark Danner, *The Massacre at El Mozote: A Parable of the Cold War* (New York: Vintage Books, 1994) 229–33.

6. Golden, "Salvadoran Skeletons Confirm Reports of Massacre in 1981."

7. Danner, *The Massacre at El Mozote;* Rufina Amaya, Mark Danner, and Carlos Henríquez Consalvi, *Luciérnagas en El Mozote* (San Salvador: Ediciones Museo de la Palabra, 1996).

8. Guillermoprieto, "Shedding Light on Humanity's Dark Side."

9. Douglas Martin, "Rufina Amaya, 64, Dies; Salvador Survivor," *The New York Times* March 9, 2007: A21, May 20, 2007, www.nytimes.com/2007/03/09/world/americas/09amaya.html?ex=1 331096400&en=2f997d367c323c32&ei=5088&partner=rssnyt&emc=rss.

10. Martin, "Rufina Amaya, 64, Dies; Salvador Survivor."

11. Jeffrey L. Gould, "El Mozote after 25 Years: The Capital of Salvadoran Memory," *Counterpunch* 23/24 Dec. 2006; May 20, 2007, www.counterpunch.org/gould12232006.html.

12. Ibid.

13. Michael Hirsh and John Barry, "What to do about the deepening quagmire of Iraq? The Pentagon's approach is being called 'the Salvador option,'" *Newsweek,* January 14, 2005; May 20, 2007, www.msnbc.msn.com/id/6802629/site/newsweek; Thomas Riggins, "Remembering Rufina Amaya, Survivor of U.S.-Inspired Slaughter in El Salvador," *political.affairs.net,* March 21, 2007; 20 May 2007, www.politicalaffairs.net/article/articleview/5020/1/248.

14. Alicia Partnoy, "On Being Shorter: How Our Testimonial Texts Defy the Academy," *Women Writing Resistance: Essays on Latin America and the Caribbean*, Jennifer Browdy de Hernández, ed. (Cambridge, MA: South End Press, 2003), 185.

15. Ibid.

16. Alicia Partnoy, "*Cuando Vienen Matando*: On Prepositional Shifts and the Struggle of Testimonial Subjects for Agency," *PMLA* 121.5 (Oct. 2006): 1666.

17. Arturo Arias, ed., *The Rigoberta Menchú Controversy* (Minneapolis: University of Minnesota Press, 2001); David Stoll, *Rigoberta Menchú and the Story of All Poor Guatemalans* (Boulder, CO: Westview Press, 1999).

18. John Beverley, "What Happens When the Subaltern Speaks: Rigoberta Menchú, Multiculturalism, and the Presumption of Equal Worth," *The Rigoberta Menchú Controversy*, Arturo Arias, ed. (Minneapolis: University of Minnesota Press, 2001), 220.

19. Ibid.

20. Ibid., 223.

21. Ibid., 221; my emphasis.

22. Ibid., 221.

23. Partnoy, *On Being Shorter,* 1667.

24. See Danner's *The Massacre at El Mozote* for a book-length account on the massacre. A number of original documents, newspaper articles, and communiqués are compiled as appendices to the book.

25. For a retrospective look at how journalists Alma Guillermoprieto and Raymond Bonner were censored for writing about the massacre, see Hoyt 1993 (see Works Cited).

26. Alma Guillermoprieto, "Salvadoran Peasants Describe Mass Killing; Woman Tells of Children's Death," January 27, 1982, reproduced in Danner's *The Massacre at El Mozote*, 185.

27. Ibid., 185.

28. Raymond Bonner, "Massacre of Hundreds Reported in Salvador Village," reproduced in Danner's *The Massacre at El Mozote,* 188.

29. "Tres Vidas" has been performed at many university venues, such as MIT, Suffolk University Law School, Wellesley University, Jacksonsville University, Sonoma State University, and the University of the Pacific in Stockton, California. Georgina Corbo plays the three women and is accompanied by the Core Ensemble, a chamber music ensemble composed of cello, piano, and percussion. May 20, 2007, www.core-ensemble.cc/tv.htm.

30. *Homeland,* dir. Doug Scott, prod. Daniel Flores y Ascencio and Lisette Marie Flanary (Huevos Indios Productions, 1999); J. C. Mendizabal and Trip Tech, *La masacre del Mozote* (BlackNote Music, 1999); OnRamp Arts, "Tropical America," 2002; May 20, 2007, www.tropicalamerica.com.

31. Amaya's testimonio, translated to English, has been published in Danner 1994; for original in Spanish, see Amaya, Danner, and Consalvi 1996.

32. Rufina Amaya, "Solo me embrocaba a llorar/Testimonio de Rufina Amaya," January 1981; May 20, 2007, http://groups.msn.com/verdad-ES/elmozote1981.msnw; Amaya, Danner, and Consalvi 1996; my translation.

33. Alexander Wilde, "Irruptions of Memory: Expressive Politics in Chile's Transition to Democracy," *Genocide, Collective Violence, and Popular Memory: The Politics of Remembrance in the Twentieth Century,* David E. Lorey and William H. Beezley, eds. (Wilmington, DE: Scholarly Resources, 2002), 4.

34. For a discussion of the postwar context of El Salvador and Central America, see James Dunkerley, *The Pacification of Central America: Political Change in the Isthmus, 1987–1993* (London: Verso, 1994).

35. See official governmental documents: Decree No. 55, *Diario Oficial,* Vol. 313, No. 206, San Salvador, November 4, 1991; *Noticoncultura* 1.2 (1992); Claudia Allwood de Mata, "Mensaje de la presidenta de Concultura," *La prensa gráfica,* November 3, 1993.

36. Supporting organizations include the Asociación de Mujeres por la Dignidad y la Vida, Asociación Probúsqueda, Asociación Yek Ineme, Centro para la Paz, Centro para la promoción y defensa de los Derechos Humanos "Madeleine Lagadec," Comisión no gubernamental

de Derechos Humanos, Comité de Familiares de Víctimas de violaciones a los Derechos Humanos, Comité de Madres de Desaparecidos y Asesinados Políticos "Monseñor Oscar Arnulfo Romero," Museo de la Palabra y la Imagen, and the Oficina de Tutela Legal del Arzobispado de San Salvador. See CEJIL (Centro por la Justicia y el Derecho Internacional), "Monumento a la memoria y la verdad en El Salvador: un gran paso en la dignificación de las víctimas y en la construcción de una sociedad en reconciliación y paz," May 20, 2007, www.cejil.org/comunicados.cfm?id=492.

37. See Amnesty International, 20 May 20, 2007, http://web.amnesty.org/library/Index/ESLAMR 290112003?open&of=ESL-SLV.

38. "Salvadoreños conmemoran 15 años de la masacre de 1.000 campesinos," *La Prensa*, San Pedro Sula, Honduras, December 9 1996, May 20 2007, www.laprensahn.com/caarc/9612/c09001.htm.

39. See "Salvadoreños conmemoran 15 años de la masacre de 1.000 campesinos" 1996.

40. Gould, "El Mozote after 25 Years."

41. Visit the website of the Museo de la Palabra y la Imagen. May 20, 2007, www.museo.com.sv.

42. Amaya, Danner, and Consalvi, 1996.

43. See Carlos Henríquez Consalvi, "Las palabras," March 15, 2002, www.museo.com.sv/opinion.html. Translation into English is mine.

44. Elizabeth Jelin and Susan G. Kaufman, "Layers of Memories: Twenty Years After in Argentina," *Genocide, Collective Violence, and Popular Memory: The Politics of Remembrance in the Twentieth Century*, David E. Lorey and William H. Beezley, eds. (Wilmington, DE: Scholarly Resources, 2002), 41.

45. Ibid.

46. Guillermoprieto, "Shedding Light on Humanity's Dark Side."

47. Ibid.

48. Ibid.

49. Partnoy, "On Being Shorter," 176.

50. Ibid.

51. Partnoy (2006), 1666.

52. Ibid., 175.

"COMFORT WOMEN" WANT JUSTICE, NOT COMFORT

1. "Abe Rejects Japan's Files on War Sex," *The New York Times,* March 2, 2007.

2. "Philip Roth interviews Milan Kundera (November 30, 1980), www.kundera.de/english/Info-Point/Interview_Roth/interview_roth.html.

3. "A Landmark Ruling on Rape," *The New York Times* editorial, February 24, 2001.

4. John Dower, *Embracing Defeat: Japan in the Wake of World War II* (New York and London: W.W. Norton and Company, 1999), 138.

5. Ibid., 124–5.

6. Ibid., 127.

7. Dower, *Embracing Defeat,* 129–130.

Chapter 4. Messages of Pain

A STATE OF RAGE

1. In this choreopoem, I consciously use the words Black and African American interchangeably to describe the descendants of enslaved Africans who were brought over, against their will in chains, to the Americas and landed on the mass of land now known as the United States of America. In this context Black is not a color, it is a political racial identity; that is why I chose to capitalize it.

2. "African American Women in Defense of Ourselves," *The New York Times,* November 17, 1991, 47.

MAINTAINING THE CASUALTIES OF SILENCE

1. Thanks to María Ochoa, Nandini Gunewardena, Renny Christopher, and Stephan Teodorovich for their patience and comments on this article. To all of my students, the greatest teachers of all—in particular, to the special student who transformed the day, the lives of many, but most importantly, herself.

2. Janice Mirikitani, "Prisons of Silence," *We, the Dangerous: New and Selected Poems* (Berkeley: Celestial Arts, 1995), 60–5.

3. Paulo Freire, *Pedagogy of the Oppressed* (New York: Continuum Press, 1988), 66.

4. Audre Lorde, "Poetry Is Not a Luxury," *Sister Outsider: Essays and Speeches* (Freedom: The Crossing Press, 1984), 37.

5. Mirikitani, "We, the Dangerous," 26–7.

6. League of Women Voters of Honolulu, "Report: Domestic Violence Family Court Monitoring Project" (Honolulu: Hawaii State Commission on the Status of Women, 1996), 3.

7. Freire, *Pedagogy of the Oppressed,* 28–9.

8. I intentionally shift from plural to singular and use the gender-specific pronouns of "her" and "she" in order to complement the topics and particular contextual situations.

9. Lorde, "Poetry Is Not a Luxury," 41.

10. Ibid.

11. Ibid.

12. Ibid., 42.

13. Ibid., 42.

14. League of Women Voters, 2.

15. Mirikitani, "Insect Collection," 33–4.

16. Ibid., 33.

17. In order to protect the student's identity, I have used the pseudonym "Grace" and have changed some of the specifics of her story.

18. Lorde, "The Transformation of Silence," 41.

19. Mirikitani, "Without Comfort," 84–5.

20. Mirikitani, "We, the Dangerous," 26–7.

21. Mirikitani, "Prisons of Silence," 60–5.

THE RAPE OF AN OBSTINATE WOMAN

1. Karima Bennoune, "Algerian Women Confront Fundamentalism." *Monthly Review* 46, no. 4 (1994): 26.

2. Ibid.; Marnia Lazreg, "Gender and Politics in Algeria: Unraveling the Religious Paradigm." *Signs: Journal of Women in Culture and Society* 15, no. 4 (1990): 755, 776-778; Bart Moore-Gilbert, "Frantz Fanon: En-gendering Nationalist Discourse," *Women: A Cultural Review* 7, no. 2 (1996): 125.

3. Azizah Al-Hibri, "Tear off Your Western Veil!" and Nada Elia, "A Woman's Place is in the Struggle: A Personal Viewpoint on Feminism, Pacifism and the Gulf War." In *Food for our Grandmothers: Writings by Arab-American and Arab-Canadian Feminists* Ed. Joanna Kadi (Boston: South End Press, 1994).

4. Avery Gordon, *Ghostly Matters: Haunting and the Sociological Imagination* (Minneapolis: University of Minnesota Press, 1996) 15, 17. Gordon offers: "the ghostly haunt gives notice that something is missing—that which appears to be invisible or in the shadows is announcing itself... that which appears absent can indeed be a seething presence."

5. Assia Djebar, "Blood Does Not Dry on the Tongue" *Research in African Literatures* 30, no. 3 (Fall 1999): 18-22; Daniele Djamila Amrane-Minne, "Women and Politics in Algeria from the War of Independence to Our Day." *Research in African Literatures* 30, no. 3 (Fall 1999): 62; Bennoune, 26.

6. Frantz Fanon, *Wretched of the Earth* (New York: Grove Press, 1963) 251. Fanon writes: "Firstly as a general rule, clinical psychiatry classifies the different disturbances shown by our patients under the heading "reactionary psychoses" ... It seems to us that in the cases here the chosen events giving rise to the disorder are chiefly the bloodthirsty and pitiless atmosphere, the generalization of inhuman practices, and the firm impression that people have of being caught up in the veritable Apocalypse."

7. Bennoune, 26.

8. Ibid.

9. Francoise Verges, "Chains of Madness, Chains of Colonialism: Fanon and Freedom." In *Fact of Blackness: Frantz Fanon and Visual Representation* Ed. Alan Read (Seattle: Bay Press, 1996) 61.

10. Lazreg, 764. Lazreg writes: "Thus, upgrading women's status did not stem from an interest in women as women but from a concern for men's cultural identity."

11. Frantz Fanon, "Algeria Unveiled." In *A Dying Colonialism.* (New York: Grove Press, 1965) 37; Elia, 114-119.

12. "Gender Violence and the Prison Industrial Complex: A Joint Statement by Critical Resistance and INCITE!" *INCITE! Women of Color Against Violence.* Accessed 14 July 2007 <http://www.incite-national.org/involve/statement.html>.

13. Kimberlé Williams Crenshaw, "Demarginalizing the Intersection of Race and Sex: A Black Feminist Critique of Antidiscrimination Doctrine, Feminist Theory, and Antiracist Politics." In *Critical Race Feminism* Eds. Adrien Wing, et al. (New York: NYU Press, 2003) 23.

14. Madhu Dubey, "The 'True Lie' of the Nation: Fanon and Feminism." *differences: A Journal of Feminist Cultural Studies* 10, no.2 (Summer 1998): 1.

15. Fanon, "Algeria Unveiled," 41.

16. Verges, 49.

17. Fanon, "Algeria Unveiled," 41.

18. Dubey, 2. Dubey suggests: "Indeed, in most crucial respects, Fanon's account of Algerian nationalism...can be closely aligned with recent feminist critiques of decolonizing nationalisms."

19. Ketu H. Katrak, "Decolonizing culture: toward a theory for postcolonial women's texts." *Modern Fiction Studies 35*, no. 1 (Spring 1989): 157.

20. Fanon, *The Wretched of the Earth*, 257.

21. Ibid.

22. Fanon, "Algeria Unveiled," 42.

23. Ibid., 45.

24. Fanon, *The Wretched of the Earth,* 256.

25. Eddy Souffrant, "To Conquer the Veil: Woman as Critique of Liberalism." In *Fanon: A Critical Reader*, Eds. Lewis R. Gordon, et al. (New York: Blackwell, 1996), 177.

26. *Tongues Untied,* directed by Marlon Riggs. New York: Cineaste, 1992.

27. Fanon, *Wretched of the Earth,* 258.

28. Moore-Gilbert, 128. Moore-Gilbert writes: "Fanon appears to excuse, even naturalize, rape in certain circumstances or, at least, to hold certain women responsible for being raped."

29. Ibid., 128.

30. Darlene Clark Hine, "Rape and the Inner Lives of Black Women in the Middle West: Preliminary Thoughts on the Culture of Dissemblance." In *Unequal Sisters: Multicultural Reader in U.S. Women's History* First edition. Eds. Ellen DuBois and Vicki Ruiz (New York: Routledge, 1990),

295. A very careful analysis is offered in T. Denean Sharpley-Whiting's *Frantz Fanon: Conflicts and Feminism* (Lanham, MD: Rowman and Littlefield, 1997).

31. Fanon, "Algeria Unveiled," 47.

32. Ibid., 37.

33. Fanon, "Algeria Unveiled," 44.

34. Ibid.

35. Fanon, *The Wretched of the Earth,* 258.

36. Ibid.

37. Souffrant, 177; Moore-Gilbert, 126.

38. Albert Memmi, *Colonizer and Colonized* (Boston: Beacon Press, 1965), 17.

39. Angela Y. Davis and Elizabeth Martinez, "Coalition Building among People of Color," *Inscriptions* 7 (1994), <www.ucsc.edu/cultstudies/PUBS/inscriptions/vol_7/Davis.html>; Audre Lorde. "There is No Hierarchy of Oppressions," *Interracial Books for Children Bulletin* 14.3 (1983): 9.

40. Clark Hine, 292.

"I WILL DO A DEED FOR FREEDOM"

1. Fisher argued that the "evidence" also should inform the sectional crises. He wrote, "On the inherent, unalterable qualities of the negro hinges the whole question of slavery. Fortunately for our justification, unfortunately for our country, all the researches of science, all the annals of the past, and all the facts of the present hour, prove that the negro is fit for servitude, that he requires guidance and protection, naturally seeks them, and renders in return, labor and obedience. Servitude arises from the relation of strength to weakness; and the negro is adapted to it, by want of his intellectual power, his feebleness of will, his docility, his god nature. He is submissive, and neither hates nor inspires hatred. Sidney Fisher, *The Laws of Race as Connected with Slavery* (Philadelphia: Willis P. Hazard, 1860), 46–7.

2. Steven Weisenburger, *Modern Medea: A Family Story of Slavery and Child-Murder from the Old South* (New York: Hill and Wang, 1998), 72–4.

3. George Fitzhugh, for example, asserted, "'[I]t is the duty of society to protect the weak': but protection cannot be efficient without the power of control; therefore, 'It is the duty of society to enslave the weak.'" George Fitzhugh, *Cannibals All! Or Slaves without Masters,* C. Vann Woodward, ed. (1856), rpt. (Cambridge: The Belknap Press of Harvard University Press, 1980), 187.

4. Darlene Clark Hine, "Female Slave Resistance: The Economics of Sex," *Hine Sight: Black Women and the Re-Construction of American History,* Darlene Clark Hine, ed. (Bloomington: Indiana University Press, 1994), 34–5.

5. For a discussion of black women's critical role as subject in abolitionist literature, see Amy Dru Stanley, "'The Right to Possess All the Faculties That God Has Given': Possessive Individualism,

Slave Women, and Abolitionist Thought." *Moral Problems in American Life: New Perspectives on Cultural History,* Karen Halttunen and Lewis Perry, eds. (Ithaca: Cornell University Press, 1998), 126–7, 129; Edward E. Baptist, "'Cuffy,' 'Fancy Maids,' and 'One-Eyed Men': Rape, Commodification, and the Domestic Slave Trade in the United States," *The American Historical Review* 106 (December 2001): 53; Deborah Gray White, *Ar'nt I a Woman?: Female Slaves in the Plantation South* (New York: W.W. Norton & Co.), 15–6.

6. George Fredrickson, *The Black Image in the White Mind: The Debate on Afro-American Character and Destiny, 1817-1914* (Hanover, NH: Wesleyan University Press, 1971), xiii.

7. Mia Elisabeth Bay, *The White Image in the Black Mind: African American Ideas about White People, 1830–1925* (New York: Oxford University Press, 2000), 16. In her dissertation, Joan Bryant also explores African American notions about racial character. See Joan L. Bryant, "Race Debates among Nineteenth-Century Reformers and Churchmen," PhD dissertation, Yale University, 1996.

8. Fredrickson, xviii.

9. Ethnology was defined as the comparative study of human cultural variation, change, and development. Ethnologists attempted to uncover stages and meanings of human developments in cultural, physical, and historical terms.

10. In a description of her mother's preemptive attack on two men sent to whip her, Ophelia Settle Egypt asserted, "She knew what they were coming for and she intended to meet them halfway. She swooped upon them like a hawk on chickens. I believe that they were afraid of her or thought she was crazy. One man had a long beard, which she grabbed with one hand, and the lash with the other. Her body was made strong with madness." In *Black Women in White America: A Documentary History* Gerda Lerna, ed. (New York: Vintage Books), 37.

11. Adrienne Davis, "Don't Let Nobody Bother Yo' Principle": The Sexual Economy of American Slavery, Sharon Harley and the Black Women and Work Collective, eds., *Sister Circle: Black Women and Work* (New Brunswick: Rutgers University Press, 2002) 103–27.

12. I am grateful to Joy James, "Searching for a Tradition: African American Women Writers, Activists, and Interracial Rape Cases," *Black Women in America,* Kim Marie Vaz, ed. (Thousand Oaks, California: Sage Publications, 1995), 150–1. This piece greatly influenced both this study and my understanding of the tradition of black female resistance and activism. My work also is informed by the scholarship of Mia Bay, *The White Image in the Black Mind;* Lauren Berlant, "The Queen of America Goes to Washington City: Harriet Jacobs, Frances Harper, Anita Hill," *American Literature* 65, no. 3; *Subjects and Citizens: Nation Race, and Gender from Oronooko to Anita Hill* (September 1993), 554; Adrienne Davis, "'Don't Let Nobody Bother Yo' Principle': The Sexual Economy of American Slavery," *Sister Circle: Black Women and Work,* Sharon Harley and the Black Women and Work Collective, eds. (New Brunswick: Rutgers University Press, 2002), 103–27; Angela Davis, "Reflections on the Black Woman's Role in the Community of

Slaves" and "Rape, Racism, and the Capitalist Setting," *The Angela Y. Davis Reader,* Joy James, ed. (Malden, Mass: Oxford Blackwell Press, 1998), 111–28 and 129–37; George M. Fredrickson, *The Black Image in the White Man*; Darlene Clark Hine, "Female Slave Resistance: The Economics of Sex," 27–36; Dorothy Roberts, *Killing the Black Body: Race, Reproduction and the Meaning of Liberty* (New York: Pantheon Books, 1997); Deborah Gray White, *Ar'nt I a Woman,* 62–90.

13. Saidiya V. Hartman, *Scenes of Subjection,* 3–4.

14. Hammonds, *Toward a Genealogy of Black Female Sexuality,* 177–8.

15. Darlene Clark Hine, "Introduction," xxviii.

16. Darlene Clark Hine, "Rape and the Inner Lives of Black Women: Thought on the Culture of Dissemblance," 41.

17. Deborah Gray White, *Ar'nt I a Woman,* 24.

18. Linda Brent, *Incidents in the Life of a Slave Girl, in The Classic Slave Narratives* Henry Louis Gates, Jr., ed. (New York: Penguin Books, 1987), 362.

19. Keckley, *Behind the Scenes,* 38.

20. In *We Are Your Sisters,* 25; Aunt Jane: Rawick, vol. 8 Charles Perdue L. Thomas E. Barden, and Phillips Rovert K. eds. *Weevils in the Wheat* (Charlottesville, 1976).

21. Josiah C. Nott, "The Negro Race: Its Ethnology and History," By the Author of "Types of mankind." To Major General O.O. Howard, Superintendent, Freedmen's Bureau (1866), 25.

22. Josiah Nott and George R. Gliddon, *Indigenous Races of the Earth* (Philadelphia: J. B. Lippincott, 1857), 454.

23. Ibid.

24. For a discussion of the term as used by John C. Calhoun in 1837, see Fredrickson, *The Black Image in the White Mind,* 47.

25. Fisher compared the queen of the Antilles, and her charming sisters in their ambrosial summer sea, to Cleopatra. "'Tis the old story; the Cleopatra of the South, the serpent of the Nile, entangling sensual, brave, athletic and conquering northern Anthony, in her silken meshes of dalliance, lapping him in the luxury and sloth, kissing away his manhood, courage, glory, power, and provinces." Fisher, *Laws of Race,* 40.

26. Ibid.

27. Truth grew up in a Dutch community in New York. Sojourner Truth, "Abolition of Slavery," New York City Anti-Slavery Society, Metropolitan Hall, New York City, September 4, 1853. *New York Tribune,* September 5, 1853: 5, in *Sojourner Truth as Orator, Wit Story and Song,* Suzanne Pullon Fitch and Roseann M. Mandziuk, eds., *Great American Orators 25* (Westport, Connecticut: Greenwood Press, 1997), 109.

28. Charles Caldwell, *Thoughts on the Original Unity of the Human Race,* 2nd ed., (Cincinnati: J.A. & U .P. James, 1852), iii. In reference to Smith's work, Caldwell wrote, "But of sound science of any description, it possessed not a fragment."

29. Henry S. Patterson, "Memoir of the Life and Scientific Labors of Samuel George Morton," *Types of Mankind,* xiv.

30. George Fitzhugh, "Sociology for the South; Or the Failure of Free Society"; published at Richmond Virginia, 1854, quoted in Lydia Maria Child, ed., "The patriarchal institution as described by members of its own family," 6.

31. Sterling, *We Are Your Sisters,* 57.

32. William Wells Brown, "The History of the Haitian Revolution," (1855) in Pamphlets of Protest, 251.

33. James Redpath, *The Roving Editor, or Talks with Slaves in Southern States* (New York: Burdick, 1859), 141, quoted in Deborah Gray White, *Ar'nt I a Woman,* 30.

34. Weisenburger, *Modern Medea,* 8.

35. Amy Dru Stanley, "'The Right to Possess All the Faculties That God Has Given,'" 127–9.

36. Editorial. *Provincial Freedman,* February 2, 1856.

37. The term "conceived violently," as used by T. Denean Sharpley-Whiting, raises questions about black motherhood that creative writers and literary theorists have explored. In Toni Morrison's *Beloved,* for example, Sethe is told that her mother "threw away" children conceived during the horrific middle passage. See Ann Folwell Stanford's discussion of Sethe and other black women in the novel who struggle with the legacy of violent conceptions in *Bodies in a Broken World: Women Novelists of Color and the Politics of Medicine* (Chapel Hill: University of North Carolina Press, 2003), 71–2, 82–3. Gayl Jones also explores in *Corregidora* (Boston: Beacon Press, 1987) three generations of women who wrestle with a legacy of violent conceptions and loss. The critical implications of the impact of these conceptions warrant further historical research and analysis.

38. Joshua D. Rothman, *Notorious in the Neighborhood: Sex and Families across the Color Line in Virginia 1787–1861* (Chapel Hill: University of North Carolina Press, 2003), 133.

39. Alonzo Alvarez, for example, offered this description of slavery: "In the slave States, it is seldom that our ear is pained in hearing chastisements; the masters are lenient and seldom overexacting. If the negro is sick, he is cared for immediately, and the best medical talent is generally brought into requisition. He is well clothed, fed and housed; for all these requirements appeal to humanity and interest. The licentiousness of the sex is restrained by the planters, inducing their negroes to choose companions and live respectably with each other." Alonzo Alvarez, *The Progress and Intelligence of Americans, Written by a Mexican Now Residing in the U.S. as a Result of the French Invasion* (translated, printed, and published by the author, 1865), 35.

40. Van Evrie, *White Supremacy and Negro Subordination*, 227.

41. Ibid., 229.

42. Ibid., 226–7.

43. Ibid., 227.

44. Van Evrie, *White Supremacy and Negro Subordination,* 226.

45. Ibid., 232.

46. Van Evrie, *White Supremacy and Negro Subordination,* vol. 3 The New Proslavery Argument, part 1, John David Smith ed., (New York: Garland Publishing, 1993), 2nd ed. (New York: Van Evrie, Horton and Co., 1868), 90.

47. Ibid., 121.

48. Ibid., 122.

Chapter 5. Defining a Principled Peace

SO

1. *Haha,* Japanese endearment for "mother."

2. *Akachan,* Japanese endearment for "baby."

3. *Obasan,* Japanese for "aunt."

4. *Okasan,* Japanese for "mother"; *Onesan,* Japanese for "sister."

5. *Kazoku,* Japanese for "family."

6. *Familia,* Spanish for "family."

7. *Jya ren,* Chinese for "family."

Sources

Chapter 1

WHAT IS IT ABOUT THE WALLS?

Daniels, D. M., and Sandy, C. *Souls of My Sisters: Black Women Break Their Silence, Tell Their Stories and Heal Their Spirits.* New York: Kensington Publishing Corporation, 2000.

Ianno, L. Professional conversation. Family Violence Council. Lincoln Medical Education Foundation. June 25, 2003.

Jordan, L. M. "Domestic violence in the African American Community: The Role of the Black Church." Retrieved June 3, 2003 from www.hds.harvard.edu/cswr/projects/healing_reports/05 .Jordan.pdf

Kelley, V. A. "'Good speech': An interpretive essay investigation and African philosophy of communication." *The Western Journal of Black Studies* (2002): 26.

VOICES OF THE PIONEERS

Abraham, Margaret. "Ethnicity, Gender, and Marital Violence: South Asian Women's Organizations in the United States." *Gender & Society* 9 (1995): 450–68.

Abraham, Margaret. "Speaking the Unspeakable: Marital Violence against South Asian Immigrant Women in the United States." *Indian Journal of Gender Studies* 5 (1998): 215–41.

Dasgupta, Shamita Das. "Charting the Course: An Overview of Domestic Violence in the South Asian Community in the United States." *Journal of Social Distress and the Homeless* 9 (2000): 173–85.

Fisher, Maxine P. "Creating Ethnic Identity: Asian Indians in the New York City Area." *Urban Anthropology* 7 (1978): 271–85.

Prathikanti, Sudha. "East Indian American Families." *Working with Asian Americans.* New York: Guilford Press, 1997. 79–100.

Tolson, Mike. "When Hope Dies." *Houston Chronicle.* July 7, 1996.

Vaid, Jyotsna. "Seeking a Voice: South Asian Women's Groups in North America." *Making Waves: An anthology of writings by and about Asian American women.* Boston: Beacon Press, 1989. 395–404.

Vaid, Jyotsna. "Beyond a Space of Our Own: South Asian Women's Groups in the U.S." *Amerasia Journal* 25 (1999/2000): 111–26.

DOMESTIC VIOLENCE IN AFGHAN HOUSEHOLDS

Roberts, Albert. 1996. *Helping Battered Women: New Perspectives and Remedies.* New York: Oxford University Press.

Bogard, Michele. 2005. "Strengthening Domestic Violence Theories: Intersections of Race, Class, Sexual Orientation, and Gender." Ibid.

DasGupta, Shamita. 2005. "Women's Realities: Defining Violence against Women by Immigration, Race, and Class." Ibid.

Ahmad, Farah, Sarah Riaz, Paula Barata, and Donna Stewart. 2004. "Patriarchal Beliefs and Perception of Abuse Among South Asian Immigrant Women." *Violence against Women* 10 (3): 262–82.

Liang, Belle, Lisa Goodman, Pratyusha Tummala-Narra, Sarah Weintraub. 2005. "A Theoretical Framework for Understanding Help-Seeking Processes among Survivors of Intimate Partner Violence." *American Journal of Community Psychology* 36 (1 & 2): 71–84.

Chapter 2

SPIRITS IN TRAFFIC

Altink, Sietske. *Stolen Lives: Trading Women into Sex and Slavery.* London: Harrington Park Press, 1995.

Bales, Kevin. *Disposable People: New Slavery in the Global Economy.* California: University of California Press, 1999.

Bishop, Ryan and Robinson, Lillian. *Night Market*. New York: Routledge Press, 1998.

Frank, Marcus Sgt. "Asian Criminal Enterprises and Prostitution." Westminster Police Department, 2002.

Frederick, John. "Deconstructing Gita." *Himal Magazine* Oct. 1998, vol. 11, no. 10.

Human Rights Watch. *Owed Justice: Thai Women Trafficked into Debt Bondage in Japan*. USA: Human Rights Watch, 2000.

Kempadoo, Kamala & Doezema, Jo. *Global Sex Workers: Rights, Resistance and Redefinition*. New York: Routledge, 1998.

SELECTIVE STORYTELLING

Agnes, Flavia. "Violence against Women: A Review of Recent Enactments." *In the Name of Justice: Women and Law in Society*. ed. Swapna Mukhopadhyay. New Delhi: Manohar Publishers, 1998. 81–116.

Ahuja, R. C. et al. "Domestic Violence in India a Summary Report of a Multisite Household Survey." International Center for Research on Women, 2000.

Amanpour, Christiane. 2003. "For Love of Money." CBSNews.com. October 5, 2003. www .cbsnews.com/stories/2003/10/03/60minutes/main576466.shtl.

Dave, Anjali, and Gopika Solanki. "Journey from Violence to Crime: A Study of Domestic Violence in the City of Mumbai." Department of Family and Child Welfare Tata Institute of Social Sciences, 2001.

Diwan, Paras, and Peeyushi Diwan. *Law Relating to Dowry, Dowry Deaths, Bride Burning, Rape, and Related Offences*. Delhi: Universal Law Publishing Company, 1997.

Greenberg, Judith G. "Symposium: Criminalizing Dowry Deaths: The Indian Experience." *American University Journal of Gender, Social Policy and the Law* 11 (2003): 801–46.

Grewal, Inderpal, and Caren Kaplan. "Warrior Marks: Global Womanism's Neocolonial Discourse in a Multicultural Context." *Camera Obscura* 39 (1996): 4.

Horon, I., and D. Cheng. "Enhanced Surveillance for Pregnancy-Associated Mortality—Maryland, 1993–1998." *Journal of the American Medical Association* 11 (2001).

Hutchinson, Sue. "Again, Abuse Masquerades as Love and a Woman Dies." *San Jose Mercury News.* August 1, 2003.

"Intimate Partner Violence 1993-2001." Ed. Bureau of Justice Statistics U.S. Department of Justice, 2003. Vol. NCJ 197838.

Jaswal, Surinder, et al. "Domestic Violence in India a Summary Report of Four Records Studies." International Center for Research on Women, 2000.

Kapur, Ratna. "The Tragedy of Victimization Rhetoric: Resurrecting the 'Native' Subject in International/Post-Colonial Feminist Legal Politics." *Harvard Human Rights Journal* 15 (2002): 1–37.

Lawrence, Sonia N. "Cultural (in)Sensitivity: The Dangers of a Simplistic Approach to Culture in the Courtroom." *CJWL/RFD.* 13 (2001): 107–36.

"Lisa Ling Investigates Dowry Deaths." *The Oprah Winfrey Show.* ABC. January 16, 2004.

Mani, Lata. *Contentious Traditions: The Debate on Sati in Colonial India.* Berkeley: University of California Press, 1998.

Mitra, Nishi, and Tata Institute of Social Sciences. Women's Studies Unit. *Domestic Violence as a Public Issue: A Review of Responses.* Mumbai, India: Unit for Women's Studies, Tata Institute of Social Sciences, 2002.

Mohanty, Chandra Talpade. *Feminism without Borders: Decolonizing Theory, Practicing Solidarity.* Durham: Duke University Press, 2003.

Narayan, Uma. *Dislocating Cultures: Identities, Traditions, and Third World Feminism.* New York: Routledge, 1997.

Natarajan, Mangai. "Women's Police Stations as a Dispute Processing System: The Tamil Nadu in Experience in Dealing with Dowry-Related Domestic Violence Cases." *Women and Criminal Justice* 16.1/2 (2005).

Oldenburg, Veena Talwar. *Dowry Murder: The Imperial Origins of a Cultural Crime*. Oxford/New York: Oxford University Press, 2002.

Palkar, Vineeta. "Failing Gender Justice in Anti-Dowry Law." *South Asia Research* 23.2 (2003): 181–200.

Parameswaran, Radhika. "Coverage of 'Bride Burning' in the Dallas Observer: A Cultural Analysis of the 'Other.'" *Frontiers: A Journal of Women Studies* 16.2/3 (1996): 69.

Patel, Julie. "When Culture Rejects Divorce: For Indo-Americans, Breakup Can Be Risky." *San Jose Mercury News*. August 3, 2003.

The Protection of Women from Domestic Violence Act. No. 43 (2005).

Sitaraman, Bhavani. "Law as Ideology: Women, Courts and 'Dowry Deaths' in India." *International Journal of The Sociology Of Law* 27.3 (1999): 287–316.

Stites, Roxanne. "Milpitas Husband Kills Estranged Wife, Self; Man Distraught over Breakup of Arranged Marriage." *San Jose Mercury News*. July 22, 2003.

Tjaden, Patricia, and Nancy Thoennes. "Extent, Nature, and Consequences of Intimate Partner Violence: Findings from the National Violence against Women Survey." Pub. No. NCJ 181867. Washington: DOJ, 2000.

———. "Full Report of the Prevalence, Incidence and Consequences of Violence against Women: Findings from the National Violence against Women Survey." Pub. No. NCJ 183781 Washington: Department of Justice, 2000.

U.S. Department of Justice, Bureau of Justice Statistics. "Supplementary Homicide Reports, 1976–2004." ed. Federal Bureau of Intelligence.

Visaria, Leela, et al. "Domestic Violence in India: A Summary Report of Three Studies." International Center for Research on Women, 1999: 1–52.

Volpp, Leti. "Essay: Blaming Culture for Bad Behavior." *Yale Journal of Law & the Humanities* 12 (2000): 89–116.

————. "Symposium: On Culture, Difference, and Domestic Violence." *American University Journal of Gender, Social Policy and the Law* 11 (2003).

HIDDEN TRANSCRIPTS

Agarwal, Ravina. "At the Margins of Death: Ritual space and the politics of location in an Indo-Himalayan border village." *American Ethnologist* 28.3 (2001): 549–74.

Coomaraswamy, Radhika. Women of the LTTE. *Frontline*. Jan 10, 1997: 61.

Council on Foreign Relations (n.d.). "Terrorism: Questions and Answers." September 2, 2004. www.terrorismanswers.com/terrorism/suicide2.html.

de Alwis, Malathi 1997. "The production and Embodiment of Respectability: Gendered Demeanours in Colonial Ceylon". *Sri Lanka: Collective Identities Revisited, Vol. 1.* ed. Michael Roberts. (Colombo, Sri Lanka: Marga Institute, 1997). 105–143.

Eddleston, Michael, M. H. Rezvi Sheriff, and Keith Hawton. 1998. "Deliberate Self-Harm in Sri Lanka: An overlooked tragedy in the developing world." *British Medical Journal* 317 (1998), 133–135. Sept 23, 2004. http://bmj.com/cgi/content/full/317/7151/13.

Edirisinghe, Neville. *Poverty in Sri Lanka: Its Extent, Distribution, and Characteristics.* (Washington, D.C.: The World Bank, 1990).

Goody, Jack. "Bridewealth and Dowry in Africa and Eurasia." *Bridewealth and Dowry.* ed. Jack Goody and Stanley Tambiah. (Cambridge Papers in Social Anthropology, Cambridge: Cambridge University Press, 1973). 1–58.
Goody, Jack. *Production and Reproduction.* Cambridge: Cambridge University Press, 1976.

Haraway, Donna. "Situated Knowledges: The Science Question in Feminism and the Privilege of Partial Perspective." *Feminist Studies* 14.3 (1988): 575–99.

Kearney, R. N. and Barbara Miller. "The Spiral of Suicide and Social Change in Sri Lanka." *Journal of Asian Studies* 2.1 (1985): 81–101.

Kearney, Robert N., and Barbara D. Miller. *Internal Migration in Sri Lanka and Its Social Consequences*. (Boulder, CT: Westview, 1987).

Marecek, Jeanne. "Culture, Gender and Suicidal Behavior in Sri Lanka." *Suicide and Life Threatening Behavior* 28.1 (1998) Spring: 69-81.

Miller, Barbara D. and Robert N. Kearney. "Women's Suicide in Sri Lanka." *Women and Health: Cross-Cultural Perspectives*. ed. Patricia Whelehan. (Boston: Bergin and Garvey, 1988). 110–23.

Murdock, George P. "Cultural Correlates of the Regulation of Premarital Sex Behavior." *Process and Pattern in Culture*. ed. Robert A. Manners. Chicago: Aldine Publishing, 1964. 399–410.

Obeyesekere, Gananath. "The Vicissitueds of the Sinhala-Buddhist Identity through Time and Change." *Sri Lanka: Collective Identities Revisited, Vol. 1*. ed. Michael Roberts. (Colombo, Sri Lanka: Marga Institute, 1997). 355–384.

———. *The Cult of the Goddess Pattini*. Chicago and London: University of Chicago Press, 1984.

———. *Medusa's Hair: An Essay on Personal Symbols and Religious Experience*. Chicago: University of Chicago Press, 1981.

———. "The Fire-Walkers of Kataragama: the Rise of Bhakti Religiosity in Buddhist Sri Lanka." *Journal of Asian Studies*, 37.30 (1978): 457–76.

———. "Pregnancy Cravings (dola-duka) in Relation to Social Structure and Personality in a Sinhalese Village." *American Anthropologist* 65 (1963): 323–42.

Ortner, Sherry. "The Virgin and the State." *Feminist Studies* 4 (1978): 19–37.

Ratnayake, Tilak, and L. Siyambalagoda. *A Guide to Prevention of Teen Suicide*. Sri Lanka: (Department of Health Services, North Central Province, 1998).

Schelegel, Alice. "Status, property, and the value on virginity." *American Ethnologist* 18.4 (1991): 719–34.

Silva, Kalinga Tudor and W. D. N. R. Pushpakumara. "Love, Hate, and the Upsurge in Youth Suicide in Sri Lanka: Suicide Trends in a Mahaweli Settlement." *Sri Lanka Journal of Social Sciences* 19.1–2 (1996): 73–92.

Sunder Rajan, Rajeswari. *Real and Imagined Women: Gender, Culture and Postcolonialism.* (London and New York: Routledge, 1993).

Van Vleet, Krista E. "The Intimacies of Power: Rethinking Affinity and Violence in the Bolivian Andes." *American Ethnologist* 29.3 (2002): 567–601.

Weiner, Annette B. "Toward a Theory of Gender Power: An Evolutionary Perspective." *The Gender of Power.* ed. Monique Leijenaar, et al. Leiden: Vakgroep Vrouwenstudies FSW en Vrouwen Autonomie, 1988: 41–77.

Winslow, Deborah. "Rituals of First Menstruation in Sri Lanka." *Man* 15 (1975): 603–25.

Zhang, Li. "Migration and privatization of space and power in late socialist China." *American Ethnologist* 28.1 (2001): 179–205.

Chapter 3

COMPETING MASCULINITIES

Abusharaf, Rogaia Mustafa. "Sudanese" In C. Ember and M. Ember (Eds.) *Encyclopedia of Medical Anthropology: Health and Sickness in the World's Cultures.* NY: Plenum, in conjunction with Human Relations Area Files: Yale University. 2004. Pages 964-971.

Agger, I. *The Blue Room: Trauma and Testimony Among Refugee Women.* London: Zed Books. 1992.
Amnesty International. Sudan Report. 2001. Internet sources, www.amnesty.org.
Amnesty International. Sudan, Darfur. Rape as a Weapon of War: Sexual Violence and its Consequences. New York: Amnesty International 2004.

Bales, K. *Disposable People: New Slavery in the Global Economy.* Berkeley, CA: University of California Press. 1999.

Baya, Philister. "Seeking a Refuge or Being a Displaced: Analysis of a Southern Woman's Personal Experience". In M. Elsanousi (ed). *The Tragedy of Reality: Southern Sudanese Women Appeal for Peace.* Khartoum: Open Learning Organization. 1999.

Beshir, M. *The Southern Sudan: Background to Conflict.* New York: Praeger. 1965.

Deng, Francis. *The Dinka of the Sudan.* Illinois: Waveland. 1972.

Deng, F. and R. Cohen. *Masses in Flight: The Global Crisis of the Internally Displaced.* Washington, D.C.: The Brookings Institution. 1998.

_____. *The Forsaken People.* Washington, D.C.: The Brookings Institution. 1995.

Dudu, C. "Southern Sudanese Displaced Women: Losses and Gains." In M. Elsanosi (ed*.). The Tragedy of Reality: Southern Sudanese Women Appeal for Peace.* Khartoum: Sudan Open Learning Organization. 1999.

Eastmond, M. "Reconstructing Life: Chilean Women and the Dilemmas of Exile." In G. Bujis (ed.) *Migrant Women: Crossing Boundaries and Changing Identities.* Oxford: Berg. (1993): 35-55.

Eisenbruch, M. "From Post-Traumatic Stress Disorder to Cultural Bereavement: Diagnosis of Southeast Asian Refugees." *Social Sciences & Medicine* 3 (1991): 673-680.

El-Hassan, Yahya. "Sudanese Women as War Victims." *PANA.* March 6, 2000.

Habib, A. "Effects of Displacement on Southern Women's Health and Food Habits." *Ahfad Journal* 12(2).(1995): 30-52.

Hackett, B. *Pray God and Keep Walking: Stories of Women Refugees.* London: McFarland & Company Publishers. 1996.
Hamid, Sulieman. *Darfur.* (Forthcoming from Elmeidan, Sudan 2004).

Indra, D (Ed.) *Engendering Forced Migration.* New York: Berghahn. 1998.

International Crisis Group. Crisis in Darfur. www.crisisweb.org. 2004.

Jok, Jok Madut. *War and Slavery in Sudan.* Philadelphia: University of Pennsylvania Press. 2001.

Khalid. Mansour. *War and Peace in Sudan: The Tale of Two Countries.* London: Kegan Paul (2003).

Kukathas, Chandran. "Are There Any Cultural Rights?" Political Theory 20 no. 1. (1992): 105-139.

Kukathas, Chandran. "Cultural Rights Again: A Rejoinder to Kymlicka." *Political Theory* 20 no. 4. (1992): 674-680.

Kushner, T. and K. Knox. *Refugees in an Age of Genocide*. London: Frank Cass. 1999.

Kymlicka, Will. *The Rights of Minority Cultures*. Oxford: Oxford University Press. 1995.

Leaning, Jennifer. Diagnosing Genocide- The Case of Darfur. *New England Journal of Medicine* 351:8. Pages 735-8.

Leckie, Scott. "Another Step Towards Indivisibility: Identifying the Key Features of Violations of Economic, Social, and Cultural Rights." *Human Rights Quarterly* 20 no. 1. (1998): 81-124.

Levey, Geoffrey Brahm. "Equality, Autonomy, and Cultural Rights." *Political Theory* 25 no. 2. (1997): 215-248.

Long, Lynellyn. *Ban Vinai: The Refugee Camp*. New York: Columbia University Press. 1993.

Loveless, Jeremy. "Displaced Populations in Khartoum." Report for Save the Children Denmark. Channel Research 1999.

MacKinnon, Catharine. "Rape, Genocide, and Women's Human Rights." In *Violence Against Women: Philosophical Perspectives*. Stanley French et al. (eds.) Ithaca: Cornell University Press. (1998): 43-57.

Malwal, B. "Sources of Conflict in the Sudan." Paper presented at the United States Institute of Peace, Washington D.C. 1993.

Morawska, E. "Intended and Unintended Consequences of Forced Migrations: A Neglected Aspect of East Europe's Twentieth Century History." *International Migration Review* 34(4).(2000): 1049- 1087.

Nordstrom, Carloyn. *Another Kind of War Story*. Philadelphia: University of Pennsylvania Press (1997).

Power, Samantha. "A Reporter at Large: Dying in Darfur." *The New Yorker Magazine* August 30, 2004: 57-73.

Ruiz, H. "The Sudan: Cradle of Displacement." In F. Deng and R. Cohen (eds.). *The Forsaken People*. Washington, D.C.: The Brookings Institution. 1997.

Sen, Amartya. *Development as Freedom*. New York: Knope. 1999.

Sudan Demographics and Health Survey. Baltimore: Institute for Resource Development/Macro International, Inc. 1995.

Turner, Terrence. *The Kayapo*. The Disappearing World Series: Granda TV 1997.

UNESCO. *Cultural Rights as Human Rights*. Paris: UNESCO. 1970.

UNESCO. *Defending Cultural Rights*. UNESCO Asia and Pacific Regional Bureau for Education. Thailand, Bangkok.

UNHCR. *Sexual Violence against Women: Guidelines for Prevention and Response*. Geneva, Switzerland. 1995.

U.S. Committee for Refugees. *Follow the Women and the Cows: Personal Stories of Sudan's Uprooted People*. Washington, D.C. 2000.

Wani, Mary Hillary. "Women's Agenda for Peace." Paper presented at the Sudanese Women's Peace Forum, Grand Holiday Villa, Khartoum, October 29, 2001.

LAYERED VIOLENCE, IMPERIALISM, OCCUPATION, AND RELIGIOUS FUNDAMENTALISM

Amnesty International. "Iraq: Iraqi Women—the need for protective measures." 2005. http://web.amnesty.org/library/index/engmde140042005.

Amnesty International. "Israel and the Occupied Territories: Israel must end its policy of assassinations." 2003. http://web.amnesty.org/library/Index/ENGMDE150562003?open& of=ENG-ISR.

Cooke, M. "Wo-man, Retelling the War Myth." *Gendering War Talk.* M. Cooke & A. Woollacott, eds. Princeton: Princeton University Press, 1993. 177–204.

Ewan, M. *Afghanistan: A Short History of Its People and Politics.* New York: HarperCollins, 2002.

Gerami, S., and M. Lehnerer. "The Blackwell Encyclopedia of Sociology." *Gendered Aspects of War and International Violence.* G. Ritzer, ed. Oxford: Blackwell Publishing, 2007. 1885–8.

Gerami, S., and M. Lehnerer. "Women's Agency and Household Diplomacy: Negotiating Fundamentalism." *Gender and Society* 15 (2001): 556+.

Hatem, M. "Arab Americans and Arab American." *The MIT Electronic Journal of Middle East Studies* 5 (2005): 39.

Helie-Lucas, M. "Women, Nationalism and Religion in the Algerian Struggle." *Opening the Gates: A Century of Arab Feminist Writing.* Margot Badran and Mirriam Cooke, eds. London: Indiana University Press, 1990. 104–14.

Palestinian Central Bureau of Statistics. "Democratic and Social Consequences of the Separation Barrier on the West Bank." 2004. http://womenwarpeace.org/opt/docs/pcbs_wallstudy_april2004.pdf.

Rasekh, Z. "Women's Health and Human Rights in Afghanistan." *The American Medical Associations* 5 (1998): 449.

Rubenberg, C. *Palestinian Women: Patriarchy and Resistance in the West Bank.* Boulder: Lynne Rienner Publishers, 2001.

UNICEF and CDC. "Afghanistan is among worst places on globe for women's health." 2002. www.unicef.org/newsline/02pr59afghanmm.htm.

UNIFEM. "Question of the violation of human rights in the occupied Arab territories, including Palestine: Report of the Special Rapporteur of the Commission on Human Rights on the situation of human rights in the Palestinian territories occupied by Israel since 1967." 2001. http://domino.un.org/unispal.nsf/a39191b210be1d6085256da90053dee5/43fc268b1bf484fd85256c610065c63a!OpenDocument

UNHCR, BADIL Resource Center. "Palestinian Refugees and Durable Solutions." 2002. www
.badil.org/Publications/Briefs/Brief-No-07.html.

UNHCR, BADIL Resource Center. "Palestinian Refugee Facts & Figures." 2004. www.badil.org
/Refugees/facts&figures.htm.

WomenWarPeace.org. "Occupied Palestinian Territory: Country Profiles, Reports and Fact Sheets
on the Occupied Palestinian Territory." 2004. http://womenwarpeace.orgopt/opt.htm#country
_team.

Woollacott, A. "Sisters and Brothers in Arms: Family, Class, and Gendering in World War I Britain."
Gendering War Talk. Cooke, M. and Woollacott A., eds. Princeton: Princeton University Press,
1993. 128–47.

RUFINA AMAYA

Allwood de Mata, Claudia. "Mensaje de la presidenta de Concultura." *La prensa gráfica.* November
3, 1993.

Amaya, Rufina. "Solo me embrocaba a llorar/Testimonio de Rufina Amaya." January 1981; May 20,
2007. http://groups.msn.com/verdad-ES/elmozote1981.msnw.

———. *Testimonio de Rufina Amaya (Parte uno).* YouTube. May 20, 2007. www.youtube.com
/watch?v=-6MywPoe-9U.

———. *Testimonio de Rufina Amaya (Parte dos).* YouTube. May 20, 2007. www.youtube.com
/watch?v=F0KaAVVu2No.

Amaya, Rufina, Mark Danner, and Carlos Henríquez Consalvi. *Luciérnagas en El Mozote.* San
Salvador: Ediciones Museo de la Palabra, 1996.

Amnesty Internacional. "El Salvador: Monumento a la Memoria y la Verdad: Hacia la dignificación
de las víctimas del conflicto armado." December 12, 2003; May 20, 2007. http://web.amnesty
.org/library/Index/ESLAMR290112003?open&of=ESL-SLV.

Arias, Arturo, ed. *The Rigoberta Menchú Controversy.* Minneapolis: University of Minnesota Press,
2001.

Beverley, John. "What Happens When the Subaltern Speaks: Rigoberta Menchú, Multiculturalism, and the Presumption of Equal Worth." Arias. 219–36.

Bonner, Raymond. "Massacre of Hundreds Reported in Salvador Village." *The New York Times*. January 27, 1982.

CEJIL (Centro por la Justicia y el Derecho Internacional). "Monumento a la memoria y la verdad en El Salvador: un gran paso en la dignificación de las víctimas y en la construcción de una sociedad en reconciliación y paz." December 8, 2003. May 20, 2007. www.cejil.org/comunicados. cfm?id=492.

Comisión de la Verdad, 1992–1993. *De la locura a la esperanza: La guerra de 12 años en El Salvador*. San José, CR: Editorial Departamento Ecuménico de Investigación (DEI), 1993.

Consalvi, Carlos Henríquez. "Las palabras." March 15, 2002. www.museo.com.sv/opinionhtml.

Danner, Mark. "The Truth of El Mozote." *The New Yorker*. December 6, 1993: 50–133.

———. *The Massacre at El Mozote: A Parable of the Cold War*. New York: Vintage Books, 1994. 188–92.

Decree No. 55. *Diario Oficial*, 313.206. San Salvador. November 4, 1991.

Denial. Dirs. Daniele Lacourse and Yvan Patry. New York: First Run Icarus Films, 1994.

Dunkerley, James. *The Pacification of Central America: Political Change in the Isthmus, 1987–1993*. London: Verso, 1994.

Golden, Tim. "Salvadoran Skeletons Confirm Reports of Massacre in 1981." *The New York Times*. October 22, 1992: A1:4; May 20, 2007 www.newslinx.org/articles/10-22-1992ElMozotehtm.

Gould, Jeffrey L. "El Mozote after 25 Years: The Capital of Salvadoran Memory." *Counterpunch* 23/24 Dec. 2006. 20 May 2007. www.counterpunch.org/gould12232006.html.

Guillermoprieto, Alma. "Shedding Light on Humanity's Dark Side: The Outspoken Survivor of Slaughter." *Washington Post*. March 14, 2007: C01. 20; May 2007. www.washingtonpost.com /wp-dyn/content/article/2007/03/13/AR2007031301826.html.

———. "Salvadoran Peasants Describe Mass Killing; Woman Tells of Children's Death." *The Washington Post*. January 27, 1982.

Hirsh, Michael and John Barry. "What to do about the deepening quagmire of Iraq? The Pentagon's approach is being called 'the Salvador option.'" *Newsweek*. January 14, 2005. May 20, 2007. www.msnbc.msn.com/id/6802629/site/newsweek.

Homeland. Dir. Doug Scott, Prod. Daniel Flores y Ascencio and Lisette Marie Flanary. Huevos Indios Productions, 1999.

Hoyt, Mike. "The Mozote Massacre: It was the reporters' word against the government's." *Columbia Journalism Review*. Jan/Feb 1993; May 20, 2007. http://archives.cjr.org/year/93/1/mozote.asp.

Jelin, Elizabeth and Susan G. Kaufman. "Layers of Memories: Twenty Years After in Argentina." *Genocide, Collective Violence, and Popular Memory: The Politics of Remembrance in the Twentieth Century*. David E. Lorey and William H. Beezley, eds. Wilmington, DE: Scholarly Resources, 2002. 31–52.

Martin, Douglas. "Rufina Amaya, 64, Dies; Salvador Survivor." *The New York Times*. March 9, 2007: A21; 20 May 2007. www.nytimes.com/2007/03/09/world/americas/09amaya.html?ex=13310 /6400&en=2f997d367c323c32&ei=5088&partner=rssnyt&emc=rss.

Menchú, Rigoberta with Elizabeth Burgos Debray. *I, Rigoberta Menchú: An Indian Woman in Guatemala*. Trans. Ann Wright. London: Verso, 1984.

Menchú, Rigoberta with Elizabeth Burgos Debray. *Me llamo Rigoberta Menchú y así me nació la conciencia*. Mexico: Siglo XXI Editores, 1983.

Mendizabal, J. C. and Trip Tech. *La Masacre del Mozote*. BlackNote Music compact disc. 1999.

Museo de la Palabra y la Imagen. 2006. May 3, 2007. www.museo.com.sv.

Noticoncultura, 1992: 1.2.

OnRamp Arts. "Tropical America." 2002. May 20, 2007. www.tropicalamerica.com.

Partnoy, Alicia. "*Cuando Vienen Matando*: On Prepositional Shifts and the Struggle of Testimonial Subjects for Agency." *PMLA* 121.5 (October 2006): 1665–69.

———. "On Being Shorter: How Our Testimonial Texts Defy the Academy." *Women Writing Resistance: Essays on Latin America and the Caribbean.* Jennifer Browdy de Hernández, ed. Cambridge, MA: South End Press, 2003. 173–192.

———. *The Little School: Tales of Disappearance and Survival.* San Francisco: Cleis Press, 1986.

Riggins, Thomas. "Remembering Rufina Amaya, Survivor of U.S.-Inspired Slaughter in El Salvador." *political.affairs.net.* March 21, 2007. May 20, 2007. www.politicalaffairs.net/article /articleview/5020/1/248.

"Salvadoreños conmemoran 15 años de la masacre de 1.000 campesinos." *La Prensa*, San Pedro Sula, Honduras. December 9, 1996. 20 May 2007. www.laprensahn.com/caarc/9612/c09001.htm.

Stoll, David. *Rigoberta Menchú and the Story of All Poor Guatemalans.* Boulder, CO: Westview Press, 1999.

"The Media's War." Editorial. *The Wall Street Journal.* February 10, 1982.

Chapter 4

THE RAPE OF AN OBSTINATE WOMAN

Al-Hibri, Azizah. "Tear off Your Western Veil!" *Food for our Grandmothers: Writings by Arab-American and Arab-Canadian Feminists.* Ed. Joanna Kadi. Boston: South End Press, 1994. 160-64.

Amrane-Minne, Daniele Djamila. "Women and Politics in Algeria from the War of Independence to Our Day." *Research in African Literatures.* 30. 3 (1999): 62-77.

The Battle of Algiers. Dir. Gillo Pontecorvo. Chicago, Ill.: International Historic Films, 1985.

Benslama, Fethi and Salah Khellaf. "Identity as a Cause." *Research in African Literatures* 30.3 (1999): 36-50.

Bennoune, Karima. "Algerian Women Confront Fundamentalism." *Monthly Review* 46.4 (1994): 26-39.

Bergner, Gwen. "Who is that Masked Woman? Or the Role of Gender in Fanon's 'Black Skin White Masks.'" *PMLA* 110.1 (1995): 75-88.

Clark Hine, Darlene. "Rape and the Inner Lives of Black Women in the Middle West: Preliminary Thoughts on the Culture of Dissemblance." *Unequal Sisters: Multicultural Reader in U.S. Women's History.* Ed. Ellen Carol DuBois and Vicki Ruiz. New York: Routledge, 1990. 912-20.

Crenshaw, Kimberlé Williams. "Mapping the Margins: Intersectionality, Identity Politics, and Violence against Women of Color." *Critical Race Theory: The Key Writings That Formed the Movement.* Ed. Crenshaw, et al. New York: The New Press, 1995. 357-83.

———. "Beyond Racism and Misogyny: Black Feminism and 2 Live Crew." *Words That Wound: Critical Race Theory, Assaultive Speech, and the First Amendment.* Ed. Mari J. Matsuda, et al. Boulder: Westview Press, 1993. 111-32.

Daniel, Jean. "Introduction." *Research in African Literatures.* 30.3 (1999): 15-17.

Djebar, Assia. "Blood Does not Dry on the Tongue." *Research in African Literatures* 30.3. (1999): 18-22.

Dubey, Madhu. "The 'True Lie' of the Nation: Fanon and Feminism." *Differences: A Journal of Feminist Cultural Studies* 10.2 (1998): 1-29.

Elia, Nada. "A Woman's Place is in the Struggle: A Personal Viewpoint on Feminism, Pacifism and the Gulf War." *Food for our Grandmothers: Writings by Arab-American and Arab-Canadian Feminists.* Ed. Joanna Kadi, Boston: South End Press, 1994. 114-19.

———. "Violent Women: Surging in Forbidden Quarters." *Fanon: a Critical Reader.* New York: Blackwell, 1996. 163-69.

Fanon, Frantz. "Algeria Unveiled." *A Dying Colonialism.* New York: Grove Press, 1965.

————. *Black Skin, White Masks.* Pluto Press, 1991.

————. *The Wretched of the Earth.* New York: Grove Press, 1963.

Frantz Fanon: Black Skin, White Mask, directed by Julien, Isaac. UK: Arts Council of England, 1996.

Farred, Grant. Book Review of Barbara Harlow's "After Lives: Legacies of Revolutionary Writing." *Research in African Literatures.* London: Verso, 1999. 229-32.

Goldberg, David Theo. "In/Visibility and Super/Vision Fanon on Race, Veils, and Discourses of Resistance." *Fanon: a Critical Reader.* NY: Blackwell, 1996. 179-201.

Gordon, Avery. *Ghostly Matters: Haunting and the Sociological Imagination.* Minneapolis: University of Minnesota, 1996.

hooks, bell. "Feminism as a persistent critique of history: What's love got to do with it?" *Fact of Blackness: Frantz Fanon and Visual Representation.* Ed. Alan Read. Seattle: Bay Press, 1996. 76-85.

Katrak, Ketu H. "Decolonizing culture: toward a theory for postcolonial women's texts." *Modern Fiction Studies* 35. 1 (1989): 157-79.

Lazreg, Marnia. "Gender and Politics in Algeria: Unraveling the Religious Paradigm." *Signs: Journal of Women in Culture and Society* 15. 4 (1990): 755-78.

Memmi, Albert. *Colonizer and Colonized.* Boston: Beacon Press, 1965.

Moore-Gilbert, Bart. "Frantz Fanon: En-gendering Nationalist Discourse." *Women: a Cultural Review* 7.2 (1996): 125-35.

Narayan, Uma. *Dislocating Cultures: Identities, Traditions, and Third World Feminism.* NY: Routledge, 1997.

Oyewumi, Oyeronke. *Invention of Women: Making an African Sense of Western Gender Discourses.* Minneapolis: University of Minnesota, 1997.

Robinson, Cedric. "The appropriation of Frantz Fanon." *Race and Class* 35. 1 (1993): 80-91.

———. "Frantz Fanon." Unpublished article, 1980.

Saliba, Therese. "Arab Feminism at the Millennium." *Signs: Journal of Women in Culture and Society* 25.4 (2000): 1087-92.

Sanchez, George. "'Go After the Women': Americanization and the Mexican Immigrant Woman, 1915-1929." *Unequal Sisters: A Multicultural Reader in U.S. Women's History.* Ed. Vicki Ruiz, et al. New York: Routledge, 1990: 250-63.

Schemla, Elisabeth. "A Battle of Sexes in Algeria: Interview with Militant Khalida Messaoudi." *World Press Review* 42.1 (1995): 19-20.

Sharpley-Whiting, T. Denean. "Anti-Black Femininity and Mixed Race Identity: Engaging Fanon to Reread Capecia." *Fanon: A Critical Reader.* Ed. Lewis R. Gordon, et al. New York: Blackwell, 1996. 155-62.

Stora, Benjamin. "Women's Writing between Two Algerian Wars." *Research on African Literatures* 30.3 (1999): 78-94.

Souffrant, Eddy. "To Conquer the Veil: Woman as Critique of Liberalism." In *Fanon: A Critical Reader.* Ed. Lewis R. Gordon, et al. New York: Blackwell, 1996. 170-78.

Tongues Untied. Dir. Marlon Riggs. New York: Cineaste, 1992.

Verges, Francoise. "Chains of Madness, Chains of Colonialism: Fanon and Freedom." *Fact of Blackness: Frantz Fanon and Visual Representation.* Ed. Alan Read. Seattle: Bay Press, 1996. 46-75.

Yacine, Tassadit. "Is a Genealogy of Violence Possible?" *Research on African Literatures* 30.3 (1999): 23-35.

Young, Robert Clark. *One of the Guys.* New York: Harper Collins, 2000.

Chapter 5

USING POETRY TO REDUCE SHAME

Jordan, J. V. 1989. *Relational development: Therapeutic implication of empathy and shame.* Wellesley, MA: The Stone Center.

About the Contributors

Rogaia Mustafa Abusharaf is the director of the Brown University Pembroke Center's research initiative on Gender and "Traditional" Muslim Practices, where she teaches courses in the Gender Studies program. Among Abusharaf's publications is *Wanderings: Sudanese Migrants and Exiles in North America,* one of the first books devoted to the experience of Sudanese immigrants and exiles in the United States. She is editor of the anthology *Female Circumcision: Multicultural Perspectives.* Her work has received support from the Guggenheim Memorial Foundation, the Royal Anthropological Institute and the Durham University Anthropology Department in England, the Bellagio Study Center, the Mellon Foundation, and the MIT Center for International Studies. She is a former postdoctoral fellow of the Pembroke Center and was previously affiliated with the Carr Center for Human Rights, the W. E. B. DuBois Institute, and the Francois-Xavier Bagnoud Center for Health and Human Rights, Harvard University.

Born in Hyderabad, India, and raised in the United States, **Sham-e-Ali al-Jamil** is a poet, writer, and public interest lawyer. Her work has appeared in *SALT Journal, SAMAR, Roots & Culture,* and *Mizna* and can be found in anthologies such as *Shattering the Stereotypes: Muslim Women Speak Out* (Olive Branch Press, 2005) and *Living Islam Out Loud: American Muslim Women Speak* (Beacon Press, 2005). Sham-e-Ali performed her poetry with the Sister Fire Cultural Arts Tour of Radical Women of Color Artists and Activists in 2004.

Anida Yoeu Ali is an interdisciplinary artist whose individual performance repertoire synthesizes performance poetry, movement, video, and site-specific installations. Anida has toured over a hundred universities, theaters, and high schools as a member of the multimedia theatrical ensemble Mango Tribe and with performance poetry quartet I Was Born with Two Tongues. Anida's writings and performances transform personal stories into compelling political commentaries. She is a participant of Dance Theater Workshop's Mekong Project Artist Residency program in Thailand and Cambodia. Her current work investigates the poetic potential of the body through the incorporation of Butoh and experimental movement theater. Her art continues to explore diasporic issues of displacement, spiritual turmoil, and loss within exiled bodies. You may visit her website for more information: www.atomicshogun.com.

Alisa Bierria is an experienced grassroots organizer with expertise in working against domestic violence, sexual violence, white supremacy, misogyny, and internalized oppression. She is an active member of many liberation-based movements and values critical thinking and analysis, popular education, and collective action. Alisa is currently the Program Coordinator of Communities Against Rape and Abuse (CARA), a vibrant antirape organizing project in Seattle, and she is on the Steering Committee of INCITE! Women of Color against Violence, a national activist organization of radical feminists of color advancing a movement to end all forms of violence against women of color and our communities.

May Chan is a sculpture and installation artist who holds an MFA in Media Arts from the Massachusetts College of Art (1998) and a BFA in Painting from the University of Iowa (1995). Her awards include a Eureka Fellowship from the Fleishhacker Foundation in San Francisco, a 2002 Artists-in-Residency fellowship at Kala Art Institute in Berkeley, and a 2004 Artists-in-Residency at WORKS/San José. Her work is in the collections of the Denver Art Museum and Norlin Library of the University of Colorado and in the Richmond Health Center.

Sharline Chiang is a writer and journalist based in San Francisco and Vancouver. Born in New York City and raised on the Jersey Shore, Sharline is the only daughter of Chinese immigrants. A graduate of Rutgers University, she holds a master's degree from Columbia University's Graduate School of Journalism. She is deeply indebted to her literary writing mentors, authors Junot Diaz, David Mura, Gail Tsukiyama, and Elmaz Abinader, with whom she studied at VONA, the Voices of Our Nation Arts Foundation's Writing Workshops for Writers of Color (www .voicesatvona.org). She is currently writing a memoir about her one-year adventure as a journalist in China and her lifelong journey toward self-discovery as a Chinese American woman. To learn more about Sharline and her work, please visit www .sharlinechiang.com.

Alexandra Cornelius-Diallo is an assistant professor of African– New World Studies and History at Florida International University. Currently, she is working on a book that explores African American men's and women's resistance to scientific racism during the 19th century.

Keina Davis-Elswick has been painting since age seven. Her work is shown in museums, galleries, and alternative spaces throughout the United States, as well as internationally. She received her Bachelor of Fine Arts in painting from the University of Florida and her MFA from the School of the Museum of Fine Arts–Tufts University, in Boston. She has also traveled and studied in Europe. One of the major goals of Keina's work is to "inspire us to make connections between our ancestors and ourselves, between one culture and another, between the community and the individual." Mrs. Davis currently lives in San Francisco with her husband, Benjamin. To learn more about her work visit www.sivadart.com.

Aya de Leon is a Bay Area writer/performer who has received acclaim in the *Village Voice*, *The Washington Post*, *American Theatre Magazine*, and *East Bay Express* and has been featured on *Def Poetry* and in *Essence*. Her performance of *Thieves in the Temple: The Reclaiming of Hip-Hop* is about fighting sexism and commercialism in hip-hop, and won awards from the *San Francisco Chronicle* and the *San Francisco Bay Guardian*. She was an artist in residence at Stanford University and is currently the director of the June Jordan Poetry for the People program, teaching poetry, spoken word, and hip-hop at

UC Berkeley. Aya is finishing her first novel. In 2007, she released the video version of *Thieves. . . .* Visit www.ayadeleon.com for more information.

Deidra Suwanee Dees, Muscogee Nation, is a doctoral candidate at Harvard researching the impact of colonization on indigenous education. She is a storyteller, stomp dancer, and scholar who worked as the director of education at Poarch Muscogee Nation, developing a culturally appropriate curriculum for indigenous students. Her research has been published in many publications, including *The Diversity Factor,* the University of Arizona's *Red Ink,* and Harvard's *The Appian.* She has edited a number of publications and is a reviewer for *Postcolonial Text,* in Canada. The People's Poet in the United Kingdom honored her for creative writing, and she received the Mirrors International Tanka Award. TA Publications published her first book, *Vision Lines: Naïve American Decolonizing Literature,* in 2004. As the winner of New Dawn Unlimited's annual writing contest in 2005, she is working on her second book, *Indian Ice.*

Adriane Shown Deveney (Cheyenne and Hodulgee Muscogee) is a curator, performance poet, and an artist of 2D and 3D collage. Her most recent poetry work, *Fire & Ash,* has been presented by The Black Cat and D.C. Arts Center, in Washington, D.C.; Freak Planet and Indian Art Northwest in Portland, Oregon; and Paramount in Santa Fe, New Mexico; among other places. Excerpts have been featured on *Coffee House TV* and in several publications, including *Red Ink* and *Potomac Review.* She has published five chapbooks of her poetry, and her visual art has appeared in several group shows and one-woman exhibits, as well as in the American Psychological Association's 1998–2000 exhibit called Healing Art.

Chitra Lekha Divakaruni, PhD, is an award-winning author and poet. Her works have been translated into fifteen languages, including Dutch, Hebrew, and Japanese. She was born in India and lived there until 1976, at which point she left Calcutta and came to the United States. She continued her education in the field of English an received a MA from Wright State University in Dayton, Ohio, and a PhD from the University of California, Berkeley. Divakaruni teaches at the University of Houston in its nationally ranked creative writing program. She serves on the board of Maitri in the San Francisco Bay Area and on the Advisory Board of Daya in Houston. Both of these are organizations that help South Asian or South Asian American women who find themselves in abusive or domestic violence situations. She is also on the board of Pratham, an organization that helps educate children—especially those living in urban slums—in India. Her book *Mistress of Spices* (now also a film) portrays a character who breaks out of an abusive situation; the book was named one of the "100 Most Important Books to Read in the 20th Century" by the *San Francisco Chronicle*. Divakaruni lives in Houston with her husband, Murthy; her two sons, Anand and Abhay (whose names she has used in her children's novels); and Juno, the family dog.

Hosai Ehsan is a graduate student in sociology. A native of war-torn Afghanistan, she spent most of her life as a refugee in Pakistan, and later, in the United States. Until her refuge to the United States, Hosai had only received two years of formal education. In 2003, she revisited Afghanistan and volunteered for the United Nations, as well as the Ministry of Finance. Such experiences caused Hosai to pursue a career that would place emphasis on gender equality and social change. Hosai is the founder of the Ehsan Family Microgrant Project, which gives grants to individuals in Afghanistan to improve/develop small businesses. An active community member, a dedicated citizen, and a motivated student, Hosai plans to use her graduate studies to teach and conduct research.

Darrell Ann Gane-McCalla is an artist in the movement for radical social change. She was born in Boston in 1978 to a (white) South African mother and (black) Jamaican father and was raised in Cambridge, Massachusetts. While growing up, she also spent time with family in Jamaica, England, and Swaziland. She is a sculptor, painter, muralist, and art teacher. She has been an artist all her life and has been involved with consciousness raising and community activism and organizing since high school. For more information, check out www.in-d-visible.com

Professor **Shahin Gerami** is director of Women's Studies at San José State University. She holds a law degree from the University of Tehran and a doctorate in sociology from the University of Oklahoma. Her research on religious fundamentalist movements resulted in the book *Women and Fundamentalism: Islam and Christianity*. Since 2001 she has worked with the United Nation's High Commission for Refugees in conducting needs assessments of Afghani refugee families in Iran. Her research on Islamic masculinities has resulted in three publications. In 2005, she delivered a keynote address at the University Centre St. Ignatius, in Antwerp, Belgium, and in 2007, she delivered the keynote at the International Conference on Migration, Islam, and Masculinities in Oldenburg, Germany.

Janice Gould is of mixed Konkow and European descent and grew up in Berkeley, California. She graduated magna cum laude with distinction in scholarship from the University of California, Berkeley, where she received degrees in linguistics (BA) and English (MA). She earned her PhD in English at the University of New Mexico. Janice has won awards for her writing from the Astraea Foundation and from the National Endowment for the Arts. Her books of poetry include *Beneath My Heart, Earthquake Weather,* and *Alphabet* (an art book/chapbook). She is the coeditor of *Speak to Me Words: Essays on American Indian Poetry*. Janice is also an accomplished musician who plays guitar and accordion. She is currently pursuing a master's degree in library science at the University of Arizona.

Nandini Gunewardena, PhD, is a sociocultural anthropologist with expertise in transnational feminist concerns. She has been engaged in pragmatic, hands-on strategies to address women's poverty, reproductive health and nutrition, and economic empowerment in Asia, the Middle East, and North Africa. Her work links cultural gender ideologies to material conditions as evidenced in social institutions and everyday practices. She has taught applied anthropology courses on gender and development, gender and poverty, and global poverty issues at UCLA. She recently joined the faculty at Western Washington University. Her recent publications include a coedited volume on gender and globalization, *Gendered Globalization: Women Navigating Cultural and Economic Marginality* (forthcoming, SAR Press), and on disaster assistance, *Capitalizing on Catastrophe: Disaster Assistance in a Neoliberal Era* (forthcoming, Alta Mira Press).

Suzan Shown Harjo (Cheyenne and Hodulgee Muscogee) is a poet, writer, curator, lecturer, and policy advocate who has helped Native peoples recover over one million acres of land and numerous sacred places. She also has developed the most important modern federal laws to protect Native cultures and arts. President of The Morning Star Institute, in Washington, D.C., she is lead plaintiff in a groundbreaking lawsuit regarding the disparaging name of the Washington football team. An award-winning columnist for *Indian Country Today,* her columns can be found at www.indiancountry.com. She was a School of American Research 2004 poetry fellow and summer scholar, a founding trustee of the National Museum of the American Indian, and executive director of the National Congress of American Indians.

YK Hong has been doing trainings in organizational change, antioppression, and community organizing since 1996. Through her work abroad and nationally, she has been committed to developing a radical political education curriculum and organizing for marginalized communities. She works as the lead trainer for Freedom Trainers, a national training collective, and also travels independently talking about her experiences, lessons, and work. In her other time, she is also a freelance writer, web and graphic designer, Mac techie, personal trainer, bartender, cultural worker, and trapeze trainee currently residing in Brooklyn. You can learn more about YK's journey at www.ykhong.com.

ku'ualoha ho' omanawanui is Kanaka Maoli (Native Hawaiian) born in Kailua, O'ahu, and raised in Wailua, Kaua'i. A poet and artist with a love for diverse genres of music, ku'ualoha is also the chief editor of *Oiwi: A Native Hawaiian Journal,* the first contemporary journal featuring Native Hawaiian writers and artists. With a PhD in English, an MA in Hawaiian Religion, and BA in Hawaiian Studies, all from the University of Hawai'i at Manoa, she has taught a variety of courses at different levels over the past decade, focusing on Native Hawaiian mythology, literature, and indigenous perspectives on literacy.

Akasha Hull, PhD, is a writer, poet, lecturer, and consultant who has widely presented on women, literature, power, and spirituality at conferences and workshops. Her books include *All the Women Are White, All the Blacks Are Men, But Some of Us Are*

Brave (coediter); *Color, Sex, and Poetry: Three Women Writers of the Harlem Renaissance; Healing Heart: Poems;* and *Soul Talk: The New Spirituality of African American Women* (Inner Traditions, 2001). She has received numerous prestigious fellowships and was a professor of literature and women's studies at the University of California, Santa Cruz. A native of Shreveport, Louisiana, and mother of one grown son, Akasha currently resides in Little Rock, Arkansas, where she is completing her first novel.

Jackie Joice likes to make things up. She also enjoys photography, travel, and filmmaking. Joice was a 2004 participant in the Hurston/Wright Writer's week at Howard University.

Venita Kelley, PhD, is Associate Dean of Leadership and Student Services at Spelman College. Her background includes an Administrative Fellowship at Harvard University and positions as a professor of communication and ethnic studies, with affiliated status in film and women's studies programs. Her scholarly foci include intercultural and inter/intragender competencies, images of culture and gender in media, leadership development, the impact of African American rhetoric and culture in the United States and globally, African American women's communication strategies; and the presentation of culture in media. She speaks, consults, and has an award-winning local and national service background. The essay whose findings were included in this anthology were made possible because of the invaluable assistance of Dr. Kelley's co-researchers/co-facilitators, who contributed enlightened discussion and insight during the research and writing of the original report: Myesha Albert, S. Lateefah Coleman, Debbie Gaspard, Cindy Grandberry, Tekla Ali Johnson, Wendy Smooth, Renita Tyrance, and Franchell Watson.

Dai Sil Kim-Gibson is an independent filmmaker who is widely known for championing the voiceless and the oppressed, marked by her imprint of humanizing the storytellers and an inventive format. Her film credits include *America Becoming; Sa-I-Gu; A Forgotten People: the Sakhalin Koreans; Olivia's Story; Silence Broken: Korean Comfort Women;* and *Motherland (Cuba Korea USA).* Her films were critically acclaimed here and abroad ("a film translating mute statistics into human terms," by the *Business Week*

Magazine for *Sa-I-Gu;* "a classic work of oral history," by the *Washington City Paper* for *A Forgotten People;* "a wrenching and formally inventive film," by the *Village Voice;* "A hauntingly brilliant film," by *Asian Week, Los Angeles,* for *Silence Broken*). All of her films garnered many awards and were screened at numerous festivals worldwide, in addition to receiving national broadcast on PBS and on the Sundance Channel in the United States. Among many awards, she received a Rockefeller Fellowship for *Silence Broken* and a production grant from the MacArthur Foundation for *Sa-I-Gu.* She is an author of numerous articles, and *Silence Broken: Korean Comfort Women* is her first book (*The Philadelphia Inquirer* called it "unforgettable"). She is a former professor of religion at Mount Holyoke College, with a PhD from Boston University, and a federal and state employee; filmmaking is her third career.

Yvonne S. Lee is a Korean American journalist based primarily in the United States. She is currently working on a documentary about transgender sex workers in Cambodia, where she was a reporter. She has covered a range of major historic events, including two U.S. presidential elections, the 2003 Iraq War, and the September 11, 2001, attack on the Pentagon, for which she won an Emmy award. She was also selected for the CDC Knight Public Health Journalism Boot Camp in 2006 and a Jon Davidoff Journalism Scholarship in 2004. She has interviewed senators and world leaders, including former Defense Secretary Donald Rumsfeld and Senator John Kerry. One of her most memorable interviews was with Supreme Court Justices Stephen Breyer, Ruth Bader Ginsburg, and Anthony Kennedy.

Sharmila Lodhia is a PhD candidate in women's studies at the University of California, Los Angeles. She received her law degree from Hastings College of Law, in San Francisco, and before returning to graduate school, she worked as a civil rights attorney for women at the California Women's Law Center. Sharmila's doctoral research examines law and advocacy responses to violence against Indian women through a transnational lens. This analysis of migrating spouses, traveling cultures, and shifting bodies of law suggests that new types of legal subjects are emerging in local and global spaces, which undermines the meaningfulness of advocacy conceived within the boundaries of the nation-state.

Leticia Manzano is the manager of counseling and advocacy services for the Houston Area Women's Center. In addition to providing counseling, she also supervises staff, interns, and volunteers, who provide counseling to women, men, and children who are victims of domestic violence and/or sexual assault. Additionally, she does in-service training on topics relating to sexual and domestic violence to teachers, counselors, social workers, and groups. Leticia is currently a board member of Latinas on the Rise, a mentorship program for young women. She was the coordinator of Youth Service Providers Network in the Greater Houston Area and has also been the cochair of Allies for Children and Teens of the Texas Council on Family Violence. She also provided parenting classes at Depelchin Children's Center.

Consuelo Méndez earned her bachelor's and master's degrees in printmaking and is a professor of art at the Institute of Superior Studies of Fine Arts Armando Reverón, in Caracas, Venezuela. She teaches, as well, at the International Summer Courses of Expression at the Municipal School of Barcelona, Spain. Méndez's art received prizes in the Michelena National Show, Graphic Biennal of Maracaibo, and Miniature Graphics TAGA. Her work has exhibited in Bulgaria, Puerto Rico, Colombia, the United States, Cuba, Mexico, Poland, and Belgium, and she has performed solo performance pieces in the Contemporary Museum of Caracas, Los Teques Museum, the National Art Gallery, the First International Encounter of Body Art, and the Alejandro Otero Museum. Méndez is a cofounder of Mujeres Muralistas in San Francisco, California.

Janice Mirikitani, a *sansei* (third-generation) Japanese American, is recognized as a poet, editor, and community activist. Appointed San Francisco's second Poet Laureate, she is author of four books of poetry—*Awake in the River; Shedding Silence; We, the Dangerous;* and *Love Works*—and is the editor of nine groundbreaking anthologies. She is the founding president of the Glide Foundation. During her tenure there as the executive director for almost forty years, Janice developed more than eighty programs for the poor and marginalized, including free primary and mental health clinics, violence prevention programs, and innovative multicultural programs for women and children. During World War II, Mirikitani and her family were incarcerated in a camp in Rohwer, Arkansas.

Ana Silvia Monzón is a Guatemalan sociologist and communicator. She is a host and founding member of *Voces de Mujeres,* a weekly radio show now in its fourteenth year of existence. She is a researcher, reporter, mother, student, activist, and the author of *Las viajeras invisibles,* a report about migrant women from Guatemala and Southern Mexico. In addition she coedited *La encrucijada de las identidades,* a book about ethnicity and feminism in Guatemala. Ana Silvia is a member of organizations such as Red Mujeres al Aire, Convergencia Ciudadana de Mujeres, Mujeres contra el racismo y la discriminación, and *La Cuerda,* a feminist newspaper. She is also a founding member of Instituto Universitario de la Mujer and a cofounder of Mujeres Abriendo Caminos, a communication initiative that links women living in Guatemala and migrant women residing in Los Angeles via a weekly radio show.

Lucía Morán was born in Guatemala in January 1968. She is a lawyer with a postgraduate degree in Labor Relations and Human Resources from the UN-sanctioned University for Peace in Costa Rica. She has published nine books of poetry, and her work is found in three anthologies—two published in Guatemala and one in Spain—as well as in various periodicals. She is a member of the Women in the Arts Collective.

Deborah Okrina, LCSW, received her master's in social work at the University of Texas in Austin. She worked as a counselor and educator at the Houston Area Women's Center for more than nine years. She has been a dedicated advocate, fighting to end violence against women and all forms of oppression. She currently works at Cadwalder Behavioral Clinics in Tomball, Texas, where she does equine-assisted psychotherapy, combining her love for horses with her passion for helping women heal.

Lakshmy Parameswaran emigrated from India to the United States in 1973. She is a founder of Daya Inc., a Houston-based nonprofit organization serving South Asian victims of abuse and violence. She obtained her MA in Family Therapy from the University of Houston–Clear Lake and is a counselor with a private practice specializing in domestic violence and sexual assault issues. She has conducted numerous workshops on gender-based violence. Her writings have appeared in the *Houston Chronicle* and *Texas Psychologist,* and she has appeared on local ABC television programs as an expert on domestic violence. Lakshmy considers her commitment to Daya in bringing awareness to domestic violence issues as the most significant aspect of her work. For more information on Daya, visit www.dayahouston.org.

Ishle Yi Park is a Korean American woman who is the Poet Laureate of Queens, New York. Her first book is entitled *The Temperature of This Water* and is published by Kaya Press. For more information, please go to www.ishle.com.

Teresa Pedrizco Romero is a passionate Chicana feminist who received her bachelor's in social science with an emphasis in women's studies. This degree, and the ones to come, she owes to her mother, Margarita Romero Medina. Teresa understands the circumstances why her mother is not too expressive in encouraging her to reach her potential. However, Teresa believes that her mother's second-grade level of education, unskilled hard service work, and experience with violence speak loud and clear. Unlike her mother, now Teresa has access to share her experience with violence against women with others outside her net of close friends and counselors. Teresa acknowledges that privilege, and dedicates her education and participation in *Shout Out* to her mother.

Ana Patricia Rodríguez, associate professor of U.S. Latina/o and Central American literatures in the Department of Spanish and Portuguese at the University of Maryland, College Park. Her doctorate is from the University of California, Santa Cruz. Her research focuses on U.S. Latina/o and Central American literary and cultural production. Her forthcoming book, *Dividing the Isthmus: Central American Transnational Literatures and Cultures,* examines narrative geographies of economic, symbolic, and human excess in Central American isthmian and diasporic texts. She is working on a second book, tentatively titled *Same Story, Different Endings: Trauma, Cultural Memory, and Narrative in the Salvadoran Diaspora,* which explores the construction of Salvadoran posttraumatic memory through representations in film, music, performance art, and testimonial texts. Her work is found in *American Literature, Latino Studies, Life Writing, and Istmo.*

Rogers Park Young Women's Action Team (YWAT) is a youth-led, adult-supported social change project that empowers young women to take action on issues that affect their lives (particularly issues of violence against girls and young women). The YWAT believes that girls and young women should be free from violence. We believe that through collective action, consciousness raising, and organizing, we can end violence against girls and young women. For more information about the YWAT, visit www.youngwomensactionteam.org. The YWAT collective poem included in this book was written in 2004 by members Joyce, Shannon, Karia, Shay, Renee, Ronnett, Jasmine, Christine, Daphnee, Jackquette, Jonnae, Emilya, Crystal, and Geri, with support from their adult ally, Mariame Kaba.

Mukta Sharangpani has been actively engaged with the issue of family violence as artist, activist, and academic. Her interest in this work began with her participation in street-theater projects in Mumbai over two decades ago. Currently, she volunteers as board member with Maitri and is finishing her doctoral requirements at Stanford University. She is particularly interested in the intersections of class, modernity, and violence, and her dissertation examines domestic violence among middle-class families in Mumbai, India. She continues to be deeply engaged with theater for social change and her performative poetry, spoken word, and monologues about issues such as sexual abuse, human trafficking, marital violence, and cultural alienation have been very well received.

Nalini Shekar worked as the director of advocacy at NextDoor Solutions to Domestic Violence and volunteered as a board member of Maitri in San Jose, California. Her extensive experience for more than five years in the United States includes advocacy work with victims of domestic violence and trafficking. Ms. Shekar is a key member of the team that rescued and rehabilitated Indian women trafficked into the United States by a Berkeley landlord.

Elena Shih is originally from Queens, New York, and received her BA from Pomona College, where the focus of her work was transnational women's migration. She has explored the influence of the politics of globalization on the migration and trafficking of Asian women and girls as a Freeman summer research fellow to Belleville, Paris, where she explored the migratory trends of Wenzhou immigrants to Paris, and subsequently as a Fulbright scholar in the People's Republic of China, where she conducted research on human trafficking, working alongside local NGOs in Beijing and Yunnan Province. She cofounded a project called Border Statements, which connects local and international contemporary artist/activists with communities on the China–Myanmar border in order to run community art trainings that engage issues of displacement, disease prevention, and education.

Aishah Shahidah Simmons is an award-winning Black feminist lesbian independent documentary filmmaker, international lecturer, and activist from Philadelphia. An incest and rape survivor, she spent eleven years—seven of which were full-time—to produce/write/direct *NO!*, a feature-length documentary that explores the international reality of rape through testimonies, scholarship, activism, spirituality, and cultural work of African Americans. *NO!* also examines how rape is used as a weapon of homophobia. Since its official release in 2006, *NO!* has been used as an educational organizing tool with racially and ethnically diverse audiences at community centers, colleges/universities, high schools, juvenile correctional facilities, rape crisis centers, battered women's shelters, conferences, and film festivals across the United States, Europe, Africa, and South America. For more information visit www.notherapedocumentary.org.

Teresia Teaiwa I am of mixed African American, Banaban, and I-Kiribati Pacific Islander heritage. I was born in Honolulu, Hawai'i and raised in the Fiji Islands. I now live in Wellington, Aotearoa/New Zealand with my partner, Sean, and my sons, Manoa and Vaitoa. Mana/South Pacific Creative Arts Society published my first collection of poetry, *Searching for Nei Nim'anoa,* in 1995. My work also features alongside the poetry of Samoan writer Sia Figiel on a CD of spoken word titled *Terenesia,* released in 2000. More recently, I have had poetry published in *Tinfish,* a literary journal of the University of Hawai'i, and *Women's Studies Quarterly,* an educational project of the Feminist Press at CUNY in cooperation with Rochester Institute of Technology.

Lisa Valencia-Svensson is a Filipina Canadian half-breed dyke based in Toronto. She recently produced a short film on undocumented workers in Canada and has a TV series in development about writers in exile. When not working on documentary films, she loves to salsa dance.

Blue Wade My work is in response to African American art history and culture. Black art began as soon as Africans arrived in America and is now firmly rooted in African and American traditions. Because of this, Black art possesses African roots, transatlantic reality, and a diasporic nature. As an artist I am interested in furthering the visual language of Black art. I work from a neocolonial perspective, questioning the effects of our history on our current lives. By doing this I hope to continue the Black-art tradition of creating pieces that speak to the community, as well as sharing with others the global implications that are intrinsic in this work.

Tiffany Willoughby-Herard is an assistant professor of comparative political thought in the Department of Political Science at San Francisco State University. My work speaks to the lessons of postapartheid South Africa for an apartheid globe and the newest incarnation of development studies: democratization from above. I am an interdisciplinary political scientist who studies political theory, comparative politics, and feminist antiracist political philosophy, and I am deeply committed to political organizing around social and economic justice, community development, and artistic expression.

Merle Woo is an acclaimed activist, poet, and essayist. A lesbian of Chinese/Korean descent, she is a member of both Radical Women and the Freedom Socialist Party. She received her bachelor's and master's in English from San Francisco State University. In 1982, the University of California, Berkeley, refused to rehire her because of her political beliefs and activism. In a series of protracted legal proceedings, she successfully sued the university for practicing discriminatory personnel policies. She is the author of numerous works, including the book *Our Common Enemy, Our Common Cause: Freedom Organizing in the Eighties*, which she coauthored with the late Audre Lorde.

Victoria Lucia Ybanez (Navajo, Apache, and Mexican) is the executive director of Red Wind Consulting, coordinating tribal technical assistance for grants recipients of the Office on Violence against Women. She brings firsthand experience with domestic violence, racism, and poverty to her work and has been working to end violence against women for twenty-four years. During her career, she has worked extensively in housing and advocacy for battered women. She frequently works with national Native technical assistance domestic violence organizations such as Mending the Sacred Hoop, Sacred Circle, and the Tribal Law and Policy Institute. She holds a bachelor's in economics from the University of Minnesota, Duluth, and is a graduate of the 1997 Institute for Renewing Community Leadership, at the University of St. Thomas, in Minneapolis.

Lily Yeh is an internationally celebrated artist and the award-winning founder and former executive and artistic director of the Village of Arts and Humanities. From 1986 to 2004, with the help of neighborhood children and adults, Yeh built the Village from an empty lot in inner city North Philadelphia into an organization and a community that transformed abandonment and despair into abundance and joy. In 2002, Yeh formed the Barefoot Artists, an international organization that brings the transformative power of art to impoverished communities through participatory, multifaceted projects that heal the wounded, reconnect the broken, and make the invisible visible. Her current work includes the construction of the 1994 Genocide Memorial and the transformation of a survivors village in the Rugerero district in West Rwanda. She has worked in China, Colombia, Ecuador, Ghana, Italy, Ivory Coast, Kenya, the Republic of Georgia, Rwanda, and the United States.

About the Editors

María Ochoa, PhD, is a writer who teaches at San José State University in the Department of Social Science/Women's Studies Program. Recent publications include the books *Voices of Russell City: An Oral History of a Town and Its People* and *Creative Collectives: Chicana Artists Working in Community,* as well as poetry in the anthology *Oakland Out Loud.* In 1999 the California State Assembly named her a Woman of the Year for her contributions to the visual arts.

Barbara K. Ige, PhD, has at every stage of her academic and administrative career demonstrated an unwavering commitment to diversifying the student population. She has taught multicultural North American literature, Asian American studies, and popular culture at the University of Hawai'i, Pitzer College, and the University of California, in Santa Cruz, Santa Barbara, and Los Angeles.

Credits

Selected Titles from Seal Press

For more than thirty years, Seal Press has published groundbreaking books.
By women. For women. Visit our website at www.sealpress.com.

Voices of Resistance: Muslim Women on War, Faith, and Sexuality edited by Sarah Husain. $16.95, 1-58005-181-2. A collection of essays and poetry on war, faith, suicide bombing, and sexuality, this book reveals the anger, pride, and pain of Muslim women.

Colonize This: Young Women of Color on Today's Feminism edited by Daisy Hernandez and Bushra Rehman. $16.95, 1-58005-067-0. An insight into a new generation of brilliant, outspoken women of color and how they are speaking to the concerns of new feminism, and their place in it.

Listen Up: Voices from the Next Feminist Generation edited by Barbara Findlen. $16.95, 1-58005-054-9. A collection of essays featuring the voices of today's young feminists on racism, sexuality, identity, AIDS, revolution, abortion, and much more.

Getting Free: You Can End Abuse and Take Back Your Life by Ginny NiCarthy. $16.95, 1-58005-122-7. This straightforward and motivational book provides all the tools and advice you need to help yourself recognize, respond to, and overcome domestic violence.

Helping Her Get Free: A Guide for Families and Friends of Abused Women by Susan Brewster. $13.95, 1-58005-167-7. This straightforward and compassionate book offers the information needed to help give strength to women who are trying to break free of harmful relationships.

You Can Be Free: An Easy-to-Read Handbook for Abused Women by Ginny NiCarthy and Sue Davidson. $13.95, 1-58005-159-6. In this best-selling guide, the authors give practical and gentle guidance to help women work toward building relationships that are healthier and, most importantly, safer.